Joachim Prinz, Rebellious Rabbi

AN AUTOBIOGRAPHY—THE GERMAN AND EARLY AMERICAN YEARS

Edited and introduced by
MICHAEL A. MEYER

Indiana University Press

BLOOMINGTON AND INDIANAPOLIS

Published with the generous support of the Rabbi's Discretionary Fund
of Temple B'nai Abraham, Livingston, New Jersey

This book is a publication of
Indiana University Press
601 North Morton Street
Bloomington, IN 47404-3797 USA

http://iupress.indiana.edu

Telephone orders   800-842-6796
Fax orders   812-855-7931
Orders by e-mail   iuporder@indiana.edu

The paper used in this publication meets the minimum requirements of American National
Standard for Information Sciences—Permanence of Paper for Printed Library Materials,
ANSI Z39.48-1984.

Manufactured in the United States of America

Library of Congress Cataloging-in-Publication Data
Prinz, Joachim, 1902-1988.
Joachim Prinz, rebellious rabbi : an autobiography : the German and early American years /
edited and introduced by Michael A. Meyer.
p. cm.
Includes index.
ISBN 978-0-253-34939-2 (cloth)
1. Prinz, Joachim, 1902-1988. 2. Rabbis—Germany—Berlin—Biography. 3. Rabbis—United
States—New Jersey—Newark—Biography. 4. Berlin (Germany)—Biography. 5. Newark
(N.J.)—Biography. I. Meyer, Michael A. II. Title.
BM755.P74A3 2008
296.8'342092—dc22
[B]
2007009435

1 2 3 4 5 13 12 11 10 09 08

CONTENTS

PREFACE

WHEN, A FEW YEARS AGO, it was suggested to me that I look at a manuscript of an autobiography by Rabbi Joachim Prinz (1902–1988), my assumption was that, as is true of most such writing, it would be of interest to family and friends, perhaps belonged in an archives, but was unlikely to attract a larger readership. To my surprise, I found the life story of this provocative Liberal and Zionist rabbi in Germany and later in America extraordinarily fascinating, had difficulty putting it down, and soon resolved to prepare it for publication. My reading had convinced me that the Prinz story had broader significance for at least two reasons. First, Prinz had been one of the foremost spiritual leaders of German Jewry during its darkest years. His experiences shed light on that community's struggle to maintain its self-respect when Nazi authorities were making every effort to extinguish it. From the pulpit and in the lecture hall, Prinz provided what can properly be called a form of spiritual resistance. Second, Joachim Prinz was a most extraordinary rabbi. He brought innovations to the Liberal rabbinate that in large measure still characterize it today. His uninhibited lifestyle, a product of Weimar culture, broke clerical taboos to the point where he was discharged from rabbinical duties, and his candid description of his sex life is astounding. Finally, his commitment to universal values led him to become a leader of the Civil Rights movement in the United States, a friend and co-worker of Martin Luther King, Jr. Thus Prinz's autobiography possesses attraction not only for the members of Temple B'nai Abraham, which he served for nearly forty years, first in Newark and then in Livingston, New Jersey, many of whom still remember him fondly. Rather, his recollections will likewise draw in students of modern Jewish history and of Nazi Germany, as well as general readers interested in the human struggle for spiritual self-assertion in the face of unprecedented oppression.

The process of preparing the manuscript for publication took somewhat longer than anticipated, requiring careful editing of a dictated and probably never reviewed text to correct spelling and syntactical errors and to eliminate repetition. It was also necessary to check all the historical references that could be located and supply explanatory notes relating to persons and events. Obvious factual errors that seemed revealing have been corrected in the notes but are left standing in the text. In general, I have kept the oral style of the original with its immediacy and impact and made the notes as brief as possible in order not to impede the reader.

Prinz dictated this autobiography to his secretary around 1977, probably very shortly after his retirement from the rabbinate of Temple B'nai Abraham. He began the story with his birth in 1902 and carried it forward to the death of his mentor and idol, Rabbi Stephen S. Wise, in 1949. Regrettably, Prinz did not continue the account further, into his career as a prominent leader of American Judaism, specifically to his roles as president of the American Jewish Congress and chair of the Conference of Presidents of Major Jewish Organizations. Nor does the autobiography include his relationship with Martin Luther King, Jr. and Prinz's own dramatic speech at the March on Washington for Jobs and Freedom on August 28, 1963. However, as Prinz indicated in his remarks on that occasion, his work on behalf of African Americans rested upon his experience as a rabbi in Nazi Germany, which forms the central chapter of his autobiography.

I should like to express my gratitude, first and foremost, to Ina Maria Remus, who served as my research assistant, locating Prinz's contributions to various periodicals, tracking down obscure references, and helping with the task of editing. I am grateful to Rabbi Jonathan Prinz and Deborah Prinz Neher, custodians of the Joachim Prinz estate, for allowing me to publish their father's autobiography without editorial restrictions. The current rabbi of Temple B'nai Abraham, my student and friend Clifford Kulwin, has been most helpful in facilitating the publication project. In addition to Jonathan and Deborah Prinz, the following family members and friends of Joachim Prinz were kind enough to submit to interviews: Muriel Bloom, Lucie Prinz, Jo Seelman, Gerda Schultz, and Joachim Silberman. I am grateful to the anonymous readers selected by Indiana University Press for their helpful suggestions and to its editors for their courtesy and efficiency in bringing the manuscript to publication. My research was facilitated in various ways by Irene Awret, Jacob Borut, David J. Goldberg, Katrin Janson, Robin Judd, Peter Klein, Ann Millin, Rachel Nierenberg Pasternak, Anna Ornstein, Eli Prinz, Carl Rheins, Monika Richarz, Jean Rosensaft, Peter Rubinstein, Michael Stanislawski, Yitzhak Steiner, and Robert Williams. I would also like to express thanks to the staffs of the Leo Baeck Institute and the Ratner Archives of the Jewish Theological Seminary in New York; the Jacob Rader Marcus Center of the American Jewish Archives and the Klau Library of Hebrew Union College-Jewish Institute of Religion in Cincinnati; the Yad

Vashem and Zionist Archives in Jerusalem; the Weizmann Archives in Rehovot; the Stiftung Neue Synagoge-Centrum Judaicum Archives in Berlin; the archives of Temple B'nai Abraham in Livingston; and the Jewish Historical Society of Metrowest in Whippany, New Jersey. Without the assistance of these individuals and institutions, it would not have been possible to place Prinz's account of himself against the backdrop of his actual life and the times in which he lived.

EDITOR'S INTRODUCTION

AUTOBIOGRAPHY, ITS STUDENTS agree, is a problematic genre of literature. One cannot expect it to be a balanced and wholly accurate representation. Remembering and forgetting are determined not only by temporal distance from the events described, but also by psychological factors that often unconsciously push certain recollections into the foreground and bury others. Autobiographers are explorers of the self, but they are also its fashioners. They configure the tale of their personal development and character in a manner that is both most easily acceptable to themselves and that presents the self-image that they wish to convey to succeeding generations of their family or to a larger readership. The process begins before the text is produced. Frequently told tales are reshaped, embellished, and become exemplary for the life even as others are suppressed. In addition, literary motives play their role as the autobiographer seeks to create a coherent and intrinsically interesting narrative, omitting distractions, limiting qualifications, exaggerating importance. As one scholar of the subject has put it, "The self that is the center of all autobiographical narratives is necessarily a fictive structure."[1] But at the same time, as another scholar reminds us, "Even if what they [the authors] tell us is not factually true, or only partly true, it always is true evidence of their personalities."[2] In a sense, the writing of autobiography is a kind of performance, a dramatization of the writer's life for the readers' entertainment. Like a film or play, its success depends on its holding the interest of those exposed to it. Not surprisingly, autobiographies written by Jews follow the general pattern. Their stories are traceable to the model of Rousseau's *Confessions* and, in the Jewish sphere, to the famed eighteenth-century autobiography describing the acculturation in Germany of the Eastern European Jew Solomon Maimon. By the nineteenth century, there is a variety of Jewish autobiographies and, in the twentieth, a plethora of memoirs written by Jewish survivors of the Holocaust.[3]

The recollections of Joachim Prinz display the characteristics of the autobiographical genre that literary scholars and scientific investigators of memory have described and analyzed. His work is focused upon the self. It fashions an imagined persona that must be differentiated from the historical person, whose identity is only partially revealed by a selective use of memory. Although there are occasional descriptions of milieu, especially of the village of his childhood, the autobiography is less a memoir of his times than a relation of his own development and activity within a changing environment. The autobiography presents Prinz as he would like to be remembered: as the possessor of a meaningful and interesting life; a breaker of taboos; a man whose life was filled with experiences that were out of the ordinary. He was not, the autobiography repeatedly impresses on the reader, a mere run-of-the-mill rabbi. The frequent instances of self-dramatization, of setting the self apart from others without qualification, create a more powerful, if not always historically accurate or carefully qualified narrative. Despite the occasional note of self-deprecation with regard to irresponsibility and insensitivity, the dominant mood is one of self-confidence and self-admiration. Although there are occasional critical reflections, the autobiography gives little evidence of inner struggle; unlike Rousseau's, its mood is not confessional, but triumphant, more a celebration of his qualities of character than of deeper introspection. Known as an excellent raconteur, Prinz here presents stories that must have been often told and hence most easily remembered, no doubt restructured and stylized in the course of repeated retellings. Since the autobiography was created shortly after his retirement from a very successful rabbinical career, producing it may have been a way of coping with the crisis of retirement, which had closed off most opportunities for public display and induced an inward focus as well as the desire to leave a personal legacy.

Given the uncertainties of autobiography in general and of this one in particular, the reader must come to the text with a measure of suspicion. However, this necessity in no way invalidates the importance of the work, which lies not only in what it reveals of the facts of Prinz's life and his interactions with his environment, but also of the nature of the man as he understood himself. Moreover, while some incidents arouse skepticism, others do not, or at most require a determination of where the factual core has been subject to distortion or embellishment. In what follows in this introduction I shall be asking Roy Pascal's question: "Does the author's representation of himself as a personality correspond to what we can get to know of him through other evidence?"[4] Such evidence consists of Prinz's published writings, correspondence, background information, and the views of his contemporaries expressed in writing and interviews. I have attempted to relate the autobiography to the somewhat differently shaped framework of the life insofar as that is determinable from other sources, and to round out the picture it presents.

The effort to contextualize Prinz's autobiography within his life and his changing milieu seems worthwhile because Joachim Prinz, the historical figure, was indeed a significant presence in Jewish history both in Germany and the United States. His reinterpretation of the role of the rabbinate had a broad influence and the Jewish spiritual life in which he participated has yet to be fully integrated into portrayals of German Jewry during the Nazi period.[5] Among German Zionists, Prinz was the movement's most popular propagandist; among rabbis, his part in the spiritual resistance to Nazism is second only to that of the leader of German Jewry during the Nazi period, Rabbi Leo Baeck. Finally, in the United States, Prinz became one of the foremost Jewish leaders of the Civil Rights movement. Yet there has not been so much as a single critical article dealing with his life and achievements. The discovery of Joachim Prinz's autobiography provides a window into a fascinating life as well as the opportunity to assess his significance for Jewish history.

The initial section of the autobiography, dealing with the first seven years of Prinz's life in the small village of Burkhardsdorf in Upper Silesia and the following eleven years in the town of Oppeln, draws upon distant memories to create lively images of the milieu and experiences of a sensitive Jewish child. Prinz knows that "memories taken from childhood often cause us to forge facts and to remember things as being very large when, in fact, they are quite small," and no doubt some of the tales are embellished to make them more dramatic. But the substance of the descriptions and the personal interactions offer genuine insight into his early life with family and neighbors.

This portion of the text has particular value for its account of Jewish daily life (*Alltagsgeschichte*), first in the countryside, isolated from other Jewish families, and later in a town with a relatively small Jewish community. Remarkable during these last years of the Second Reich were the excellent day-to-day relations between Jews and Christians in both village and town, the casual encounters between religious groups, the banding together of educated persons from both religions, and the universal respect for the clergy of both faiths. No less noteworthy is the degree of religious assimilation, even in the village, where Prinz's family is more observant of Christian than of Jewish holidays, and especially in the town, whose nineteenth-century rabbi had written a tract against the Jewish dietary laws and where Prinz's father made a slice of ham, consumed at a second breakfast, a part of his daily routine.

Whereas the village narrative is mostly taken up with recollections of the world around him, when Prinz comes to his adolescent years in the town, he begins to focus more on his own development. Repeatedly, he returns to his strained relationship (or nonrelationship) with his father, whom he paints as a generous individual, who always provided him with his material needs, but failed to supply the more important gifts of tenderness and love. He was, according to Prinz, typically Prussian in his authoritarian attitudes and, with the exception of a few Jewish residues, entirely a product of his non-Jewish environment and its values. Prinz portrays his father as the foil for his own rebellious development away from everything that his father stood for. There are at least five elements to Prinz's revolt: his father was typically bourgeois whereas Prinz rejected bourgeois morality; his father was a fervent supporter of Germany in World War I, Prinz was not; his father was a virulent anti-Zionist, Prinz joined a Zionist youth group and later became a leading German Zionist; his father was at best lukewarm to religion whereas, for three years, Prinz would not eat the nonkosher meat in his home, began to put on tefillin (phylacteries), and eventually became a rabbi; his father was authoritarian, stiff, and cold in his personal relationships, while Prinz tried to be the opposite. As the autobiography conveys it, the young boy terribly resented this dominating father whose death many years later produced little sorrow.

Even as his biological father pushed the maturing boy into various forms of opposition, a father substitute appeared to whom Prinz was greatly drawn. Felix Goldmann, the rabbi of Oppeln when Joachim moved there in 1910, was one of the most capable of the German Liberal rabbis and also one of the most innovative. Prinz was impressed by him, especially for two reasons. Goldmann had reconceived the sermon, not as inspirational and edifying, which had been its role in the nineteenth century as both Orthodox and Liberal rabbis adopted the sermonic form from Protestantism, but rather as an educational and advocative tool. And he placed service to the poor at the center of his rabbinate. A eulogy upon Goldmann's death in 1934 called him "not a holiday rabbi but an everyday pastor."[6] When this youthful rabbi took Joachim with him on secret early morning deliveries of food and clothing to the non-Jewish poor, it made a lasting impression on the boy. Goldmann also had high regard for the Yiddish language and valued Eastern European Jews, of whom there were many in the Leipzig community that he later served. Though a foe of ideological Jewish nationalism, he became a supporter of Jewish settlement in Palestine. In one of two eulogies that Prinz himself published, he wrote: "Felix Goldmann was my teacher. I owe him everything. It was he who made me into a Jew. It was he who drove me to my rabbinical profession."[7]

However, seemingly no less influential in Prinz's decision to become a rabbi was his attachment to his mother and his sadness at her early death.

She represented for the growing boy all the qualities that were lacking in the father: tenderness, love, and emotional support. Prinz recalls the privilege of cuddling with her in her bed on every birthday and terms her early death in childbirth "the most important event of my life." When his mother died in 1915, a few months before Prinz's Bar Mitzvah, he went to synagogue daily to mourn her. There one morning, the rabbi decided to substitute a Torah scroll for the tenth man required for a prayer quorum and asked Joachim to hold it on his lap. In a poignant recollection that bears the ring of truth, Prinz describes how the soft covering of the Torah became his mother's warm skin, as he remembered it from his visits to her bed. He continues: "I celebrated some sort of wedding with her, the Torah becoming a symbol of my mother. I was determined to devote my life to her. The Torah and my mother—they had become one. Then and there I determined to become a rabbi."

An earlier formative experience, according to Prinz's recollections, occurred when he became infatuated with the music of a café fiddler. He asked his father to buy him a violin and arrange lessons, "for I wanted to become a first fiddler standing on a little pedestal playing a solo and being applauded by an audience as was my hero." However, when not long thereafter Joachim brought home poor grades from school, his father trampled the violin to pieces and the lessons were abandoned. Recalling these events, Prinz believes that his desire to be a public personality stemmed from his longing to perform on the violin. If he could not be an applauded violinist, he would instead be an applauded public speaker.

Thus, by the time Prinz left Oppeln to study in Breslau in 1921 at the age of nineteen, his character and goals had been shaped in the crucible of familial distance-and-love relationships and he had been given a model for his rabbinate. He had also gained the extraordinary self-confidence that would characterize his later years. When a teacher in the Oppeln high school questioned his return to school after a failed attempt to be a businessman, Prinz casually replied: "I was born to be something more exalted."[8]

Prinz's account of his student years is especially valuable for what it tells us of the conservative Jewish Theological Seminary of Breslau and the life of its professors and students—though we need to keep in mind that Prinz is at pains to show how different he was from his colleagues. Homiletics was apparently taken very seriously, with intimidating critiques by professors and colleagues and with students required to memorize their texts and to speak without notes—as Prinz in fact did henceforth when delivering his sermons. The environment at the seminary synagogue, where women sat in a section behind the men that was even supplied with a curtain—albeit never drawn—points to the traditional cast of the institution. The professors, as Prinz describes them, were both brilliant and endowed with memorable foibles. Although under considerable academic pressure because of the requirement simultaneously to obtain both a doctorate and rabbinical ordination, students nonetheless had time for a fraternity, to which they gave a Latin rather than a Hebrew name. In the company of fraternity brothers, they sang only non-Jewish songs and reveled in the quantity of beer they could consume. Like his fellows, Prinz got a doctorate, in his case from the University of Giessen after deciding against the University of Jena on account of the latter's pervasive antisemitism. Although even later in the United States he would always prefer to be called Dr. Prinz, rather than Rabbi Prinz, he admitted that his doctorate was nothing to be especially proud of. It was a hurdle to be surmounted with a philosophical essay of less than one hundred pages (dedicated to the memory of his mother), which, in addition to examinations in two minor subjects, was the standard requirement at the time.

Unlike his fellow students in Breslau, who mostly came from impoverished, Eastern European families, Prinz could, thanks to his father's generosity, live in very comfortable quarters. While his colleagues were almost fully absorbed with their studies, Prinz at age twenty-two found time to edit a new weekly Zionist newspaper, the *Jüdische Zeitung für Ostdeutschland.* On its pages, he regularly published articles on a variety of Jewish and general subjects, for example in 1925 advocating the election of the republican candidate Wilhelm Marx for president of Germany over his opponent, General Paul von Hindenburg.[9] One such article made a strong case for the establishment of a Jewish teacher-training institution in Breslau, in conjunction with the seminary, which would prepare educators for Jewish schools. Such an institution seemed badly needed on account of the Christian atmosphere then prevalent in non-Jewish training institutions.[10]

Like most students of his day, Prinz studied at a number of universities: Breslau, Berlin, and Giessen. By chance he was in Berlin on June 24, 1922, the date on which the Jewish foreign minister, Walther Rathenau, was assassinated. Not only does the Prinz autobiography present a fascinating account of the reaction of his professor at the time, the prominent scholar and thinker, Ernst Troeltsch, but he repeatedly thereafter makes the assassination the symbolic focus for his Zionist argument against a Germany inherently unfriendly to the Jews. The animosity, he suggests, was easy to ignore since Jewish artists and intellectuals were enthusiastically celebrated in the liberal capital city of Berlin.[11]

Throughout his autobiography, but especially in the section dealing with his student years, Prinz devotes a surprising amount of attention to sexuality and especially to his own views and experiences. It is surely remarkable that a rabbinical autobiography should repeatedly and in some detail deal with sexual matters. That the Weimar years were marked by revolt and innovation, not only in literature, art, music, and theater, but also in relations between the sexes, is well known. The Jewish writer Stefan Zweig, for example, spoke of this rebellion at length in his own autobiography where he described the preceding generation of the Second Reich as decrying every form of free and extramarital love as contrary to middle-class respectability even as it engaged in a "morality of secrecy" that allowed men to fulfill their desires surreptitiously while proper young women were expected to remain chaste until marriage. By contrast, the German capital of the 1920s was a place where "to be sixteen and still under suspicion of virginity would have been considered a disgrace in any school of Berlin at that time. Every girl wanted to be able to tell of her adventures and the more exotic the better."[12] During the Weimar years, the alleged hypocrisy and duplicity of the earlier generation gave way in urban circles to unshielded and unfettered relationships.

It is common knowledge that some leading religious figures, both Christian and Jewish—one thinks, for example, of Paul Tillich, Martin Buber, and Martin Luther King, Jr.—were less than faithful in their relationships, but it is unusual to find an explicit disavowal of monogamy among rabbis along with specific attention to their own sexuality. Prinz begins this subject by describing the sexual games played with the maids in the village, the first kiss, and the conflict between his inclinations and the strict code of the Zionist youth movement to which he belonged. When he comes to his seminary and university years, his sexual attitudes become yet another way of distinguishing himself from his fellow students. But he is inconsistent, at one point writing of the seminarians that "probably very few of them had had any sexual experiences" and that they sublimated their desires through rowdyish behavior, but writing less than a page later that "although there were some theology students who remained 'pure,' they were a distinct minority." He not only describes the first time he slept with his wife-to-be, the seminary professor's daughter Lucie Horovitz, whom he married in 1925 when she was twenty-three, but also notes that she was at the time sexually much more experienced than he. And he goes on to tell us that his first marriage, as well as his second to Hilde Goldschmidt, were egalitarian "open" marriages in which neither partner felt bound to a monogamous relationship. As we shall see, however, Prinz's participation in the unrestrained lifestyle of Weimar urban culture did not diminish his standing as a rabbi, especially among the youth who shared his values. But it did upset the older generation and it became a factor in his dismissal from his position in 1935. It was also the subject of a caution expressed by Rabbi Stephen S. Wise in a letter to the relative who would make it financially possible for Prinz to flee to the United States two years later.[13]

Prinz came to Berlin in 1926, three years before receiving a formal ordination certificate, in order to serve as rabbi of the Friedenstempel, a private congregation that stood outside the framework of the organized Jewish community and whose rabbi was therefore not subject to its discipline. His inaugural sermon, delivered on January 7, 1927, when Prinz was twenty-four years old, was printed in the Breslau paper that he had earlier edited.[14] Here, at the beginning of his formal rabbinical career, Prinz laid out basic principles that would govern his rabbinate henceforth. "Who should the rabbi be?" he asks in this programmatic sermon. And he answers: "The rabbi needs to be someone who is able to see into his time and to render judgment upon it. He needs to be and should be a critic of his time." In order to do that the rabbi must be entirely free to speak his mind. The pulpit must be a place of truth, where not so much as a single step departs from it. Later Prinz would become a friend and admirer of Rabbi Stephen S. Wise, who had earlier insisted on freedom of the pulpit when he left Temple Emanu-El in New York and established the Free Synagogue in the same city. So, too, Prinz insisted from the first upon his right to express unpopular views that he believed to represent truth.

Having asserted his right to say what he pleased, Prinz went on to make a provocative statement—as he always loved to do. The rabbi, he insisted, is not a preacher. Inspirational preaching has no lasting influence. It may momentarily exalt the soul, but it does not have long-term effects on those who hear the sermon. "A rabbi hasn't had a beneficial effect if he has inspired people of his congregation through his sermons, if he has won over a few individual souls. Rather he has been effective if he is successful in making his congregation into a living link in the chain of Jewish tradition. . . . It is necessary to attach the present to the past." That act required a rabbi who was, above all, a teacher—not simply of children, but also of adults. And indeed throughout his life as an active rabbi, in Germany and in New Jersey, Prinz would regularly use the pulpit to give instruction in Judaism and in contemporary Jewish life, thereby linking the generations. In Germany this use of the sermon, which he claimed to have learned from Felix Goldmann, was a novelty, although other rabbis soon adopted it as well.

Prinz concluded his inaugural sermon with a statement on the importance of paying more attention to Jewish youth. "To be a rabbi," he noted, "means to me to be an educator. Being a rabbi means taking responsibility for the Jewish reality of the future." For his last sentence, Prinz chose to say: "All of my work shall be directed to the youth."

Of course, Prinz did not direct all of his work toward young people, but he did devote more attention to them than did most of his colleagues. Without question he was their favorite rabbi. Both in Berlin and later in Newark, New Jersey, young people—young women, in particular—would come to the synagogue, not so much for the service, but to hear Prinz, in some cases to absorb what he had to say about contemporary issues, in others because they were secretly in love with the handsome young rabbi.[15] On Saturday afternoons, beginning in 1928, an average of 150 of them went "to Prinz" for the Oneg Shabbat (Sabbath social hour) celebration. One participant recalled that the synagogue vestibule teemed with young people. Prinz led discussions and Hebrew songs and taught a bit of modern Hebrew.[16] He was also a master storyteller who could make the biblical tales come alive. Younger children flocked to his classes and Prinz was able to bring his retellings to a larger audience by publishing them in illustrated volumes. In the first book, intended to be read aloud, he expressed his desire to bring the biblical characters to life so that children would remember them as they remembered Little Red Riding Hood. The purpose was not to rationalize the stories but to appeal to the child's imagination and evoke a sense of wonder.[17]

Prinz flouted regnant custom by greatly diminishing the distance between himself and the young people, utterly demolishing the stereotype of the solemn and dignified religious leader. He would wear casual clothing, take young people ice-skating, and in other ways participate in their lifestyle and activities. Well aware of his being different, he once distinguished his own approach from that of Rabbi Leo Baeck, who was still a representative of the older generation and its rabbinical self-image. Of Baeck, whom he highly respected, Prinz noted: "He was a leader of the people without being of the people. He never danced or laughed with the people."[18]

Prinz enjoyed great popularity, not only among the young people, for whom he created a youth club[19] and a school,[20] and for whom he served as a Jewish chaplain at the University of Berlin.[21] Adult members of the community flocked to him for weddings and funerals, the latter described in interesting detail in the autobiography.[22] Yet Prinz was consistently ambivalent about being a rabbi and went out of his way to avoid the stereotyped view of a clergyman. No longer convinced of the religious importance of the dietary laws, he kept kosher because that tradition was demanded of rabbis in Europe. On Sabbaths he drove to synagogue, parking a short distance away. And he spent his evenings at cafés with intellectuals and artists, not at home studying sacred texts. Less than his professional career, it was his nightlife, which also included frequent parties, attendance at theater performances, and occasional costume balls, that later made Prinz say to an interviewer, "If I could choose a time to live in, any time, any place, I'd choose the 1920s in Berlin."[23] His marriage to Lucie was a very happy one, her loss in childbirth—paralleling the death of his mother—was a traumatic experience, which the autobiography relates in detail. By and large, Prinz avoided the company of fellow rabbis, from whom he felt a personal distance despite their common profession. The sole exception may have been Malwin Warschauer, a fellow Zionist and practitioner of the pastoral rabbinate, whom he chose to officiate at his second marriage, to Hilde Goldschmidt, in 1932.[24]

Prinz's pulpit served him as a stage, an opportunity to present himself to an audience as does an actor, but within the framework of Judaism and for the sake of the Jewish people. To his brother-in-law Max Gruenewald, then the rabbi in Mannheim, he wrote in 1930: "The holidays were exciting and taxing, with services conducted in large spaces. Like a wandering preacher.[25] Again and again I regret that applause is prohibited in synagogues, but sometimes am glad it is likewise prohibited to throw eggs. I would have endured both with the same vanity. The one because I gladly allow myself to be spoiled, the other with the ominous premonition that one always throws eggshells at great men when they are about to hatch something new."[26]

Politically, Prinz was a socialist and a Zionist. In 1930, he spoke to a meeting of the Jewish Peace Association, in which Albert Einstein and Leo Baeck also played a role and which was headed by the Jewish banker Oscar Wassermann.[27] For Prinz there was a distinct connection between social inequality and militarism. Explicitly declaring that, although a theologian, he would be speaking "entirely un-theologically and only as a young person to his own generation," he asserted that "the shortcomings of our social and economic order stand opposed to peace. It is necessary to transform it in such a way that it will cease to be the seedbed of militaristic entanglements and become instead the soil for a peaceful order."[28] Later, in the United States, Prinz would express similar views in favoring greater economic equality and in opposing the Vietnam War.

During the Weimar years, Prinz's Zionism gave him a second major channel of self-expression alongside his sermons. And it also provided him with his social circle. The German Zionists during that period were a small minority of German Jewry, mostly young and highly rebellious against the non- or anti-Zionist older generation. Although he was not a major officer of the Zionist Association in Germany, Prinz became one of its most popular speakers. It was as a Zionist that Prinz claims to have foreseen the danger that Hitler would constitute for Jews once he came into power. Prinz asserts in the autobiography that he declared Hitler's rule a realistic possibility as early as 1929, when most German Jews were making light of the mustached madman.[29] Mistakenly, they assumed that the liberal Berlin, where a third of them lived, was representative of Germany, while he paid more attention to the far different mood in the countryside. Prinz claims also to have recognized that Nazism was more than a political ideology. It could penetrate so deeply because it was a "new political church."

Hitler's appointment as chancellor of Germany on January 30, 1933, unleashed a crisis within German Jewry, especially among the Liberals, who had remained optimistic about the future of Jews in that country. Increasingly driven out from the public sphere, German Jews were forced to seek psychological sustenance from within a Jewish community that hitherto had been at best peripheral to their daily lives. As their long-standing ideology of complete equality within German society lay in ruins, they turned to the abandoned synagogue as a place of refuge where they could be among their own. Large numbers turned to Prinz as the rabbi who would dare to address their concerns the most honestly, directly, and dramatically.

Never was this more true than on Friday evening, March 31, 1933, the night before the boycott of Jewish stores that by two months followed Hitler's ascent to power. Prinz referred to the service he conducted that evening as the most memorable in his life, especially when the worshippers in a packed synagogue shouted the watchword of the Jewish faith, the Shema Yisra'el ("Hear, O Israel"), with such fervor that it drowned out choir and organ.[30] From the recollections of Prinz's rabbinical colleague, Hans Tramer, we learn more than what is contained in the autobiography about how Prinz chose to dramatize the crisis for the congregation. Tramer remembers that earlier that day he had met with Prinz at his home and asked his more senior colleague what he should say at the services. Prinz replied that he himself would simply read a proclamation circulated to all synagogues by Rabbi Leo Baeck and add two or three sentences about its contents. It was, he added, a time not for speaking, but for silence. That, in fact, is exactly what Tramer did in his synagogue. The next day, however, he learned what Prinz himself had done. This is Tramer's account: "Prinz entered the synagogue, called the shammes [the caretaker of the synagogue] and had him call up the three oldest men in the congregation. He then removed the Torah scrolls from the ark. They stood, two next to him and one in front of him. Then before the open ark he read [Baeck's] letter, had the scrolls solemnly replaced in the ark, whereupon he spoke for forty minutes or even an hour saying: 'We Jews will defend our Judaism; we have no weapons, for THIS is our weapon.' Thereupon he wheeled around and tore open the ark containing the Torah scrolls!"[31] When Tramer later asked Prinz why he hadn't suggested something similar to him, Prinz replied innocently: "All of that occurred to me only at the last minute." He claimed to have improvised the performance spontaneously.[32]

That summer, Prinz wrote his most successful—and most controversial—book: *Wir Juden* (We Jews). Upon its appearance toward the end of 1933, it quickly sold thousands of copies and created a considerable stir. Jewish assimilation in modern times had been a failure, this historical polemic proclaimed; German Jews had always remained on the margins of German society, their identification with Germany a psychopathological flight from self, their modern history a *Krankengeschichte*, a history of the sick. And now that the so-called liberal era was suddenly reaching a dramatic end, Liberal Judaism, as it had developed in the nineteenth century, needed to give way to the only philosophy of Judaism that made sense in Nazi Germany, namely the recognition that the Jews were themselves a nation. Given the new situation, the only salvation for the Jews lay in emigration to Palestine. The book represented a clear example of a genre that Prinz would later defend as legitimate: the use of historical writing for the purpose of propaganda.[33] Not surprisingly, critics in the Zionist camp praised the little volume; advocates of Jewish integration in Germany were more critical, though they could not just dismiss its arguments.[34] The right-wing Jewish theologian Hans Joachim Schoeps wrote an entire countervolume entitled *Wir deutschen Juden* (We German Jews) in which he branded Prinz's book an example of Nietzschean paganism and plaintively asserted: "Even if our fatherland repudiates us, we remain ready to serve it."[35] *Wir Juden* even came to the attention of the German novelist and poet Hermann Hesse who, though describing Prinz's prose as not on the same spiritual level as Martin Buber's writings, declared the book "an honest, warm and sympathetic effort to lead the Jews back from adaptation to foreign peoples to their own Jewish nationalism"—and, moreover, it was more accessible to assimilated Jews than was Buber's work.[36] Almost six years later, after Prinz was established as a congregational rabbi in New Jersey, Stephen Wise proposed that the book be published in

English in a translation by his wife, Louise. "This would be your valedictory to Germany," Wise proposed, "and your salutatory to America." However, the translation, to which Prinz was supposed to add a chapter, remained in manuscript.[37]

The overflow crowd that had come to hear him speak on March 31, 1933 became almost standard in the weeks and months that followed. Prinz's sermons now focused even more on the contemporary situation of German and world Jewry, less on the weekly reading from the Torah, and hardly at all on strictly religious or philosophical subjects.[38] His words were pressed into the service of two partially contradictory goals. On the one hand, as a Zionist, Prinz preached the full severity of the new situation and the need to seek refuge in a land where Jews could determine their own fate. The effectiveness of that message required shaking up his listeners. But, on the other, he had to avoid inducing despair, the more so as emigration to Palestine—or anywhere else—became increasingly difficult. And that demanded compassion. "The anvil is stronger than the hammer," Prinz reminded his listeners. The flight from despair—and in many cases suicide—required the creation of a fervently held positive self-image that contradicted the abhorrent caricature projected by Nazi propaganda. The press and radio depicted Jews as ugly, groveling, lecherous, power-hungry, and devious. They needed to hear the opposite: that they were beautiful, noble human beings and that they had made a magnificent contribution to Western civilization. While swimming in a sea of hostile propaganda, they needed to nurture self-respect. His sermons, Prinz suggests in the autobiography, were a form of collective therapy.

Since Prinz did not usually publish, or even write out, his sermons, we can determine their content only from reactions in the Jewish press. One sermon, a worshipper recalled, suggested that it was necessary to create a new German Jew who would cease trying to shine (*scheinen*) outward toward the non-Jewish world, but rather focus inward, simply trying to exist (*sein*).[39] Another sermon was self-critical. Not only the Jews of the world, it suggested, but also the Jews of Germany spoke in so many languages that they failed to understand each other. Unity among Jews was required, now more than ever.[40]

As Prinz relates in the autobiography, the presence of two Gestapo officials at every service required ingenuity in delivering an unvarnished message. He effectively achieved that by using negative biblical images symbolically: Haman for Hitler, Amalek for the Nazis, and the like. Among the Jewish holidays, Passover attained central significance; a new pharaoh had

arisen to enslave the people of Israel. A Passover seder held at the Friedenstempel in 1934 drew 350 participants with "many hundreds" turned away
for lack of space.[41]

Forced to retreat into what for many German Jews was a nearly empty
Jewish identity, they began to attend classes on Judaism in unprecedented
numbers. In the expanding scope of adult education Prinz played a central
role. He spoke frequently in gatherings of the Kulturbund, the Jewish cultural association, where he argued provocatively on one occasion that a non-
derivative Jewish culture was possible only in Palestine or Eastern Europe,
but not in Germany.[42] Already in 1930 he had published a popular history
of the Jews, which appeared three years later in a more extensively illustrated
version. Laying no claim to original research, Prinz's preface declared that his
purpose was simply to convey the "suspense, dynamics, and drama of this
singular community."[43] Reading such a history could evoke deeper identification. Toward the end of his stay in Germany, when Jews had already
been forced into an invisible ghetto, Prinz gave them parallels from Jewish history in a book entitled *Life in the Ghetto.*[44] Prinz was a pioneer in
advocating experiential learning and using audiovisual aids in education.
His initial lecture series in the Bialik Adult Education Institute featured
color slides and was entitled "Jewish History in Contemporary Images."[45]
Once again challenging customary norms, he proposed a de-theologized Jewish cultural history that would include the secular culture of average Jews
and embrace such nonnormative figures as Jesus and Spinoza.[46] Perhaps his
most striking suggestion was to imitate a Ministry of Education directive for
the Hitler Youth that designated Saturdays henceforth as a day devoted to
instilling Nazi values. So too, Prinz argued, Jewish educators should specify
the Jewish Sabbath as a day for instilling Jewish values. The authorities could
hardly object to the Jews taking up the same idea for indoctrinating their
own youth.[47]

No less provocative was Prinz's assault upon the most influential and es-
teemed of the German Zionist and religious thinkers, Martin Buber. At one
time Prinz and his Zionist friends had regarded Buber's writings as "sacred
texts," and they admired the novelty of his Bible translation. Moreover, Buber's new book of essays[48] indicated that he had once more become "a great,
courageous, and fearless preacher." But Prinz and his circle had also been disappointed by Buber and turned away from him. Increasingly, they had concluded that his work was too ethereal, too lacking in concrete substance.
Prinz claimed that when Buber dealt with the practical consequences of religious belief, he often spoke of "life within Jewish law," but, according to
Prinz, his own life showed no evidence of it. He was disappointed that Bu-

ber did not take his own words seriously. "How, then, could he lead us?" he asked. In response, Buber distinguished between divine and codified law in Judaism. The former demanded listening (*horchen*) and then, if the divine voice reached the individual, obedience (*gehorchen*). That was a position Prinz too could accept: the choice and adoption for life of that which is personally heard as representing God's will. The extended, sometimes heated discussion thus ended in agreement.[49]

At the time of his interchange with Martin Buber in 1936, Prinz was no longer a rabbi of the Berlin Jewish community, but had returned to his early interest in journalism and was spending most of his time as the political editor of an important Jewish newspaper published in Hamburg called the *Israelitisches Familienblatt.* A year earlier he had been summarily fired as community rabbi, a position he held from the time the initially independent Friedenstempel had been integrated into the community in 1929. Since many of the documents concerning his dismissal have survived, it is possible to reconstruct its background and causes—which vary in their nature and complexity from what Prinz offers in his autobiography.[50]

Despite his extraordinary sermonic abilities and the ego pleasure he received from speaking in the largest Berlin synagogues, Prinz was a critic of the long-standing system that sent rabbis weekly from synagogue to synagogue to provide "variety" for the worshippers. He declared this practice "a pernicious custom," appropriate perhaps for a theater audience but not for a religious community. "Not every filled synagogue is a community," he wrote. It is only a public gathering. Moreover, the system makes preachers into prima donnas. In place of the regnant norm, Prinz proposed the creation of small organic communities within the larger organized Berlin community, each with its own rabbi, who would be able to know his congregants with greater intimacy, sharing their joys and sorrows. The *kehillah* (the organized community), Prinz claimed, had become a bureaucracy that paid little attention to the rabbis, and, as such, was unable to meet religious needs.[51] On May 17, 1935, Prinz made critique of the community's administration the topic of a sermon in which, according to the written version he produced later, he said: "The pens of bureaucrats can stifle human hearts and kill living organisms."[52] Community officials claimed that the orally delivered sermon was even more derisive and insulting in its attack. Moreover, Prinz continued his campaign to the point where a foreign newspaper picked it up and transformed it into a personal attack upon the head of the community, Heinrich Stahl (whom Prinz mentions twice in the autobiography). Such attacks could not sit well with the community's administration, which was accustomed to treating rabbis as paid employees. Prinz and his fellow Zionists also claimed that his Zionism was a factor in the dismissal, which may have been the case, though by 1935 he was by no means the only Zionist rabbi in Germany.[53]

However, neither his critique nor his Zionism seem to have been the determining causes of Prinz's dismissal. In fact, even Zionists on the community executive voted for the initial unanimous decision to suspend him from office. The record of charges consisted of a long list of complaints. Crucial to his dismissal was the easily substantiable claim that Prinz was negligent in carrying out the duties of his office. Specifically, he had overextended his vacation and missed religious school classes for which he was responsible. For years he had flouted community regulations regarding weddings and funerals. His remarks about the death of German civilization at the funeral of a physician murdered by the Nazis (recorded in the autobiography) had gone too far, creating a danger for the community in such perilous times. More generally, his personal conduct for years had violated the dignity of the rabbinical office. It was only on account of his extraordinary popularity that action had not been taken earlier.[54] Now it was decided that Rabbi Prinz was incorrigible—he was a rebel by nature, and such a religious leader was regarded as especially undesirable at a time when Jewish unity was deemed essential.

Prinz's colleagues and supporters came to his defense. They attempted, ultimately in vain, to mediate the dispute. One of them, fellow Zionist Rabbi Max Elk, declared that Prinz's loss to the German rabbinate would be immense as he was currently the most active and effective force within it. A petition on Prinz's behalf gathered more than ten thousand signatures.[55] In order to avoid the charge of infringing freedom of the pulpit—a value upheld also by the Liberal Jewish press—Prinz was for a time allowed to continue preaching while absolved of other rabbinical functions. But that too ended after a few months. Fortunately for Prinz, however, by the time of his final departure from the Berlin rabbinate at the end of September 1935, he had already been able to find new employment—as the fund-raising representative in Europe for the Hebrew University in Jerusalem.

As early as March of that year, Prinz had spoken on behalf of the university in Germany, afterward printing his remarks in the Jewish press.[56] Toward the end of the year, as he recorded in his autobiography, he traveled on its behalf to Eastern Europe, where he combined fund-raising with Zionist propaganda. A contemporary report indicates that in Yugoslavia he drew enormous crowds, packing synagogues and requiring transmission of his speeches by loudspeakers to adjoining rooms. In Belgrade, the senate of the university held a special session in his honor.[57] He was equally well received in Romania and Czechoslovakia. However, his work for the Hebrew University lasted only a few months. In the autobiography, Prinz attributes that short tenure to his reluctance to do much traveling, but there is also evidence that, at least on a trip he took to Switzerland for the university, he failed to raise any money.[58]

Returning to the German scene, Prinz began to focus on his duties as editor and also on a busy lecture schedule that took him all over Germany. By this time, Prinz had ceased to be enthusiastic about the Jewish revival in which he himself had played such a major role. Now he noted that in 1933 large numbers of Jews had fled from Judaism through conversion or by leaving the organized community. Even for those who had sought to strengthen their Jewish identity, their "return to Judaism," he now suggested, was at best superficial. By the end of 1936, attendance at adult courses had decreased drastically, down to a few hundred in Berlin with some courses having to be canceled.[59] Jewish existence in Germany, as Prinz now saw it, was life in a ghetto without walls, a life without gentile neighbors. When the Olympics were held in Berlin in 1936, Prinz wrote: "We Jews exist alongside the celebrations, just as for some time now we have, as it were, been living alongside life."[60]

As the situation of German Jewry worsened and morale began to sink, Prinz wondered whether the new self-confidence he had sought to instill was not an illusion. Writing in the *Israelitisches Familienblatt*, of which he had become the editor, he complained in March 1937 of the negative effects of living in a spiritual ghetto and of the bureaucratization of the Jewish revival. He also recognized that the needs of the body were rapidly pushing aside those of the spirit. "Thus the dream of renewal came to naught," he wrote. "Our people, who in 1933 eagerly took in everything called Judaism, have today often internally abandoned it. Being Jewish is no longer a challenge but a [constricting] form of life. Having become bored, they leave the courses and the lecture halls and often also the schools and don't perk up their ears until they hear the words 'certificates for entry to Palestine, affidavits, transfer,[61] authorization and work permits.' That is our life."[62] Spirituality and Jewish learning sank beneath the need to leave Germany as soon as possible. One was preoccupied now not with reconstituting oneself as a religious and educated Jew but with saving one's life.

Despite his involvement in Jewish spiritual resistance, Prinz had all along advocated systematic emigration to Palestine as the best solution, especially for the young.[63] Although not in a major position of organizational leadership in German Zionism,[64] he wrote on the subject, preached it from the pulpit, and was among its most popular lecturers.[65] When he spoke at a gathering marking the thirty-second anniversary of Theodor Herzl's death, the largest hall available to the Berlin Jewish community proved much too small.[66] But did such Zionist propaganda make sense when there was already angry competition for the few certificates for entry to Palestine granted by the British mandatory government? Prinz believed that it did, since association with the movement, beyond all practical consequences, was an inner source of strength. As he put it, "Even in the face of apparent hopelessness, we must win people over to the idea and thus preserve the utopian power of Zionism."[67]

As Prinz traveled around Germany speaking on Zionism to large audiences—in Dresden, Bremen, Düsseldorf, Leipzig and elsewhere—his listeners invariably included Nazi watchdogs, who reported on the content of his addresses. Their reports indicate that on no occasion did they find reason to object to his remarks. The Zionist goal, after all, at this point coincided with that of the Nazis: to remove Jews from Germany as quickly and as efficiently as possible. Moreover, on at least one occasion Prinz spoke about the acuteness of the Jewish question also in other lands, a reassurance to his Nazi listeners that they were not alone in detesting Jews. In a speech delivered in Königsberg in May 1935, Prinz supposedly said the following, which apparently impressed the Nazi reporter sufficiently for him to cite it: "Let Germany do what it must. . . . We are a burden for this people, a people that, as it always stresses, would be happy if we did not exist. . . . I am not reproaching this land since one can do as one wants in one's own country. The world can manage without Jews. That is something we must always consider."[68] It is hard to imagine a stronger Zionist message, or one more in agreement with Nazi views at the time.

Prinz did, however, on frequent occasions arouse the ire of the authorities in Berlin. Regrettably, because of the loss of Gestapo files, it is not possible to verify the accounts of his arrests that Prinz presents in such detail in the autobiography. However, his acquaintance and apparent protector, Gestapo Obersturmbahnführer Kuchmann, is mentioned in the Eichmann trial, and Prinz's rabbinical colleague, Hans Tramer, relates how the Gestapo in 1933 arrested Prinz, wearing casual clothing and without documents, along with members of his youth club. When Tramer went to bail them out, affirming that Prinz was a rabbi, one Nazi allegedly said to him in the prevalent Berlin dialect: "We never believed him [*jarnicht jeglaubt*]. He's a young man. How could he be a clergyman?" Both Prinz and the youth club members were thereupon quickly released. The reason for the arrest was apparently something the young people had done, and Prinz had simply volunteered to accompany them to the Gestapo. Tramer also substantiates Prinz's account of his brief arrest following the report by a stool pigeon of his earlier mentioned provocative remarks at the physician's funeral. In the early days of Nazi rule, Tramer notes, one could still argue freedom of the pulpit.[69]

Prinz's autobiographical account of various arrests gives the reader a fuller understanding of the author's character. The recollections seem to fill him with admiration for his own cleverness. Although he also admits to the role of luck, according to his entertaining descriptions he repeatedly managed to outsmart the authorities who arrested him, in one case by declaring his status as clergy, in another by laying out his rank as a Ph.D. In a manner reminiscent of the way the psychoanalyst Bruno Bettelheim describes outwitting the SS in the concentration camps of Dachau and Buchenwald by acting counter to their stereotype of the Jew, Prinz claims success in avoiding peril at the hands of the Nazis by playing upon their mentality. He remains the master of every situation. But perhaps this attitude was not fashioned only in retrospect for the autobiography. Although we might imagine complex feelings, including fear, Prinz may be correctly recalling what he felt at the time, for example, when he writes of experiencing "a strange sense of elation whenever I was arrested; I was always so sure I would be released. It seemed to be some sort of psychopathological attitude I had adopted at that time, but it was very helpful to me." However, his success with Nazi authorities could not last indefinitely. In the end, for reasons that cannot be determined with certainty, Prinz was forced to leave Germany. The obvious question, one that dogged Prinz his entire life, was why, as a confirmed Zionist, he chose America over the Land of Israel.

Repeatedly, Prinz had considered the possibility of aliyah, of immigration to Palestine. As recorded in the autobiography, a few months after Hitler came to power, Prinz wrote to the Zionist leader Chaim Weizmann suggesting the establishment of a boarding school in Palestine, for which he would raise money from the German Zionists and whose directorship he would presumably assume.[70] But nothing came of that scheme. In the winter of 1934, Prinz and his wife Hilde visited Palestine, and although he was critical of some aspects of what they saw, he waxed enthusiastic about the work of the pioneers.[71] Had he chosen aliyah, it would not have been difficult for Prinz to gain entry to the country, as there was a special quota for rabbis. Why, then, did he prefer to remain in Germany until he was forced to leave and then choose emigration to the United States, much to the dismay of his German Zionist associates, most of whom settled in Palestine? A number of considerations were involved. As the autobiography suggests, Prinz, like his senior colleague Leo Baeck, felt a responsibility to remain at his post. But perhaps most crucial to his ultimate choice of America over Palestine, as Prinz himself saw it, was the question of what he would do there as a Liberal rabbi. It is also true, as is so apparent from the autobiography, that Prinz enjoyed the good life—fine food and drink, modern furniture, an apartment in the fashionable Dahlem neighborhood of Berlin, and first-class accommodations on his travels. But Palestine of the 1930s was not a place of luxuries. Life could be far more comfortable in America. Moreover, at least initially, it would have been difficult for the eloquent speaker to express himself well in Hebrew.

Prinz's ambivalence about aliyah is perhaps most apparent in an essay that first criticizes the bourgeois values he found among the Jewish city dwellers in the Jewish homeland, then suggests the necessity of "Zionizing the German Jews in Palestine," and finally projects a pastoral vision as the only real Zionism: "For the establishment of an industrial state one need sing no songs, and sowing the land with smokestacks and factories does not demand summoning up the moral powers of our people. From such a conception we expect absolutely nothing. The wonderful élan and the amazing enthusiasm that until now have built the land arose from conceptions of a new Jewish people that plows its own soil. Without these ideas the dream vanishes and its realization disappears."[72] Since Prinz was clearly not cut out to realize the pioneering ideal, he could at least distance himself from the Palestinian urban culture that he believed violated it and thus provide himself with another justification for choosing America. In the wake of the Arab riots in 1936, he also began to argue that one should not cast Zionist aspersions on those German Jews who chose to emigrate to destinations other than Palestine.[73] Nor should Zionists deprecate the feelings that German Jews still harbored for Germany, not as fatherland, but as an internalized homeland, a place of birth, family, and memories.[74] Already in *Wir Juden* he had argued that even in their own land, in the Land of Israel, German Jews would not forsake German culture, which was their "holy and unforgettable possession."[75]

By early 1937, Prinz was preparing for emigration to the United States, encouraged by Rabbi Stephen S. Wise of New York, whom he had met at a Zionist congress in Switzerland two years earlier. As Prinz tells us in the autobiography, he began to take English lessons, and in mid-March 1937 undertook a four-week exploratory visit. Despite his earlier views, he had come to believe "that it was no exaggeration to say that the future of the Jews may some day be determined in America."[76] And now, increasingly, he began to think of himself as participating in it.

As the date of his departure approached, Prinz's Zionist friends arranged a grand farewell evening on June 26, 1937, at which, as Prinz correctly notes in the autobiography, Adolf Eichmann was present. It was a Saturday evening, and according to his friend Benno Cohn, Prinz quoted a phrase from the havdalah service that separates the Sabbath from the rest of the week— "He [God] who distinguishes the holy from the profane." Prinz then went on to say: "All around us is profanity, but our Jewish nationality is holy."[77] After the meeting, Eichmann came up to the speakers' table and made some unfriendly remarks, but Prinz was allowed to depart from Germany a few days later. Even in leaving, he had managed once more to raise the Jews above the "profanity" of their environment.

After what Prinz describes in the autobiography as a sometimes scary but also quite comfortable trip, he arrived in New York on August 1, 1937, accompanied by a pregnant wife, two children, and their faithful Christian maid. The day after, the *New York Times* carried a brief article and photograph, which cited Prinz as saying that "German Jewry has died." To the *Newark Evening News* he said at the time: "Germany will be and should be a country without Jews." That was a view he maintained even later when visiting the new German-Jewish communities that sprang up after the war. Offered the opportunity in 1956 to reoccupy a rabbinate in Berlin, Prinz declined the offer and was still convinced even in 1969 that the postwar community would "die out within less than a generation."[78] Unlike his brother-in-law, Max Gruenewald, who would become president of the Leo Baeck Institute for the History and Culture of German-Speaking Jewry, Prinz devoted little time to émigré organizations or to preserving the German-Jewish cultural heritage. In his autobiography, he curiously and erroneously pushed laws from the year 1938, like that requiring the insertion of a "J" into all Jewish passports and the provision that Jewish men add the name "Israel," Jewish women "Sarah," to their given names, back to the beginning of the Nazi regime. Perhaps—whether conscious or not—it was a way of suggesting that conditions at the time of his departure were already worse than they were in fact. Whether he felt any survivor guilt is a matter of dispute within the family.

Once in the United States, Prinz participated actively in fighting against the isolationist America First Committee and the leading protagonist of Nazi Germany in America, Charles Lindbergh. To deaf ears he warned American Jews about Hitler. As one who had experienced Nazi Germany firsthand, he soon became a major New Jersey spokesman for American intervention in Europe.[79] Yet he derided American culture as inferior to its German counterpart, the latter having the benefit of a rich and varied history, especially in

the arts. Even the political life of America, as Prinz first encountered it, re-
pelled him on account of its corruption. Not least bothersome about his new
home was its attitude toward the black population. In a rather balanced report on his initial trip to the United States, Prinz had called attention to the
prevalent attitude of arrogance toward blacks that was shared by American
Jews.[80] In the autobiography he tells a likely embellished but fundamentally
credible story about his encounter, some months later, with Jewish racism in
Atlanta.

The initial months in America were the most difficult of Prinz's life. For
the first and only time, he suffered economic deprivation. The lectures that he
undertook for the United Palestine Appeal took him away from his growing
family, but no other source of income beckoned on the horizon. He was not
eager to take a permanent position with the impecunious High Holiday congregation of German-Jewish immigrants for whom he conducted services in
1938. Always ambivalent about his rabbinical role, he hoped for some alternative within the Jewish community, but to no avail. When Stephen Wise
came up with a very attractive rabbinical position, Prinz could not turn it
down.

Although the dramatic manner in which Prinz was offered the Newark
pulpit, as described in the autobiography, is not documented elsewhere, the
match was certainly an excellent one, coming at a time when Prinz was without other prospects and the congregation was desperately in need of an outstanding personality who could lead it out of a financial crunch brought
about by economic depression and imprudent, lavish spending. Temple B'nai
Abraham of Newark, New Jersey, was proud of its 2,000-seat sanctuary and
its social center wing that, like other large synagogues of the time, boasted a
gym and a full-sized swimming pool. Its rabbi for thirty-seven years, Julius
Silberfeld, was not a great orator and had proven himself unable to draw in
new members whose dues could cover the growing deficit. But he was a Zionist and socially progressive, so that the tenor of the congregation was well
suited to Prinz's own inclinations.[81] The $6,000 salary he was offered was
most generous for an untried immigrant.[82]

Stephen Wise honored Prinz by giving the main address at his inaugu-
ration on September 1, 1939, remembered especially for the "rude slight of
Dr. Wise" when, on the pulpit and in the sight of all, the anti-Zionist local
Reform rabbi, Solomon Foster, refused to shake Wise's hand.[83] Like many
non-Orthodox congregations of that age, B'nai Abraham was a synagogue
based more on ethnic than on religious ties. Though at the time a member of
the Conservative movement, it was to become wholly independent during
Prinz's tenure, in that respect taking on the initial status of the Friedenstem-

pel in Berlin when Prinz had become its rabbi in 1926. As Prinz's oratorical skills in English were soon on a par with those he had displayed in Germany, the synagogue began regularly to draw large numbers for Sabbath services. The fact that the congregation was composed almost entirely of Jews from Eastern Europe seems not to have created any barriers between them and their German-born rabbi. As in Germany, here too Prinz spoke on the Jewish and general issues of the day, and once again drew young people attracted by his ability to express his views clearly and relevantly on current events. And, as in the past, he thrived on controversy. The lay leader of the congregation, Michael Stavitsky, could write to Wise a few months after Prinz's installation that the new rabbi was fulfilling all their expectations: the synagogue was regularly full, young people were coming in large numbers, the religious school had full registration, and—most important—new members were joining the congregation. Prinz too was pleased, "happier than ever" in his new position.[84]

Since he cared a great deal about good synagogue music, Prinz employed a professional (gentile) choir and the noted composer of Jewish music, Max Helfman. He cared much less about theology and religious piety. Prinz professed belief in God but not in the afterlife or in the efficacy of prayer. Tellingly, his autobiography does not attribute Prinz's escape from Germany in any manner to God's providence.[85] His Jewish focus was consistently far more on the people of Israel than on its God or even on Torah. Synagogues exist, he wrote on one occasion, "for the purpose of making the Jewish spirit survive among the people who willingly and enthusiastically call themselves Jews."[86] In a "Guide for Jewish Living" that he compiled for a weekend seminar in 1955, Prinz defined his congregation as "traditional progressive" and its faith as belief "in the Jewish people."[87] Very much in the manner of the Reconstructionist movement and its founder Mordecai Kaplan, Prinz avoided terms such as *commandment* and *chosenness*. Nor did he regard observance as essential to Judaism. He did not restrict his own activities on the Sabbath or advocate a life governed by Jewish law. Although his Guide called for the exclusion of pork products and shellfish from the dinner tables of congregants, Temple B'nai Abraham did not have a kosher kitchen and his family attests that Prinz himself cooked lobster for consumption in his home. On rare occasions he was also willing to preside at mixed marriage ceremonies, though not in the synagogue.

Successful as Prinz was in his American rabbinate, as in Germany so too in America, rabbinical functions could not fully satisfy his quest for both public recognition and broader avenues of service. He soon became active in the larger Newark Jewish community, managing to raise unprecedented sums for local and international Jewish needs. The autobiography relates in entertaining, though probably dramatized, detail an additional role that he began to play: as rabbi for the Jewish mob in Newark and its boss Longy Zwillman. But it was to the national and international Jewish scene that Prinz began to turn his attention soon after the end of the war.

In the United States, as in Europe, Prinz chose to remain religiously on his own. Although he joined the Reform Central Conference of American Rabbis (CCAR), he seldom attended their meetings. Nonetheless, he was invited to address the CCAR, as well as the Conservative Rabbinical Assembly.[88] He was also the speaker at the second graduation ceremony of the Reconstructionist Rabbinical College in 1974. Prinz's message in each instance was similar: the task that lay before American Jewry was to survive as a people, not for the mere sake of survival, but in a meaningful way—which for Prinz meant especially a commitment to social activism, to Jewish education, and to creative continuity (a term Prinz used long before it became a slogan of the American Jewish community).[89]

Initially, Prinz remained a fervent Zionist. During his first months in America he spoke to seven hundred delegates at the convention of the Jewish National Fund in Detroit and gave radio addresses urging more support for the Jewish settlements in Palestine.[90] Together with his mentor Stephen Wise, he attended the first Zionist Congress held after the war. But, as Prinz indicates in the autobiography, Wise's star at the time was on the descendant and the Congress was controlled by his Revisionism-leaning right-wing rival Rabbi Abba Hillel Silver.[91] Zionism in the United States was moving to the political right, and Prinz was rapidly becoming disenchanted with it. "American Zionism is driving rapidly toward Revisionism," he wrote to Wise shortly before the Congress. "The people are bewildered. Nobody knows where he stands."[92] Once the State of Israel was established, Prinz did two things: he left the Zionist Organization of America in 1948 and a year later made a final attempt "to find a position that would permit me to settle in Israel." This time his job would be to take charge of propaganda and organization for the Jewish National Fund at its head office in Jerusalem.[93] But once again the effort foundered. In 1949, Prinz was quoted by the *Jerusalem Post* as saying—in line with David Ben-Gurion's views—that "a Jew who takes his Zionism seriously should prepare himself for emigration to Israel."[94] Since Prinz had now finally determined to remain in the United States, consistency required that he seek national prominence in channels of the Jewish community that lay outside of Zionism. He soon found such channels in the American and the World Jewish Congress. Through the World Jewish Congress, which focused on the Jewish people as a whole, Prinz could still act in support of Israel (and sometimes criticize its policies), but from a position of greater independence than from within organized Zionism.[95] Through the American Jewish Congress he could extend his activities to issues that affected life in the United States beyond the confines of the Jewish community.

In the summer of 1948 Prinz joined the aging and ailing Stephen Wise at the plenary assembly of the World Jewish Congress in Montreux, Switzerland, where he served as leader of the U.S. delegation. Prinz describes the meeting in detail in his autobiography.[96] Thereafter he continued to be active in the World Jewish Congress, which brought him nearer to the man who would be one of his closest friends in the postwar years, its president following Wise, Nahum Goldmann. In his own autobiography Goldmann praised Prinz's courage, rhetorical skill, and personal loyalty. However, to Prinz's disappointment, he did not pave the way for him to be his successor as president of the World Jewish Congress.[97] Prinz's fame in America rested rather upon his activity in the American Jewish Congress.

Like the World Jewish Congress, the American Jewish Congress was the creation of Stephen Wise, the Jewish leader for whom Prinz had the highest regard.[98] Surprisingly, Prinz chose to end his autobiography not at any milestone in his own life but with the death of his mentor on April 19, 1949. Prinz's American career, however, was at that point only beginning to take off and it is regrettable that he did not extend his recollections to the years that followed. From 1958 to 1966, he would serve as president of the American Jewish Congress and from 1965 to 1967 as chair of the Conference of Presidents of Major Jewish Organizations, arguably the most important post in American Jewry. He would also continue to serve as rabbi of Temple B'nai Abraham, which moved to Livingston, New Jersey in 1973,[99] until his retirement in 1977.

It was through the American Jewish Congress that Prinz reached the pinnacle of his fame in the United States beyond the Jewish community. In 1963, when he was its president, the Congress served as one of the co-organizers of Martin Luther King's memorable March on Washington. A friend of King, Prinz was asked to deliver a short address to the more than 200,000 demonstrators immediately preceding the speech by King himself. Prinz, who had been an opponent of racial discrimination in America since his arrival and had participated in demonstrations and sit-ins against segregation,[100] gave a remarkable, very brief, talk in which he recalled his experience with racism of a different kind in Germany and insisted that the gravest sin at a time of injustice was the sin of silence. His few well-chosen words (see Appendix B), linking his own past with America's current problems, brought together the historical experiences of Jews and African Americans. The March, he later recalled, was "the greatest religious experience of my life."[101]

In appearance, Prinz was a short but handsome man. He spoke with a British inflected slight German accent; his powerful personality created a measure of distance between himself and those he led. Yet despite his love of speaking to large audiences from the raised pulpit at B'nai Abraham, he was no less devoted to playing the rabbi's pastoral role. In his comfortable home, enhanced by exquisite modern art, he preferred to speak in German with his wife Hilde. In general, he remained very European, and nearly every summer would spend two months in Europe. Despite his commitment to the Jewish people, he remained—like other early Zionists—at heart a cosmopolitan. Although not monogamous, he was very much a family man, finding time in a busy schedule to "have fun" with his children, including an adopted young Holocaust survivor who was a relative of his wife. As a parent, Prinz tried hard not to imitate the lack of communication he had experienced from his own father. Those who knew Prinz attested to his vanity and self-absorption, even to his arrogance, but also to his generosity and empathy with others.

As Prinz had been, after Leo Baeck, the best known of the German rabbis during the Nazi years, so he now became one of the most prominent figures in American Jewry in the generation after Stephen Wise and Abba Hillel Silver. At a meeting of the Rabbinical Assembly in 1971, Arthur Hertzberg said of him to his fellow Conservative rabbis that Prinz was "an astute mind and the most distinguished and beloved of our colleagues, revered in the American Rabbinate, the man who, I think, most of us would most like to be."[102] Perhaps that was an exaggeration, but the words also possessed some measure of truth. The career of this audacious and talented German and American Jew is certainly one of the more significant in modern Jewish history.

Notes

1. John Paul Eakin, *Fictions in Autobiography: Studies in the Art of Self-Invention* (Princeton, N.J., 1985), 3.

2. Roy Pascal, *Design and Truth in Autobiography* (New York, 1985), 1.

3. On Jewish autobiographies, see Alan Mintz, *"Banished from Their Father's Table": Loss of Faith and Hebrew Autobiography* (Bloomington and Indianapolis, 1989); Michael Stanislawski, *Autobiographical Jews: Essays in Jewish Self-Fashioning*

(Seattle and London, 2004); Guy Miron, *From "There" to "Here" in the First Person: The Memoirs of German Emigrants in Israel* [Hebrew] (Jerusalem, 2004); and the articles included in the *Jewish Quarterly Review* 95:1 (Winter 2005).

4. Pascal, *Design and Truth in Autobiography*, 188.

5. Religion is given but scant attention in two recent studies of the Jews in Nazi Germany: Saul Friedländer, *Nazi Germany and the Jews. Volume 1: The Years of Persecution, 1933–1939* (New York, 1997) and Marion A. Kaplan, *Between Dignity and Despair: Jewish Life in Nazi Germany* (New York and Oxford, 1998).

6. Alfred Hirschberg, "Felix Goldmann. Ein Gedenkblatt," *Gemeindeblatt der Jüdischen Gemeinde zu Berlin* (*GJGB*), October 20, 1934, p. 2.

7. Prinz in *C.V. Zeitung* (*CVZ*), October 11, 1934. See also Joachim Prinz, "In Memoriam Felix Goldmann: Mein Lehrer," *Jüdische Rundschau* (*JR*), October 16, 1934, p. 5. Later in Prinz's life, Rabbi Stephen S. Wise would become his role model.

8. Interview with Prinz in Herbert Fraenkel, "Joachim Prinz" [typescript] (Newark, NJ, 1947), p. 3.

9. On the newspaper see Joseph Walk, *Die "Jüdische Zeitung für Ostdeutschland" 1924–1937* (Hildesheim, 1993).

10. Dr. Joachim Prinz, Breslau, "Der jüdische Lehrer," *Jüdische Zeitung für Ostdeutschland* (*JZO*), January 22, 1926.

11. For example, in his book, *The Dilemma of the Modern Jew* (Boston and Toronto, 1962), 125–126.

12. Stefan Zweig, *The World of Yesterday: An Autobiography* (New York, 1943), 67–91, 313–314.

13. Wise, who himself was known to have had extramarital relations, wrote the following to Ludwig Bendix, the uncle of Prinz's second wife, Hilde Goldschmidt, on December 3, 1936: "If, of course, [Prinz] is ultimately to take his place where he really belongs, in a Jewish pulpit, he must avoid those things which have raised certain questions with regard to his personal life. There is still something of puritanism in the American viewpoint and it must be reckoned with—quite apart from the morals of the case." Stephen Wise Papers, "American Jewish Affairs," American Jewish Archives (AJA), Cincinnati, Microfilm 2356.

14. "Beginn und Rückblick. Antrittsrede," *JZO*, January 7, 1927.

15. See, for example, Irene Awret, *They'll Have to Catch Me First: An Artist's Coming of Age in the Third Reich* (Madison, Wis., 2004), 77; *JR*, February 26, 1929, p. 102. Prinz's cantor at the time, Manfred Lewandowski, recalled of Prinz that "his sermons were in the tradition of the great prophets and the power and fire of his words so stirring that soon Jews from all parts of Berlin made pilgrimage to the Friedenstempel to join in this enthusiasm for everything Jewish. Often the police had to shut the gates of the temple because the synagogue was filled beyond its capacity." Cited in Max Sinasohn, *Die Berliner Privatsynagogen und ihre Rabbiner 1671–1971* (Jerusalem, 1971), 81.

16. Cilli Cohen, "Erinnerungen an Rabbiner Prinz," *Aufbau*, December 2,

1988, p. 12; Joachim Prinz, "Zur Berliner Jugendarbeit," *GJGB*, May 20, 1930, pp. 239–240. The content of the sessions also included discussion of the weekly Torah reading as well as of contemporary Jewish issues. They concluded with the havdalah ritual. Prinz believed them to be more effective than the usual "youth services."

17. *Helden und Abenteurer der Bibel. Ein Kinderbuch* (Berlin, 1930), Preface.

18. Cited in Leonard Baker, *Days of Sorrow and Pain: Leo Baeck and the Berlin Jews* (New York and London, 1978), 169–170.

19. As Prinz relates in his autobiography, in 1932 a Christian woman had given him use of a piece of property she owned in the Grunewald in Berlin. There Prinz founded a youth club for boys and girls from the ages of thirteen. See also the recollections of Hans Tramer, Yad Vashem Archives, 0.1/145, who places the gift a year earlier.

20. At the School for Jewish Youth in 1929, Prinz taught classes in Jewish history, including a survey, a history of the Jews in Christian Spain, and a history of Jewish heretics of the seventeenth century. In the following year, the school had five hundred students ranging in age from fifteen to twenty-five. *JR*, January 8, 1929; May 31, 1929; *Jüdisches Jahrbuch 1930*, 148. The teachers were, if possible, to come from the ranks of the young people themselves or to have a strong connection to them so that the presentations would differ from formal lectures. Joachim Prinz, "Die Schule der Jüdischen Jugend," ibid., 72–73.

21. Liberal Jews were perturbed when Prinz indicated his intention to use his position at the university not only to counsel students but also to preach Zionism. *CVZ*, August 28, 1931.

22. A popular wedding jingle went: "Bei Prinz getraut ist gut getraut" ("when you've been married by Prinz, you've been married well").

23. Otto Friedrich, *Before the Deluge: A Portrait of Berlin in the 1920s* (New York, 1972), 11.

24. The memoirs of the somewhat older Warschauer (1871–1955) have been published as *Im jüdischen Leben. Erinnerungen des Berliner Rabbiners Malwin Warschauer* (Berlin, 1995). Unlike Prinz, Warschauer did not devote his sermons to topics of current interest.

25. During the fall holidays, community rabbis, to which Prinz belonged in 1930, went for the various services from one large community synagogue to another.

26. Prinz to Gruenewald, October 9, 1930, Max Gruenewald Collection, Leo Baeck Institute Archives, New York, Box 5, Folder 4.

27. On the Association, see Virginia Iris Holmes, "Integrating Diversity, Reconciling Contradiction: The Jüdischer Friedensbund in Late Weimar Germany," *Leo Baeck Institute Year Book* (*LBIYB*) 47 (2002): 175–194.

28. "Kundgebung des Jüdischen Friedensbundes," *JR*, January 17, 1930. See also Prinz's short piece on this subject in *Jüdisches Jahrbuch 1932*, 21–22.

29. For a defense of the German Jews for not seeing the handwriting on the

wall, see Peter Gay, *My German Question: Growing Up in Nazi Berlin* (New Haven and London, 1998).

30. See Joachim Prinz, "A Rabbi under the Hitler Regime," in Herbert A. Strauss and Kurt R. Grossmann, eds., *Gegenwart im Rückblick: Festgabe für die Jüdische Gemeinde zu Berlin 25 Jahre nach dem Neubeginn* (Heidelberg, 1970), 231–238; idem., "The Time was Midnight," *Jewish Spectator*, February 1972, pp. 15–19; idem, *The Dilemma of the Modern Jew*, 132–133.

31. Kurt Jakob Ball-Kaduri, *Das Leben der Juden in Deutschland 1933* (Frankfurt a/M, 1933), 90–91.

32. As a community rabbi at the time, Prinz had been assigned to the Lützowstrasse synagogue for that evening but persuaded Tramer to switch with him so he could preach in his "home" synagogue, the Friedenstempel. When some worshippers, expecting Prinz, saw Tramer on the pulpit, they walked out "since they had come to hear the great speaker Prinz." H. Tramer Recollections, Yad Vashem Archives 0.1/145.

33. Joachim Prinz, *The Dilemma of the Modern Jew*, 17.

34. Even the organs of the integrationist Centralverein deutscher Staatsbürger jüdischen Glaubens published reviews by Rabbi Manfred Swarsensky and Eva Reichmann-Jungmann that recognized the value of Prinz's book and agreed with it in part. *CVZ*, Nr. 44, 2. Beilage, 1933; *Der Morgen*, January 9, 1934, 435–436. Other reviewers, however, were more unmitigatedly critical. See *CVZ*, Nr. 46, November 30, 1933, and Guy Miron, "Emancipation and Assimilation in the German-Jewish Discourse of the 1930s," *LBIYB* 48 (2003): 165–189. For the significance of the book as seen by an American historian visiting Germany in 1935, see Koppel S. Pinson, "The Jewish Spirit in Nazi-Germany," *The Menorah Journal*, October–December 1936, 235–237, 243.

35. Hans Joachim Schoeps, *Wir deutschen Juden* (Berlin, 1934), 51.

36. Hermann Hesse, "Erinnerung an ein Paar Bücher," *Die neue Rundschau* 1(1934): 456–457.

37. Stephen Wise to Joachim Prinz, July 18, 1939; Prinz to Wise, January 29, 1941, Stephen Wise Papers, AJA, Microfilm 2356.

38. "Dr. Prinz hält Rückschau," *JR*, September 17, 1935.

39. Dr. N., "Berliner Kanzelredner. Ein kritischer Bericht," *JR*, October 31, 1933, p. 732.

40. —t. —l., "Rabbiner Dr. Prinz predigt wieder," *JR*, July 2, 1935.

41. N., "Seder der Dreihundertfünfzig," *JR*, April 5, 1934.

42. *Israelitisches Familienblatt* (*IF*), September 10, 1936; October 7, 1936. For a report on one such lecture see Herbert Freeden, "A Jewish Theater under the Swastika," *LBIYB* 1 (1956): 149–150.

43. Prinz's popular history of the Jews was one of a number that appeared in Germany of the 1930s, one of which, by the rabbi and novelist Emil Bernhard Cohn, especially evoked Prinz's admiration. *IF*, September 16, 1936.

44. For a listing of these volumes see Appendix C.

45. *JR*, November 1, 1935; *CVZ*, November 7, 1935.

46. "Zur Kulturgeschichte," *IF*, January 21, 1937.

47. *JR*, June 22, 1934; October 23, 1934. Although Prinz's suggestion was favorably received in some quarters, the community leadership did not act on it. See also his proposal for a religious ceremony in the synagogue for Jewish youth graduating from high school. *IF*, July 25, 1935.

48. Martin Buber, *Die Stunde und die Erkenntnis. Reden und Aufsätze 1933–1935* (Berlin, 1936).

49. The discussion, which took place on the pages of the *Israelitisches Familienblatt* in the summer of 1936, was reprinted in the *Bulletin des Leo Baeck Instituts* 10 (1967): 221–231. Buber and Prinz were also occasionally in contact after the war. See the correspondence in the Buber Archives at the Hebrew University in Jerusalem, Arc. Ms. Var. 350/5946.

50. With the exception of cited newspaper items, the following account is based on the records of the Allgemeiner Rabbinerverband in Deutschland located in the archives of the Stiftung Neue Synagoge-Centrum Judaicum, Berlin, 1, 75 C Ra 1.

51. *IF*, June 13, 1935; July 4, 1935; November 5, 1935.

52. "Umstrittene Predigt," *JR*, May 28, 1935.

53. Prinz himself recalled the case of Rabbi Emil Cohn, whom the Berlin Jewish community had dismissed in 1906 on account of his openly expressed Zionism. *IF*, June 4, 1936.

54. When negotiations for the integration of the Friedenstempel into the community began in 1928, the community executive demanded that it first fire its current rabbi. But, in the end, it backed down. *JR*, January 6, 1928.

55. *JR*, August 16, 1935.

56. His ten-year review of the university's work, printed in *IF*, March 28, 1935, most probably originated as a fund-raising talk.

57. *IF*, November 28, 1935; *JR*, December 12, 1935. Prinz sent back reports on the governments and Jewish communities of the countries he visited, which were published in the *Israelitisches Familienblatt*.

58. Julius Bär to Chaim Weizmann, February 19, 1936, Weizmann Archives, Rehovot.

59. *IF*, December 12, 1935; November 19, 1936; May 21, 1936; Jacob Boas, "The Shrinking World of German Jewry," *LBIYB* 31 (1986): 246–248.

60. "Das Leben neben der Wirklichkeit," *IF*, July 30, 1936.

61. The scheme that allowed German Jews to transfer funds to Palestine provided they were used to purchase German goods.

62. "Bilanz der Erneuerung," *IF*, March 11, 1937.

63. For example, *JR*, August 16, 1935.

64. He was elected a member of the steering committee of the Zionistische Vereinigung für Deutschland in 1936, but is mentioned only once, in passing, in

Hagit Lavsky, *Before Catastrophe: The Distinctive Path of German Zionism* (Detroit and Jerusalem, 1996), 244.

65. According to a contemporary, Prinz was "the most effective propagandist that the ZVfD possessed; he was really the first and only speaker to the masses [*Massenredner*] that German Zionism produced." Walter Gross in Tel Aviv to Hilde Prinz in New Jersey, October 7, 1988, Prinz family archives. For an example of his Zionist writings, see his "Ueber Grundsätze einer Jüdischen Politik," *Der Morgen* 12 (October 1936): 289–300.

66. *JR*, July 17, 1936.

67. *JR*, February 4, 1936.

68. Otto Dov Kulka and Eberhard Jäckel, eds., *Die Juden in den geheimen NS-Stimmungsberichten 1933–1945* (Düsseldorf, 2004), Document 854 on the inserted CD.

69. Ball-Kaduri, *Das Leben der Juden in Deutschland*, 43–44, 109–110. The burial incident was also reported by another eyewitness: Arthur Stern, *In bewegter Zeit. Erinnerungen und Gedanken eines jüdischen Nervenarztes* (Jerusalem, 1968), 126.

70. Joachim Prinz to Chaim Weizmann, October 20, 1933, Weizmann Archives, L13/156.

71. His impressions appeared in *JR*, April 5, 1934; April 13, 1934; April 17, 1934.

72. *JR*, April 13, 1934; *IF*, February 18, 1937. Prinz attributed the industrialization program to the Revisionist Zionist, Vladimir Jabotinsky. The ambivalence is also apparent in an undated letter to his father's second wife, Gertrude. Here Prinz discourages her from settling in Palestine, mentioning political, economic, cultural, and linguistic difficulties, as well as recurrent Arab riots. "I would rather go today than tomorrow, but it is nothing for you," he concludes. She and her husband nonetheless settled in Palestine in 1938. The letter is in the archives of Temple B'nai Abraham, Livingston, New Jersey.

73. *IF*, May 7, 1936. Already in 1936, Prinz was on the liberal side of the Zionist spectrum, recognizing the claims of the Arabs even as he argued for the right of the Jews to the Land of Israel and that the future of the Jewish people lay there. See his "Unser Recht auf Palästina," *IF*, June 18, 1936.

74. "Heimatlosigkeit," *IF*, January 7, 1937.

75. *Wir Juden*, p. 157.

76. *IF*, November 12, 1936.

77. State of Israel Ministry of Justice, *The Trial of Adolf Eichmann. Record of Proceedings of the District Court of Jerusalem*, vol. 1 (Jerusalem, 1992), 220–221, 230. See also the report of the meeting in *IF*, July 1, 1937.

78. *Newark Evening News*, March 24, 1945; *Jerusalem Post*, September 14, 1956; Joachim Prinz, "Germans and Jews—Is There a Bridge?" in Herbert A. Strauss and Hanns Reissner, eds., *Jubilee Volume dedicated to Curt C. Silberman*

(New York, 1969), 56. Only after Germany and Israel established diplomatic relations did Prinz moderate his views about Germany. See his "Germans and Jews,"
Congress Bi-Weekly, September 20, 1965, 5–6.

79. Warren Grover, *Nazis in Newark* (New Brunswick and London, 2003),
201, 270, 300 n. 100, 317. Prinz appears as the anti-Lindbergh rabbi in Philip
Roth's novel *The Plot against America* (Boston and New York, 2004).

80. "Amerika—hast Du es besser?" *Der Morgen* 13 (1937): 104–111.

81. See the history of the congregation at http://www.templebnaiabraham.
org/images/TBA%20History.pdf

82. Michael A. Stavitsky, chairman of the board of trustees, to Julius Silberfeld, July 18, 1939, Archives of the Jewish Historical Society of Metrowest, Whippany, New Jersey.

83. Stavitsky to Rabbi Solomon Foster, September 11, 1939, Archives of the
Jewish Historical Society of Metrowest; William B. Helmreich, *The Enduring Community: The Jews of Newark and Metrowest* (New Brunswick and London, 1999),
250.

84. Stavitsky to Wise, October 12, 1939; Prinz to Wise, July 12, 1939, Stephen
S. Wise Papers, American Jewish Archives Microfilm 2356.

85. Unlike his Berlin colleague Malwin Warschauer who, in his own autobiography, thanks God for "His rescuing hand." Warschauer, *Im jüdischen Leben*, 120.

86. *B'nai Abraham News*, January 1950.

87. "A Basis for a Discussion on a Guide for Jewish Living, B'nai Abraham
Weekend Seminar, April 15–17, 1955, Lakewood, New Jersey," B'nai Abraham
Congregational Archives.

88. Although Prinz did not lead the halakhic life expected of Conservative
rabbis, during the 1940s he was on good relations with the chancellor of the Jewish
Theological Seminary, Louis Finkelstein, who spoke at Temple B'nai Abraham on
one occasion and for whom Prinz gave several brief addresses following the dramatic
presentations on the seminary's radio program *The Eternal Light*. See the Finkelstein
correspondence in the Ratner Archives of the Jewish Theological Seminary.

89. "Who is a Jew?" *Central Conference of American Rabbis Year Book* 69
(1959): 248–256; "An Agenda for the Jewish People," *Proceedings of the Rabbinical
Assembly (PRA)*, 1971, 15–28; "A Rabbi in the Twentieth Century," *Reconstruction-
ist*, September 1974, 7–15. As early as 1949, Prinz had called for a "Congress of
Jewish Survival," which, however, did not come about. Joachim Prinz, "The Jewish
Revolution," *Congress Weekly*, April 4, 1949, 8.

90. *JR*, October 15, 1937; October 29, 1937.

91. See the daily mimeographed bulletins of the congress entitled "Congre-
zion" and also Raphael Medoff, *Militant Zionism in America: The Rise and Impact of
the Jabotinsky Movement in the United States, 1926–1948* (Tuscaloosa, Ala., 2002),
131–142; Marc Lee Raphael, *Abba Hillel Silver: A Profile in American Judaism* (New
York and London, 1989), 154–155; Melvin Urofsky, *A Voice that Spoke for Justice:
The Life and Times of Stephen S. Wise* (Albany, N.Y., 1982), 353–355. Prinz does

not appear on the list of elected members of the congress, but perhaps he was an alternate delegate.

92. Even more outspokenly critical of Silver than Prinz, Wise replied to Prinz calling Silver "the Führer." Prinz to Wise, October 29, 1946; Wise to Prinz, October 30, 1946, Wise Papers, AJA, Microfilm 2356.

93. See the correspondence between Prinz and Abraham Granovsky (Granott), in Central Zionist Archives, A 202.

94. *Jerusalem Post*, July 6, 1949.

95. See, for example, Prinz's *The Dilemma of the Modern Jew*, 208–212. In the mid-1970s, he was a member of Breira, the dovish, highly critical but pro-Israel group of American rabbis and intellectuals. He resigned from the organization when its stance became more radical. Michael E. Staub, *Torn at the Roots: The Crisis of Jewish Liberalism in Postwar America* (New York, 2002), 291, 304.

96. See also David Petegorsky, "World Jewish Unity Established," *Congress Weekly*, July 16, 1948, 7–9.

97. Nahum Goldmann, *Mein Leben. USA—Europa—Israel* (Munich and Vienna, 1981), 130–131. Prinz did serve from 1967 to 1969 as the chair of the WJC's governing council.

98. See Prinz's eulogy, "Man of the People," *Congress Weekly*, May 30, 1949. Born on St. Patrick's Day, Wise characteristically signed his letters in green ink. For a time after Wise's death, Prinz did so as well. Like Wise, Prinz also signed his letters "Faithfully yours."

99. The move was prompted by the diminishing number of Jews who continued to live in what had become a dominantly black city and a focus of racial strife. Prinz, who had been an advocate of black–Jewish cooperation, told an interviewer: "Jews had been here for many generations. I felt they belonged here. But I was wrong. It was a European romanticism that was ill-placed." Cited in Helmreich, *The Enduring Community*, 41–42.

100. Staub, *Torn at the Roots*, 64–65. Prinz's activity on behalf of American blacks remained incomprehensible to one of the leading German Zionists, who was then living in Israel. Kurt Blumenfeld wrote to Prinz on April 19, 1960, questioning whether as a Jew he had a right to intervene in American affairs, and added, "I am very sad when I see how the oldest Zionists, who today are in leading positions, have learned nothing with regard to the Jewish question." Kurt Blumenfeld, *Im Kampf um den Zionismus. Briefe aus fünf Jahrzehnten*, ed. Miriam Sambursky and Jochanan Ginat (Stuttgart, 1976), 289. Although Prinz had on his first visit called attention to the presence of discrimination against Jews in the United States, in his later writings he tended to minimize it and certainly did not believe that it should serve as a brake on Jewish political activism whether on behalf of blacks or in opposition to the Vietnam War.

101. Joachim Prinz, "An Agenda for the Jewish People," *PRA* 34 (1971): 28.

102. Arthur Hertzberg, "An Agenda for the Jewish People: A Response," *PRA* 34 (1971): 33.

Joachim Prinz,
Rebellious Rabbi

1

Childhood and Youth

BURKHARDSDORF

THE VILLAGE IN WHICH I was born cannot be found on any map. Even on the most minute maps of Upper Silesia,[1] in the province in which it was situated, it is not even a dot. The name was Burkhardsdorf. The original name, however, dated back to the eighteenth century when Upper Silesia was a part of the kingdom of Poland, and at that time it was called Bierdzan.[2] Evidently, nobody who was born there ever moved away. It is because of this fact that the peasants who lived in this tiny village still spoke a German mixed with many Polish words, and those who spoke Polish spoke a jargon which was a distorted language mixed with many German words. There were nine hundred people in the village. The peasants were serfs and depended upon the count who lived in a lovely eighteenth-century chateau, built on a hill and visible from every part of the little village, which was built around a pond. The count actually owned all the land and leased it to the people who worked diligently from early in the morning until the beginning of the night, taking home whatever fruit, vegetables, or wheat were harvested. I am sure that a considerable portion of the fruits of their labor had to be delivered to the count. I often saw his carriage drawn by four horses rush through the village, with him and his family sitting there stiffly, smiling from time to time, as the peasants stood around bowing their heads in reverence to the man who held them in some sort of beneficent slavery.

The houses in which the peasants lived looked decent and sturdy. They were neither dilapidated huts nor hovels or village slums. They were nicely

1. Upper Silesia is the southeastern portion of the region of Silesia. In 1742, Frederick the Great annexed most of Silesia to Prussia and it was part of the German Second Reich when Prinz was born there. Today Upper Silesia is part of Poland.
2. Burkhardsdorf (today Bierdzan) is a village in the district of Oppeln (today Opole in Poland), which in 1885 had 832 inhabitants. In 1939, there were 1,151 residents, of whom 49 were Jews.

kept. The gardens were cultivated and there were flowers all over the place. Nobody starved and nobody suffered. They were all pious Catholics who had a quiet and convincing form of rustic piety with many superstitions, strictly adhered to since the Middle Ages. None of them had gone to school longer than the prescribed years, which meant graduation at the age of fourteen. The son usually followed in his father's footsteps with regard to his work, as he had been doing since early childhood. It was a peaceful village, and I do not remember any kind of quarrel or loud noises. We must have had the proverbial village idiot, but I don't remember him. There were only two establishments accessible to the people, the inn and my father's general store. We were the only Jewish family; my parents were among the few who spoke nothing but German and who wrote clearly and spelled properly. The other two persons who were educated were the parish priest and the director of the school. Once every week my father met with these two gentlemen. The meeting was usually held in our home in the big living room, which was properly and formally furnished, with kerosene lamps standing on a covered table. I do not remember what kind of card game they played, but play they did, from shortly after suppertime until midnight. I always saw the two men come and watched my mother offer them refreshments and liquor, but, of course, I was fast asleep when they left.

The small one-room school was typical of villages all over the world. Since the village's inhabitants were Catholic, classes were usually taught by a priest. Like all German schools, it was orderly and very well disciplined. No one dared to talk during class hours. When the teacher came in, we all rose and stood until he asked us to sit down. But we were not permitted to sit without joining him in pronouncing the sacred words, "In the name of the Father, the Son and the Holy Spirit." He would ask us to put our thumbs up to our foreheads and then make the sign of the Cross on the forehead, the mouth, and the chest. Only after we had done that were we allowed to sit down for the beginning of the class. We[3] went to that school only for a bit over a year, but it was a sacred place, not merely sparklingly clean, but also somewhat divine. For to have a book and learn how to read and write was not merely an exercise of the mind but a personal involvement. I was probably more efficient at that than my classmates, for I came from a cultured family whereas they were the children of peasants. I was always properly dressed. I rose early in the morning and was dressed by one of the maids.

Our house, when I think back to it, appears to have been very large, although I am sure that memories taken from childhood often cause us to

---

3. The use of the first person plural may be intended to include his siblings.

forge facts and to remember some things as being very large when, in fact, they are quite small. But small it was not. It had many rooms. I was the eldest of three children, all born in a succession of one-and-a-half-year intervals, as though it had been carefully calculated.[4] I believe that we had a large room together at first. It was only later that I had my own room, long after we left the village. So I must have shared a room with my brothers until that day.

The house was surrounded by a very large courtyard. Next to the house was a well from which we pumped water. There was no water in the house, nor were there flush toilets. The courtyard led to a large barn where we kept our horses. I don't remember whether we ever had cattle. The most important part of the barn, however, was the upper floor because my father was a pigeon fancier and bought all kinds of pigeons, some of them rather fancy. There must have been several hundred of them. It was the only hobby he really had, or at least the only one I remember. All his time was given over to our general store.

There were large tracts of land: gardens for flowers and others for vegetables, a field with wheat and large meadows, and a little brook in which we played and caught fish. The water needed in the house for cooking and washing was brought in by one of the many servants we had. We never had less than three or four in addition to one or two young girls who were in charge of the children. They used to take us out for long walks in the fields and forests and introduced us rather early in life to sexual experiments of which we understood very little. They asked us to crawl underneath their skirts and play with their private parts, which we found rather amusing and sometimes a burden of our day, but which nevertheless, at least at that time, played no part in our lives. The smell of the blueberries and wild strawberries, and the many kinds of mushrooms we found in the forest, were more important to us than the little sex games the girls evidently expected us to play with them.

My father had inherited all of his property from his father. His mother was always very sickly and had died in the village long before my birth. My grandfather had left the property to his eldest son. Apparently, he was the only one determined to stay in the village; his brothers and sisters had moved away to larger towns, married there, and founded their own families. Only my father stayed on. Whether he did so because he loved the village and the simple life we lived appealed to him more than the great adventure of establishing a new life in a larger city, I do not know. The village was very close to him and everybody in the village knew him, of course. The store was the

4. First Kurt, then Hans.

only place where one could buy things. There was no other within a radius of a hundred miles.

The store, founded by my grandfather, was very profitable. Naturally, it would have been ridiculous to carry such items as butter, milk, or bread in the store. All these staples of life were produced by the peasants themselves and they would not have dreamed of buying them in a store. Of course, there was no one in the village who did not have many chickens that provided the family with eggs. Our courtyard was replete with them. Every morning one of the maids would collect the eggs, which we ate for breakfast. I do not know where we bought our meat. There might even have been a butcher in the village, but I do not remember. I only know that food was plentiful, and some of the peasant dishes, which were served regularly in addition to the typical meals of that time, I still remember fondly. Once in awhile I try to recreate them in my present life. Our food was very German. We never had any notion of Jewish food, although I do not believe that in the village my father ate ham every day as he did in later years or that we served pork. Money was never discussed, nor was it ever an object of any kind of serious consideration. We got a new outfit of clothes every year; we knew nothing of monetary restrictions, or poverty, or any kind of need. We were always well provided for as befitting a middle-class family living in the midst of a population of peasants.

Somehow I knew that I was a Jew, but not because of any Jewish customs that were observed in the house. I remember that we had a Hebrew prayer book, but it was only taken out when there was a thunderstorm. I remember that whenever there was loud thunder and frightening lightning, my mother would take out the prayer book, open it to a certain prayer, put it on the table, and tell me that the prayer on that page would protect our lives. Evidently it did because the house was never struck by lightning.

We felt that we were Jews especially when our relatives would visit, maybe once or twice a year. We knew we were different from the others, but it was simply that the others were Catholics and we were not. This did not prevent us from observing certain Catholic customs. Whenever we met peasants in the street or walking in the fields, they would say, "In the name of the Father, the Son, and the Holy Spirit," and we would answer, "In all eternity may it be so. Amen." I never forgot that sentence. It was said with great sincerity, and I learned early in life to respect the faith of others. My first religious experiences, if they can be called that, were in the Catholic church.

The church was a lovely little village church without any architectural significance. I write this although I knew very little about architecture at that time. It might very well be that it was an old church, for the village was old. The church was surrounded by the churchyard, which served as a cemetery. During the cold autumn months, we commemorated the day of All Souls.[5] The maids would take us to the cemetery after sunset to the graves of their ancestors or members of the family, and each of us would light a candle on the graves. It was one of the most profound and solemn memories of my youth. The churchyard was rather small, but there was not a single grave without many candles. Although the wind sometimes blew them out, they were immediately lit again. Remembering it now, it seemed to me then as though the cemetery were an ocean of light. The light was not merely beautiful but also very comforting because the nights were cold and warmth came from the burning candles. We were all bundled up and it was pleasant to come home, where we were given a plate of soup to warm us up until we undressed and crawled into the big beds, covering ourselves with down quilts. They were not the kind we have today, however; they were very heavy and caused us to dream terrible dreams.

We were brought into this world by a midwife. If we needed a doctor, as we sometimes did, he had to be called from the town,[6] which was many miles away. I remember that one of them later told me one day he had received a call from our village that Prince Joseph (my father's first name was Joseph) was ill and needed medical attention. He immediately had his horse-drawn carriage prepared, put on his best suit and his high hat because he was about to examine and probably cure a real prince. He must have been terribly disappointed when he discovered that it was not a prince, but a family by that name that he had to attend to.[7] A reasonable bill came, as was the custom in those days, at the end of a year. My father was in the habit of paying his bills on the same day they arrived.

When my father was old enough to look for a wife, he found her in a small town not too far from us by the name of Guttentag.[8] My maternal grandfather, Liebermann Berg, was a landholder, who had a large farm with hundreds of people working for him, as well as a moving business. He was a very important person in the town and one of the streets was named for him. He had two daughters and several sons. I do not know how my father discovered the Berg family, perhaps through a marriage broker. They were well-to-

---

5. All Souls' Day is a day set apart in Roman Catholicism for commemoration of the faithful departed. It occurs early in November.
6. Presumably Oppeln.
7. The German word for *prince* is *Prinz.*
8. Guttentag was the name of both a rural district and a town in Upper Silesia. In 1925, the dis-

do. Before my grandfather moved to that town, he had been a manufacturer of cigars; he was rich enough to retire at the age of fifty and to live on the interest that had accumulated from his life's fortune. As was usual in those days, my mother had to have a dowry that was rather large and that my father never touched. It was Rabbi Leo Baeck,[9] who later became very famous, who performed the wedding ceremony in 1901. He was a Liberal rabbi. I do not know where the ceremony took place. A year later I was born.

I do not now remember ever having seen my mother in the kitchen. I suppose she did some of the cooking, but most of it was done, under her supervision, by our cook. My mother helped my father in the store. She was very petite, soft-spoken, and terribly affectionate. Once in awhile I would hear her quarrel with my father who was stern, punctual, and completely dedicated to what he considered to be his duty. He was very Prussian. His father was born in an Eastern European[10] province, but I am sure his grandfather was born in Poland. We never spoke about it. Polish Jews were not among my father's favorites. He never spoke about the fact that his grandfather might have been an Eastern European Jew. This may very well have been so because of my mother's family. They were very German, one of the old German-Jewish families. In the early seventeenth century, they lived in Upper Bavaria; how and why they moved to Upper Silesia I do not know. Their name was Fraenkel, and my great-grandfather's name was Joachim Fraenkel. He served as an inspector for the manufacturing of alcohol on the estate of a German count. I was named for him. I never knew him, but people who did used to tell me stories about him. He was a great wit and very well educated. He had seven children. His five sons went to universities, which was rare in the middle of the nineteenth century, particularly for Jewish families. The two girls went to public schools, but they also had a French governess. I remember my grandmother, my mother's mother, who was to play a very important role in my life, spoke French and recited French poetry. Later, when I knew some French, I was appalled at her German accent. My great-grandfather, who was born in a very old German enclave in Upper Silesia, lies buried in a cemetery there, where his parents are buried. I was always fascinated by the stories of the Fraenkel family. One of my great-grandfather's sons had become a famous lawyer who was in charge of the

trict had 18,088 inhabitants. In 1939, the population of the district was 21,892, of whom only 12 were Jews, while the town had 4,305 inhabitants.

9. Leo Baeck (1873–1956) served as the rabbi of Oppeln from 1897 to 1907. He later held rabbinates in Düsseldorf and Berlin and gained fame both as a theologian and as the head of the representative organization of German Jewry during the Nazi years.

10. Probably an error for "East Prussian."

property of the French government in Germany, which went back to the days of Napoleon. All members of the family did very well, and my great-grandfather's children, particularly the sons, were very tall and looked very distinguished. None of them was poor; all of them were well educated.

My father was very much the father figure and the authority whom I respected more than I loved. His stern demeanor prevented me from ever speaking intimately and personally with him. But my mother made up for it. On every one of our birthdays, we were permitted to come into her bed in the early morning and lie there close to her warm, tiny body, and she always told us the story of our birth. I am sure that it was not biologically a good story, but it was always very sweet, and throughout the year we looked forward to that moment. It may have been the warmth of her body that attracted us. Although I am sure that occasionally we were permitted to sleep next to her, it was the birthday that was the important day, as it has remained in our family. Everybody knew that I was born on the tenth day of the month of May, and I still remember that my mother was born on the second of September in 1877. My great-grandfather was born in the middle of April of 1814. I have his birth certificate in my possession and I hope it will somehow remain in the possession of my family. The name of Fraenkel is probably derived from the fact that they used to live in Franconia,[11] probably in the city of Augsburg.

Very early in my life, I grew terribly attached to my mother. It was she who told me my first fairy tales and it was she who embraced me as often as she saw me. She was not an authoritative figure but a figure that stood for great affection and love. She was always warm and understanding. I remember her taking me by the hand on my first school day and giving me a large colorful bag of candy.[12] It was a special kind of pointed bag that she had ordered for me. I kept it as one of my most precious possessions for a long time. I still remember the red and blue flowers on it. To my father it was an ordinary day, for he, too, had once gone to school for the first time, but my mother understood that to me it was a very great event. For as long as she lived, which was not long enough, she always understood what a certain day or a certain event meant to me personally; she always identified herself with me and with my most personal feelings.

The most important events, however, were the Catholic holidays. Since we had no Jewish customs at home and no Jews but ourselves lived in our vil-

11. Franconia is a region in Bavaria, in southeastern Germany.
12. It was a widespread German custom to give children a cone full of candies to mark their first day of school.

lage, I had no notion of Judaism and what the Jewish service would be like. I remember now very faintly that my mother took me to the town some fifty miles away, to which we finally moved,[13] and that I attended a Jewish service in the synagogue there. But it was all very strange to me. It must have been on a Sabbath morning, for they took the Torah scrolls out.[14] Of course, I did not know what the Torah scrolls were. It was a Liberal synagogue with organ and mixed choir, but I could follow neither the service nor the customs. When I came home, I told my brothers about it. Since I was five years old, they must have been almost infants. I imitated the procession with the Torah scrolls by taking sticks of wood and carrying them around, singing something in a gibberish language that nobody understood, just as I had not understood the Hebrew chants.

The Roman Catholic church was not far from our house and our housekeeper took me there very often. For many years, the scent of incense remained in my nostrils, and whenever I attend a Catholic service now I experience all kinds of dreams of my childhood. Of course, I did not understand the priest's sermons—which I think were rarely given—but I remember the cross, the crucified Christ, the stained glass windows, and the reverence of the assembled congregation. Peasants are still part of my vivid memory of childhood. I did not ask any questions. It was so natural to my parents and me that I should "go to church." We had a Christmas tree during the Christmas season, which I decorated together with "the girls."[15] We had no menorah,[16] no Sabbath, no seder,[17] nothing whatsoever that was Jewish. During Passover we ate certain foods, but bread as well, though it may very well be that we also had matzos.[18] My father never ever read the Haggadah[19] to us, although strangely enough his Hebrew was very fluent, at least the liturgical part of it. For a long time he put tefillin[20] on his head, saying the appropriate prayers. But all that took ten minutes or less. After he put the tefillin away, he attended to his mustache, which took him much longer to get it all fixed than it did to pray.

13. Oppeln.
14. One or more scrolls, consisting of the Pentateuch, are removed from the ark that contains them for reading on Sabbath morning.
15. The servant girls.
16. The eight-branched candlestick that is used for the Hanukkah festival.
17. The home ceremony on the first two evenings of the Passover festival.
18. Unleavened bread.
19. The special prayer book for the Passover seder, which recounts the redemption of the Israelites from Egyptian slavery.
20. Phylacteries, small boxes containing biblical passages worn at daily prayers on the arm and forehead.

My family actually came from an Orthodox background. My grandfather must have been very Orthodox, or at least adhered to Orthodox customs or beliefs. During one of the rare conversations I had with my father, he told me that his father had once tied him to a chair with leather straps and punished him physically because he had done something on the Sabbath that was not permitted by Jewish law. But what it was I do not know, nor would he talk about it. I only gathered that his father, coming from an Eastern European family, must have observed some Jewish customs. When I was born, my grandfather was already dead or died shortly afterwards. He had left the village long ago and lived in the city of Breslau,[21] which had a population of one-half million, and I never saw him. He had married a rich widow with two children. All I know of him is that he died in an epidemic and that there was not much love lost between him and his children.

But there are very many things that I still remember now when I think back to almost seventy years ago. There was a rhythm of events, happenings that occurred at a certain time and at regular intervals, and always in the same manner. One of them was Friday. One would imagine that Friday would be the day of preparation for the Sabbath in a Jewish home, and that the table would be set in the evening with the challah[22] and wine for kiddush. That this did not happen was strange because my mother came from a home where challah was baked at home. I am not sure that my maternal grandfather ever recited the kiddush, but nevertheless something of the atmosphere of the Sabbath must have been preserved there. Either my mother was not strong enough to insist upon it, or my father simply did not care. I sometimes felt, and still feel, that his rejection of all that was in reality an expression of his rejection of his father, although he had inherited a great deal of his stern attitude.

Friday was important for us because it was the great day of the bath. There was no bathtub in the bathroom. As a matter of fact, I do not think we had bathrooms in the village. I am not even sure that we had toilets in the house, for I distinctly remember the outhouses. Whether these were for the use of the maids or for us, I no longer know. The taking of a bath every Friday afternoon was a great event. It started on Friday morning when some of the maids and we went out into the fields to pick a certain plant that went by the strange name of *Quendl.*[23] I have not been able to find the En-

---

21. The largest city in Silesia, today: Wrocław.
22. The braided loaf of egg bread over which a blessing is said by Jews prior to the meal on Friday evenings following the Kiddush, the blessing over wine.
23. *Quendl* is a medicinal herb, sometimes baked into bread.

glish equivalent for it. But it smelled beautiful. Later my mother added some extract from the sap of pine trees which, together with the *Quendl,* made a marvelously smelling bath. The huge wooden bathtub (at least I thought it was huge at that time; it might have been rather small, for I was small and my brothers even smaller) was filled with hot water. The water had been brought in by the maids from the water pump, heated in the huge kitchen, and brought in in pails. It was poured over the aromatic plants and steamed for a while, for the water was much too hot for us to get into the tub. I always remember my mother coming in, dipping her finger into the tub, and when she was satisfied, giving the signal for us to be lifted into the bath. It was one of the great pleasures of the week, and we all looked forward to Friday. The soap that was used profusely on us—for we were rather dirty—was not at all perfumed. It was a big, yellow piece of ordinary soap we sold in our store. It was used for washing clothes as well as our bodies. But it certainly got the dirt out of our ears. Every morning my mother inspected our ears, and I still wonder how it was that when we were little so much dirt should have accumulated that thorough cleaning was absolutely necessary.

The second great thing was the kitchen. As I think back to it now, it appeared to have been as large as a ballroom. Most important was the huge stove where something was always boiling or cooking. I remember the bright, hot fire with huge pieces of wood thrown in along with a bit of coal. One of the bigger attractions was the huge tables. None of them stood in the center of the room. They were all placed against the walls; the tabletops were made of unpolished wood. It was on these tables that food was prepared, for we never ate at them. No meal was taken in the kitchen. It was always properly served in the dining room. My father, until the day of his death, remained particular about the manner in which food was served. It had to be good and hot. If it was not, he sent it back to the cook, sparing no words of displeasure and anger. It was at a certain time and under circumstances that I no longer now remember that I discovered the big kitchen tables were not merely tables. One of the maids had taken ill and I saw that the tabletop had been removed, revealing a bed underneath it for one of the servants. I don't remember the woman in the bed, but the bed itself was made so differently from ours. All the maids had a different kind of bedding. Ours was white, but theirs was always covered in red or blue patterns, which indicated lower class. I also believe the maids ate food different from ours. They were, after all, peasant girls and preferred their own kind of cooking rather than ours, which was made according to family recipes. But I don't think that the difference in bedding and food was due to a particularly kind consideration for the maids; it was rather a declaration of social distinction. This does not mean that the maids were treated badly or looked down upon. They were part of our family and I remember that our cook, whom we took on when we moved to the town some years later, stayed with us for thirty years. When she retired, she received a pension from my father. They were really members of the family and treated as such, but their status as servants was strictly observed. This was not a time of social rebellion. They were probably much better off in our house than in their own. They were the children of neighbors with whom my father had gone to school. In a community of nine hundred people, probably less than two hundred families, there was a close relationship among them. I do not remember any harsh words, loud arguments, or rebellious behavior.

I remember two incidents that I will never forget and of which I sometimes dream, although they happened so many decades ago. I was standing in the kitchen when suddenly the door opened rather abruptly. Nobody had knocked at the door. A man came in, pale and out of breath, and immediately sat down. At first he could not speak. Apparently, he had not eaten for a long time, and I remember one of the maids giving him a plate of hot soup. He drank it with gusto and asked for another one, for he must have been very hungry. No one spoke. Then one of the maids asked: "Who are you? You are not from our village." He said: "I am not from this village. I am from far away and I had to run through the woods, for they are after me." "Who?" asked the maids. He stared at them and at me, and he did not answer. After having eaten, he asked for a slice of bread, which he hastily put into his pocket, and said that he had to run again. He went out through the back door. Evening had come on in the meantime, and it was dark outside. It was wintertime and heavy snow was falling, covering everything with a thick, white sheet. We opened the door cautiously. Although he was wearing boots we could hear him walk down the steps, and in a few moments he was out of sight. We looked at each other and talked about the strange man, why he was running and out of breath, and why he was so hungry and thirsty. I think the girls had also given him a large glass of some schnapps that he had hastily poured into his mouth. But he was no longer there and the wildest stories were told. After a while, somebody knocked at the kitchen door. Two policemen who were part of the "gendarmerie," in fact the entire police force of the village, came in. We knew them well and they said to us: "We found tracks in the snow that led to this house. Was there a man here whom you did not know and who rushed in out of breath and hungry?" We could not figure out how these men should have known about our strange visitor, and then we asked who he was. And I will never forget how they answered, matter-of-factly and with great emphasis, and a sense of horror. "He was a famous murderer. Yesterday he killed three people." I could not sleep all night. The next morning when we all got up and the mailman brought us our daily mail, he told us that the man had been caught and that he would be hanged.

The second unforgettable and even more gruesome experience concerned a young man from the village who came to our house for some strange reason. He was a youngish man, and he was standing with my mother on the exterior landing on which the water pump stood. It was a winter day. Winters were very cold in those days, lasting for many months. The wind was blowing sharply and cruelly, and we all had to be dressed very warmly with many sweaters and woolen underwear. I stood next to my mother. Why the young man was carrying an ax I never knew, nor do I remember what he intended to do with it. I only recall that he suddenly chopped the ice, which had accumulated on the water, with his ax so that chunks of ice were still clinging to the blade, and then—God knows why—he stuck out his tongue and put the ax blade on it. Because of the extreme cold the ax froze to the tongue, and in trying to tear it loose he cut into the tongue. He must have cut it in half, for blood was spurting out covering the whole landing. My mother stormed into the house to get some cotton bandages, calling for help. The young man was carried out by other men, among whom was his father. Since there was no physician in town and the hospitals were many miles away, he was probably taken by sled, for I vividly remember the horses and the bells, the sled speeding away, and the horrible sounds that came from the injured young man who, having lost his tongue, had lost his speech as well.

Since I was little I was never involved in any kind of planning on the part of my parents. However, I noticed that something was going on, something that would change my life radically, taking me away from the village and the friends whom I had made there, the surroundings which were so much my own, the hundreds of pigeons flying around our barn, the horses and the stables, and everything else that had become so familiar to me and so much a part of my existence. But what was actually being planned I did not know. I remember only that my father once remarked to my mother that "the children must get a better education than I did. We can't give it here in our one-room school. We have to move to the nearest town where there are schools and the children can learn." I know nothing about the sale of the house and the store. I have only a photograph of our store with my father's name still on it. This photograph was taken some thirty years or more after we had left the village. Nor did I know anything about my father's purchases in the new town: a house to live in, a store to work in that would provide bread to eat. It would be a whole new life.

OPPELN

I started my second year of school in January, and nothing strange or unusual seemed to happen. However, at the beginning of May my mother told me that by my birthday, which occurs on the tenth of that month, we would all have moved away. Father and the little ones would go first, but on my birthday I would be put on a coach that would take me to the new town, the name of which I heard for the first time. It was called Oppeln and was the capital of Upper Silesia. It had a population of 35,000.

Whether my mother was still in the village when I left I do not remember, but I assume that she had remained in order to look after many things. I remember only that I sat all by myself next to the coachman and that there were four horses. There were other passengers sitting in the back while I sat in the front, holding on to a bag of candy and bread that my mother had given me.

It was a long trip, the town being some fifty miles from the village. On this trip I had the first of my very basic experiences, which will remain with me forever. The horses trotted along, not too slowly but also not too fast. Spring had just come. There were flowers all over. The landscape was undistinguished and very familiar, the fields flat brown and huge forests everywhere. All this had been part of my life for the first seven years of my existence. Suddenly, something happened that I can still hear clearly. There was a certain strange clattering sound coming from underneath the horses. It was long after we had left the village. I looked down and discovered their hooves were hitting some stones. I asked the coachman what they were and he, who very rarely talked to me, said: "Son, this is pavement." I said: "Pavement for what?" He answered: "We are approaching the town, and the roads to the town are paved so that horses and coaches can move more smoothly." I sat there in great amazement. Pavement was the first indication that our life would be radically changed. No longer would we have to wade through the wet dirt in the autumn and the high snow in the winter, the puddles that formed on the dirt roads that I had known—and had not minded at all. The pavement became a symbol of the new order and a new, more orderly life, as well. It did not take too long before we arrived in town. All the roads were paved and the coachman told me they were called streets. Many houses stood there, one next to the other. Although there were trees and green places, it was not like the village. The people were dressed differently and I saw men tipping their hats or taking them off when they met other people. Suddenly, the coach stopped. We had arrived at my new home.

This was no longer called "my house." No stable, no barn, no horses, no pigeons, no trees. and no flowers. It was a house four stories high that my father had bought. We had one of the apartments in the house. I do not remember now the number of rooms we had, but the accommodations were ample. We three boys had a large room where we all slept together, each in his own bed. When I arrived, my father was already in the house, which had been cleaned up. On the first floor was a saloon. We had had one in the village[24] and so I remembered the smell of liquor. When I looked in, I saw many people standing around drinking beer or something else and my father standing behind the counter together with other people serving the customers. When I entered, he immediately took me upstairs, and there I experienced two additional events that I will never forget. He took me into the kitchen and showed me the sink, but above it I saw something metallic. "Look at this," he said. I looked, and to my amazement he touched a piece of metal, turned it around, and water flowed out of it. I asked my father, "What is it?" He told me it was a faucet, that it was the great advantage of living in a town that the water was supplied to us. No longer would we have to ask the maids to bring in water. Of course, there was no hot water, but I discovered that the house had many faucets and a bathroom with flush toilets. I marveled at this and used the toilet immediately out of curiosity and probably also necessity. That a mere touch of a button should flush everything down was a source of great wonder to me. I remember going from room to room wherever there was a faucet and letting it run to convince myself that the faucet was not an extraordinary thing but could be taken for granted. From now on I would have water that came from God-knew-where.

In the meantime, the rooms darkened. There were two maids, our old furniture, and some new pieces of furniture as well. Our beds were made. At that moment, my father approached a lamp on the wall, the one above the table. He turned the little key attached to the lamp, then held a burning match to it, and suddenly there was light. My father said to me: "You never saw that before. We will no longer use kerosene here, for this is a great new invention. It is called gas. And when you go to the kitchen you will find that the stove has gas, and all over the house you will see gaslight. Be careful with it for it is dangerous, and none of you children is permitted to light

24. There was a tavern in the village, but not run by Prinz's father.

a lamp." We walked by the many lamps in the house with a great deal of respect and looked at them shyly, as though they were something divine and to be worshipped. Something very new, something very revolutionary, something very exciting.

I began to hate my father's saloon. The door was almost always open. I would watch my father standing behind the counter handling all the beer and glasses of liquor that the customers demanded. I admired him for his ability to adjust so quickly to something so new. Then I began to think that he might have gone to the saloon in our village without my knowing and might have served some sort of apprenticeship there. At any rate, I did not like it a bit. I was nauseated by the smell of it. It was a mixture of tobacco and liquor, and even passing by the open door made me dizzy and half intoxicated. But the most unbearable experience for me was the noise and the coarse language that came from the lips and throats of half-drunk people who could hardly walk and had to be asked by my father to leave as quickly as possible. Leave they did, but not terribly quickly, for the alcohol they consumed seemed to have created wooden legs that would not move swiftly.

There was one comforting thought about the saloon. Every Saturday night a man appeared there to sell all kinds of things to customers, including chocolates and other sweets. He was evidently one of those traditional figures in German saloons. The man had a rather poetic-sounding name for his profession, but I have forgotten it. The nice thing about it was that my father would bring some things up to our room and place them next to each of our beds, something for Sunday morning that tasted and smelled good. My father had changed. He was less stern, but also less reliable. The saloon was kept open until well after midnight, or so it seemed to me. At any rate, he came home late, and home was only one story above the saloon. I do not remember ever seeing my mother in the saloon. It may well be that the kitchen was attached to it and that she attended to things that had to be done there in order to satisfy the customers. But everyone could see that she was very unhappy with the new business. The only advantage was that it apparently was very profitable. There was a distillery in the backyard where certain liquors were manufactured and then sold to the customers. I don't know whether the saloon ever closed and when there was ever a free day for my father. He kept it for only two years, but although these two years coincided with the first years in the new town, the making of new friends, attending a new school, learning new things, I vividly remember them as most disagreeable. For a long time, the smell of liquor and tobacco and the rough voices of the men did not leave me.

I had a very well-developed sense of smell. I longed for our old street in the village and for its odors. They were a mixture of the scent of coffee and spices, of sugar and flowers, of all the good things in life. The most exciting event for me there was the day the postal coach stopped in front of our store and the man brought in sacks or boxes with strange imprints. Some of them had Chinese words on them, others French, or another language I did not understand. What I did understand was their strangeness, and I was overcome with a sense of yearning for places like Hong Kong and Paris. The sacks contained things produced in these countries, from which they were imported. When the sacks were opened, the sweet smell of the foreign spices gave me the feeling of reading a fairy tale. I could close my eyes and see palm trees, feel the hot sun, and forget the village with its dreariness and its flat fields. I could dream of high mountains and desert sand, veiled women, and strange-looking brown-skinned men. I had read about these things in my books, and before that my mother had read fairy tales to me, particularly from the *Arabian Nights*.[25] Foreign lands sounded very attractive to me, and I had the great desire to go from land to land, meeting all kinds of people, particularly those whose language I did not understand and who looked so different from us. This remained the theme of my many dreams of those later years. They gave me the opportunity to balance the stench from the saloon with the scent of the foreign spices from our old store.

Next door to the saloon was a lovely bakery. It was my job to go down there early in the morning before I went to school, to pick up fresh rolls and, once a week, buttery croissants. Behind the counter stood the baker and his wife, both well nourished and properly rotund, dressed in white. They must have worn new, white coats every morning, for they looked as fresh as the lovely wares they sold. The old shop, which was rather small, smelled of a beautiful combination of fresh butter, sugar, and chocolate. Inside the glass case were all kinds of goodies, and once in a while the baker's wife, who liked me very much, would give me a little cookie with an unforgettable smile. They had become our neighbors and friends on a street that was not particularly distinguished by its beauty.

Our stay in the house was not long. Plans for the move started with whisperings between my mother and my grandmother. We had moved to the town because my mother's family lived there. Her parents were settled in another part of town in a small apartment full of lovely things, which had been provided by the rather successful and affluent sons. My grandfather was an inaccessible man who never smiled, never laughed, and scarcely talked, who would go for long walks with a walking stick that could be transformed into

25. A collection of Persian, Arabic, and Indian folktales, also called *1001 Nights*.

a little stool. He had brought that from the little town where they had lived and where a street was named for him; he had acquired considerable capital there. I never saw any sign of tenderness in him. He sat at the table ready to be served, and was critical of what he was served by an old maid whose name was Bronislava. Several times during the day, while he was sitting in a big chair smoking one of his many cigars, his voice would roar through the apartment, asking Bronislava to bring in the spittoon. I recall that I never saw him touch my grandmother's hand or exhibit any kind of sweetness or tenderness to her.

Actually my grandmother was the head of the family. She had black hair and I often saw her do it up in the morning. She had a little jar with grease that she rubbed into her hair so that it looked smooth and shiny. She used perfume every day and I can still remember her favorite perfume, lilac. It came in a flask inserted into a lovely wooden case, which stood in her boudoir where she dressed and made herself as beautiful as she could. She was in fact very beautiful, had large black eyes, a sweet smile, and an even sweeter disposition. When I was little she frequently sang songs to me, some of them in French, some of them part of little games we played with my fingers. I never forgot the tunes of the songs, nor the words or the games. Later I recited them to my children and grandchildren when they were little. She was also a woman of courage and common sense. Two of her sons lived in the same town. One of them had a rather flourishing shoe store; the other one was married to a very lazy, aggressive woman, and had it not been for his mother he would never have made a living. The other two sons, who lived in Berlin, were very successful in their various professions. However, by the time she had moved to the town, they had both died, one at the age of thirty-two and the other at twenty-nine. My grandmother had to carry this burden of her life, and later added another one.[26]

The whispering between my mother and my grandmother, which I overheard once in a while, amazed me. They talked about my father as having gotten used to the saloon and even liking it to such an extent that he would come home slightly tipsy and sometimes rather drunk. For a man as straitlaced as my father, this was a rather dramatic change in character. My grandmother decided that this could not go on without ruining the family and that she would not permit my parents to stay where they were. Evidently she also had enough influence on my father to convince him that it was not good for his health to indulge in alcohol. My father was a great hypochondriac, and the argument my grandmother advanced regarding his

26. Prinz is referring to the early death of his mother.

health must have persuaded him. He began to look for another opportunity to invest the money he had made in a new house and a new store. I do not know of any details as to how he went about it, but finally we were simply informed that we were moving from the house in which we lived to a house not too far away, completely different, a different kind of street, larger and more pretentious. The ground floor contained a very large store. When we moved into the house, new furniture had to be bought. I remember the very heavy pieces that my father had ordered from one of the cabinetmakers. At that time, furniture was not bought in a store. All of our furniture was hand-made. The new pieces for the salon were hand carved and black.

The huge store suddenly came to life. As my father knew little about managing a large store with more than thirty employees standing there be-hind the counters ready to serve customers, he had entered into an agree-ment with a large firm, which established similar stores all over the country, to take care of buying the merchandise and training the new proprietor in handling his business. I remember that before the opening of the store there were large posters all over town showing three rings in three different colors bearing the name of my father and telling people about the opening of the new department store where merchandise could be bought that was of good quality at a reasonable price. I don't exactly remember the opening of the store, although I know that large crowds of people came, my father stand-ing at the door greeting every one of them. The most elegant division was the men's department; my mother was in charge of the millinery. It was not really a department store in the modern sense because neither glassware nor housewares, nor many other items that are part of a department store were sold. My father insisted upon strict pricing. I still remember a large sign hanging from the center of the huge store saying that our prices were firm and that there was not to be any attempt to whittle them down. Our sales-people, all of whom were women, had to be dressed properly and among themselves spoke only in whispers. My father had an office. The store was opened at eight in the morning, right after breakfast. Our apartment was right above the store. By now each of us boys had a separate room. There were two bathrooms, both of them with huge tubs, and a kitchen over which our cook Maria presided. We had only two servants, one being the cook and the other in charge of cleaning the apartment. In addition, we always had a young teenage girl who was in charge of the children.

Our daily schedule at home was not very different from the old one. My brothers now went either to kindergarten or the first grade in school, but we always came home for lunch, which in Europe is the main meal. My father had a "second breakfast" served in his office at exactly ten o'clock. It always consisted of a slice of ham, coffee, bread and butter. It never varied. The food at home was plentiful and good, but not terribly varied. There was always a dairy meal on Friday because all the servants were Catholic and did not eat meat, and that had become our custom as well. Supper always consisted of a large ham and other cold cuts or dairy dishes. The meal was invariable, solemn, and boring.

That which made life in the town completely different from what I had been accustomed to was the fact that I suddenly discovered I was a Jew. I was old enough to understand that that was something of importance, and certainly something that distinguished me from the other students. The Jewish community was small and I very rarely had Jewish classmates. However, the Jewish young people kept together, visited each other, played with each other, and went to the synagogue together. Our town[27] had a particular importance in Jewish life. Although it dated back to the Middle Ages and the seventeenth-century chateau was still its center, with some old buildings formerly inhabited by Mennonites, the Jewish community went back only to the early eighteenth century.[28] For a hundred years or so it had been a leading Liberal Jewish community.[29] There was no kosher butcher because only a very tiny group of people kept a kosher home. There was hardly a single poor Jew in town. The Jewish community consisted of two hundred families, all of whom were very affluent or at least middle class. All the big stores were owned by Jews. Many Jewish doctors and lawyers practiced their professions, and all of them were highly respected. There was not the slightest trace of antisemitism. There was, of course, no Jewish neighborhood. There was a relationship between Jews and gentiles that could be considered ideal. The funeral processions always went through the town, and whether they were Christian or Jewish all the people who watched the hearse, followed by the limousines or the mourners, uncovered their heads. The Christians made the sign of the Cross whether the funeral procession was Christian or not. We, too, took off our hats when a Christian funeral procession moved slowly through the streets. Christian holidays were often elaborately observed. For one of them, which occurred during the autumn and was celebrated in the marketplace where the old town hall stood, the house in the center of the

27. The reference is to Oppeln, which at the time had about 750 Jews in a population of 30,000.
28. There had been a small medieval Jewish community in Oppeln, which in the sixteenth century numbered seventeen taxpayers. However, in 1565 all Jews were forced to leave the territory of Oppeln and they are not mentioned again until Silesia comes under Prussian rule in 1742.
29. A new Oppeln synagogue was dedicated in 1842 by the Jewish religious reformer Rabbi Abraham Geiger. A succession of Liberal rabbis thereafter made Oppeln the center of religious reform in Upper Silesia.

block would be decorated. It was a stipulation of the deed signed by the proprietor of the building. Incidentally, that building belonged to a Jew, and invariably he would decorate it on that Christian holiday. I never heard a single word said against the Jews. They were and had been for two hundred years[30] part of the community's life. They played their role in civic affairs, were generous contributors to all kinds of causes, and, of course, maintained the Jewish community.

In accordance with Western European law, Christians and Jews paid additional taxes for the maintenance of their respective houses of worship. The rabbi and the cantor were civil servants and entitled to a pension fund from the state. Both Christian and Jewish clergymen, as well as all schoolteachers, were highly respected people and played important roles in the community. There was a bookstore across the street from our store where I bought my first books and which was sort of a cultural center of the town. I still remember the young women who sold the books, most of whom stayed with the store for many decades. The Jewish community was liberal in its outlook, headed by a rabbi who played a significant role in Jewish national life. One of the rabbis of the late nineteenth century wrote the first book by a Jewish theologian against dietary laws.[31] Rabbis had life tenure from the first day of their service, and the relationship between them and the families of the community was most intimate. They, in turn, were received and treated with the utmost respect. It was unthinkable for a rabbi to enter a room or a hall without everyone rising and waiting to be spoken to. It was an unwritten law observed by Jew and Christian.

The synagogue was built on a little hill overlooking a lake. It was a red brick building of Moorish architecture with a beautiful dome on which the Star of David seemed to overlook much of the town. Although it was a Liberal synagogue, men and women did not sit together. The women sat in the balcony. There was an organ and a mixed choir and the services were held with great dignity. Never was a word spoken between the worshippers until the services ended. From the moment we entered the synagogue we were silent and kept this silence and solemnity until the services were over. Our community always had particularly great rabbis. One of them was Dr. Leo Baeck, whom I already mentioned because he officiated at my parents' wedding ceremony. He was soon to become the leading spirit of European Jewry,

---

30. Slightly more than 150 years.
31. Adolf Wiener (1811–1895), who served as rabbi in Oppeln from 1845 until his death, was the author of *Die jüdischen Speisegesetze* (The Jewish Dietary Laws; 1895), which constituted a severe criticism of these laws.

and one of the great figures in the intellectual and spiritual life of European society. The prayer book was abridged. The congregation joined in the singing with the choir, which was always a choir of volunteers but well trained. The tunes were always the same, written by the nineteenth-century composer Lewandowski.[32] No other melodies were ever used and we all knew them by heart. The Saturday afternoon service was for young people, conducted by them, and in later years I was the one chosen to conduct the youth service every week.

My parents very rarely went to services. My grandmother, however, went every Saturday morning. She carried a German prayer book bound in green velvet. It was called *Hannah* in memory of the prayer that Hannah of the Old Testament offered to God when she was so eager to have a child.[33] This was the prayer book for the women who usually knew little or no Hebrew and prayed in German, which they were sure God understood as well as any other language. Although my grandmother, I think, never missed a Saturday morning service, her husband did not go to services even on Yom Kippur. My parents, however, did attend services during the High Holy Days.[34] On such days the tables were always festively decorated, and different kinds of food were served. Although no prayers were said, it was noticeably the time of the Jewish holidays, and before Rosh Hashanah my mother would take all three of us children to buy new outfits for the entire year. Everything had to be of the best quality, and money played no role whatsoever. She paid the merchant whatever he asked, and each of us got a new suit, a new winter coat, and all the underthings and shirts we needed. She bought so much that it had to be delivered to our house, for it was too heavy to carry home. We wore our new things on the High Holy Days with a great deal of pride. We all had the same suits. The only difference was that when we went to high school each of us wore a distinctive class hat, which differed each year in color. Otherwise we were dressed alike.

My puberty years were quite normal. They presented the usual difficulties, but they were made easier because the young girls in charge of us children took care of that. I still remember how one of them introduced me to the secret world of sex, willingly and joyfully offering her services as a matter of course. She was not much older than we were, but certainly much

---

32. Louis Lewandowski (1821–1894) was the chief choirmaster of the Liberal synagogue in Berlin and one of the most important nineteenth-century composers of Jewish liturgical music.

33. The story of Hannah is to be found in I Samuel 1–2. No published prayer book by that name is known. Perhaps this was a name given by Prinz's grandmother to her own personal copy of the prayer book.

34. The Jewish New Year (Rosh Hashanah) and the Day of Atonement (Yom Kippur).

more knowledgeable. There were also sex games among us and our friends, sometimes carried out in great secrecy, and more often than not discovered by our friends who did the same things. There was a lot of laughter about it. Nobody really took it terribly seriously, and all this was done as though it were a matter of natural routine. Neither of my parents ever spoke to me about sex. It was the Catholic priest who taught in one of the schools who, at least once a month, spoke very gravely about the great sin of masturbation. I can still remember how my face reddened when he spoke about the great sin with which we burdened ourselves by indulging in what he called "self-satisfaction." My heart beat rapidly, but he was, after all, not my priest; my rabbi never talked about it. We no longer believed that it was the stork who brought the children. In the drawer of my father's night table I discovered packages of condoms—and I knew what they were for. Sex education in schools did not exist. At home it was unnecessary. It was assumed by the parents that the sweet secret of the relationship between boy and girl, man and woman, had already been divulged to us, that we were sufficiently knowledgeable about the subject, and probably practiced it already.

My greatest and most important experience in the new town was the relationship with my rabbi. Although he appeared to me as a grown-up man and rather elderly, he probably was not older than thirty when I met him. He was married to the daughter of one of the Jewish millionaires. He had three children, whom he named for us. The oldest son was Joachim, the second Kurt, and his youngest Hans. He liked the names in our family. Very soon I discovered that he hated his wife. He was bright and she was dumb. He made fun of her and it soon became known that he had affairs with other women, one a very serious one with the very beautiful daughter of an affluent member of his congregation. But no one really cared. I did care about him, perhaps more than about anyone else with the exception of my mother. Looking back to this time, I begin to understand that he was a father substitute for me, a father to whom I could talk and discuss all kinds of things, and this I did. He was a very extraordinary and excellent man.

He had been born in London, England and his German still had some English accent in it. He had been brought to Germany as a young man and had studied there, gaining a doctorate in philosophy and a completely new outlook on things Jewish. He was contemptuous of Orthodoxy, and called the bowing and *shokling*[35] during the prayer "pious calisthenics." Although he was not Orthodox at all, he understood that living at the beginning of the twentieth century required an interpretation of Judaism, and to me he was

35. Swaying back and forth in prayer, as is customary among some Orthodox Jews.

the most pious man I ever met. He soon took a liking to me. Several times during the year he would ask me to get up in the morning at five o'clock and come to his house. In front of his house was a horse-drawn carriage loaded with packages. He came down smilingly and said to me: "Get up there, I need your help." Then the driver took us to the districts of the town where the poor people lived. Almost all of these people were Christians, but Dr. Felix Goldmann[36] (that was his name) knew the names of the poorest of the poor. Whenever we stopped in front of a house, he would ask me to place one of the packages in front of it. Then we left. The packages contained food and clothing, and very often his own clothing. These were unforgettable morning hours, for here was a man who practiced what he preached, and piety suddenly became an act of love. Love, not charity, for the first thing he made me understand was that one does not give charity. Giving was an expression of love for one's neighbor. It did not matter to him whether the neighbor was Jewish or not, a believer or an atheist. He was a human being.

After these experiences, I listened to his sermons quite differently. I now shared a secret with him and he with me. I was bound to secrecy and was never permitted to speak about what happened in those morning hours, sometimes in the middle of winter. I never told my parents or my brothers why I got up so early. It was I and Dr. Goldmann, and nobody else. I soon began to understand things a little better. I listened attentively to his sermons. He was extraordinarily eloquent and had done away with the false solemnity and pathos of the nineteenth-century preacher. He talked in his normal tone of voice, and often was more forensic[37] than anything else. This had something to do with the fact that he had also studied law. When he wanted to make a point, he did so clearly and unafraid of any kind of criticism, with a great deal of courage and a brave attempt to address himself to the problems of the time. Even today I can recite the main points of a sermon he delivered about the coming of the Messiah. It was an anti-Christian sermon. To him the Messiah belief was the very core of Judaism. It called for justice and peace. There was something in him that reminded us of his English heritage, the spirit of the Magna Carta and the eloquence of Shakespearean poetry. I began to love him, and love him I did until he died. This although I became an early Zionist, as we shall see, and he was a rabid anti-Zionist. When he died, at a time when I was already a rabbi and writer, he

36. Felix Goldmann (1882–1934) served as rabbi in Oppeln beginning in 1907 and later in Leipzig from 1917. He played an active role in combating antisemitism and was also a productive Jewish scholar. When Goldmann died in 1934, Prinz published a eulogy entitled "My Teacher" in the Zionist newspaper, *Jüdische Rundschau* (October 16, 1934).

37. He made arguments rather than attempting to inspire, as other rabbis did.

left the manuscript of a book attacking one that I had written,[38] but his manuscript was not published because he had passed away. As he approached death it had seemed senseless to publish a polemical book against the man who until his last day remained his most faithful and favorite student.

It is very difficult to imagine the enormous influence Goldmann had over me. He remained my ideal as a rabbi because he combined so many human traits with his ministry. His style of preaching has remained meaningful to me until this day, and no one had a greater influence on my own style of preaching than he. He rejected the false tone of sermonizing, which at that time was the accepted method of Christian and Jewish messages from the pulpit. It was, in fact, an imitation of the Protestant style of preaching. Most rabbis and ministers shied away from the problems of the day. They were satisfied to interpret a biblical verse in order to please the congregation. Their goal of preaching was "spiritual elevation of the congregation." Goldmann's goal was to teach, to interpret, and to state a position. He persuaded me at an early age that when standing in the pulpit wearing the garb of a "godly man" one must remain human, more so than anyone else, that decency and human behavior were more important than ritualistic organized religion. He was careless with money and died a poor man, having cosigned numerous bank loans for students and poor people and in the end having to pay it all. He must have spent his wife's entire dowry, which was considerable. He gave the equivalent of thousands of dollars to poor people; they all came to him, knowing they would be helped whether they were Jewish or not. When he died, he left behind a large sum of debts, which I think were never paid. But he also left behind the name of an extraordinary human being who expressed his humanness in the kind of religious terms that are the only acceptable ones to me as they were to him. He left me when I was young, but we remained in contact even after I had become a rabbi. When he died in 1934, it was as though I had lost a very close relative, although in terms of Jewish attitudes I had drifted far away from him and he from me.[39]

By now I was twelve years old. A few months after my twelfth birthday in 1914, the war broke out. It was an unforgettable day. I had very little knowledge of the incident in Sarajevo.[40] Very few people expected the death of a grand duke to cause the beginning of a world war. In the early morning of the first of August, 1914, we three boys left with one of our young girls to

38. The reference is doubtless to Prinz's *Wir Juden* (We Jews; 1934), a Zionist tract that caused tremendous consternation in anti-Zionist circles.
39. The reference is to Zionism.
40. The assassination of Archduke Francis Ferdinand on June 28, 1914, which was the immediate cause for the outbreak of World War I shortly thereafter.

go into the woods to pick blueberries and mushrooms. It was, after all, vacation time and this was our daily routine. It was pleasant to walk in the woods barefoot, to cool off in the many rivers and brooks, and it was not very far away from the town. In the afternoon of that day, we returned and found the town in turmoil. The reason became quite clear. The proclamation of war had been read in the public squares. People stood around in groups and discussed the seriousness of the situation. Upon our return home, my father informed us excitedly that war had broken out and that Germany would win the war because it was the greatest of nations, the most powerful and the best in the world. It was on that very day that we began to collect the extras that were printed and distributed by the newspapers. They contained a summary of the events of the day. My father had a special place in his office where he collected the daily editions and kept them for four years. By the end of the war they had become quite voluminous. His belief in the victory of Germany never lessened; he was a very ardent German patriot. He was, however, not so patriotic as to want to serve in the army and tried every trick in the book to evade conscription. He joined the voluntary fire brigade hoping that would exempt him from service. He cultivated his imagined frailty, which he called pneumonia. He was really never sick, but there was not a single week I can remember when he did not stay in bed for a whole day, applying cold compresses to cure his imagined feverish condition. His body was in perfect shape. He was slim, and he died at the age of eighty without ever having been in a hospital or seriously ill at home.

Our new business had developed extraordinarily well and the family became rather affluent. For many years now my parents had been taking four weeks off from work and going to spas. Because one of them had to be in the store, they went away separately. I was sometimes taken along with my mother and grandmother who went to a spa that specialized in heart disease and rheumatism. It was expensive and frequented by people from many countries. I still remember the rich Russians who came there with their families. The boys wore the uniforms of their Russian schools. In the afternoon, we all went to the park of the spa where a band played pleasantly. We walked around drinking from the "waters" that were supposed to have a curative effect on whatever ailed us. We took various kinds of baths in the large establishment, the main attraction of the mountain village, which was attractive in many other respects, as well. My father always thought I had a heart murmur. Although that was a natural thing for young people during their puberty, he took it very seriously. I was exempt from participating in the physical exercises that were part of the curriculum of the school. He thought his son was so ill that he ought not to indulge in such strenuous exercises, but all this was pure imagination. There is no doubt that my father cared for me and was worried about anything that happened to any one of us. He was extraordinarily generous with money as long as he had it. There was never any doubt that if we needed something, even for our sheer enjoyment and entertainment, he would not hesitate to pay for it.

When I was ten years old or even younger, I went with my father and my brothers every Sunday afternoon to a café situated on the second floor of a building. This was the main attraction of the town, particularly on a Sunday afternoon. It was called Café Residence and was a typical European café where only coffee and all kinds of delicious cakes and tarts were served. The main attraction, however, was a little orchestra that played while the burghers and their families sipped their coffee and ate enormous portions of cake with whipped cream. I was particularly drawn to the first fiddler. He stood on a little stand, and once in a while he played a solo. The music was always light, saccharine, nostalgic, and musically mediocre. But to me it was great music, and the young man standing there performing his art on the violin became my hero. After a few weeks of such visits I asked my father to buy me a violin, for I wanted to become a first fiddler standing on a little pedestal, playing a solo and being applauded by an audience as was my hero. My father immediately bought me a lovely little violin and engaged a teacher who came to the house two or three times a week. I was very ambitious and eager to advance beyond the first attempts to play the violin, trying to imitate the fiddler of the café, but without much success. I practiced for hours every day since I was trying to reach that stage of accomplishment as soon as possible. Of course, I did not succeed. The only thing I did succeed in was neglecting my schoolwork.

Around Christmastime I got my report card from school, which showed I failed in every subject. As was the custom, I had to show my report card to my parents and have my father sign it, indicating that he had seen it. I brought it tremblingly to my father. I forgot to mention that my father was very hot-tempered and had no patience with either his wife or his children. All the physical punishment we ever got came from him. My mother never touched us other than in love and with sweet caresses. My father owned a cat-of-nine-tails, an instrument of torture that consisted of eight long leather strips. Very often he beat us with it, until much later when I rebelled and cut off the strips. After reading my memorable report card, my father looked at me sternly. I was sure he would now take his cat-of-nine-tails, ask me to undress, and treat my naked behind in the usual fashion. I was already prepared for the pain it caused. But diabolically my father had something else in mind. He asked me to bring him my violin, which I did.

When I came back, he was still holding my report card in his hands. He looked foreboding when he asked me to hand over the violin. He then took it, threw it to the floor, and stepped on it. There on the floor was my beloved violin, or rather the corpse of a violin, with the strings torn and the wooden case broken. He stormed out of the room in great anger, possibly because he was angry at himself and his lack of control. But I stayed with my broken violin as though I were keeping watch over a dead body. I remained there for many hours crying until my mother came in. She was aghast at what my father had done. She knew how much the violin had meant to me and that it had become part of the dreams for my life. She comforted me sweetly, but the violin was never repaired. It was indeed beyond repair, nor did my father ever buy a new one. The instructor was informed that he need not come any more. I then decided that some day, even without a violin, I would be standing on a pedestal, performing a solo, and acknowledging the applause of my audience. This incident was in reality a very important factor in my decision to become a public speaker. That I should ever want to become a rabbi was probably very far from my thoughts at that time. I was still too young.

When the war broke out, all the young men went to fight. Many of our teachers were conscripted. A few weeks later we received the news that some of those who had gone had been killed in action. One of my teachers was among them. Patriotic speeches were delivered in school. Our main enemy was Britain. I still remember the first speech my mathematics teacher delivered, in which he said: "Whenever you speak of lies in your life, say your lies like a young man."[41] A few months later he was killed. He had volunteered to serve in the army and was killed in action.

I was twelve years old when the war broke out. Our town was not far from the Russian border, probably less than a hundred miles away. Oppeln was an important town in terms of industry and it was the seat of the provincial government. The bridges had to be watched and guarded against possible attack or sabotage, and soldiers were stationed at every bridge with machine guns propped up for defense. My mother, appalled at the war and the deaths of so many people, would arise early in the morning and with our two maids carry large baskets of sandwiches and hot coffee to the bridges to refresh the soldiers who had spent the cold night there. It must have been at five or six in the morning when she did so. It became a routine of hers for a whole year, three times a week, and it had the same effect on me as the little packages for poor people Dr. Goldmann used to distribute. She did it quietly and without fanfare. It had become her habit, and I am sure the food and

41. The meaning of this citation is not apparent.

drink she brought to the soldiers were not merely generous in quantity but also very carefully prepared, so that something good and strong and tasty should get into the stomachs of these young men who suddenly had become the heroes of the nation.

Two important things happened during that year. First, my mother became pregnant. She was already thirty-six years old and evidently her pregnancy was due to an accident. She suffered from some kidney trouble and had to be carefully watched. We had a family physician who was particularly careful and a bit worried about her pregnancy. In addition, she had an obstetrician who was the head of the department of the hospital in our town. Since she was very petite, her belly was even bigger than normal. She began to walk with some difficulty, but never lost her native sense of humor, which meant so much to me. She had inherited this trait from my great-grandfather, who was well known as a man of wit, telling jokes and funny stories as did my mother. She made light of her kidney condition and carried the fetus in her body with great expectation. I knew that it was not a baby that she would have wanted to have at such a late date after having given birth to three boys. She was hoping to have a daughter. We were therefore looking forward to the birth in our family, and there were preparations for the room in which the new baby would live.

The second event was the farewell service for Dr. Goldmann, who had been called to a much larger pulpit in the city of Leipzig, which had a community of many thousands of families.[42] Goldmann had become very well known not merely as a speaker and lecturer, but also as a writer. I am sure that the salary he received in his new job was three times as large as the one he had earned in my community. At any rate, he accepted, and the farewell service was one of the saddest days of my life. He left and we did not have a rabbi. It was difficult to get one to fill his shoes. In fact, it was altogether not easy to get a rabbi to come to a town that had a reputation for radical liberalism. One of the Jewish teachers accepted the responsibility of filling in for a while until a new rabbi was elected. He was a typical German teacher with an unpleasant rasping voice, and knowing that he would officiate at my bar mitzvah made me even sadder. Goldmann gave me his picture. It was on a Saturday night, and since he wanted to write something on the picture, he changed the date to Sunday, saying to me, "I do this because I don't want people to say later that Goldmann wrote on the Sabbath."

As I was twelve years old, I began to think of my approaching bar mitzvah. It was not necessary for me to take special lessons for it since the bar

42. The Leipzig Jewish population in 1910 was 9,728.

mitzvah service consisted mainly in the recitation of a Torah blessing. Nothing else had to be done. The rabbi delivered a speech to the bar mitzvah boys, but neither a speech nor anything else had to be done by the bar mitzvah boy himself.

Since I was born in May, my bar mitzvah would take place in that month, but long before then my mother had bought me a navy blue suit, a white shirt, and a conservative tie—my first suit with long trousers. It was customary at that time for young boys to wear short pants. The suit was of a particularly good quality and I got new black shoes with it. January was the last month of my mother's pregnancy. At the beginning of the month of February she felt uncomfortable, and climbing up the stairs to our apartment was quite a chore for her. Her kidneys did not function well and she stayed in bed a great deal. There was very little to be done about the infected kidneys; neither sulfa drugs nor antibiotics existed at that time. Our family doctor, a very serious, bearded man with silver-rimmed eyeglasses, examined her often. Apparently, he was not very happy with what he found. There was no way of preventing the birth, which was to take place in a few weeks. February came and my mother went to the hospital on the thirteenth of the month. On the fifteenth, the baby was born. It was a girl. My mother was very happy. Since my father's mother was called Dorothea, the baby was named for her. She did not get a Hebrew name. It simply was not our family tradition.

My mother's condition became alarming almost from the first day. I visited her every day, often with my grandmother. It was a Sunday, the date was February 14th, and my grandmother told me that I could visit my mother wearing my bar mitzvah suit. I put it on and appeared in her room in my brand-new navy blue suit, long trousers, a white shirt, and new tie. She was in bed and very weak. She looked at me and said: "You look very handsome and you will have a very nice bar mitzvah." This was her last clear sentence. She then said a few confused words, which I still remember. Every word was distorted. I knew that she was very ill. Upon leaving the room, I looked back at her, knowing instinctively that I would never see her again. She had fallen into a semi-coma. The next day she died.[43] She was not even thirty-seven years old; she would have been thirty-seven on the second of September.

For a young child, the death of a mother is always a painful and traumatic experience. For me it became the most important event of my life. I doubt that I would be the person I am without this great and tragic event. It became more tragic because of my complete lack of relationship with my

43. Joachim's mother died in the process of childbirth on February 15, 1915.

father. This has to be explained. My father was a very good man. Although he had gone to school in a one-room village school, his handwriting was extraordinarily beautiful, and he never made a spelling mistake. I was amazed how this man, born in a little village and accustomed to the ways of life in such primitive, rural surroundings, was able to adjust to life in town, the handling of a rather big business, and the organization that was necessary for it. He was also a man of great generosity. The older I became, the more conscious I became of the fact that money was never discussed in our house and that much more than we actually needed was given to us. My father was not a very rich man, but he was always very comfortable. I don't know whether he ever developed any personal and intimate relationship with anyone, including my mother. In many ways he was reticent and narrow. He was a great patriot and a believer in Germany, a royalist who could never understand the meaning of the revolution of 1918, an assimilated Jew to whom Zionism was anathema, and religiously quite mixed up. I do not believe that either of my brothers had any relationship with him—perhaps Kurt, who later was in charge of the men's department of our store. But my relationship to him was nonexistent.

It is for this reason that my relationship to my mother was extraordinarily close. But I hate to think that it was due to my lack of relationship to my father. It was mainly due to the fact that she was warm, capable of great love and compassion. I am sure her relationship to my father was perfunctory. It was the spirit of the times which upheld marriages that were not very successful, and which substituted marital duty for love and affection. My mother always related to her marriage with a sense of great integrity, probably never looked at another man; but very often I would see her crying because of my father's lack of understanding, his stubbornness, his hotheadedness, and his exaggerated sense of duty and order. He was very Prussian indeed, while my mother knew that love was an important factor in the upbringing of her children. She was very impartial, of course, and all of us benefited from her love. Still, since I was the oldest, she could communicate with me better than with the others. I spent as much time as I could with her. That she could have died at the age of thirty-six was something that I never contemplated, and I have not been able to comprehend it even to this very day.

My father's reaction was, again, one of order and discipline. After the burial he took us to the cemetery every Sunday morning at eleven o'clock sharp. There we stood at her grave not knowing what to do. He had a little book from which he read a prayer unintelligibly and quite meaningless. Going to our mother's grave was unproductive. I knew that my mother was not in this grave but in my heart, and the grave itself was without meaning. The very large black marble tombstone with the gold lettering was erected a year later. Her first name was Nani, a rare name, but one that became very dear to me. I do not know for whom she was named. Since she died in the hospital, her body had to be taken to the Jewish cemetery chapel where the ritual cleansing was performed. It was customary for a Jewish family to be present when the body was taken to the cemetery, following behind the hearse. The body had been placed in a long, covered basket. We waited downstairs in the street or in the courtyard of the hospital. As the basket was being brought down, there was a slight wind that blew the cover away so that I could see her face. I had never before seen a human corpse. Her face was peaceful, but it took many decades for me to forget its yellowness. The blood had gone out of her body, and there she was, cold and stiff and dead. Instead of her rosy cheeks, so much a symbol of her life, her quick, lively motions so character-istic of her, and the smile on her face whenever she told us funny stories—all that was gone, and here she was in a basket being lifted into the hearse. It drove off and, as was the custom, we followed on foot. I still remember how I trembled at the thought that the curtain of the hearse might be blown away by the wind, and again I would have to see her. But it did not happen, and I was glad of it.

The funeral services were held three days after her death. This was the rule at that time. No one could be buried before the end of a three-day pe-riod.[44] Bodies were not embalmed. We waited at home and relatives began to come. However, I do not believe that our store was closed until the day of the burial. What we did during those three days of waiting I do not recall. My father was really very sad and often cried. Maria, our cook, was now in full charge, and all the maids showed a great deal of tenderness and under-standing. My brothers were too young to understand; Kurt was eleven and Hans was nine. They did not realize what had happened, and continued to play and laugh and fight and do what they always did. I was closeted in my own world, a little island of mourning and despair. I could not imagine that I could continue to live without her. I did not speak to my father, nor he to me. The relatives annoyed me. Many of them came and necessitated large-scale activities in the kitchen. Huge amounts of food had to be served; it was something in between festivity and mourning, but I could hardly eat.

Then the day of the funeral arrived. It was customary for mourners to wear a black ribbon around one arm, a "mourning band," to be worn throughout the year. I still remember how much satisfaction it gave me to

---

44. Jewish law, however, requires burial on the day of death except under special circumstances.

wear it. It was almost like a badge of honor for my mother. (We carried it in our store, for it was a popular item.) The several horse-drawn carriages took us and the relatives to the cemetery. We all sat there in the small chapel. I think that the whole Jewish community was present, for she was loved by all people, and every one of our Christian neighbors came. Unfortunately, the rabbi, my friend Dr. Goldmann, had already left the community, and the substitute rabbi officiated. Although he knew my mother and us, he was a very mediocre man and read a eulogy of which I do not recall a single sentence. I recall only that whenever he mentioned her children, I whispered to my brothers that we must weep. It was rather a whimperish weeping; I was too desperate to cry. For me the burial service was particularly painful since Dr. Goldmann was not there. He therefore said[45] a few loving sentences that helped me since I had spoken to him about my close relationship with my mother. But he was not there and it made the event particularly painful. We buried her in the cemetery. Now the cemetery no longer exists; it was covered over by the Communist regime established in our town after the Second World War. I was told that my mother's large tombstone was among the many Jewish tombstones used to pave the square under which she and hundreds of other Jews lie buried.

The house was now very empty. Busy and empty. My mother's sister stayed with us for a few weeks, but she was nauseatingly sentimental and did not help me at all. It was the month of February, and the little newborn baby was brought home. A wet nurse was engaged to take care of her. I helped to diaper her, and I did so because I thought my mother would have wanted me to. As my aunt was not much comfort, I now turned more than ever to my grandmother, my beautiful, understanding, and compassionate grandmother, who more and more became for me the mother of my mother, as though she could be a substitute for her. But she was not that, for there could be no substitute. However, she certainly made my life much easier; she was capable of great love and indescribable humanity. She lived with her husband in a constant state of civil war. She had borne him seven children, but she hated him, and he deserved to be hated.

My mother was the third child my grandmother had lost. Before that, and not too many years earlier, an uncle of mine died of a disease that at the time was incurable. He suffered from diabetes and died at the age of twenty-nine. My other uncle had died seven years earlier. He had been my grandmother's most beloved son and had spoiled her all the time. Most of her possessions came from him. The first phonograph, large and elegant, was his

45. The intention is probably "wrote," since Goldmann had left the community.

gift. He took my grandmother to the Berlin Opera and bought a whole box for her just opposite that of the Kaiser, who he knew would attend that performance. My grandmother could not stop telling me about the opera, which was very popular at that time. It was *Mignon*, and my grandmother always sang the famous aria from it. She had no voice and could not carry a tune, but she sang it nevertheless. I sat at her feet. Very often she was knitting something and I was permitted to hold the ball of wool. These were great moments that are completely unforgettable.

Toward the end of the first year after my mother's death, while sitting and talking with my grandmother at her home, I said to her: "You have now lost three children, all of whom were grown up and very close to you. But you continue to live and I have not seen you cry. How can you take all that and continue to live?" She looked at me with her big brown eyes, thought for a while, and then said a sentence that I have never forgotten. In order to understand this sentence you must realize that she had lived a rustic life on a farm with cows and horses. So she said to me: "I want you to understand and promise me that you will never forget that a human being is much stronger than a young colt." Upon saying this, she rose and went into the next room, returning with a silver cup. It bore the engraved date of 1670. "When our ancestors used to live in Bavaria," she said, "one of them had this cup made in 1670, and every one of us recited the kiddush[46] with this cup. You are my eldest grandson and I want you to have it and use it, and maybe you will also use it for the kiddush on a Friday night." I still do.

Sometime later she gave me two paintings. My great-grandfather Joachim Fraenkel had his and his wife's portraits painted by an artist. They were beautifully done. It showed him as a young man with a cleft in his chin, which I inherited from him. His wife was blonde and very beautiful. My grandmother told me on this occasion that my great-grandfather saw her once and thought that she was not Jewish, but he had decided to marry her anyway. She was so beautiful. I, of course, never knew either of them, but I took the pictures for my own room and later, when I got married, transferred them to my own home. Unfortunately, in the turmoil during the Hitler time the two pastels were lost.

Life at home was pretty sad. The day of my bar mitzvah was approaching, and although in those days nobody thought of big parties, things had all been arranged. Finally, the day did come and there was hustle and bustle in the house, but we still had no rabbi. As I said before, there were no par-

46. The cup used for recitation of the blessing over wine at the ceremony of welcoming the Sabbath on Friday evenings and holidays.

ticular preparations for the bar mitzvah boy. He would be called to the Torah and then stand at the lower pulpit while the rabbi, standing in front of the ark,[47] would talk to him. Alas, there was no Goldmann to do it, but only this rather boring and mediocre man. I did not particularly look forward to that day. Without my mother it was utterly meaningless for me. After the service, we came home and a luncheon was served. My presents were brought to the house, all of them being books. I think I received a hundred books for my bar mitzvah—whole sets of classics with particularly beautiful bindings. A bookshelf was made for me in my room. It made me very proud and very fond of books, for I began to read at every free moment. The books formed the beginning of my library and I still have many of them today.

My social life was restricted to the small group of people who were my friends. I have forgotten all their names with the exception of one girl who I discovered was madly in love with me. She was a famous ice-skater. Her father had a large business in town and we, of course, knew the family well. Ice-skating was one of the great pastimes of that town. We had a famous ice rink. It was on the lake, which was situated in a large valley and bordered on the left side by a park containing the very well-preserved, seventeenth-century chateau of the duke who used to live there, but no longer did. On the other side there was a hill on which our synagogue was built. The lake was used by famous ice-skating societies who came from as far away as Austria and Hungary and participated in yearly contests there. The ice was always beautifully kept. In my early days in the village, we did not have ice-skates; we used to skate on wooden pieces from cigar boxes. I loved skating and also did some figure skating, which I have not forgotten how to do until this very day. My girlfriend, however, was a great figure skater. She was very pretty with two dimples and long black hair, and she was very aggressive. She was a Jewish girl, of course, a bit older than I. Very often we used to go home together from the pond. No one ever drove home. There were no automobiles. And the town was small. We had to cross a bridge over the river Oder on which the town is situated. One day, when it was already dark at five o'clock in the afternoon as we started for home, she suddenly stopped at a gas lamppost, looked at me, and then kissed me. I was all of fifteen years old and probably very eager to be kissed. But what I remember is not merely her passion, but that some gas had leaked out of the street lamp, and for many years after that whenever I kissed a girl it smelled of gas. It is amazing for how long that persisted. I was already a grown-up man and kissing women was not an unusual or extraordinary activity of mine. But whenever

47. The shrine at the front of the synagogue sanctuary that contains the Torah scrolls.

I did it, I thought back to that great day of my first kiss and the odor of gas that had emanated from the street lamp. However, nothing serious developed from this friendship. It was customary for friends to give someone who played the guitar silk bands that were to be fastened to it. As I played that instrument, she gave me many of them, and they were among the most beautiful that I possessed. At that time I did not think of sexual activities, for I was a member of a youth movement that frowned on such things.

I was now fifteen years old and deeply involved in Judaism. I had already decided to become a rabbi. This was not only because I thought I should do something for my mother instead of the perfunctory things that had been done for her at the funeral service, but something much more enduring and much more meaningful. My actual decision had come about earlier and in a strange manner. There were daily services in our synagogue, which were held in the little chapel. So when my mother died, I decided to attend services every day. On a Monday morning, when the Torah was being read, we noticed we had only nine men. I had not yet celebrated my bar mitzvah and therefore was not counted among the minyan.[48] The rabbi looked at me and said, "We have only nine men and you will not be bar mitzvah for a month. But I will follow an old Jewish custom." He went to the little ark and took out a Torah scroll. He gave it to me to hold and sit with it during the service. It was a little scroll, not too heavy for a young boy, with a beautiful velvet mantle adorned with golden letters and symbols. It must have been pretty old. I was sitting during the service when suddenly my cheek touched the velvet. It was so soft. Suddenly, it reminded me of my mother's warm skin, which I had felt whenever, during our birthdays, we visited her when she was still in bed. I actually felt that I was sitting with my mother since the velvet was as soft as her skin. I celebrated some sort of wedding with her, the Torah becoming a symbol of my mother. I was determined to devote my life to her. The Torah and my mother—they had became one. Then and there I determined to become a rabbi.

I informed my father of my decision and it made him very unhappy. He told me that under no circumstances would I be permitted to become a rabbi. I would finish the first part of my high school studies when I would be sixteen years old, serve an apprenticeship at one of the large department stores, and then join the business. And when the time came, I, the oldest, would take over. My father was very determined, and I thought it futile to continue the discussion. My mother was dead and I had no one to turn to.

---

48. The quorum of ten men traditional Judaism requires for certain public prayers. If only nine men are present, the Torah scroll can take the place of a tenth man.

I tried to proceed as though I were preparing for my rabbinical career. This was necessary because my knowledge of Hebrew was very limited and I had hardly any familiarity with Jewish customs. But in the meantime the community had engaged a new rabbi who was much more scholarly than Goldmann, but also less attractive.[49] Nevertheless, I decided to take private Hebrew lessons from him and I began as soon as I could arrange it. I learned a great deal from him. He was a Bavarian by birth, the son of a Jewish scholar, and knew a great deal. He really laid the foundation for whatever I later studied, and I am very grateful to him although we never established an intimate relationship.

I continued to go to services, but I began to find the Liberal service empty and shallow. Goldmann, who had fascinated me with his sermons, was no longer there; the new rabbi's sermons were ordinary and mediocre. The services were not very well attended and the contrast between the organ and the choir and the paucity of the attendance began to annoy me. By accident I found a rather strange way out of this spiritual wilderness into an oasis of religious experience. One day, while entering the house through the back door and standing in front of the second house my father had rented to some people, I noticed a man. He was a rather simple person, a carpenter by profession. As I came closer to him, I saw that his daughter was also there. In her hand she was holding a picture of a Christian saint, which I saw agitated her father very much. He spoke loudly and angrily to his child, insisting that to carry such pictures, which she had gotten in school, was sheer idolatry and in violation of the Ten Commandments in which he believed. The child cried bitterly, but he tore up the picture. I then spoke to him and asked what had motivated his action. He told me that he was a Seventh-day Adventist, observed the Sabbath, and knew the Old Testament by heart. I was very curious about all this and found out that their services were on Friday nights. An itinerant preacher would conduct them and deliver the sermon. I asked whether I could be present at the next service. It was held in a small hall of a hotel. I decided to attend.

When next Friday came, I did not to go to the synagogue but to the service of the Seventh-day Adventists. It may very well be that my Roman Catholic experience in the village still influenced me, and the great solemnity of the large congregation in the village church impressed me more favorably than the small group that assembled in the synagogue on Friday nights. I needed the warmth of religious experience, which my Jewish community

49. This rabbi was David Braunschweiger, who served in Oppeln from 1917 to 1928.

could not provide for me. As I entered the small hall, I discovered that I knew most of the people. All of them were artisans of some sort, men and women sitting together, all of them simple folk, many having done work for my parents. I sat next to the seamstress who would come to our house once or twice a month to do the necessary mending and sewing. With her were other people—shoemakers, carpenters, cabinetmakers, all of them dressed in their best suits, sitting and waiting for the preacher to arrive. A young man finally came and conducted the service. Whereas in the synagogue the members of the congregation relied on the choir and hardly participated in the service, here I found the whole congregation singing together. They had neither organ nor piano. They sang with so much fervor that I was deeply impressed. Even the portion of the service before the preacher stood up in front of a table to deliver his sermon remained for me for many years to come a memory of great spiritual enjoyment. Although the preacher spoke about the New Testament, as well, his main source was the Old Testament, and his theology was a confirmation of the strictest possible monotheism, rejecting many of the Christian dogmas and adhering very closely to a narrowly interpreted Old Testament. He rejected Sunday and praised Saturday as the holy day. He also explained the dietary laws of Seventh-day Adventists, which excluded pork as food and were almost as strict as the ritual code of Orthodox Judaism. I made friends with the people who worshipped there and for a long time I alternated between the Friday night service in the synagogue and the service of the Seventh-day Adventists. What I had missed in the synagogue I found there.

My Jewish emptiness, which was caused by the perfunctory and assimilationist Jewish attitude of my community, including my own father, left a void inside me that made me search for something to fill it. It was at that time that I began to discover there was something in Jewish life that was new, but rejected by the vast majority of the Jewish people. It was the Zionist movement. I ordered Theodor Herzl's *The Jewish State*[50] from our bookstore since the library of the Jewish community did not carry it. I read it feverishly, including the last sentence: "If you will it, it will not be a fairy tale."[51] I was convinced that he was dealing here with a utopian idea and that the Jewish state would never be founded. But I was attracted to it as an idea because

50. Theodor Herzl published his *Judenstaat* (more properly translated: "The Jews' State") in 1896. It became the principal text for political Zionism.
51. This sentence does not occur in Herzl's *The Jews' State*. It appears as a motto on the title page of his novel, *Altneuland*.

it was completely utopian, something never to be fulfilled, a political Jewish notion that never could be attained. It was that very thing that attracted me to the movement. In speaking to my rabbi about it he warned me against such a foolish idea that could only lead to a Jewish disaster and create a situation of dual loyalty, a betrayal of the German patriotism to which we were all wedded because we enjoyed freedom and full citizenship.

As I began to examine these ideas, it became very clear to me that, although we were formally and legally emancipated, during the First World War, which was still going on, now in its last year, hardly any Jew could become an officer,[52] and that the government was free of Jews. It was the beginning of my complete rejection of Germany and the German people. In my search for fellow Zionists I found three people in the community who were Zionists, albeit clandestinely. Two of them were lawyers, the third a physician. They were very happy about my decision to join them. I asked whether there was a youth movement that I could join. They told me about a movement called "Blue-White,"[53] the colors of the flag of the Zionist movement, which at that time was only twenty years old. Immediately, I went about founding a very small chapter and got in touch with the national organization, which consisted mainly of children of very assimilated families. Most of the boys had not even been circumcised. In comparison with their parents, my father could have been an Orthodox Jew. They had chosen Zionism because it gave them some content and a goal. They had their own book of songs and their main activity was similar to that of the German youth movements: the discovery of nature and gaining closeness to it. They held that it was great to be a Jew. As they put it, "It's beautiful to be Jewish."

After joining the Zionist movement, I ceased to sing the German national anthem and developed a sense of distance from the German people. I watched my father collect the daily dispatches about the war, which was beginning to look rather dismal. But it was not my war and Germany was not my country. I was fifteen years old. My country was nowhere. It was just a dream and a goal, but one that became more attractive and concrete to me the more I read; and I read all of the Zionist literature and the proceedings of the Zionist congresses. Our main activity was to hike in the woods and later in the mountains, to be self-reliant, cook our meals, and never to use a

52. In fact, during World War I about 2,000 Jews served as officers.
53. The German Zionist youth movement, Blau-Weiss, was founded in 1913. At its peak in the 1920s it reached a membership of about 3,000 young people.

vehicle. It was a basic experience for my life. I began to resent the customs of my family, which relied upon servants. I moved closer to the socialist movement, which was finally victorious on November 9, 1918.[54]

A few months after my sixteenth birthday the Germans lost the war and the German Republic was established. I obtained the blue box of the Jewish National Fund into which I put my money. I asked my father to do likewise, but he refused since he would not help finance an idea so outrageously insane. That his eldest son had joined that movement was further confirmation for him that I was a little bit out of the ordinary, probably slightly disturbed. He was determined that I take over his business and forget about these Jewish dreams of Zionism and the rabbinate. My father forced me to leave school after I had graduated from the first part of high school and was about sixteen years old. He was determined to apprentice me to one of the large department stores where I could learn the trade.

One of our relatives owned a very large store of that kind about a hundred miles away from our town. Compared with our store, the six-story building was a commercial palace. However, I did not make a good impression on the man who owned the store and who was a distant cousin. Obviously he realized that I was not really interested in the work. I was rejected and left the town. I hoped that my father would get the idea, but I was mistaken. Soon after that, he took me to the largest store in the city of Breslau, which had a population of half a million. The store was a famous commercial establishment, and much to my surprise I was accepted. I left my family without much regret and began an apprenticeship with that large firm. The year was 1918 and I was there during the last months of the war. Food was still very scarce and most of the young men had gone off to war.

It was there that I experienced the great excitement of the revolution. Officers were assaulted in the streets, some of them badly beaten up. The old flag had been removed and socialist groups, many of them still in uniform, marched singing through the streets. I still remember that first revolutionary experience—the speeches about freedom, equality, and democracy. This was the first time in my life that I heard the word *democracy*. It appealed to me greatly, but I soon discovered that many of the people I met, including members of my family who lived in Breslau, spoke with great horror about it, as though it were the beginning of the end. The Kaiser had abdicated and a labor leader had become the president of the country. For the first time Jews were elected to the parliament, and not many years later one of them became

54. On November 9, 1918, socialists overthrew the German imperial regime.

the Minister of Foreign Affairs.[55] A year earlier, a famous jurist had become the Minister of Justice.[56] Although this did not cause me to identify with Germany, it nevertheless brought me closer to it, for Zionism itself contained a great many socialist ideas. In fact, the first flag Theodor Herzl selected for the Jewish state contained six stars because he believed that no one should work more than six hours a day.[57]

My few months as an apprentice in the department store were of great importance to me. I had gotten a room with a Jewish family that had several roomers. I also ate there, but I was completely intoxicated with the Zionist idea and more than ever opposed to becoming a merchant. I developed a heart murmur, which I exaggerated when I spoke to my father, who used to come to the town once a week to buy merchandise for the store. In order to counteract the commercial aspects of my new life, I read classical literature every free moment, and I recall that it was at that time that I managed to learn the first part of Goethe's *Faust* and whole acts of the German translation of Shakespeare's plays.[58] I also began to write, which created an island for me outside the commercial world. A few months later, an aunt of mine, who was very fond of me and who was married to a rather affluent merchant, disclosed to my father that I was extremely unhappy and that I simply did not want to become a merchant.

It was during this time, at a meeting of Jewish young people, that I met a very beautiful girl, as old as I was, with long blonde hair and blue eyes. I became rather friendly with her although I met her rarely. I did not at that time realize that I would marry her some day. She was the daughter of the most famous Jewish scholar of the time. He was the Professor of Medieval Philosophy and Talmud at the Jewish Theological Seminary.[59] She, too, was a Zionist so that we had many things in common. But my attraction to her was really to her face and body and smile, rather than to anything else. When we sang together, I discovered she could not carry a tune. I didn't care. Her name was Lucie Horovitz. At that time I could hardly imagine how close our relationship would become, how very much her family would mean to me—and still does.

55. Some Jews had served in leading positions in the parliament of the Second Reich. The Jew who became Foreign Minister of the Weimar Republic was Walther Rathenau. He was assassinated by rightist extremists in 1922.

56. The reference is to Hugo Preuss (1860–1925), who became minister of the interior after the war and had earlier headed the committee that drafted the Weimar constitution.

57. Herzl proposed a flag with seven stars for the seven hours of the working day.

58. The text does not say "learn by heart," though that may be the intention.

59. The reference is to Saul Horovitz (1859–1921). At the Breslau rabbinical seminary, he at first

It was at that time that my father decided to remarry. As always, my grandmother, who was the person to arrange for it, was of the opinion that since the baby[60] was only a few years old, a mother was necessary. She found one of my mother's cousins, the daughter of my great-grandfather's son, a spinster, and decided that my father should marry her. She lived in Berlin and must have been in her forties at the time. The very fact that my father remarried seemed to me to be a betrayal, and I spent many hours of childish reaction to a rather reasonable decision on the part of my father, crying about the fact that he was betraying my mother. He went to Berlin to be married to her and returned after a brief honeymoon trip with a lady who was rather tall, buxom, energetic, and very "Berlinish." She brought some of her own things, among others a large number of books bound in leather. They were written by the most popular and worst novelists of that time, books resembling the soap operas of our time, so that I did not like seeing them at all. But she was that kind of person, and although I had a great deal of respect for her because she had become our mother, until her death I never established a relationship with her. She was not an unkind woman, nor was there any real objective reason why I did not take to her. She simply was no substitute for my mother, and although I called her that, as did the other children, none of us ever established any closeness with her. For my father she was evidently a very good companion. She was interested in business and showed great ability in that field. Otherwise, she was no factor in my life. She treated me well, as she did all the others, brought up the little girl, and did everything she was supposed to do.

It was then that my father finally became convinced that I should not remain with the department store since I would never amount to anything as a merchant. Whether it was this reason that swayed him or whether he was alarmed at the doctor's finding of the condition of my heart, I do not know. At any rate, I packed up and was sent to a spa that specialized in cardiac diseases. I spent a month there in great comfort with all financial matters generously taken care of by my father. While there, I met an old man who revealed to me that he had performed my circumcision. It was a rather comical encounter. Much less strange was my meeting a young lady from Berlin who was also a Zionist and who evidently had a great many emotional problems.

taught philosophy of religion and homiletics and in 1917 he succeeded to the position of Seminary Rabbi. In addition to philosophy, he published numerous scholarly writings in the field of rabbinic literature.

60. Dorothea (known in the family as Thea), the girl whose birth had brought about his mother's death.

She became my first pastoral case. I did not think of her in terms of a young woman with whom I could have started some sort of an affair, but as an object of my ability to help her out of a deep depression. I remember giving her Helen Keller's little book entitled *Optimism*,[61] and to my surprise it cured her. Several decades later she reminded me of it, and at that time my relationship with her was not merely therapeutic.[62]

Later, after I had taken the "cure" in that boring spa where people strictly adhered to the therapeutic routine the doctors prescribed, I went home. My father had given up talking me into going into the business. During one of his many imaginary illnesses, he asked me to come to his bedside. Since he thought he was going to die soon, he wanted me to swear a solemn oath, a deathbed oath. He wanted me to swear that I would never become a rabbi. Since I had already delivered several speeches in the community and he was aware of my oratorical talents, he asked me to solemnly promise him in the face of his imminent death that I would become a lawyer specializing in criminal law. I did so, keeping my fingers crossed[63] and knowing that I was lying to him.

The last three years in high school, which after graduation would permit me to attend a university, were among the most satisfying of my life. I suddenly discovered the world of science, literature, and art. I was particularly attracted to philosophical works. During all the years prior to that time I had been a mediocre student, neither very good nor very bad, and with little interest in specific fields. But now, after spending that time in the department store, I was thirsty for knowledge and passionately eager to get into a different kind of world where knowledge was more important than money. So with uncontrolled and uncontrollable passion I threw myself into this new world.

I was lucky that these years coincided with a major educational reform movement in Germany. Schools were completely under the influence of great and creative educators. Our school building was brand new and built in the architectural style of the twentieth century with all kinds of facilities. The students had their own government. Classes were extremely small. There was complete freedom of expression, and we were permitted to exert our influence on the curriculum. The relationship between the students and the teacher became very close. No longer was there any Prussianism in educa-

---

61. Helen Keller's *Optimism, An Essay* had appeared in 1903.
62. Her name was Grete. She is mentioned again later in Prinz's narrative when he writes of his year as a student in Berlin.
63. As children do to remove the onus of the lie they are telling.

tion. We very often met in the homes of the teachers, and each of us was permitted to develop his particular talent in his respective field of interest. In the type of school I attended, it had been impossible to graduate with a failing mark in mathematics—which I continued to flunk. But on account of our school reform, it was now nonetheless possible for me to be graduated since the fields of my extracurricular activities and interests were considered and graded. I received "A"s in art, philosophy, and history of religion. One of the most exciting and important events was that the school, originally only for boys, suddenly began to admit girls, at least in the higher classes, and four young ladies entered our class. Since we were sixteen or seventeen years old, you can imagine that our interest in the girls was not merely in their scholastic achievements.

This period coincided with the occupation of our province by Allied soldiers. There were regiments from England, Italy, and France. It changed life in our town completely. Suddenly, a rather conservative town became loose and permissive. The number of children born out of wedlock grew tremendously. Every foreign soldier had a German girlfriend. In our own class, there was a girl of Polish descent, who was flippant, attractive, and promiscuous. Some of my classmates knew of her promiscuity, but then she began an affair with a French officer with whom she evidently spent almost every night, for in the morning hours she was usually late for class and her face and disheveled hair betrayed the amorous activities of the preceding night.

My friend among the girls was a completely different sort of person. She was over six feet tall, much older than the others or myself. She was a member of the nobility. Her father owned large tracts of land and they lived in an eighteenth-century chateau with a host of servants. She came to school in a horse-drawn carriage, very conservatively, expensively, and elegantly dressed, and very serious indeed. She took a particular interest in me. Strangely enough, it had something to do with the fact that I was a Jew. I was the only Jew in the class, as usual. But she was seriously interested in theology and was particularly enamored of Martin Buber.[64] It was a time when I was very deeply influenced by Buber, who had just begun to write and to become a great literary figure of Western Europe. I was often invited to her chateau, and was picked up at my house by the elegant coachmen. Very often I drove with her through the family's village in a carriage with only two wheels. I have forgotten what it was called, but it was the most expensive and

64. The Jewish philosopher Martin Buber (1878–1965) had gained considerable attention in Germany by the end of World War I, even though his best-known work, *I and Thou*, did not appear until 1923.

most elegant of carriages. As we moved slowly through the village, which apparently had only one street, the farmers would line up along the road, the men removing their hats and the women curtseying. My first trip to the chateau was an awe-inspiring introduction to the kind of life I found within the house. It was all very friendly, but at the same time very formal. I don't think her parents had ever seen a Jew before, so that I was some sort of exotic and exciting experience for them. Special food was prepared for me as they were very eager not to serve me ham or something that would be in violation of the Jewish dietary laws. I maintained a very close intellectual relationship with her until graduation and saw her again many years later. She had become a famous physicist in one of the northern universities.

My life was now very serious and heading toward my goal. I increased the number of Hebrew lessons I took and began to study not merely the Hebrew text of the Bible but rabbinic literature as well. I must have been quite unbearable in those days, terribly serious, not given to any kind of levity or fun, and suffering silently and quietly the pangs of body and soul that are so much a part of the life of an adolescent boy. I had little fun and used every minute to study. The youth movement continued to play an important role in my life. A few more men and women joined the Zionist movement, which was a tiny, insignificant movement, not merely in my town but in the country as well. A kind of brotherhood developed among us so that when we said *shalom*[65] to one another, it was a bond very similar to that of a closely knit family. Once in a while, the rabbi permitted me to deliver a sermon at the youth group services, which I very carefully prepared and which made me the object of great admiration on the part of the young people. But in the community itself, as well as in my family, I was considered some sort of outcast, or at least someone who did not quite fit into the pattern of our family life. Family affairs bored me. My relationship to my brothers was close enough for me to finally convince them to join the Zionist movement, but their participation in it was not as ardent as mine. My brother Kurt left high school at the age of sixteen, was apprenticed to a large store in Breslau, and was trained to take over my father's business since the eldest son had failed him so tragically.

During those years, people who lived in other cities came to our town to visit their families. Some were interested in Jewish scholarship, and I usually spent a great deal of time with them, studying together. One was a hunchback who later became a famous lawyer. During the time I studied with him, I discovered how sharp and concise his mind was. I met him many de-

65. The Hebrew greeting, meaning *peace*, then used in Zionist circles.

cades later and was not surprised that he occupied a position in the judiciary in Israel, which afforded him an opportunity to develop his creative, legal mind.[66]

On the last Passover before my graduation, a rabbinical student was sent from the seminary in Breslau to occupy the pulpit. He was a good-looking young man who delivered a number of very fervent sermons. The one I remember vividly was preached on the biblical Song of Songs, which is so full of erotic allusions. He was to become a good friend of mine and later became my brother-in-law. His name was Max Gruenewald.[67] I told him that I had never seen a seder in my father's home. Although we did eat Passover food on that night, my father never really conducted a seder. I could not go to my grandfather's home for he, too, had no seder. By that time, I had already established a new rule in my home. Since the food in our house was not kosher, I did not eat any meat. For three long years I lived on vegetables and fish much to the annoyance of my father and stepmother who had to cook separate foods for me. Altogether I was leaning toward Orthodoxy. I remember studying the book of Jewish laws, which enumerated and dealt with all the Jewish customs to be observed.[68] I discovered how many, on account of my ignorance, I had not kept. Whenever I learned of a new one, I immediately observed it. I remember very vividly learning that on the Sabbath one is not to ring a doorbell or carry anything. Since we had school on Saturday and had to bring books there, I asked my father to buy me a second set so that I could walk to school on the Sabbath without carrying a book. My father acceded to my wishes since he had given up trying to change me. My mathematics teacher, a veteran of the First World War who had lost one arm, was a very Orthodox Jew and did not write on the Sabbath, but had to teach. He looked at me in amazement when I asked him whether I could leave my books in school with him during the week so that on the Sabbath I would not have to carry them. Much more annoying to my father was the fact that I refused to ring the doorbell. Upon entering the house on Friday night or on the Sabbath I would knock on the door instead. Even touching the bell I regarded as prohibited. My father thought me crazy and said so in no uncertain terms. But to me it was an affirmation of my life's most ultimate goal.

66. It has not been possible to determine this jurist's identity.
67. After his ordination from the Breslau seminary in 1926, Rabbi Max Gruenewald (1899–1992) served as a Liberal rabbi in Mannheim before emigrating to the United States, where he occupied a pulpit in Millburn, New Jersey and later served as the New York and International President of the Leo Baeck Institute.
68. Probably a shortened version of the *Shulhan Arukh*, the sixteenth-century compendium of Jewish law.

My religious fervor was expressed in my daily morning prayers when I put on the tefillin with great vigor. This was all part of a new serious phase in my life and in preparation for what I considered to be a great and unusual future.

I have always considered my turn to Orthodoxy as an attempt to substitute for the lack of Jewish environment I experienced in my own home and the negative attitude of my father to any kind of observance. I was particularly turned off by his habit of not permitting us to speak about Jewish subjects during dinnertime when the meal was being served by the maids. I considered it a matter of personal cowardice. Altogether his attitude was that of an assimilationist. His rejection of Zionism hurt me deeply, and it is probably because of the degree of his rejection that I became a very ardent Zionist. My membership in the Blue-White movement helped me greatly. The Zionists at that time were a small family, almost a clan. They rejected any kind of German patriotism and identified themselves with the Jewish people as such. It was at that time that I began to deliver speeches for Jewish groups in our town, and even outside of it, which dealt with the Zionist ideal and which met with violent opposition. My new rabbi was also an anti-Zionist. There was hardly anyone in town who shared my views with the exception of a Christian friend. He was my classmate and understood the Zionist aspirations of the Jewish people better than most Jews.

I was very curious about our own Jewish background. My father never spoke about his parents or grandparents. I think he was a little ashamed of the fact that his great-grandparents had been Polish Jews. I made many attempts to press him for some information, but apparently he didn't have any, or if he did, he did not want to speak about it. His father, who was already born in Germany, was a rather Prussian type as he himself was, with great emphasis on punctuality and a code of honor so typical of the Germans. I then began to inquire into the background of my mother's family. Unfortunately, my mother was dead and I could not talk to her about it. Her brothers knew very little, and so I turned to my grandmother, who became my main source. My great-grandfather played a very important part in this whole story. After all, I had been named for him and some people claimed that I resembled him. He interested me as a Jew who was born in 1814 and was never a merchant. He lived close to the land, serving that German count I mentioned earlier. He left a little library after his death. I remember having been given a dictionary of some kind from it. But I do not remember whether it was an etymology or a French–German dictionary. At any rate, I lost it. On his birth certificate, which I have, it is noted that his father was a merchant. But outside of the fact that his parents were buried in the same cemetery in which he and his wife were laid to rest, I knew little.

I began to collect material, and the first writing that I ever did was an effort to write the history of the Fraenkel family. Because of the lack of material, I did not get far. I gave it up as I began to write, or at least sketch, other books. I had a very large notebook that, by the end of the first year after I started, was filled with all kinds of subjects for new books. Of course, I was too young to publish them, nor would they have been any good. At that time there was really very little Jewish material available. I wrote an outline of a book called "To Be a Jew," but I discovered that in order to write a book you have to acquire not merely much more knowledge but also the ability to organize the material.

My last years in high school were years of very intensive study. I have already mentioned the fact that our province was occupied. The Allies prepared for a plebiscite to be held in our province, which would give the people an opportunity to opt for either Germany or Poland.[69] At the end of a long process, half of the province went to Poland, but our half remained German. I remember that an Apostolic delegate, representing the Pope in Germany, visited our town. It was Cardinal Pacelli, who later became Pope Pius XII. He stayed in our town for many weeks. I remember that he once fainted in the street and had to be carried into a Jewish school near our house. He was a famous mountain climber and our bookstore exhibited his books about that subject to honor him. For many years he was the Papal Nuncio in Germany, soon becoming a Germanophile and speaking the language fluently. When he became Pope, he surrounded himself with German nuns and monks who served him in his chambers.

STUDIES IN BRESLAU AND BERLIN

My school years were coming to an end. Upon completion of our high school careers, we received a graduation paper that enabled us to attend a university. Colleges were and still are unknown in Western Europe. The curriculum of the last years of our high school corresponded to that of our American colleges so that I could matriculate in the equivalent of a graduate program at a university. It was understood that I would also attend the Jewish Theological Seminary in Breslau, the leading conservative seminary.[70] Since Breslau was only an hour by train from my own town, it was also practical for me to go there. The seminary was the first modern theological seminary in the world

69. A plebiscite held in Upper Silesia on March 20, 1921, produced a majority of votes for Germany over Poland.
70. Opened in 1854, the conservative Jüdisch-Theologisches Seminar in Breslau was until 1872 the only modern rabbinical seminary in Germany.

and had a very high reputation. But its leading spirit, Prof. Horovitz, who taught Talmud and medieval philosophy, had died just a few weeks before I arrived in 1921. At that time, of course, I did not know that I would marry his daughter. This was the beginning of the period of inflation, which was to have a devastating effect on the economy.

The seminary was a rather interesting place. The building, which we called the Gray House, had been erected at the beginning of the eighteenth century. It was four or five stories high and, of course, there was no elevator. On the first landing, there was an eighteenth-century clock, which always stood still; nobody ever thought of having it repaired. On the upper floor was a small synagogue that was the seminary's chapel where we as students delivered our first sermons. The seminary itself, in addition to its classrooms and a very famous library, contained apartments for the professors, and almost every one of them lived in that building. There was a large garden, and each of the professors "owned" a little part of it where he built his own sukkah.[71] The trees were tall and old. It was a beautiful place; in between classes we used to spend a great deal of time there. The classrooms were equally old fashioned. I sat on a bench into which the famous historian Heinrich Graetz had carved his name when he had been a student there.[72] The old place was full of history. However, there were very few young people who wanted to enter the rabbinate. Almost every student was the son of a cantor or a Jewish teacher. I was the only one who was the son of a merchant, the only one who was a Zionist, and the only one who did not need any kind of financial help from the institution.

I must have looked strange to my fellow students, for I wore an open shirt as a member of the youth movement, and the suits I wore were of a better quality. Also my way of living was different from that of my fellow students. My father insisted that I rent two furnished rooms. He sent me a rather large check every month, which made it possible for me to live at great leisure. My colleagues called it luxury. The rooms that I rented were part of an apartment belonging to two spinsters, very lovely people probably in their early thirties, who worshipped me. We ate at a certain place maintained by the seminary where excellent food was served at very modest prices. Most of the students did not have to pay at all. I paid my way. The fact that we ate our main meal together at 12:30 in the afternoon made us a kind of family,

71. The outdoor booth observant Jews construct and dwell in during the fall festival of Sukkot.
72. The historian Heinrich Graetz was for many years a professor at the Seminary, but he had not been a student there. More likely, one of the students carved Professor Graetz's name into the bench.

small, intimate, very warm. Strangely enough, although we came from different backgrounds, there was no tension among us, except that once in a while we fell in love with the same girl. The student body was very small. When I came to the seminary there were twelve students and eight professors.[73] During the first year, I often had the professors all to myself. My background was much less thorough than that of my colleagues. They had come from Jewish homes and had studied Hebrew, the Bible, and even Talmud long before they came to the seminary. I had to receive some very thorough and basic training.

I had the great fortune of sitting at the feet of extraordinary teachers, each of whom was an authority in his field and an internationally recognized scholar. They taught me a great deal of respect for scholarship. One of my professors was a specialist in the field of Hellenism whose main interest was late Greek literature.[74] But he also taught homiletics, the art of preaching. He was himself one of the greatest preachers I ever heard. He came from Frankfurt and his way of preaching had a major influence on me. It was his rule that none of us was permitted to take a paper with notes to the pulpit. He insisted on our writing out the sermon in advance and then memorizing it. If we got stuck, it was just too bad. But use of a text was strictly forbidden. Manuscripts were to be filed away. He instilled something in me that later became a phobia about having any piece of white paper on the pulpit. Until this very day I remove whatever paper is lying there.

We had a "homiletics association" where each of us took turns preaching. It was a devastating experience. Our audience consisted of our fellow students and the professor of homiletics. We prepared our sermons carefully and were very fervent about it, for we considered that the result had to be a masterpiece. When we came to delivering the sermon, having finally completed something of which we were extremely proud, our fellow students would fall upon us and rip us apart. I remember very vividly delivering a sermon on the schizophrenic situation of the Jew who has a German and a Jewish calendar, thereby living in two different worlds. I thought it a very original idea, and since psychiatric training was part of our curriculum, I was particularly proud of the fact that I had applied my meager knowledge of psychiatry to a Jewish situation. However, both my colleagues and my professor thought it a perfectly horrible sermon. I remember that after

73. According to its annual report, in 1921 the Jewish Theological Seminary in Breslau had only four regular faculty: Michael Guttmann, Isaac Heinemann, Albert Lewkowitz, and Israel Rabin. There were nineteen regular students and twelve auditors, some of whom were women. A portion of the students, however, may not have been in residence.

74. The reference is to Isaac Heinemann, who taught at the seminary from 1918 to 1938. He

the session I went to my room and wept. The other opportunity we had to preach was even more demanding. Twice a year we were required to speak in the synagogue of the seminary. It was a small room. The women sat in the back in a separate part of the synagogue, and there were curtains to separate the women's synagogue from that of the men. But the curtains were never drawn, so we could see the women who were the wives, widows, and daughters of our professors—plus certain outstanding women of the community. To preach before that kind of a congregation was sheer torture. After we were through with the sermon and had returned to our seats, we would wait for the reaction of our professors, which was not always very enthusiastic. Each of them shook our hand, but their handshakes were often very cold and discouraging. Today I know how very important it was to have had that kind of severe criticism.

Not every one of my professors at the seminary was a charismatic figure, and there was certainly no hero worship on our part for any one of them. To a very large extent we lived on the memory of the great ones, including Prof. Horovitz, Lucie's father, about whom everyone told stories and whose universal knowledge was often discussed. He had a fabulous memory; as a child of thirteen he knew more than a thousand pages of the Talmud and its commentaries by heart. He had a very small library because every book he read he knew by heart, and very often he would throw it away. Once, after reading a book written by my university professor of philosophy on the philosophy of antiquity, Horovitz called him angrily and asked to see him, whereupon he told him that he had misinterpreted Aristotle completely. The name of my philosophy professor was Richard Hoenigswald.[75] I will say more about him later. At this meeting, Hoenigswald expressed his amazement at my father-in-law's audacity to accuse him of misinterpretation. Hoenigswald listened very carefully as Horovitz recited by heart, and in Greek, twenty pages from Aristotle. Hoenigswald was flabbergasted, not merely at the exhibition of so rare a memory, but at himself and the misstatement that he had made in his book.

There were also stories about Prof. Israel Lewy, who preceded my father-

served simultaneously as professor of Hellenism at the University of Breslau and died in Jerusalem in 1957.

75. Richard Hoenigswald (1875–1947) was an increasingly popular and respected scholar. From 1919 to 1930, he was Professor of Philosophy, Psychology, and Pedagogics at the University of Breslau. From 1930 until his forced retirement as a non-Aryan by the Nazi regime in 1933, he taught at the University of Munich. In 1939, he left Germany for Switzerland and then for the United States.

in-law as Professor of Talmud.[76] He was an extraordinary man who had written only one book, while Horovitz had written very many volumes. Lewy
was hesitant to write because he conceived of writing as an act of imper-
tinence. He was one of the greatest Jewish scholars of the last century, and
he combined his great learning with a mystical concept of Judaism. He was
probably in great need of psychiatric treatment, full of guilt, and conscious
of many sins he had committed. On Saturday nights he used to call students together for a ceremony of forgiveness, which was described in great
detail amidst a mixture of laughter and admiration. When, for instance, he
touched his hair by mistake while praying in the synagogue, he considered
this an act of impurity and wanted to be forgiven by ten men who, because
they studied theology, were therefore able to understand the great sin he had
committed. Unlike Lewy, Horovitz was a rationalist and skeptic. No wonder
it was he who discovered the relationship between the skeptical philosophy
of Greece and that of the Arabs.[77] He was, among other things, an Arabist
who had written his doctoral thesis at the University of Munich on some
Arabic problem.[78]

The University of Breslau was very old. The complex of buildings invited students of art to an analysis of baroque architecture. The auditorium
of the university was a beautiful example of the decorative and dramatic
style of the baroque. I studied philosophy, art history, Arabic, and Syriac
there. The most important field for me was philosophy, which at that university meant Kantian cognition. My professor, whom I mentioned before, was
Richard Hoenigswald. Although there were other professors of philosophy
who were more eloquent than he, and certainly more entertaining, I chose
him. He was a Hungarian Jew who had converted to Christianity, but the
baptismal water was not able to dilute the keen mind of the man, which
could be traced to Talmudic studies and tradition. He was without any sense
of humor. His lectures were attended by hundreds of students, and he required and requested the kind of concentration of mind that is very rarely
necessary for those who listen to a lecture at a university. It was disastrous
to miss even one sentence, for the whole lecture was based on a sequence of
such overwhelming logic that you lost him if you did not listen to each sen-

76. Israel Lewy (1840–1917), Seminary Rabbi and Professor of Talmud in Breslau from 1883 to
his death, published a number of important studies, especially on the Palestinian Talmud.
77. In 1915, Horovitz published *Der Einfluss der griechischen Skepsis auf die Entwicklung der Phi-
losophie bei den Arabern.*
78. Horovitz's doctoral dissertation, accepted by the University of Halle in 1883, was entitled
"Die Prophetologie in der jüdischen Religionsphilosophie." It was not on an "Arabic problem."

tence carefully. His philosophy was terribly rigid. He had invented his own terminology, which those of us who attended his lectures translated into Talmudic Aramaic. Although he could not have been described as a beautiful man, he was a charismatic figure in terms of his clear and critical thought. I shall be indebted to him for the rest of my life, since it was he who taught me to think clearly and to organize my thoughts logically and in an orderly way. He was extraordinarily strict about definitions and insisted upon complete and uncompromising clarity of thought. To his mind thinking was identical with criticism. I learned from him not only the systems of the great philosophers, but also the methodology of cognition.

When I studied at the University of Berlin[79] I had two fascinating teachers, both of whom were world renowned. One of them was a very old man, Prof. Alois Riehl,[80] who rejected the school of "Realistic Kantianism." He sat there like an eighteenth-century scholar. His pants were always too short so that we could see his long underwear; his socks, more often than not, were of different colors, one green and the other white. He taught us Kant, never using a book. He evidently knew the *Critique of Pure Reason* by heart, and although his teachings were directed toward transmitting knowledge of the text, he was also a sharp thinker. I could not call him charismatic, although I had profound reverence for the old man, who did not give up teaching despite the fact that he must have been at least seventy-eight years old.[81] He was a professor emeritus of a great university, but he was as active as any other professor. His lessons in Kant were almost religious exercises, and the words he recited sounded like a proclamation of religious wisdom. Kant was his Bible.

I cannot write about the University of Berlin without mentioning the lectures of Prof. Ernst Troeltsch.[82] He was really a theologian but lectured on philosophical and general themes. His was the largest hall in the university, and he taught a special course (the title of which I now have forgotten) every Saturday morning from ten to twelve. Although he was a scholar of note, having written at least ten or twelve volumes most of which were translated into many languages, he was also a fascinating speaker and an en-

79. Prinz studied in Berlin in 1922. It was not unusual for German university students to spend time at more than a single university.

80. Alois Adolf Riehl (1844–1924) was a representative of the Neo-Kantian School of philosophy, which, though following Kant in most matters, did not accept the existence of the "thing-in-itself."

81. Riehl was seventy-eight years old in 1922.

82. Ernst Troeltsch (1865–1923) was a historian of religion and culture for whom religious truths had to be understood in their respective historical contexts.

thusiastically revered teacher. To have been able to attend his lectures and classes was a source of great inspiration to me. I will never forget the 24th day of the month of June 1922. It was the day on which Walther Rathenau, a German Jew who served as Minister of Foreign Affairs, was assassinated. He was one of Troeltsch's closest friends. On that day Troeltsch was late for his lecture, and when he finally arrived, ascending the stairway to his rostrum, we saw that he was pale and trembling. He said—and I will never forget his words—"We have been talking here about the philosophy of religion. What has happened today, and of which you are not informed, belongs to this topic. Walther Rathenau, one of my closest friends, was murdered by two high school students who called themselves National Socialists. They murdered him because he was a Jew. This is the beginning of the German tragedy, but it is also the beginning of a great human tragedy. I am not able to lecture this morning. If you listened to my lectures during the first month of the year and had any inkling as to what I meant to say, and was probably not always able to express, you will understand that what has happened today is an important chapter in the philosophy of religion."

Our student years were extremely serious. There was little time for play. The curriculum was strict. One could not miss a class or come to class unprepared, and there were very many nights during the week when we, as a group, studied until two in the morning and had to be ready for class at eight. The fact that we had to go to the university and attend the seminary at the same time was particularly burdensome. However, there was an unwritten law in German Jewry that no one could serve as the rabbi of a congregation without having an academic degree in addition to his rabbinical approbation. That degree, according to this unwritten law, had to be in a field other than theology. This rule was designed to enable us to have a broader view of the world and of knowledge than a theologian had. Several of us received our Ph.D.s in philosophy and related subjects; others studied law and received a doctoral degree in that field. I considered this to be a most creative idea. I find most of the rabbis in other countries, including our own, to be poorly trained and incapable of thinking in terms other than theological. I find their outlook on life limited and their knowledge of subjects beyond the sphere of theology most deplorable. I am personally very grateful that my horizon was enlarged by the study of philosophy, art, and linguistics. It has given me a completely different outlook even on theology itself. It has also prevented the kind of narrow-mindedness and limitations that are the hallmark of most theologians, Jewish and Christian, that I have known over a period of many decades.

It would be untrue, however, to say that we did nothing but study. Somebody had invented an outlet for us, which was to play an important role in our lives. We had our own theological fraternity that was called "Amicitia," which means friendship, and it certainly developed friendships. Among the many fraternities that existed at the university (Jews were excluded from most of them and had their own fraternities) ours was known to drink more beer and spirits than any other fraternity in town. Amicitia was not merely interested in drinking, although I must say that it was an extraordinary training ground for those of us who in later life loved to drink wine and spirits; it made us almost immune to alcohol. We met every Thursday night wearing our fraternity caps and a ribbon bearing the colors of our fraternity across our chests. In conducting the meetings a great deal of Latin was used in order to emphasize the academic character of the group. Once in a great while we invited ladies to an affair. Usually we met in a specially reserved room in a restaurant. The drinking consisted exclusively of beer, and it was not very rare that each of us emptied ten or twelve glasses in a single night. We sang a great deal, and not one of these songs was Jewish. We sang the old German student songs, most of which were from the late Middle Ages. They dealt with love, honor, patriotism, and some were slightly pornographic. After a while, I began to understand the meaning of these Thursday nights. Most of the students were rather shy about women, and probably very few of them had had any sexual experience. Sex was seldom discussed and probably more rarely practiced. But to sing about it, to laugh about it, and to be rather rowdyish on Thursday nights, drinking, singing, and thinking of the dark places of our lives, the pent-up desires and our growing hopes for sexual excitement and satisfaction, must have been a great relief for those to whom sex was unknown territory and the goal of their most intimate and personal dreams.

This was not true of me. Although I was brought up in the youth movement where sex was frowned upon, and at a time when "physical purity" was one of the great goals of the youth movement, I was already deeply in love with Lucie and we had a rather active sex life together. Although very young,[83] she was, I must say, extremely well trained. She was very romantic about sex, but also very experienced and far superior to me. I did not find her to be a virgin. She told me of several affairs that she had had. She was beautiful and passionate and we had already decided to get married. Altogether, the early twenties in Western Europe were years of a sexual revolution. It certainly was not customary in our circles of educated men and women to get

83. She was only two months younger than Joachim. In 1922, she celebrated her twentieth birthday.

married without having lived with each other for several years. We frowned upon virginity and rejected the moral code of our parents as being hypocritical. Although there were some theology students who remained "pure," they were a distinct minority. Lucie and I traveled together every year. I remember the first night we slept together was after a long walk through the woods and our bed was the field. The moon was shining brightly, the stars were above us, and I thought about Kant's famous sentence in his *Critique of Pure Reason* in which he talked about the relationship of moon, stars, and the moral conscience.[84] What we were doing in the field we did not consider to be immoral but rather a relationship that both of us had wanted for a long time. I must say that I was rather clumsy; she had to teach me a great many things. It took her a long time to teach me well, but she knew all the tricks in the book and some of them that she herself had invented. All this made my years at the seminary, which were so solemn and concentrated on serious academic matters, bright and enjoyable. We knew that we could not get married before I concluded my studies, and I know that she was not entirely faithful to me during that time. However, I, too, had certain moments when I preferred a different partner of whom there were very many, for virginity was no longer a great ideal. It was, after all, several years after the revolution. There was an architectural renewal; Picasso had already been painting for twenty years. Expressionism was the art the painters practiced. A new revolutionary theater had begun performing plays that were written in the spirit of the newly awakened twentieth century of which we were very much a part. Literature played a great role in this world where every new book was passionately discussed. If we had any free evenings, we went either to the theater, opera, or concerts. It was, in short, a great, creative, marvelous life, which cannot be repeated because it was a time of mankind's great hopes for a world of justice and peace.

My political outlook was very deeply affected by the spirit of the time. I was originally a member of the Independent Socialist Party but later, when the party became too radical, I switched to the Social Democratic Party. I have always sided with the left on the issues it selected as important political goals. The German democracy[85] was struggling. It was quite clear to me that democracy was not what the German people really wanted. The right-wing parties were growing and were evidently and obviously an expression

---

84. Prinz is apparently thinking of the well-known quotation from Kant's *Critique of Practical Reason* in which Kant wrote that two things filled him with wonder and awe: "the starry sky above me and the moral law within me."
85. The newly established Weimar Republic.

of what the majority of the German people really thought. The Jews were very much in the middle. The intellectual ones belonged to the left, but the majority belonged to the German Democratic Party. The National Socialist Party in Germany was small but it was certainly growing, and although Adolf Hitler was not yet a well-known personality in the twenties and was politically in the background, he seemed to me even at that time the great threat to Germany and the world. More often now we saw the brown uniforms of the storm troopers at their daily exercises. Although they were officially forbidden, the police overlooked all that and seemed to be applauding them. The political assassinations multiplied. They all came from the right-wing movements. Democracy was simply not for the Germans. What they wanted was discipline and order. In addition, the Weimar Republic seemed unable to cope with the problem of growing unemployment.

The main scourge of the time was inflation. The German people had a very large percentage of pensioners who lived on their accumulated savings and the pensions they received from the state. Of course, the savings disappeared completely and the pensions could not keep pace with the inflation, which was not merely enormous but swift. Very soon a loaf of bread cost a million marks. My father, who used to send me a check every month, now had to send me one every three days. The figures quoted for food, rent, and clothing were astronomical. Foreign currency, even a single dollar, loomed like a fortune. Foreigners came into the country to buy up whole blocks of apartment houses. Allegedly, they paid only a hundred dollars for an entire apartment house. Among them were many Jews from foreign countries. The antisemitic press, as well as the right-wing papers, emphasized the fact that the German people were being taken advantage of by rich foreign Jews. I am sure that the majority of those who purchased property were not Jews. But the Jews stuck out like a sore thumb.

To watch the political developments was fascinating and frightening. It was clear to me and to a very small group of friends that the end of German Jewry had come. In June 1922, when Rathenau was assassinated, we very carefully watched the reaction of the German people. In spite of the official state funeral accorded him and the solemn memorial service, which was held in the House of Parliament, it seemed that the majority of the German people were very happy to have gotten rid of a Jew. Everything pointed to a catastrophe. The combination of unemployment, inflation, national degradation, and native militarism was too powerful to be overcome by any democratic tendencies that might have existed. Finally, the inflation was halted through a very radical decree of the government, but that did not solve the large economic problems that had deprived the middle class of its stability.

There were already, at that time, small towns that were completely National Socialist. After the assassination of Rathenau, a few of us held a meeting in the forest near Berlin at which we decided that German Jewry was lost, European Jewry threatened, and that it would take only a few more years before all of Germany would become National Socialist and Hitler would assume the leadership. It happened eleven years later, but the symptoms were there. We were not deluded into a sense of security by virtue of the fact that the large cities were still democratic and incredibly creative.

To have lived in Berlin in the twenties was an indescribable experience. It was probably at that time the most creative city in the world. It was cosmopolitan and far removed from German nationalism. The newspapers, two of them owned by Jews,[86] as well as the magazines, were of the highest possible standards, and the intellectual life was creative in literature and the arts. It is usually not understood that the first modern church, which even today would be considered an outrageous piece of architecture, was built there in 1911. The theater, in which Jews played an important role as producers as well as actors and actresses, every night presented interpretations of new as well as classical plays. There was no season without three or four of Shakespeare's plays being produced in a completely new fashion. It was at that time that the large theater seating some four thousand people was built by Hans Poelzig.[87] The whole building looked like a cave, an enormous space. The stage moved, the settings were completely modern, and the theatrical group that performed in this repertory theater, which combined classical with modern plays, was under the leadership of the great producer Max Reinhardt.[88] He was an Austrian Jew whose real name was Goldmann. His most spectacular performance took place in 1905, which, of course, I did not see but which remained his masterpiece. It was performed on a revolving stage. In 1909, a performance of Hamlet followed with the actors wearing modern dress. These are only two examples of the simply fantastic phenomenon of the Berlin theater. Berlin had at that time three opera houses and more than twenty-five theaters. It was always difficult to get a ticket to any one of them.

The Jews played an equally important role in the publishing of books,

---

86. Prinz is probably referring to the *Berliner Tageblatt,* owned by the Mosse family, and the *Vossische Zeitung,* owned by the Ullstein family.

87. Hans Poelzig (1869–1936), a non-Jewish architect, designed the Grosses Schauspielhaus, which was completed in 1919 and deemed a masterpiece of German Expressionism.

88. Max Reinhardt (1873–1943) was one of the most innovative and influential twentieth-century stage directors. As he was a Jew, the Nazis forced him out of his position in Germany in 1933. He spent the last years of his life in California.

and were the interpreters of foreign literature that was translated into German. Thus all of Dostoyevsky, American literature, and English literature became part of our lives; the appearance of a new book, the presentation of a new play, the interpretation of a symphony were events that literally shook the town. The cafés were filled with people who discussed these important events, while continuing to live in a dream world, accepting the great cultural renaissance of Berlin and Munich, as well as other cities, as proof of a general revival in the country. Hitler appeared to be insignificant and the political movements unimportant. It is true that they felt the country had moved to the right, but in their minds the intellectuals ruled and the artists were the real arbiters of contemporary life. I participated in this life, but was painfully aware of the political developments that began to threaten not only Germany but Europe and the world.

I was in Berlin because I attended the university there, but only for a year. I had come to Berlin since Lucie and I felt that it might be good for us to be separated for a time. Although we were certain at the beginning that we would get married, there were many critical moments when we became less certain of it. Was I really the right man for her? Was she really the right woman for me? Since we were unsure, we decided that a year in Berlin would do me good. I was also thinking of my academic career and the great advantages to be had from studying in Berlin. In addition, I continued my theology studies there[89] and I met many new people who became my friends, especially from the Zionist movement, which was much larger there than in Breslau. I also met many women, among others Grete, my friend from the spa whose depression I had cured. There were now some more serious developments in my relationship to her, but I was much less certain of her than of Lucie. So I became more and more convinced that it would be Lucie whom I would marry. After a year I returned to Breslau.

This year[90] was of some importance because, although I was still a student, I had begun to write in various newspapers, and suddenly I was offered the position of editor of a Zionist weekly that was to be founded. The salary was very small and for me financially insignificant. But the opportunity to be the head of a newspaper that was just about to come into being attracted me greatly. I became the chief editor of a paper that was very successful al-

89. Prinz took some classes at the Liberal seminary, the Hochschule für die Wissenschaft des Judentums, which was located in Berlin. In the curriculum vitae attached to the précis of his doctoral dissertation (but, strangely, not in our text), Prinz not only mentions the institution by name but also notes that Julius Guttmann, who taught Jewish philosophy there, suggested that he write on the topic he chose for his dissertation. Prinz heartily thanks him for the stimulus.
90. Presumably 1923/24, after Prinz had returned to Breslau from Berlin.

most from its very beginning because I made it into an aggressive one with an editorial policy that attacked all the problems that beset the Jewish community.[91] The Jewish community of Breslau, numbering 30,000 people,[92] was completely reactionary, anti-Zionist, and authoritarian. The community itself was rather old and had a long tradition. It could be traced back to the twelfth century. It was well organized with a very large number of synagogues, some of them with seating capacities of two thousand. The appearance of a new Jewish newspaper was quite an event, and I soon became a very well-known personality in the community. I wrote the paper from beginning to end, and, of course, was responsible for the editorial, which was always very sharp and militant—and therefore controversial and the subject of many discussions.

The importance for me of my work on a newspaper cannot be overrated. It taught me to write with the kind of facility you need if you are an editor with deadlines to meet. It also had a great influence on my career as a speaker. I dictated every article and found it to be a very effective training ground for public expression. There was little time to look for words. It had to be done spontaneously, and it did not take me much time to learn this art. Until this very day I am able to dictate without much hesitation, and I owe it to the years of training as the editor of a newspaper, a position I held until my last day in Breslau, when I left to serve as a rabbi in Berlin.

It also had some political importance. Our newspaper was printed by the printing press of the socialist daily of the town, which had the newest equipment. It was there I learned the art of "making up" a newspaper. I learned all the technical expressions of the printing trade: the making up of headlines, the structure of the paper, and the appearance of the front page. It was almost an artistic job. But even more important was the fact that I met a new breed of people called printers. They were simple men but politically very alert. In spite of their simplicity in appearance and lifestyle they were very literate, great readers, and critical observers of the political and literary scenes. Altogether, this was one of the most pleasant and instructive encounters with people I have ever had in my life. Of course, I was in touch with the editorial staff of this important socialist paper, and much of my political work was done during the many conversations I had in the building of the paper or in the staff's homes. My political observations became much keener and better grounded than before, so that my career as a newspaper-

91. The newspaper referred to is the *Jüdische Zeitung für Ostdeutschland*, which began to be published in 1924. Prinz was its first editor.
92. According to the 1925 census, Breslau's Jewish population then stood at 23,240.

man, which lasted for more than three years, was an important chapter in my development, both as a human being and as a public figure.

The time had come for me to begin thinking of getting a Ph.D. From the very beginning, my major subject was philosophy, as I mentioned earlier. Since my professor[93] was a very ardent admirer of Immanuel Kant and belonged to the school of what at that time was called "Realistic Kantians," I, of course, became a member of this school. Although I am now far removed from it, it had the great advantage of forcing the student to adhere to clear definitions and a rare discipline of thought. Kant's *Critique of Pure Reason* became my Bible, and I knew many parts by heart in spite of the very difficult language in which it was written. It had long sentences in eighteenth-century German—a typical baroque habit, almost as ornamental and colorful as baroque painting and architecture. I don't know how many volumes of philosophy we had to read.

The most important part of my studies was the seminar, which only a selected group of good students attended. I was proud to be one of them. It consisted of a small group of twenty or thirty people and lasted for three hours. Prof. Hoenigswald sat there unsmilingly as we discussed the most intricate problems of cognition. He rejected the classification of psychology as a part of natural science and tried to understand it, as well as education, in purely philosophical terms. He wrote two volumes on the subject, which are almost impossible to read today. But philosophy to him was the "science of sciences," and possessed an almost religious connotation. Our relationship with professors was very formal. We would not have thought of visiting our professors at home or even being invited. They all sat on pedestals, and as far as the students were concerned, much too high for us to reach them. We hardly knew anything of their private lives, nor did they care about ours. They arrived at the expected time, a quarter of an hour after the announced time, which constituted the academic quarter, an old custom dating back to the universities in the Middle Ages. They stood or sat before their classes without moving, addressing a disciplined audience without much opportunity for us to ask questions.

My second subject was history of art, which I began to love very much. Lucie, who by then had become my fiancée, was an excellent artist. She drew very beautifully, and since her family had become rather impoverished because of the inflation, she and the other children had to earn some money. She did so by painting lampshades for a dealer, who sold them at exorbitant prices while she received a pittance. Whenever we traveled together, we

93. The aforementioned Richard Hoenigswald at the University of Breslau.

would sketch the scenery and the interesting architecture we encountered. Soon I began to paint myself. We never undertook a trip together without taking our sketchbooks along. I took several courses in art history and began to be particularly interested in architecture. Although my professor of art history was not one of the outstanding art historians of the time, I learned a great deal from him, and I have retained my interest in the subject until this day. There was a time when I decided not to become a rabbi but an art historian instead. I informed my father, but he thought that the rabbinate was sufficiently impractical, and to become a professor of art history was altogether an insane idea. I don't know whether he was right.

My third subject was Semitic languages. I studied Arabic, Syriac, Aramaic, and Hebrew. It opened a new world for me. This was particularly true of Arabic, which I learned in order to be able to read the Koran in the original language. I studied Syriac mainly for the purpose of reading the New Testament in the Syriac translation. Syriac was complicated, but Arabic was an impossible language. It was extremely difficult for me to study it. I have now forgotten both languages. I mention Semitic languages because it was one of the three subjects for my doctoral degree.

I wrote my thesis on "Cognition of Religion." When I found it in the Library of Congress[94] some ten or fifteen years ago, I did not understand a single word I had written. I was so influenced by my professor that I had not merely adopted his philosophical views but his obscure language as well. He had invented a philosophical terminology that nobody else understood.

I submitted my thesis to Prof. Bauch of the University of Jena, whose philosophy faculty was very famous; he himself was very close to my philosophical school. He had written extensively, and I thought it might be a good idea to get my doctoral degree from him. At that time it was the habit of students to leave their original universities and move elsewhere. Prof. Bauch[95] wrote me that he was interested in what I had to say. The year was 1924, eleven years before Hitler came to power.[96] At that time, however, I read in the newspapers that the students of the University of Jena had decided to set aside special benches for Jewish students, which were called "the Jew

94. It is currently not to be found in the Library of Congress catalogue. However, the University of Giessen possesses a copy as well as a printed excerpt from the year 1927. The doctoral dissertation was entitled "Zum Begriff der religiösen Erfahrung. Ein Beitrag zur Theorie der Religion." It was accepted on January 29, 1924 and was dedicated to the memory of Prinz's mother, Nani Prinz, née Berg. The referees were Professors August Messer and Ernst von Aster.
95. Bruno Bauch (1877–1942) was a prominent Neo-Kantian philosopher. During the Nazi years, he chaired the German Philosophical Society.
96. Actually nine years, since Hitler came to power in 1933.

benches." Jena had become one of the first nationalistic and antisemitic universities. I thought it beneath my dignity to attend a university where the Jews were singled out for degradation and insult.

I then decided to submit my thesis to Prof. August Messer in Giessen.[97] This university was not as great as either Breslau or Jena, nor was Prof. Messer a particularly important philosopher. But by now I had decided to make it as easy for myself as possible and to "get it over with." I moved to Giessen, a small middle-German town not far from Frankfurt in the state of Hesse. Antisemitism was rampant at that time and there were very few Jewish students. I was politically very much on the left but, amazingly, I escaped physical attacks by the nationalistic students. Although I did not do brilliantly, I received my Ph.D. there in 1924. I remember my trepidation when my professor of art history presented me with reproductions of thirty paintings that I had to interpret with the name of the painter and the time during which he lived. This was the basic requirement for passing the examination. But pass I did, even if it was without any great honors. I was not really interested in these honors. As I wanted to become a practicing rabbi, I had to have a doctor's degree, and I was very glad that I now had it.

After two semesters in Giessen I returned to Breslau to continue my theological as well as university studies. My last year was to be 1925.[98] However, before that year passed I discovered in a Jewish newspaper an advertisement calling for a rabbi in a synagogue in Berlin that was not owned by the Jewish community, but by an individual. The advertisement sounded very attractive, particularly the part that dealt with salary. I decided to try for the position and was invited to deliver a sermon. I preached in a synagogue that was comparatively small. It was called Friedenstempel, which means the "Temple of Peace." The man who owned it was some sort of a racketeer, or, at any rate, a member of the nouveau riche group, which was large at that time. Inflation had been licked and money was plentiful. The country was recovering economically, but unemployment was still very high. Going to Berlin seemed very attractive; the Jewish community numbered 175,000. The synagogue in which I was to preach had only fifteen hundred seats, which, compared to the synagogues belonging to the community, was rather small. I do not now remember what kind of sermon I delivered. I only know

97. August Messer (1867–1937) published books on the history of philosophy in ancient, medieval, and modern times. In 1922, he had published a commentary to Kant's *Critique of Pure Reason*.

98. In fact, Prinz was still in Breslau for at least part of 1926, but he may have delivered sermons in Berlin as early as the High Holidays in 1925. He delivered his official inaugural sermon there only on January 7, 1927.

that when it ended, the whole congregation rose. It was an ovation of approval. I was invited to the home of the man who owned the synagogue and who called himself Prof. Goldberg.[99] Ten years later he was in jail serving a sentence for bribery and embezzlement. He was so overwhelmed by my sermon that he offered me a salary equivalent to $15,000. It was an enormous sum of money in 1925. I told him that I would have to ask my seminary for a release as I was not yet ordained. My ordination would come in 1927.[100] It was agreed that I would begin to work in January of 1926[101] provided the seminary would release me for a year. But that was not difficult. There were so few rabbis available and so many congregations needed spiritual leaders that I got the year off during which I had to prepare for my rather difficult exam to be held at the end of the year. I married Lucie on December 25, 1925. She had been suffering from a very serious and severe cold and had a rather high temperature, but the doctor permitted her to get up for the wedding ceremony and then go back to bed.

99. Salomon Goldberg, who erected the synagogue, which was completed in 1923, in memory of his father, had made his money as owner of the local amusement park. In 1928, he ran into financial difficulties and was unable to maintain the synagogue any longer. It thereupon became one of the community synagogues and henceforth under the community's control. It was located in the western section of Berlin at Markgraf-Albrecht Strasse 11–12 and had 1,450 seats (864 for men, 586 for women). Prinz was preceded there as rabbi by Benno Gottschalk, who being an extreme reformer and anti-Zionist was uncomfortable with the synagogue's traditional liturgy.
100. In fact, it came only in 1929, probably because certain work remained outstanding.
101. See footnote 98.

The home and store in Burkhardsdorf. Courtesy of the Prinz family.

Joachim (on the left) with his younger brothers, Kurt and Hans, around 1907. Courtesy of the Prinz family.

Joachim and Lucie's wedding, December 25, 1925. Courtesy of American Jewish Archives.

The interior of the Friedenstempel, Prinz's congregation in Berlin. Photo by Knud Peter Petersen.

Lucie and Joachim on their way to a costume ball. Courtesy of the Prinz family.

Prinz addressing a Jewish Sports Rally in Berlin, 1933. Courtesy of the Prinz family.

Kurt Singer speaking at a conference of the Kulturbünde in Berlin on September 5, 1936. Prinz is at the right. Courtesy of Jewish Museum, Berlin. Photo Herbert Sonnenfeld.

Joachim and Hilde aboard the De Grasse on their way to America, July 1937. Courtesy of American Jewish Archives.

Rabbi Joachim Prinz in rabbinical attire about the time of his migration to the United States. Courtesy of Temple B'nai Abraham Archives.

2

Rabbi in Berlin

THE WEIMAR YEARS

LUCIE WAS STILL SICK when I set out for Berlin a few days before the first Friday when I was to preach, which was January 7, 1926.[1] We had rented a smallish apartment, and I had very lovely modern furniture made for us. My father had given me a rather large sum of money with which I could pay for all the furniture. My relationship to money was catastrophic and created many problems for me for years to come. I should have been able to live like a prince on the salary of $15,000, which for a student was an enormous amount. But by the end of the month I had usually spent most of my money, if not all of it.

When I preached my first sermon in the synagogue, the sanctuary was completely filled. I was twenty-three years old,[2] talented and foolish, and people began to flock to me. I was flattered. I decided at that time that I would concentrate on working for and with young people. My first gathering with them took place shortly after I arrived, and I decided to take them ice-skating. The community was up in arms. They had never seen a rabbi figure-skating with young people and considered it beneath rabbinical dignity. All my colleagues were in their fifties. Many of them had white beards. I was considered an outsider. On the other hand, many people began to love what I was doing, particularly the young people. I immediately formed youth groups and began to teach the young, even the youngest among them. I found great satisfaction in teaching children and adults, and I organized an adult school, something utterly new.[3] The service was very beautiful. There was a mixed choir and a cantor of international reputation. He was Manfred

---

1. The actual date for the inaugural sermon, as noted above, was Friday, January 7, 1927.
2. Twenty-four years old.
3. Not utterly new. Franz Rosenzweig had founded the Freies Jüdisches Lehrhaus, a school for adult education, in Frankfurt am Main in 1920.

Lewandowski, the nephew of the great Jewish composer.[4] He had a magnificent baritone voice, very similar to that of Tito Ruffo, who at that time was the world's most outstanding baritone. He was very vain and dumb, but pleasant.

After the first year I had made my mark in the community, mainly as a maverick, but I was very successful from the very beginning, and there was never a Friday night service at which not every one of the fifteen hundred seats was taken.[5] I had an average of three bar mitzvahs every Saturday morning, and sometimes ten. All young people wanted to be with me rather than with the stodgy, solemn, old rabbis who did not quite understand them. I gave them all kinds of treats, and looking back to this period I know how much I tried to live down the fact that I was a rabbi. I had great contempt for artificial solemnity and formal dress, even for the kind the Liberal rabbis used to wear. I had girls who loved me and whom I loved; Lucie and I lived an interesting, colorful, exciting, and lusty life. We surrounded ourselves with many friends, all of them as young as we were, and certainly stayed away from rabbinical families and solemn life. We spent every night in the theater and the cabarets. It was a time when Marlene Dietrich was a young woman who had just begun her career. Political cabarets were the rage of the town and Berlin was one of the most exciting cities in the world.

It was very difficult for me to establish a relationship with the rabbis and the establishment of the Berlin Jewish community. All the rabbis were at least twice my age and looked at me with great suspicion. My synagogue was probably the only private synagogue in the country, and it took several years before it was taken over by the community.[6] Even for this synagogue I was an obstacle. I was very outspoken and my lifestyle was quite different from that of the conventional rabbis. Both my political and Jewish convictions were different from the vast majority of the rabbis who had been in Berlin for many years and lived a very rabbinical life. I was not popular with most of them because I was a Zionist, and among the twenty-five rabbis who

---

4. Manfred Lewandowski (1895–1970) came to Berlin from Königsberg, where he had served as chief cantor since 1921. In 1938, he left Germany for France and then the United States, where he remained active as a cantor and composer.

5. At least one interviewee recalls that the synagogue was not always full when Prinz preached. Prinz may be projecting backward from his experience during the Hitler years.

6. There were other private synagogues in Berlin. Although most of them were Orthodox, there was also the Liberal lay-led Synagogue of the North, founded in 1923, where—uniquely at the time—men and women sat together.

formed the Rabbinical Council, only one other was a Zionist.[7] All the rest were German patriots, sold on the nineteenth-century concept of a rabbi. They preached very conventional sermons. Nevertheless, some of them, particularly Leo Baeck and Max Wiener,[8] were men of considerable knowledge. All of us observed the dietary laws and did not ride on the Sabbath. To do otherwise would have antagonized even the members of the community. The Jewish community itself served the needs of Liberal, Conservative, and Orthodox Jews, with each of the synagogues belonging to one of the three groups.[9] The ultra-Orthodox Jews formed their own community and considered themselves separatists.[10] There was only one huge cemetery and nobody could be buried anywhere else.[11] The liturgy read at the service was valid for all rabbis and no one was permitted to deviate from it. Even the Liberal synagogue did not permit the seating of men and women together. All women sat in the balconies. Most synagogues were very large. The smallest had fifteen hundred seats and the largest had thirty-five hundred.

Religious instruction for Christians and Jews was part of the curriculum of the German school system, appearing on the record of every student and listed on the report card. It was taken very seriously. Twice a week, beginning with the first grade, the Catholic students went to a room where a priest taught them, the Protestants went to their pastor, and the Jewish students were taught by a rabbi. I soon became one of these teachers. In this way, Jewish education was presented for many years. High school students received Jewish instruction for nine years twice a week. This turned out to be a very important factor in Jewish life; no Jew remained Jewishly ignorant. I soon

7. The first German rabbi who remained both a Zionist and an adherent of Liberal Judaism was Max Joseph (1894–1974), the rabbi of Stolp in Pomerania, who published a pro-Zionist work as early as 1908. Among the Liberal rabbis in Berlin, Malwin Warschauer (1871–1955), who officiated mostly at the Oranienburger Straße synagogue, was an early Zionist.

8. Max Wiener (1882–1950) served as a Liberal rabbi and taught at the Liberal rabbinical seminary in Berlin. He was among the scholars that the Hebrew Union College rescued from annihilation by bringing them to Cincinnati.

9. In fact, there were two religious groups that were part of the *Einheitsgemeinde* (the unified community) in Berlin: the Liberals and the Community Orthodox. There was also a religiously radical Reform Congregation, which was loosely associated with the community. Prinz may have intended to call the Community Orthodox "Conservative-Orthodox," yielding two groups. Alternatively, by "Liberal" he may have meant the Reform Congregation.

10. The Adass Jisroel community, founded in 1869, was independent of the larger Berlin Jewish community and served the needs of those Orthodox Jews who did not want to be forced into any religious compromise.

11. The exception to this rule was Adass Jisroel, whose own cemetery had been purchased as early as 1878 and continued to be used until the Shoah.

established a very close relationship with my students. I was assigned to the highest-level classes and I have retained my relationship with many of the students until this very day. My relationship to young people was altogether a very important part of my daily activities. To supplement the instruction they received in the public school system, we had Hebrew classes for Jewish young people in the afternoon, and many attended. Teaching in my own afternoon school was for me one of the most exciting activities of my life.

We[12] developed many friendships with members of my synagogue. Among them was a family whose twin sons I had blessed on the day of their bar mitzvah. It was shortly after this that their mother, a very young woman, became seriously ill. She was in the terminal stage of cancer. I visited her every day, and one day she asked me to find something light for her to read. I told her that I would try to give her something that I had written myself. It so happened that I had asked my secretary to accompany me to my class of six-year-olds to whom I told the stories of the Bible in my own way. I had found our textbooks to be outmoded and old-fashioned. The children did not understand the language in which they were written, and I felt that the Bible should be made an exciting book, appreciated by young and old. I therefore asked my secretary to write down the stories as I told them. I thought my sick friend would enjoy reading them, for my secretary had finished typing all of them.

In order to make it easy for my friend to read the stories, I took them to a bookbinder to have them bound for her. I did not know that this bookbinder was also a publisher. As he was interested in what I had to say, he read the manuscript and liked it so much that he decided to publish it as a book. It appeared in 1930 under the title *Heroes and Adventurers of the Bible—A Book for Children*.[13] It immediately sold more than twenty thousand copies. It was my first book and established me as someone who could write. It is, of course, no longer available; I own the only copy, which I found quite by accident in a second-hand bookstore. That book was important to me since

12. Presumably, Joachim and Lucie.
13. Dedicated to Prinz's sister Thea and entitled, in the original, *Helden und Abenteurer der Bibel,* it was published in 1930 by the Paul Baumann Publishing House in Berlin. Reproduced on the cover was the romantic portrait of *David at Prayer* by the prominent Jewish artist, Lesser Ury. The book contained eleven engaging stories featuring such "heroes" as Deborah, Gideon, Samson, David, and—in the final chapter—Moses. In the preface, Prinz claimed that the book's sole purpose was to bring these biblical figures as close to the children as were Little Red Riding Hood and the Seven Little Nanny Goats. Subtly critical of previous Jewish children's books, he added that he wished the miraculous tales, which were here purposely not given rationalistic interpretations, would enable the children to feel a breath of the Bible's eternity. Prinz did not own the only surviving copy. One is to be found in the Hebrew Union College Library in Cincinnati.

through my work on it I began to understand that I should continue to write and that writing gave me a great deal of satisfaction.

Shortly after my first book appeared, I received a telephone call from a very important publisher, the head of one of the leading publishing houses. I knew the firm was owned by the former Kaiser of Germany, who at that time lived in Holland. The publisher, whose name indicated that he was a member of the nobility, invited me to see him. When I arrived, I was royally received by a very elegant man who I learned was a Czechoslovakian. He was immaculately dressed and behaved formally and stiffly, as was the habit of people of his position. I found his behavior slightly exaggerated. Much later I learned that he was a converted Jew and that when Hitler came to power he committed suicide.[14] His secretary and mistress was the Countess Kropotkin, a member of the famous Russian family. She was a very elegantly dressed and most attractive woman. I forgot the name of the publisher, but the secretary made a greater impression on me. The publisher informed me that his publishing house had been accused of being antisemitic and that the Kaiser was very much interested in publishing a book on Jewish history as a countermeasure against the accusations, which he thought were completely unfounded. He asked me whether I could write a one-volume Jewish history. Such a one-volume history did not exist anywhere in the world. I was very excited about the idea and accepted his invitation to write it. It became an enormous success and very soon a best-seller. I had decided to write the kind of history that an educated layman could read. It was published at the end of 1931.[15] I did not know then that 1931 would become a very important year of my life.

Lucie and I wanted to have a child, but in order for her to conceive she had to undergo a gynecological operation. After this was done, she did conceive and had a marvelous pregnancy. By then she had established a very close friendship with another young woman who, being as artistically talented as she was, joined her in designing and producing necklaces. They used all kinds of material for the necklaces and they were really very exciting. The enterprise was not undertaken merely as occupational therapy. Although neither Lucie nor her friend Lotte needed the money, they thought that they should form a business and began to sell these necklaces to the most fashionable and expensive stores. They made quite a bit of money from it. Lucie's

14. It has not been possible to discover his identity.
15. The volume, published by the Verlag für Kulturpolitik in Berlin in 1931, bears the simple title *Jüdische Geschichte* and runs from biblical times through World War I in less than three hundred easily readable pages.

pregnancy did not interrupt her activities, either social or otherwise. She was an extrovert, very attractive with long blonde hair and blue eyes. Very many men were attracted to her and she to some of them. It was altogether the time of a free and uninhibited life for both of us. Life at our house was very lively. We had left our small apartment and moved into a very fashionable and expensive district of Berlin. We rented a very large and beautiful apartment and had it furnished by interior designers. Some of the furniture came from the Bauhaus.[16] There was a niche in our living room that we furnished with steel furniture and that served as a breakfast room. We had a cook and a chambermaid. Since we moved in at the beginning of Lucie's pregnancy, we furnished a special room for the baby. The floor was covered with red vinyl and the furniture was especially designed for the baby.

We were in the habit of inviting many of our friends, all of them in our age group, and had huge and wild parties at our house. There was always enough to eat and drink. We had a hilarious time. It certainly was not a rabbinical household in any respect. In the last month of Lucie's pregnancy and a week or so before she was to go to the hospital, we had a party for some thirty people. Lucie was very musical, but she could not carry a tune. One of our visitors was Lucie's brother Willy who was a young physician. In the course of the evening, during which we sang a lot, one of the people suggested that we sing the chorale of the last movement of Beethoven's Ninth Symphony. It is called "An Ode to Joy." We all sang it with a lot of gusto. It was, musically, not very good, but it expressed our zest for life. We were very young, we lived eagerly, and life itself was our greatest passion. I will never forget Lucie singing that song. In spite of the fact that she was an extrovert, very witty, and laughing most of the time, she was also sometimes depressed. She was terribly afraid of death. I once found her in bed crying. When I asked her why she was crying, she said that she was thinking that some day she and all of us would be buried and not know what had happened to us.

It was that kind of a mixture of happiness and lust for life as well as a strange premonition that prompted her to sing the way she did. That I should remember every detail of it, although it happened some forty-five years ago, is indicative of the importance of that evening. In view of what was happening, that evening has remained one of my most important and moving experiences. Our guests left at two in the morning. All of us, including Lucie, were a little drunk.

A few days later her labor pains began and I took her to the hospital. I

---

16. The Bauhaus school of art and architecture, founded by Walter Gropius, was famous for its functionally crafted and unusual furniture.

must explain here the circumstances under which we went to a certain private hospital. Because my mother had died in childbirth, this event, about which I wrote earlier, became an obsession of my life. Because of her death, I was always afraid of the moment of birth and the great dangers that existed for the mother and the baby. I therefore decided that Lucie should have particularly good care. I selected as her physician a man who at that time was probably the most outstanding obstetrician in the world. It was Prof. Bernhard Zondek who, together with Prof. Aschheim, had worked out the pregnancy test that is still used under the name Aschheim-Zondek.[17] She had gone to him throughout the nine months. Two weeks before she went into the hospital, she developed an infection. He discovered a carbuncle on her arm and she had a temperature. He told me that he was not very happy about this since he did not like a woman to be delivered while she had an infection. At that time there were, of course, no sulfa drugs and penicillin to cope with an infection. It was usually fatal. When she was taken to the hospital the fever had not abated, and we were all worried. But the baby was born during the night of New Year's Eve, 1931. I still remember sitting with Prof. Zondek during the entire time of her rather long labor. Zondek spoke to me about the miracle of birth. He had delivered thousands of babies. It still remained a mystery to him. But the baby was born, and Lucie was very happy that it was a girl. Somehow she was worried about circumcision, and although she very rarely expressed her anxiety about it, I knew of it. When the little baby girl was brought in, Lucie was hilariously happy. I never in all my life will forget her smile and laughter. She called the baby by some strange endearing name, which remained with her for many years.

The next day was a Sunday and I had to go to the cemetery to officiate at three funerals. Since I was very anxious about Lucie, I went from the funeral services to the hospital. I had taken my rabbinical robe along, and as I hung it in the closet I was suddenly overcome with great anxiety. Although I was always, and still am, free of superstition, I connected the funerals that I had attended and the robe I had worn with Lucie's condition. She was still feverish and I knew what that meant. The robe hung in the closet for two weeks until the day she died. Lucie died on January 14, 1931. She was twenty-eight years old and would have been twenty-nine in July. My twenty-ninth birthday was in May. Several other medical professors were called in during her feverish illness, but the blood was so infected that all the doctors assured

17. Bernhard Zondek (1891–1966), who together with Selmar Aschheim in 1927 developed a test for pregnancy, taught at the Berlin University until his departure for Palestine, where he joined the faculty of the Hebrew University in Jerusalem.

me they knew of no way of coping with it. Unless a miracle happened, she would die. She was not really unconscious, but since the fever was very high she spoke feverishly and slept most of the time. One day during that time the door opened suddenly and the face of my old friend Chemjo Vinaver,[18] my choir director and a very creative musician as well as a very good personal friend, said to me: "I have cooked some fish for Lucie because she liked my recipe." I had to tell him that she could no longer eat it. This, too, remained one of my many memories of those two weeks during which I brought her many delicacies that I bought at the most expensive stores. She ate some of them. I stayed at the hospital the entire two weeks, going home only to sleep. I was with her from the early morning until late at night, until the last night when she fell into a coma from which she did not emerge.

Lucie's death was unfortunately a public event, since many people knew her and many more knew me. The funeral service was attended by more than a thousand people. It was a cold winter day and it snowed all day long. The sky was as gray as our mood. Lucie's sister Resi had died only half a year earlier. She was a marvelous young woman, a pianist and a sensitive person, who had been married to a horrible man; I had buried her. She also died of an infection at a time when there were no antibiotics. Her other three sisters, a brother, and other members of the family came, of course, to attend the funeral service. I had seen to it that no eulogy would be delivered. Prayers were read and chanted by an old cantor who was the officiating cantor of the cemetery and with whom I had become very friendly. Many of my colleagues came. I had to go to the service wearing a high hat in accordance with the custom that prevailed at that time and a fur coat. Nothing could draw me out of my desperation about what had happened, and I simply did not know how I could continue living without her. She was buried in the community cemetery. I asked an architect to design a very modern tombstone for her on which I inscribed the only sentence that helped me in those days. It was taken from the Song of Songs, the biblical book that deals with love and the relationship between a man and a woman: "I am asleep, but my heart is wide awake."[19]

The new baby about whom Lucie had been very happy was still in the hospital. Because of Lucie's illness we had no time to name her on the first day after her birth. We decided to call her Renate in memory of Resi, but we never went any further, and since I wanted to be at the hospital, I had no

---

18. The prominent choir conductor and liturgical composer Chemjo Vinaver (1900–1973) left Berlin for New York in 1938. In 1967, he moved to Jerusalem, where he established a choir.
19. Song of Songs 5:2.

time to register her name at the proper office. So when Lucie died I decided to name the baby Lucie. I will never forget the moment when the baby was brought home. Again it was snowing heavily. The baby had some infection on her fingers that had to be taken care of. The house without Lucie seemed very empty in spite of the fact that I had two housekeepers and the house was very rarely empty of people who came to visit me. I never went to my office; people came to me in large numbers for consultation and advice. But, nevertheless, the house remained empty.

I had engaged a baby nurse to take care of little Lucie and she was there when the baby arrived. She was a very beautiful little baby, and in a baby contest held two years later she received first prize. I have now forgotten the name of the actress who was in charge of the beauty contest, but she was at that time a very prominent performer in Berlin. Lucie's picture was in every paper, and people congratulated me on it. Of course, Lucie was the main attraction in the house and I am afraid we all spoiled her terribly. Our first nurse proved to be the wrong choice and so I advertised for another. Among those who came was Maria Breiden, who seemed to be the best choice. I engaged her and she has remained with the family until this day; that is, for forty-five years. She has taken care of every one of our babies and those among friends and family. She had a mad crush on me, which proved to be very embarrassing. But many people had mad crushes on me who came to the house and I had affairs with some of them. But nothing was of any consequence.

I remember one incident very well. One day a Russian lady and her niece came to see me. The problem she presented seemed very fishy, but no doubt I was too young to understand that she had come to introduce me to her niece for the purpose of marriage. There were many such attempts to "fix me up" with some rich woman. However, I remember that one in particular, because a week or so after the visit I returned home late at night and found this Russian girl naked in my bed inviting me to the pleasures of the night. I was then and still am very allergic to aggressive women. I threw her out and it was many decades later that I found her in New York. I was still allergic to her and have not forgotten this attempt to rape me—as I am opposed to rape altogether. I certainly resented being raped.

But this incident was only one of many; happily, none of them so crass and unpleasant. It was understandable that many mothers of marriageable daughters would have wanted me to marry one of them since I was young and well known, although my reputation was that of a rather aggressive, fun-loving, successful, revolutionary young man. But young I was. My success was mainly due to the fact that I had introduced a completely novel style to the art of preaching, that I did not hesitate to discuss acute political problems from the pulpit. But it was also well known that I had affairs with young women, and although this was done with the approval and knowledge of my young and very pretty wife, I am sure that the average burgher did not approve of it. Nevertheless, many people wanted to marry me, but I did not want to marry any one of them.

I was determined to marry Hilde Goldschmidt. I will not forget how I had earlier met her. I came out of a drugstore where I had bought a camera and there was a young girl in a light blue dress standing with a lady who evidently was her mother. They introduced themselves to me and told me that this was Hilde Goldschmidt,[20] and that I was her brother Eric's teacher. I took out my little book, which contained the list of my students at the high school at which I taught, and I verified the fact that Eric was my student. The young girl curtsied properly and gave me her gloved hand; she looked awfully pretty to me. She was a friend of one of my young admirers, Anita, who later became a lawyer. Both of them joined my youth group. It was large, very active, and very Zionistic. Hilde at that time was about twelve years old.

My youth group in those days was quite a sensation, since the leaders of the Jewish community were virulently opposed to Zionism and Zionistic activities. I was known as a Zionist as I had joined the Zionist movement when I was fourteen years old. However, Zionism at that time was almost a family, composed of a small and selective group of people, many of them intellectuals. I was not permitted to have meetings of my Zionist youth group in any of the halls of the synagogue, so I decided to hold them on the staircase of the synagogue. The community did not realize how much this fact added to the atmosphere of youth meetings. There was a lot of singing and discussion. It was a marvelous group and I have maintained until this very day a relationship with many members of what at that time was called the Prinz Circle. Hilde was among them. Also, there was Anita, who had a mad crush on me and would have been very happy if I would have married her. But I chose Hilde.

Hilde had been part of our life during the time Lucie was still alive, and visited us almost every day. She came from a very assimilated Jewish family, which traced its German-Jewish origins back to the twelfth century. Everything in their home was very proper. They had a very large apartment and lived together with Hilde's grandparents. All of them were people of great

20. Born on July 24, 1913, Hilde Goldschmidt was eleven years younger than Joachim. She passed away on May 16, 1994, at the age of eighty.

dignity. The grandfather was born in 1831 and had celebrated the hundredth anniversary of his birth in 1931. I had buried his wife before that. I was to bury him shortly before he would have celebrated his 103rd birthday. Since his son, one of Hilde's uncles, was a very affluent banker in New York,[21] there was a formal celebration of the hundredth birthday with representatives of the government expressing their good wishes, and throngs of people coming to the very elegant reception.

Hilde's father was a remarkable man, reticent, dignified, and deeply interested in literature, particularly if the book dealt with historical facts. In his banking firm he specialized in foreign currency and made a comfortable living. He was not at all rich, but there were no financial problems. His wife came from the old Bendix family that, according to some reports, had traded in wool with England during the Middle Ages, and had had their ups and downs. Everybody was rather strict there. The two children were brought up according to the restrictive codes of German families. They had very little to do with Judaism. Of course, they lit a Christmas tree at Christmastime, but I believe they attended services during the High Holy Days. Hilde was a somewhat rebellious product of this family. She attended a very progressive high school that had a student government and many activities that only today have become part of the American curriculum.

During the years she came to our house following her thirteenth birthday, she became very close to Lucie and me. She was quiet, very pleasant, and very pretty. When Lucie died, she was in a very real sense one of the mourners. Many months after this sad event, it was clear to me that, having to take care of a baby, I would need to remarry. Since I was only twenty-eight when Lucie died, it was not unreasonable to assume that I would look for another wife. I was determined to marry Hilde.

After Lucie's death our relationship had become very close, and although I saw other women it was decided between the two of us that we would get married. We went out together a great deal and I taught her many things, took her to elegant restaurants, and spent as much time as possible with her. I was very much in love with her, and so was she with me, although for a long time I remained the popular figure she knew, and her love was probably mixed with some sense of respect. I had been successful at a very early age. I was used to jubilant crowds greeting me with loud applause when I began

21. Ludwig Bendix, who would help to support Prinz during his difficult first months in the United States.

to speak, to overcrowded synagogues, and the kind of adulation that was bound to spoil a young man.

We married in the month of July, 1932.[22] I had just turned thirty and Hilde was about to celebrate her nineteenth birthday. We decided to take our honeymoon trip on a freighter. The freighter was scheduled to leave Hamburg, which was at that time the most important harbor of Europe, and go along the coast of France, around Spain, and finally, after a bit more than two weeks, land in Genoa, Italy.

You[23] must understand that at that time in my life I still observed Jewish laws and particularly the dietary laws. We had a kosher home, and on the boat we ate only dairy food. There were only twelve passengers on the boat with not a single Jew among them. Hilde, young and pretty, and I, young and handsome, spent a fantastic time on the boat which, of course, had much influence on sex, helped along by the movement of the boat. It reminded us often of the poem dealing with the waves of the sea and the movement of the heart. There was a first officer on board ship. Hilde did not really fall in love with him but liked him very much, and we went out with him very often whenever the boat docked in some town.

Finally we landed in Italy and I only know that the place where we stayed had a balcony. Very often at night we stood there watching the beautiful Italian sky and enjoying the warm air of an Italian summer. I carried a sketchbook with me as I was always very much interested in architecture; I still have very many of the sketches I did at that time.

When we came home we began our life together as a married couple. We had a cook and a baby nurse, and later we added a second housekeeper who was particularly good with little Lucie. Our baby nurse was Maria Breiden. I was still very much attached to Lucie, and very often I called Hilde by that name. I did not realize how vulnerable she was. Since I was surrounded by many old friends, with whom I spoke the same language, we reminisced about the good old times, and Hilde felt left out. I never realized that and I paid for it dearly. It has something to do with my carelessness in those days, the lack of a sense of responsibility. I was really spoiled rotten, and I am sure that I made the first years of our marriage full of problems for young Hilde.

The year 1932 was not merely the year of my second marriage. It was the year before Hitler came to power. I had watched the development of German politics, and particularly the growing German nationalism since

---

22. An error. The wedding took place on May 24, 1932. July 24 was Hilde's birthday.
23. The "you" presumably refers to members of the Prinz family who would be reading the autobiography.

the assassination of Walther Rathenau in 1922. The number of unemployed grew and with it the collective desperation of a people who had no confidence in their government and no use for democracy at all. They were yearning for the good old days when the Kaiser was in charge and they believed only a strong government in the hands of one single man would be able to solve the problems that beset the country. There were some pseudo-religious undertones in all that; in reality, they were waiting for the savior. I watched the little insignificant nationalistic movement that started in Munich, Bavaria, whose leader was a little mustached man by the name of Adolf Hitler. Everyone made fun of this movement. How could a man, they said, who wears such a ridiculous moustache, ever make an impression on the people? But I listened to him carefully and I read the book he had written in prison.[24] I took every word of the book seriously and literally. Among the many pages that proclaimed the new German dictatorship there were odd ones written in the red blood of the Jews whom he swore to exterminate and wipe off the face of the earth.

That which to others sounded ridiculous sounded very serious to me, for he had the typical German combination of romanticism and brutality. The slogan was: "One country, one people, and one leader." I knew that to be the dream of the people. I began to talk about Hitler in 1929. Shortly after that, I published the volume of Jewish history that I mentioned earlier. I delivered public speeches all over Europe. After Lucie died, I remember taking a few months off, and on my way to Italy stopping at the German town of Kassel where I had accepted a speaking engagement. The Jews came in large numbers to listen to me, and when I told them that Hitler had to be taken seriously and that Jews had better prepare for that day, there was a storm of protest in the audience. One man, pointing at me, rose and said: "And this man claims to be a rabbi!" I left the assembly in turmoil knowing that I had spoken the truth, but the Jews did not want to hear it.

Shortly afterward, I arrived at the city of Ulm, the birthplace of Albert Einstein. I was to deliver a speech there, but before that I spoke to the leaders of the Jewish community. The Jews had been in that city for hundreds of years, and they informed me they were about to build a Jewish community center. I said to them: "This is the year 1931. Very soon Hitler will come to power, and as soon as you have finished building the new community center it will be destroyed and you will be killed." This was not a very popular talk, and I left Ulm disheartened by the utter inability of the people to face political realities and to understand the mentality of the enemy. This is

24. *Mein Kampf.*

one of the great Jewish tragedies. They trust their friends too readily and do not take their enemies seriously. I went to Italy, landed on the isle of Capri, where I stayed for a few weeks instead of one night.[25] Then I proceeded to Sicily, which I have never ceased to love until this very day, where in the early Middle Ages, and even in antiquity, there took place a cultural wedding between the Roman, Greek, Islamic, and Christian cultures. All that was expressed in architecture, and I fell in love with the mosaics of Monreale[26] near Palermo and the church, which was a living example of a creative mixture of cultures. It had been a Roman temple, later in the eighth century a mosque, and a few centuries later a church. The architecture was unforgettable, and so was its name: the church was called San Giovanni degli Eremiti.[27]

I stayed away from my work and my home for almost three months. On the way back I went to Rome and remained there for a few weeks. Although I could not possibly forget what had happened to me, this trip was of great importance, for it gave me an opportunity to look back at what had occurred and to try to look toward the many tomorrows that were to come. I was very deeply impressed with the architecture and paintings I saw; that has always been and still is a source of great amazement and inspiration to me. But in addition to that, these few months gave me an opportunity to read the foreign press, particularly Italian and French, so that I could understand what the political observers of the Western world expected to happen. Germany was of great importance to all of them, as it was located in the heart of Europe, a country in which civilization on all levels had reached its peak. Many of the political observers doubted that Hitler would come to power, but others faced the situation, analyzed the German national character, and were convinced that some day a dictatorship would be established in Germany.

I returned home shortly before my birthday in the month of May. Spring was in full bloom and our house, situated in that part of Berlin which had mostly villas and other beautiful and expensive buildings, was a particular pleasure. Little Lucie was now four or five months old and was being taken care of by Maria. I found her delightful, as did everyone else, and my old friends greeted me warmly. I was finally home.

But I was also amazed to find that most people in the middle of 1931 were little concerned about Germany's future. Nothing had changed in terms

25. Perhaps a veiled reference to the lyrics of the song "Isle of Capri," which have the lover sailing away after a single night.
26. A small town, just outside Palermo, renowned for the mosaics in its cathedral.
27. "The Church of St. John of the Hermits."

of unemployment and the general despair of the people. It was shortly after I had arrived home that I was called by someone inviting me to officiate at a funeral service some thirty miles from Berlin. It was a small town, a tiny Jewish community. It had no rabbi, and I was to officiate at the funeral service of some person whose name I have now forgotten. It was my first opportunity to see a small German town where the atmosphere was far removed from the cosmopolitan spirit of Berlin—where its beer cellars were more important than its museums. The funeral service was held in the little synagogue of the community, and according to old custom the funeral procession went through the streets of the town. I was wearing my robe as I followed the hearse on foot. The cemetery was not far from the center of town. It had been the custom in Germany for all people who lined the streets to remove their hats whenever a hearse passed by. This time there were hundreds of onlookers, curious to see the rare happening of a Jewish funeral service. But no one took off their hats. There were jeers and laughter, and some people tried to throw stones at me and at the hearse. We arrived at the cemetery and then I returned to the little hotel in town where I was staying. When I entered the dining room for dinner, I knew I was in enemy territory. I was completely isolated and it was a sheer miracle that I was not beaten up. It was an important political experience for me, for I began to understand that what was happening in Berlin was not as important as what was happening in the countryside. The little towns all over the country told the story more eloquently. People wearing the brown uniform of the storm troopers were all over and flags adorned with the swastika were exhibited without shame. Antisemitic slogans covered many walls, and the little local newspapers were full of anti-Jewish and pro-Nazi articles. I knew that Hitler had conquered Germany without conquering Berlin and without indeed having achieved any official position in the government.

This impression, which has never left me, was confirmed a few weeks later when I officiated at the funeral service of a young man and his mother. The corpses had been brought to Berlin from a little town more than a hundred miles away. The story I was told was that a storm trooper had broken into a Jewish home and killed the young man in the presence of his mother, and the mother had died of a heart attack. These were among the first victims of the Nazi regime, which was not yet even in power. They were a strong and dramatic confirmation of my fears and my predictions, which found little echo, although they were very much part of my daily thoughts and some of my nightmares.

I began to talk more and more about the coming of Hitler. The German president was General Hindenburg, a man of little intelligence in spite of his successful military exploits. After many victories Germany had lost the war, and much of the political atmosphere was a reaction to the defeat it had suffered and the peace conference at Versailles with all its restrictions limiting German military activities. I talked to Jews and non-Jews alike and found them completely unaware of the great danger that was to come only two years later.

The Jews worried me most. I always knew they had no conception of political realities. They imagined themselves to be surrounded by friends and discounted their enemies who, after all, were intellectually inferior to them. They did not know that intellectual inferiority meant political and military impotence.[28] The Jewish establishment was completely convinced that Hitler would be but an episode and soon forgotten. Their faith in Germany was so strong and so deeply embedded that they believed the German people would never vote for Hitler. This belief was maintained even though the Hitler party had in the meantime become one of the largest parties in the parliament. Jews had lived in Germany for sixteen hundred consecutive years and nearly all of them were patriots and super-Germans. My grandfather had been wounded in the war between Prussia and Austria in 1866 and wore his medals with great pride. My father, I remember vividly, collected the daily reports during the First World War, and was shattered when Germany lost the war and the Kaiser abdicated. Although our little town[29] of only thirty-five thousand inhabitants had also become quite nazified, my father noticed nothing. No wonder that when Hitler finally came to power and when my father was advised to leave the country, he had only ten dollars in his pocket; his large business had been confiscated by the Nazis.[30] But he was typical of all the other German Jews. It was only the small group of Zionists, a tiny minority in the country, that saw the tragedy that was to come and urged immigration of Jews to Palestine or other countries.

I had, as I said before, created a youth group that was completely devoted to me and my ideas. I tried to teach them the lesson of Jewish history, which was tragic because of the inability of the Jews to understand the military and political realities of the time. They all came, as I did, from completely assimilated families. As a matter of fact, the Zionist youth movement to which I belonged consisted of more than 90 percent young men and

28. In its present form, the sentence does not make sense. It probably should read: "They did not know that intellectual inferiority did not mean political and military impotence."
29. Oppeln.
30. He left in 1938, a year after his son. Ironically, while his son migrated to America, the anti-Zionist father settled in Palestine.

women from Jewish families such as mine who had in reality rejected their Jewishness and conceived of German Jews as a special elite, looking down upon Eastern European Jews, rejecting the whole notion of a Jewish people. To the older generation, Judaism was simply a religion like the others, and they considered themselves to be "Germans of the Jewish persuasion." My father never permitted us to say the word *Jew* or *Jewish* at the dining table in front of the housemaids. He was a timid and cowardly Jew.

The Jewish community of Berlin was extremely well organized. According to German law, Jews, like the adherents of other religions, had to pay an additional income tax the percentage of which was determined by the various communities. It varied around the country. Since the Jewish community of Berlin was large and prosperous, we paid only 11 percent in addition to our regular income tax. This amount was collected by the government and then transferred to the Jewish community. It accounted for the fact that huge synagogues, hospitals, homes for the aged, and all kinds of social institutions were built without having mortgages. The Jewish community had its own department of architecture and every building was paid for in cash. There was never a drive for funds among the German Jews. The Berlin community was among the youngest; it was only three hundred years old.[31]

Each of us was assigned to three synagogues in which we preached, taking turns.[32] Every month we had a free Sabbath day. We all had to accept funeral services on two days during the week, while on the other days we were at liberty either to accept or reject them. The community had a fleet of limousines and whenever I had a funeral service or a wedding, a chauffeur would stop in front of my house and take me to it. A certain amount of money was paid to the officiating rabbi for his services, not by the family but by the community, regardless of whether the people were poor or rich. Since I was very popular, my check for such services often exceeded my rather large salary. People who lacked money paid either little or nothing for the funeral service, while rich people very often paid thousands of dollars beyond what the community offered. But there was the same coffin and the same service for every person regardless of economic station. The coffins were made of pine and were manufactured by the community, which had a large department of carpentry and cabinetmaking. No one was permitted to deviate from this custom. Every Jew, regardless of whether he was

31. Jews had lived in medieval Berlin, but were expelled on various occasions in the fifteenth and sixteenth centuries. The modern Jewish community began in 1671.
32. This was the case for Prinz only after the Friedenstempel ceased to be an independent synagogue and was absorbed into the Jewish community in 1928.

rich or poor, was buried in a pine box. The ritual washing was performed professionally and death garments were used rather than suits or dresses. The funeral service took place according to German law on the third day after death. The prayers to be said were in accordance with Jewish tradition, to which everyone had to adhere. Nothing was paid for rabbinical services or the gravesite if the person was under a certain income bracket. Many rich people wanted additional services such as a choir or a string quartet, and they had to pay for them accordingly. Regardless of wealth, an employee of the community appeared at the house that was bereft and gave the mourners two silver boxes. The ones I saw were from the Baroque period. One was open and contained sufficient money for the family to buy food for the entire week of mourning. The other one was locked and people were at liberty to put into that box either the money they found in the open silver box or whatever they wished to donate to charity. This custom was old and always impressed me as particularly meaningful.

It was probably this adherence to tradition that prevented the Jewish establishment from understanding the changed conditions in the country.[33] I will never forget my talks with the president of the community, a very wealthy Jew known for his charitable contributions to all kinds of causes, and the head of one of the largest insurance companies in the country.[34] He had also assembled a very fine collection of Impressionist paintings. Once he heard me preach a sermon in which I admonished the Jews to leave the country as soon as possible.[35] The sermon was given in my largest synagogue, which had a seating capacity of three and a half thousand.[36] As always, the synagogue was opened an hour before the service was to start, and since all 3,500 seats had been taken a half hour later, the doors had to be closed. But my popularity with the Jewish people did not make me popular with the Jewish establishment.

In the sermon I delivered, I told a story that I had read in one of the books by Alfred Polgar.[37] These were stories that each covered half a page of the book. All were extraordinary in both form and content. The story I told

33. Prinz here briefly jumps ahead to the Nazi period.
34. The reference is to Heinrich Stahl (1868–1942), who headed the Berlin Jewish community from May 1933 until February 1940. He was deported to Theresienstadt in June 1942, where he died in November of that year.
35. Prinz gives us no date for this sermon, which clearly was delivered after Hitler's rise to power.
36. The New Synagogue, Oranienburger Strasse 30, in the eastern part of the city.
37. Alfred Polgar (1873–1955) was an Austrian Jewish essayist, drama critic, and prose writer known especially for his brilliant satirical style and his elegant short stories.

was as follows: "I came," Polgar reports, "to the town in which I was born. It was a medieval town with a small Jewish community that had lived there for hundreds of years. I had not been there for a long time. As I walked through the town I noticed that the clock on the Gothic tower of the church stood still. Whether that had happened recently I do not know. The clock was dead. I was struck by this strange phenomenon—whenever I looked at the clock it indicated that it was three o'clock. I went home and began to think. And I came to the conclusion that the clock was not dead. Time is never dead. The clock said three o'clock, but in reality it was three o'clock twice during a full day, once in the afternoon and once in the morning. Time is never dead. It only depends upon you and whether you look at the clock at the proper time."

I told this story to the 3,500 people, and I said, "Time is never dead. It is important to look at the clock and then know what time it really is. I am telling you," I said, raising my voice, "that the time is midnight for the Jewish people, and it is time for us to pack up and go."

The name of the president of the Jewish community was Herman Stahl.[38] After the service he came to me angry and excited, and then he said, "In as far as I and my administration are concerned, the clock is in Germany and will tell the time for us for many hundreds of years to come. My people will not be so cowardly as to leave."[39]

I made an appointment to see him at his home. When I came to his luxuriously furnished villa, I looked at the walls where I had seen his large collection of Impressionists, but the walls were bare. The paintings had been removed. I said to him, "What happened to the paintings?" He answered, "I had them sent to my son in Belgium." I then said to him, "If that is so, then there is nothing I have to tell you. Evidently the paintings are more precious to you than the people. You thought it safer for the paintings to be taken away and you are quite oblivious of the fact that the people who will not leave will die." There was nothing else I had to say. He never forgot this and thought I was irresponsible and insane. But he was a man of convictions; and while tens of thousands of people had left after Hitler became the chancellor of Germany, he remained steadfast. In the end, when in 1938 everybody was taken to concentration camps, he was sent to Auschwitz where he

38. Heinrich, not Herman.
39. However, Stahl eventually changed his mind. Toward the end of January, 1938, he said: "To those among our youth who have not yet decided to emigrate, I say, there is no future for Jews in this country. Whatever changes may be forthcoming for us will probably not be for the better." (*American Jewish Yearbook* 4 [1938/39]: 204.)

was gassed.[40] I wonder what he said and felt at the last moment of his life and whether or not he ever remembered what I had told him.

But all this happened during the Hitler regime. In 1932, Hitler had not yet come to power. The government was weak. The Weimar Republic had very small and insignificant roots in the people. Even in 1918, one could sense that the German people had no appetite for democracies. Most of them really did not know what democracy meant. The democratic values of freedom and lack of restriction in almost every field flourished after 1918, especially in the circles of intellectual writers and painters. This development was particularly significant in Germany. The theater, the newspapers, painting and sculpture, and above all, modern architecture, had begun to flourish long before such a renaissance began in other countries, and some fifty years before it came to America. Germany had become the birthplace of the new movements of Expressionism and Cubism. The Bauhaus was a center of modern architecture and altogether directed the course of modern art. The new buildings that were erected at that time were examples of the modern architecture of which Le Corbusier in France had been the father. In the realm of painting the achievements were extraordinary, creating a completely new outlook on life as it appeared on the canvasses of the leaders of the new movements. All this had started at the beginning of the century, before the First World War, but it was recognized by the government and the officials, as well as by the public, after 1918, the year of the revolution that led to the Weimar Republic. Art was also the great social critic of the time, dealing with misery, poverty, prostitution, and human degradation. It also created caricatures of the so-called Prussian spirit, the stiffness of a society built upon lies and hypocrisy. The artists George Grosz and Käthe Kollwitz were the leaders of this group of social critics. New churches and synagogues were built in the modern style. Literature was an enormously important factor, particularly in Berlin. Every new book that appeared, novel or nonfiction, seemed to make the city tremble, at least in the circles of the intellectuals among whom I lived. The literary outpouring also produced political writings of enormous importance that expounded a liberal way of thinking and were aware of the great danger in which Germany found herself. In addition to Walther Rathenau, several other political leaders of the left and the center had been assassinated. It was clear to political observers that democracy was a system that had been forced on the German people and was something they could neither stomach nor understand. They were longing for a new Kaiser.

40. Prinz is in error. See note 34, above.

The theater played an extraordinary role in all of this. One must not forget that Berlin was the world center of modern theater at that time. It must also not be forgotten that Berlin was not the only city with regular theater performances; there was a theater in almost every larger town. Most of them were experimental, a result of the "Living Theater of Russia."[41] Among the producers, Max Reinhardt was the greatest of them all. They had built a theater for him that was a completely modern building with a movable stage reaching into the audience. There I saw the most amazing performances, not merely of modern authors, but of Shakespeare, Gorky, Chekhov, and others. We went to the theater very often, as well as to the fabulous concerts performed by the Berlin Symphony Orchestra and foreign orchestras. I vividly remember the violinist Yehudi Menuhin as a young boy wearing short pants and playing beautifully. Only the other day, when I met him in Switzerland, I told him about this experience, and he told me that it was perhaps the most exciting and decisive experience of his life.

The cultural life of Berlin, as well as the existence of so many extraordinary intellectual and artistic figures, blinded the average political observer to the distinction between the artists and the people. The latter had no appetite or liking for Weimar culture and even rejected it with contempt and disgust. No wonder Hitler chased the modern artists out, had their work confiscated, and designated it as "unnatural and degenerate art."[42]

But to me and the small circle of my friends it was clear that we had to consider the people as a whole, the Germans of every description and station in life: the large group of teachers and pensioners, the officials of the German bureaucracy, and the average man and woman who eked out a rather miserable existence or stood in line for welfare payments. What they wanted was a strong hand and a strong leader. They were longing for a dictatorship by one man who could take things into his own hands and forget about the parliament and democratic decisions, who would make the decisions himself and see them through at any price.

The most astounding thing to me in the years between 1929 and 1933 was the lackadaisical attitude of the people. It did not take much time to develop a kind of antisemitism that reminded us of the 1890s when Richard Wagner's son-in-law, born in England, wrote his infamous book *The Foundations of the Twentieth Century* in which he developed a theory of the racial

41. Prinz may be thinking of a Russian theatrical company known as Living Theater, but it only came into existence in 1951. Or he may be referring to Stanislavsky's Moscow Arts Theater.
42. In 1937, an exhibit of "degenerate art" opened in Munich and later traveled to other German cities. It was intended to ridicule all modern visual art that was not in the idealized traditional style favored by the Nazis.

inferiority of the Jewish people.[43] He based his work on the writings of the Frenchman Count Gobineau,[44] misunderstanding him and misinterpreting him, but finding applause, not merely consent, among the people, including the Kaiser, high circles of the government, and the military. The ideas which had been inherited from that time had never really died; now they were allowed to come to the fore with full vigor and viciousness. It was clear that among the intellectuals, the owners of the newspapers, the directors of the film industry, the artists and the writers, there were a great many Jews. Although they were not in the majority, they nevertheless had become very visible. The satirical writer Kurt Tucholsky,[45] who wrote biting critical essays about the German people and their stupidity, was one of the Nazis' major targets. After Hitler came to power, Tucholsky went to Scandinavia where he committed suicide. He was probably one of the wittiest German writers, in the tradition of Heinrich Heine. The Jews were identified with his views although God knows the majority of German Jews, who numbered 550,000 at that time, had very little to do with socialism and communism, or even with ironic writers on the German people. Although there were Jewish socialists, and some of them were in the government, the vast majority of the Jews were middle-of-the-roaders and voted either for the Democratic Party or, strangely enough, for the Centrist Party, which was Catholic. They felt, as did the Germans—and some of them even more so—that they had a long history behind them. They never understood that the declaration of independence[46] was a piece of paper on which a decree had been written. As always, they never took the enemy seriously, and the best Jewish jokes were told at that time. But a joke is very rarely a proper response to a political reality. The German Jews were completely unprepared for Hitler, and whatever they read in Hitler's book *Mein Kampf* was considered a bizarre and eccentric notion, not to be taken at face value. That he threatened to eliminate Jews from public life, deprive them of German education, and wipe them off the face of the earth, were just words for them, and many consid-

43. In 1899, Houston Stewart Chamberlain (1855–1927) published his *Die Grundlagen des 19. Jahrhunderts,* in which he argued for the supremacy of the Teutonic race and the cultural inferiority of the mongrel Jewish race.

44. Joseph Arthur Comte de Gobineau (1816–1882) published *Essai sur l'inégalité des races humaines* (1853–1855). Although he bore the Jews no animus, he did hold, as did Chamberlain after him, that the Jews had racially degenerated since ancient times.

45. Kurt Tucholsky (1890–1935) was a journalist and sharp critic of middle-class mores, including those of the Jewish bourgeoisie. He moved to Sweden in 1930, three years before Hitler came to power, and there apparently committed suicide five years later.

46. The reference may be to the emancipation of German Jewry or possibly to the Weimar constitution.

ered him insane and therefore incapable of governing the country. But unprepared as the German Jews were, so were the Jews of the world and the democracies in which they lived. Neither England nor France was militarily prepared for the Hitler onslaught. Chamberlain of England was not the only ridiculous and tragic figure in this whole political play. Nobody thought of war and nobody took Hitler seriously. When he said: "Today Germany, tomorrow the world," that meant the threat of world conquest. But every country thought *it* was not included. This sense of unreality drove me almost insane, for I read Hitler's book again and again, and I took every line seriously. I decided to embark on a missionary campaign to convince the Jews of the Hitler reality.

It was in those days that we began to do some work within the Jewish community. Many years before Hitler came to power I had founded the Jewish School for Youth.[47] It was designed to train Jewish youth leaders who would later become the leaders of the Jewish community. The leadership we had was often Jewishly ignorant and elected because of their social status in the community. There was, after all, a very large number of Jewish bankers who owned private banks of great influence and publishers of books and newspapers who were the leading men in their profession. Some of them also became leaders of the Jewish community. But they knew very little about Judaism. I therefore decided to create in Berlin a School for Jewish Youth. Among the teachers I engaged was Martin Buber, who exerted an enormous influence upon the young people, although I doubt whether they ever understood him. I often went into the hall where he taught some five hundred young people. They listened to him expounding his theories for two or three hours. No one moved either body or lips. The boys and girls just looked at the great spiritual leader; he took great pleasure in presenting his views to them. I myself had many misgivings with regard to what he said. Later, I had a public debate about his views, which was reprinted just a few years ago.[48] We also began to think in terms of Jewish adult education, in which I became very active. I was one of the founders of the Chaim Bialik Institute of Jewish Learning.[49] I taught classes of many hundreds of people.

In the meantime, I had written my Jewish history, which under the Hit-

---

47. Prinz proposed the idea of a *Schule der jüdischen Jugend* in an address that he delivered in Berlin in 1929. The following year, it had five hundred students ranging in age from fifteen to twenty-five.

48. Prinz is referring to his 1936 debate with Buber on the pages of the *Israelitisches Familienblatt,* issues 30, 32, and 33. It was reprinted in *Bulletin des Leo Baeck Instituts* 10 (1967): 221–231.

49. The Bialik Institute was the Jewish adult education center in Berlin. It enrolled close to two thousand students.

ler regime was published anew and by another publisher.[50] Later I published two volumes of a children's Bible, which was put out by Erich Reiss, one of the most important publishers in Germany; it became a best-seller in no time.[51] I tried to teach the Jews who came to me, both young and old, not merely Jewish history, as I saw it, but my political convictions as well. A year or two before Hitler, Recha Freier[52] came to me to tell me that she expected Hitler to come to power and that we had to save Jewish children by taking them to Palestine. This was the foundation of the Youth Aliyah that was later taken over by Henrietta Szold.[53] But the real founder was Recha Freier, and the founding took place in my home. It was, I believe, in 1931. To me this idea seemed fruitful and took into consideration the reality that very few other people recognized.

Meanwhile, everyone conducted business as usual. The writers continued to write, the actors continued to perform, and the Jews involved in music and painting continued to do their thing. All that was done instead of packing up in anticipation of what was going to come. But they did not do that. Jews lived their lives as a big "as-if" proposition, based on Vaihinger's philosophy.[54] It is difficult to describe my despair when I spoke to our people and found not merely complete rejection of my ideas, but an angry outcry against the kind of nonsense they thought I was talking. Their fatherland was their surest possession and to leave it was a betrayal. Some people did indeed leave Germany before Hitler, but their number was probably less than a hundred in total. The Jewish community's leaders continued to function in the usual fashion. They did not prepare any textbooks for the time when Jewish children would have to go to Jewish schools, nor did they make any provision for the Jewish teachers who would teach them. There was no at-

---

50. This time it appeared under the title *Illustrierte jüdische Geschichte,* published by the Brandussche Verlagsbuchhandlung in Berlin with a new foreword dated November 1933 and with a great many changes and additions.

51. *Die Geschichten der Bibel* (Berlin: Erich Reiss Verlag, 1934) and *Die Reiche Israel und Juda* (Berlin: Erich Reiss Verlag, 1936).

52. Recha Freier (1892–1984) founded Youth Aliyah in 1932. Like Prinz, she was an antiestablishmentarian, whose views on the urgency of immediate emigration stood in opposition both to the official Jewish community and the Zionist movement. She settled in the Land of Israel in 1941.

53. Henrietta Szold (1860–1945) is best known for being a founder and first president of Hadassah, the Women's Zionist organization. She was one of the few American Zionists to settle in the Land of Israel. In 1933, she directed Youth Aliyah.

54. In 1911, Hans Vaihinger (1852–1933) published his influential *Philosophy of the "As If,"* in which concepts developed by the various scientific and humanistic disciplines were regarded as simply convenient fictions, devised by the human mind and removed from external reality.

tempt to prepare our people psychologically for what must have been a tremendous shock to their very existence. National Socialism was a dirty word, and to make it a dirty word was evidently enough for the Jews and a substitute for a real preparation for the time that would come.

This was also true of the labor unions and the liberal intellectuals who ridiculed Hitler, the man with the little mustache, who preached an outrageous sermon that could not be rationally interpreted. Hitler was not rational, nor was his philosophy. He lived in an irrational time that had had its fill of rationalism and wanted something emotional, indefinable and, nevertheless, activist in solving the problems. He had no party members, although they were called that; in reality, he had only disciples. More and more I recognized that we were dealing here with a new political church. Christianity was a religion that did not always appeal to the Germans. Jesus was much too meek a figure for the Germans to be their leader. There had been many instances, particularly since the last decades of the nineteenth century, when Christianity was rejected as a Jewish religion, and Jesus as an example of the very opposite of the German ideal.[55] How can a man who permits himself to be crucified be acceptable to a people who would rather do the crucifying than submit to that kind of humiliating death? It was not humility the Germans wanted and probably needed; on the contrary, it was a new pride or even a sense of superiority. In this search for superiority, which was born of a profound sense of inferiority, they needed a scapegoat, and it was only natural that the Jew should serve in that capacity, for it was a confirmation of German history and German thought. It was ridiculous for the Jews to identify antisemitism with the attitude of the untutored and illiterate people. It is a fact, borne out by history, that many of the antisemites in Germany were professors at universities and intellectuals. To us, the antisemites seemed to have been limited and illiterate persons, but in reality they had built their own system, based on the notion that a Jew poisons the German spirit. I did not like all that; but not liking it is one thing, not taking it seriously is another.

The main burden of my sermons was identification with the Jewish people and the willingness to share both Jewish destiny and fate. More and more I talked about that fate, for the days which were to come would confirm that the Jewish people had a bloody fate, and that it was time to save as many people as possible, or at least to prepare them for the time that was to come. My sermons, of course, were Zionistic and dealt with political prob-

---

55. Prinz is apparently thinking of the secular, even antireligious branch of the antisemitic movement in Germany, which arose during the last decades of the nineteenth century.

lems, both Jewish and non-Jewish. I was never able to conceive of religion, and certainly not of Judaism, as something that could continue to exist in splendid isolation. To me, the isolation of the Jews from the non-Jewish world and all Jewish problems from non-Jewish problems did not seem to be so splendid. I rejected this completely and tried to interpret Judaism in terms of a faith or a civilization that was able, or at least had to try, to supply answers to the problems that beset the people. My relationship to my colleagues was therefore very often tense and hostile. I seemed to be a man from a different world. Of course, it had something to do with the fact that I was twenty-three[56] years old when I began, and that Berlin had never had a rabbi who did not have a gray beard. It was a matter of a generation gap, but in reality it was a matter of different convictions and different approaches to my profession.

More and more I became involved in the problems of our people. One of them was death. In the eleven years of my rabbinate in Berlin[57] I buried several thousand people. I had an average of between ten and twenty funerals each week. Very often I spent almost the whole day at the cemetery.[58] There were no funeral homes. Every Jewish funeral service was held in one of the chapels of the huge cemetery. The cemetery, in which I buried many people, including my wife, was a huge and beautifully kept park. I remember being informed one day that I had just officiated at the one hundred thousandth funeral service. The park was taken care of by a large number of gardeners paid by the Jewish community, perhaps a hundred of them. The pallbearers were also officials of the community. Everything was done in accordance with the rules. There were many funerals every day so that they had to start at a certain time with utmost punctuality and strictly adhere to the rules as laid down by the community.

Since a funeral took place on the third day after death, there was much time to get involved in the life of the person who had come to an end. I had long discussions with the family, going into every possible detail of the life of the deceased. I made studies of their handwriting and photographs, and I began to understand that a eulogy was not an ordinary speech but had some psychiatric connotations. I had studied psychiatry and psychology for four years[59] and had very good training in this field. I began to develop a

56. Actually, twenty-four.
57. From the beginning of 1927 to the middle of 1937, about ten and a half years.
58. During Prinz's rabbinate, the cemetery of the Berlin Jewish community was in the eastern suburb of Weissensee. Historically, it was the third cemetery, purchased by the community in the late 1870s.
59. The reference is apparently to courses in pastoral psychology taken at the seminary in Breslau.

theory of the eulogy as instant therapy for the bereaved. I was so success-ful in this field that my late friend, Gerhart Jacobson, who very often in jest prepared slogans for me, coined one that was very well known in the com-munity: "Why live if you can be buried by Prinz!" I buried many important and prominent people. I still cannot understand when I look at photographs of myself from that time how people could have had so much confidence in me. It was true that I was in my twenties, but I looked as though I were in my teens. I remember that once during the time I taught the upper classes of the academic high school, I was asked by a teacher to leave the room during recess. He was amazed when I informed him that I was a member of the fac-ulty. He had mistaken me for a student.

Teaching at the public school was a very important experience for me in those days. I taught from the very beginning and have maintained my re-lationship with many of my former students until this day. They are now middle-aged gentlemen. Many of them died during the Hitler regime. But many also survived, having listened to me and having left Germany either through Youth Aliyah or by other means. I established a relationship with them because my concept of teaching was so liberal and informal. When the children graduated, I always gave them a drinking party, and all of us got very drunk. None of them called me by my first name, but everybody had a very close and even intimate relationship with me.

The last months of 1932 were unbearably tense. German right-wingers had taken over in parliament and the National Socialists exerted enormous power. As I said before, they had really conquered all of Germany, particu-larly the small towns, the teachers and pensioners, and also the universities. A few years before Hitler came to power I had become the official Jewish chaplain of the University of Berlin. This was a new position. The Catho-lics and Protestants had chaplains, but the Jews had never been granted this privilege. I was the first one—and I was also the last. Work at the university was very important because I finally got to the age group that was decisive. I established courses at the university, which I taught to large classes of stu-dents. At German universities there was complete academic freedom and no one had to attend classes. The most important thing was to pass an examina-tion at the end of the five or six semesters. The choice of the university was completely free; the tuition fee was very small. There was no campus and there were no dormitories. My time coincided with an era of complete sexual freedom, which fit well into the freedom in art and thought. It was a time when trial marriage was very much in vogue, and many of the students lived with their girlfriends. The women were quite emancipated, and I certainly do not remember ever having met a virgin among them. This kind of life ap-pealed to me greatly because everything else was sheer hypocrisy.

The year 1932 had come to an end. As always, we celebrated New Year's Eve. As was usual, we had a large and loud party. There was enough to drink and eat to make all of us happy. But this was a special New Year's Eve, for in spite of the large party, the loudness and the drinks, my friends who had come to the party knew that there would never be another New Year's Eve like this and that things were getting serious. Very soon we would be faced with the dreaded problem of a German dictatorship. We did not have long to wait.

THE NAZI YEARS

On January 20,[60] 1933, Hitler was appointed the chancellor of what soon became the Third Reich. Thousands of people were soon arrested. The leaders of the trade unions found themselves in concentration camps. By decree, the liberal newspapers ceased to exist. I remember coming to school to teach and seeing the majority of the professors at the school wearing the black uniforms of the SS. Many of them were officers and most of them no longer spoke to me. I was there, but I was on an island sitting in enemy territory. Hitler had come and our worst predictions had come true. The dream was over; the nightmare had become our reality.

The invitation that Hitler, as the leader of the largest party, received from the president of the German Reich[61] to serve as chancellor looked to the outsider like a normal parliamentary procedure. All of the members of parliament wore formal dress, and those who had made light of Hitler found this ceremony another affirmation of the view that once Hitler would come to power he would be tamed and controlled; the old radical programs would be forgotten. I was, of course, not of that opinion and, sure enough, shortly after his takeover as chancellor, Hitler began to translate his plans into reality.

Parliament was dissolved and all rival parties were forbidden. The National Socialist party remained the only one in the parliament. Hitler's flag, the black swastika on a red background, was adopted as the flag of Germany. Opposition to the party was forbidden, and actually there was none. Those who did try to oppose were immediately taken to concentration camps. This was the first time that we heard that term, which had no reality for us. But many such camps were established on the sites of former army camps. New barracks were built very quickly as this program of government-financed work began to develop. The streets were suddenly full of storm troopers

60. Actually, the 30th.
61. At that time Germany was still a democracy.

wearing the brown uniform and the armband with the swastika, strutting around molesting anyone they chose as they passed by. There was no due process of law; it seemed as if a storm trooper, or for that matter any German Aryan citizen, could arrest anyone. In addition to the brown uniforms of the storm troopers, we began to see the elegant black uniform of the SS, Hitler's elite guard.

Although, at the beginning, the Nuremberg Laws had not yet been written or promulgated,[62] their substance was actually being carried out. It was announced that Jewish children could no longer attend public schools.[63] Jewish lawyers could not appear in court and Jewish physicians were restricted in their practice. It was also announced that very soon Jews would not be permitted to have German Aryan maids since every Jew, usually the head of the household, was suspected of being a rapist. Also, Jewish artists in every field were suddenly prevented from exhibiting their art. Jewish art dealers closed their shops, and very soon all Jewish newspapers and other publishing houses were sold to Aryans. Use of the term *Aryan*, which had been so alien to us, became a daily reality. Slowly, the Jews began to understand what was happening. The joke was: "Are you an Aryan or are you learning English?" Emigration was very much on the minds of many.

Some Jews, not in very large numbers but nevertheless quite vociferous, joined the association of the National Socialist Jews.[64] Their leader was Dr. Max Naumann, a man with whom I had had many encounters in former years. I once discovered in the twenties that he had written an article in a nationalistic German newspaper warning against the immigration of Eastern European Jews. At that time I was the editor of a weekly[65] and wrote an editorial under the heading "The Traitor Naumann."[66] Although he had

62. The Nuremberg Laws were promulgated in the fall of 1935.

63. In fact, Jewish children did continue to attend public schools, albeit in decreasing numbers, during the first years of the Nazi regime.

64. The actual name of the organization was the Association of National-German Jews (Verband nationaldeutscher Juden). It was founded in 1920 by Max Naumann (1875–1939) and disbanded by the Gestapo in 1935 as the latter was not sympathetic to the association's insistence on the Germanness of some, though not all, German Jews.

65. *Jüdische Zeitung für Ostdeutschland.*

66. Due to the incompleteness of extant volumes, it was not possible to substantiate Prinz's claim to have written this editorial. However, there is a reference in a surviving issue that Naumann sued Prinz for libel because, as editor, he had printed and associated himself (perhaps in the mentioned editorial) with a speech by an attorney named Foerder that attacked Naumann. *Jüdische Zeitung für Ostdeutschland,* March 20, 1925, p. 1. In 1934, Prinz received a postcard threatening his life from a man who claimed to represent a "Militant Association of Jewish Germans." *Jüdische Rundschau,* August 21, 1934.

written the article under a pseudonym, I. Hobrecht (in Bavarian dialect: *I Am Right*), I found out that the real author was Naumann. I was sentenced to a fine of fifty marks for defamation of character and had a criminal record until I came under the amnesty in honor of Hindenburg's eightieth birthday.[67] Naumann's association had its own youth movement, which was super-German. They were fanatics, superpatriots, passionate anti-Zionists, and in a very real sense, antisemitic. They were self-hating Jews who thought they could save themselves by making common cause with the Nazis. It is unnecessary to add that they did not succeed. Naumann himself ended up in a concentration camp, probably singing the German national anthem as he walked to the gas chamber.[68] Among the ideologists of the movement was Hans-Joachim Schoeps who is now a professor at one of the leading universities of Germany and who, I am happy to say, wrote a book against me. It was in response to a book I had written about which I will talk later. The title of my book was *We Jews*. The title of his was *We German Jews*.[69] It was an exercise in sheer futility, morally and intellectually obnoxious, but, nevertheless, an expression of some streams within German Jewry whose adherents held stubbornly to their convictions that sixteen hundred years of German-Jewish history could not be wiped out and that they were at least as German as the others. My father, whom I had urged to sell his properties and leave the country, once said to me: "What can Hitler do to us? Hitler is, after all, a foreigner, born and raised in Austria." This was a typical expression of the opinion of a very large number of German Jews, probably the majority of them.

For us Zionists, the great time had come. Theodor Herzl's prediction, which he entered into his diary some fifty years before Hitler, had come true. Catastrophe had overtaken German Jewry and would soon overtake all of European Jewry. None of us doubted that Hitler's military plans were to conquer the world. The Zionist movement began to understand its great opportunity. We had been right in saying all along that Hitler should be taken seriously and that there was no sense in continuing life in Germany. We urged mass immigration to Palestine. In the following years we reached

67. In 1927.
68. In fact, Max Naumann emigrated to the United States after his organization, which had about 3,500 members at its height, was disbanded by the Nazis and he died there in 1939.
69. The intellectual historian and theologian Hans-Joachim Schoeps (1909–1980) founded a somewhat more moderate organization, Deutscher Vortrupp, Gefolgschaft deutscher Juden, in 1933. In 1934, he published *Wir deutschen Juden*, directed in part against Prinz's *Wir Juden*. After the war, Schoeps returned from Swedish exile to teach at the University of Erlangen.

an agreement with the German government, according to which certain transfers of money would take place from German Jews to Palestine.[70] We were criticized for this, but it did save the lives of thousands of people.

During those days the Zionist newspaper the *Jüdische Rundschau* began to play a leading role. Its subscriptions tripled within a few weeks and it became the voice of German Jewry. Its editor was one of the most gifted and best educated newspapermen in our world. His name was Robert Weltsch,[71] a Jew from Prague who belonged to the circle of Kafka and others; a Hebraist, an Arabist, and until this very day—although he has just celebrated his eighty-fifth birthday—one of the best and greatest political analysts I know. When Hitler came to power, Weltsch published an editorial on the front page with the headline across the entire paper reading: "Bear it with pride— the yellow badge." We did not have to wear the yellow badge yet, but there were rumors that soon every Jew would have to wear a yellow armband or a yellow star. At the very beginning of the Hitler regime, every Jew had the letter "J" stamped in his passport, which meant Jew.[72] Every Jewish woman had to add to her first name the name of Sarah, and every man the name of Israel.[73] Quite clearly, we had become third-rate citizens. This classification as non-Aryans, not permitted to work and not to be treated with any kindness or consideration, became a matter of daily experience. The Jews were suddenly seized by a collective neurosis of fear and trepidation, and our services at the synagogues became a refuge for our people and a source of consolation and pride.

In 1935, I wrote an article in the *Jüdische Rundschau* entitled "Ghetto 1935."[74] It became a famous piece and was translated into many languages, for I pointed out that the ghetto was outside the synagogue, in the streets, and even in the homes where everyone could be arrested at the slightest

---

70. The reference is to the so-called Ha'avarah Transfer Agreement, concluded in the summer of 1933. It permitted sums in Reichsmark deposited by Jews in Germany to be used to pay for German goods exported to Palestine. Jewish immigrants were then able to receive the equivalent value in local currency once they arrived at their destination.

71. Robert Weltsch (1891–1982) edited the *Jüdische Rundschau* from 1918 to 1938, when he was able to emigrate to Palestine. However, he spent most of the remainder of his life in London, where he edited the *Leo Baeck Institute Year Book* from 1956 to 1978.

72. The introduction of a large "J" into Jewish passports did not occur until the ordinance of October 5, 1938. It was prompted by the Swiss government's desire to determine which prospective immigrants from Germany were Jews.

73. This ordinance, too, came later, likewise in the year 1938.

74. The full translated title is "Life without Neighbors—Ghetto 1935." It appeared in the issue for April 17, 1935.

provocation, and often without any provocation.[75] But the synagogue was safe. There one was among Jews. There you heard the old melodies. There you heard, at least in my synagogue, a sermon dealing with the problems of the times. All of my synagogues[76] were so crowded that people stood in the aisles, and very often on the steps leading to the altar. Among those who came, I discovered very assimilated and often converted Jews. Something new had been added to the service. As I entered the synagogue one day, I found myself confronted by two men who informed me they were members of the Gestapo and that from now on they would be at every one of my services and would be supervising every speech I delivered anywhere. One of them was a man with a round, fat face and a charming smile, who was particularly polite to me, almost asking my forgiveness for the fact that he was one of the supervising Gestapo agents. His name was Kuchmann.[77] He listened to me carefully, and since he was not really convinced of the righteousness and verity of the National Socialist regime, I was able to convince him of the things that I tried to say to my Jews. Later he would play a decisive role in my life. He became part of the office of Adolf Eichmann[78] and very often, as we are going to see, at moments of great danger it was he who rescued me, and in the end he saved my life. I looked for him after the war, but was told that he had been found to make common cause with the Jews and that Eichmann had had him killed in Prague. I also found out later that some of the Zionist leaders undertook to bribe him with sums of money, which to him were very large and were hidden in a box of cigars. I did not know about it and I can only think of the man with profound gratitude. I always regretted that I could not express my feelings to him when I returned to Germany after the war.

Altogether every service was stirring and exciting. The one I remember best was on the evening before April 1, 1933. The first of April was a Sabbath and the government had decreed it should be proclaimed a day of boycott

75. In fact, Prinz wrote: "When [upon entry] the door of our house closes and locks behind us we come out of the ghetto." He does not mention the synagogue as a refuge.

76. Prinz means those community synagogues in which he regularly preached.

77. Gestapo Obersturmbahnführer Kuchmann's name appears in the records of the Adolf Eichmann trial. Rabbi Max Nussbaum, a colleague of Prinz in Berlin, notes that with typical German thoroughness Kuchmann had studied Jewish history and that he had fallen in love with Revisionism, the right wing of the Zionist movement. Max Nussbaum, "Zionism under Hitler," *Congress Weekly,* September 11, 1942, 12–15. Prinz was able to gain Kuchmann's favor through timely bribes.

78. Adolf Eichmann (1906–1962) headed the Gestapo's Jewish section. After the war he escaped to Argentina where he was captured by Israeli agents in 1960. He was tried and sentenced to capital punishment by an Israeli court in Jerusalem for crimes against the Jewish people.

against Jews. It was to be a national holiday. In front of every Jewish store and every office of a Jewish lawyer or physician, two or more storm troopers stood, preventing customers and clients from entering the buildings. Those who entered were photographed and later beaten and arrested. In smaller towns on the preceding evening, the storm troopers rounded up the Jews and chased them into the forests around the villages, men and women together. Then in the presence of the women, the men had to undress and stand naked throughout the night. They were beaten with steel whips. Many of them died on the spot; others were maimed for life; and even those who recovered never forgot what happened during the night of the last day of March. Since the first of April was a Sabbath, the Friday night service, which was to begin at eight o'clock, was an unforgettable experience. People stood by the hundreds outside the synagogue waiting for the doors to open. When they finally did open at seven o'clock, people streamed into the synagogue until no one else could enter, for every seat and every spot in the building was taken. There was a solemnity that had very little to do with the artificial pious experience that we call by that name. There was a mixture of hope and fear, of trembling and pride. The old prayers suddenly leaped to life and had new meaning. Verses that had been written in the Middle Ages suddenly became an interpretation of what we Jews were going through. The prayer for humility, which asks the Jew to be quiet and enduring in the face of indignities and insults, became one of the most important prayers of the whole service: "And to such as curse me let my soul be dumb."[79] It was a very difficult attitude to assume but it gave people a great deal of strength.

My Friday night service in the presence of the two Gestapo agents was a passionate attack on the government but, strangely enough, the Gestapo agents did not report me. The most stirring part of the service was the singing of the Shema.[80] We, of course, had a cantor, a choir, and an organ, but somehow when the people rose to sing the Shema, the choir could not sing and the organist did not play. I have never in my life, before or since, better understood the meaning of the Shema as an identification with our people, past and present, in joy and tragedy. All of us cried but, nevertheless, we sang. We sang through our tears, and although it may not have been musically perfect, the singing was like a great Jewish symphony that underscored our fate—that we were going to bear it with pride and dignity, and that

79. This sentence occurs in the concluding meditation following the petitionary prayers in the daily and Sabbath services.
80. The so-called "watchword" of the Jewish faith: "Hear, O Israel, the Lord our God, the Lord is One."

come what may, we would fight for our lives. It was a song of determination and rebellion. I began to understand that the Shema itself was a great revolution and that we were a part of it. These were the voices of a few thousand people—men, women and children. Leaving the synagogue after the service we all felt stronger and completely united. There was no longer a single stranger among us. We were all related, related by blood that was to be shed and by life that could be snuffed out.

Let me now add a few sentences about preaching under the Hitler regime. The sermon, as such, was a rather foreign element in the Jewish service. Until this very day, Orthodox rabbis preach only once a year, on the great Sabbath before Passover.[81] The modern sermon is a Christian invention that we added to our Liberal service at the beginning of the nineteenth century when rabbis began to wear robes, when services began to become orderly, when the organ was introduced, and a mixed choir began to sing. Nevertheless, the sermon became an integral part of the Liberal Jewish service, particularly since most Jews did not understand the Hebrew texts and were looking for something that would elevate them spiritually, giving them a moment to meditate, or for half an hour to partake in a world of which they knew little. But the sermon remained a rather stultifying, tightly structured affair consisting of three parts that were clearly defined, as taught by our professor of homiletics. I had never adhered to this structure and had always thought of such homiletics as something restrictive that prevented any kind of genius and rhetorical ability from developing. From the very beginning, I preached a different kind of sermon—but nevertheless a sermon it was. Although sometimes I dealt with problems of the day, most of my sermons were based on readings from the Torah or spiritual matters. But now that Hitler had come, all this changed radically.

The very fact that Hitler was now in power, that anti-Jewish laws had been issued and promulgated, that the danger to the lives of our people was very real, that they had been seized by a collective neurosis, a sense of inferiority and guilt that required therapy, made me feel most clearly that for me preaching under the Hitler regime had to be dedicated to the situation as it really existed. I felt very strongly about the fact that those people who came to hear me should leave the service with a feeling of physical and psychological improvement, with greater strength and courage.

It was not enough to deal with the problems that beset us. These problems were very clear. We had become third-class citizens. We also had become part of a situation of utter uncertainty. To live under a dictatorship means to be deprived of knowing what could happen the next day. Citi-

81. Actually, twice a year. Also on the Sabbath of Repentance during the High Holy Days.

zens had no rights; but the Jews, who were not even citizens—or at least had been deprived of their rights of citizenship—had no say in anything that was planned or that had already happened. It was not a government by the people. Parliament did not exist because there was no opposition. The Nazi Party itself had no voice in matters of state, either militarily or economically. Decisions were made by the Führer. Even the inner circle, which may have recognized the methodical insanity that obsessed Hitler, had little to say. Their leader was evidently a man of genius, however evil. It was he who reigned and not merely ruled. What kind of dreams or nightmares he might have would determine the situation on the following day. To preach in this kind of total uncertainty was probably the greatest challenge of my life. Jews had become a downtrodden, degraded, and humiliated clan. I considered it my task to make them into a proud people. I had to preach a sermon that was based on the notion that the anvil was nobler than the hammer, a sermon that pitied the persecutor and ennobled the victim. I found it humanly impossible for us to consider ourselves to be the selected victims of a dictator. I thought this invited collective suicide. In some cases, as we shall see, suicides took place, but I was thinking of the whole people, all 550,000 of them. If they were selected to be victims, then life made no sense at all.

It was quite clear to me what I should do in my sermons. My goal was to make my people into a group of human beings who would feel superior, not in spite of, but because they had been selected as targets of hatred and murder. I wanted them to rediscover their own nobility, then arrive personally and individually at a decision that they were infinitely superior to the so-called Aryans, that their nobility went back thousands of years—a nobility of love and not hate, of humanity and not brutality. There are a thousand variations on this topic, and I used them all in the four long years I spent under the Hitler regime. In addition, I had plenty of time to teach, and I spoke at hundreds of meetings of the Zionist organization, which had become a movement swollen in its ranks by tens of thousands who suddenly considered Zionism to be the only viable guidelines for their lives. I spoke every day, sometimes several times a day. I had no free nights.

I soon found that our people needed courage, but they also needed knowledge. I therefore began to teach large classes. My topics were Jewish history and Jewish thought. My one-volume Jewish history became a bestseller within the first three months of the Hitler regime and had to be reprinted several times.[82] There were people who kept this book on their night tables, reading it over and over again. I once received a note from Dr. Leo

82. See note 50, above. Prinz is referring to the second edition, which appeared as *Illustrierte Jüdische Geschichte* (Berlin, 1933).

Baeck, who was so much older than I and so much wiser, telling me that he had visited an old friend of his who considered my history to be his Bible. I was also aware of the fact that it was not enough to write a history. Our people needed something quite different.

I must deviate for a moment from my public life and return to my personal life, although the two were intertwined and can hardly be separated. During the month of April, toward the end of the month, Michael was born.[83] He was Hilde's first child. Since she married a widower with a child it was only natural that she should have wanted a child of her own. My premonitions about birth and its dangers were still very vivid in my mind. I have never overcome my mother's death, or for that matter, Lucie's. I therefore insisted upon Hilde being attended by an obstetrician connected with a maternity hospital so that infections from other patients could be avoided. Hilde went to the hospital twice for false alarms. She was, after all, only nineteen years old and I took her there, only to return shortly afterwards. But then the labor pains grew stronger and she knew her time had come. Michael's birth was uncomplicated. The hospital was Catholic and she was therefore given no anesthesia. But, nevertheless, she got through it well, being young and strong; she was so determined to have a child. Michael turned out to be a very sweet and lovable baby who had to spend the first years of his life under the Hitler regime. I still remember him at the age of three playing around a lake with other children when storm troopers came and chased him away, calling him all kinds of names. I have always thought that this incident left an indelible mark on him, but I cannot be sure of it. At any rate, we now had two little children in our house.

It was while Hilde was still nursing Michael, probably in the month of May, that I delivered a speech at a Zionist meeting that was attended by some two thousand people. In this speech I attacked the Jewish establishment for closing its eyes to reality. As I was talking about the Jewish leadership and the crime it committed by neglecting the real needs of the Jewish people, the meeting was suddenly invaded by a group of storm troopers who marched in, interrupting my speech and arresting me. The people were flabbergasted and the meeting was hushed. They stood there in amazement and horror watching me being led away by three storm troopers in brown uniforms. For some strange reason I was not afraid of them at all. I was young, impertinent, fresh, and aggressive and knew that nothing could happen to me. Although somehow deep within me I knew that an arrest under the Hitler regime could lead to death, even that thought did not intimidate me. I

83. Michael Prinz (1933–1998) became an accountant and then a travel agent in New Jersey. He suffered from neurofibromatosis, an incurable, debilitating disease.

waved to the people and asked them not to inform Hilde about it. Unfortunately, an idiotic cousin of mine in the audience called Hilde to tell her that I was being led away by storm troopers. What that meant to the young woman nursing Michael I can only imagine.

A car was waiting outside. I was accompanied by two storm troopers, one of them very young and one of them a middle-aged man. When the young man began to hit me, I immediately resorted, for the first time, to a method I used during the entire Hitler regime. I always understood the German mentality and knew there was no sense in arguing my case with the young man. He saw a Jew before him and so his reflexes told him to hit me. Quite loudly I yelled at him, "Don't you dare touch a clergyman!" He immediately stopped, and the older man looked at him and said to him, "As he told you, we should never touch a clergyman." For the time being this saved my life. I had to sit between the two uniformed men while the car took me far away to a place that I later discovered had formerly been a theater, but was now occupied by the storm troopers, a combination of headquarters and jail. When I arrived, I discovered that it was not only I who had been arrested but also ten other Zionists who had functioned as chairmen, ushers, and so on at that meeting. We were asked to form a line. We did so, standing there motionless and not permitted to speak. Soon there appeared an officer in the black uniform of the SS elite. He went from one man to another, asking each of them to shake hands with him. When the prisoner extended his hand to do so, he not only refused to take his hand but slapped his face with extraordinary violence. When he reached the third man, I suddenly recognized him. He was the most brilliant of my fellow students who had attended a very difficult seminar on philosophy with me at the Berlin University and had received his Ph.D. degree summa cum laude. I was amazed that a man who had studied philosophy and was so brilliant could bring himself to such brutal acts, dealing as he did with completely innocent people. It was the beginning of my skepticism toward the kind of education that I had always thought served to build human character rather than merely to hand down knowledge. What good, I thought, was philosophy if it had not influenced the student to be not merely knowledgeable but also decent?

He was coming closer to me, for he had already beaten up the man next to me who had, unfortunately, also stretched out his hand. And then he stood in front of me. We looked at each other and evidently he recognized me. I said to him, "We once studied philosophy together. You will not, I hope, expect me to afford you the opportunity to try out your philosophy, which evidently has changed from that of your former classmates." He stood there for a moment, turned quickly and left the room without touching me.

We were then taken into an almost completely dark room. In the very dim light I saw that the walls were covered with pictures of guns and very minute technical drawings. We stood there for a long time. Soon the names of several people were called out one by one and I do not know what happened to them. Finally, my turn came. I was called and was blinded by the light in the next room. I looked at it. Since this was like theater, I immediately thought of the first act of a play, for the arrangements in this large room were so theatrical. There were beds on which I saw men in uniform, some of them with women, and in the center of the room was a table around which sat officers of the SS, some of them high-ranking officers. I was asked to come forward to the table but was not asked to sit down. I heard a very gruff voice say to me, "You are herewith accused of having insulted the Führer." Here was my opportunity. I knew my forte was to speak convincingly and that his question called for the delivery of a speech to try to persuade these SS officers of my own character and of the cause for which I stood.

I immediately corrected the accusation by saying that I would in no way dare to attack the Führer of the new German Reich. They ought not to consider me so dumb and unintelligent. Even if I would want to do that, I would not do so publicly because I knew better. I knew of the fate that awaited those who had the audacity to attack the great leader of the great new German government. I had, in fact, attacked the leadership of my own people. "I am a Jew," I said, "and as a Jew I am at liberty to attack my own people." After that I began an analysis of the Jewish leadership. I told them I was a Zionist and that I had advised my people to leave Germany and leave the German people to their own fate, which they had chosen for themselves, and to the life to which they were entitled. I agreed with the Führer that Germany ought to become a country that was *judenfrei,* free of Jews. And then I began to talk about the Zionist goal of creating a state in Palestine. I had just said the first sentence about that when suddenly a colonel of the SS, a rather good-looking man, interrupted me and said, "You want your people to go to Palestine?" I replied, "Under all circumstances." He then smiled and said to me, "If you do that, promise me that you will prevent them from going to Afula.[84] That place is not good enough for anyone, even for the Jews." I looked at him in amazement. Then, changing to a conversational manner, I said to him, "What do you know about Palestine?" He answered, "During the First World War I served as an engineer in Palestine and I know a great deal about it. And as far as you are concerned, you are herewith discharged."

84. Afula is a town in the Jezreel Valley, founded in 1925.

It was two o'clock in the morning and I asked what his name was. Unfortunately, I have forgotten it, but he was later to play some role in my life. I said, "Colonel, when I leave this building, someone must take me across the courtyard. Last week I buried a man who was killed by your people while he was crossing this courtyard. I want you to guarantee my safety so that I will leave this building and courtyard alive." He was probably irked by my impudence but he called to the two storm troopers and said to them, "Take this man across the courtyard. It is very dark and if you kill him, no one will see you. But I know your names and if you kill this man, I will see to it that you will be killed immediately thereafter. I have guaranteed his life and I don't want you to betray me."

I was walked across the courtyard. In spite of their calm assurance, I was not completely certain that they would obey. On the other hand, I knew enough of the mentality of the Germans to be confident that an order given to them by a high-ranking officer would be obeyed. And it was. I left the courtyard and took a taxi home, arriving there at three in the morning. Hilde had not gone to bed; she was waiting for me. The best news was my appearance in the house.

In the summer of 1933, the inner circle of my friends decided that we should spend the summer vacation together. We did not know what would be happening in the following year, whether there would be time for us to spend a few months together, or where any one of us would be. We therefore decided to go to Denmark. We found out that on an island off the coast of Denmark called Bornholm there were lovely places where we could spend a completely carefree summer, forgetting about Hitler and our problems and not thinking of the fact that for some of us this might be the last summer of our lives. Before we left, I was contacted by Erich Reiss, one of the big publishers, who was also a literary adviser to Max Reinhardt, the theatrical producer. Reiss was a very interesting and strange man.[85] Reinhardt used to call him "my mimosa" because he was as touchy and vulnerable as the mimosa plant.[86] Reiss asked me to write a political book addressed to the Jews who had to live under the Hitler regime, who did not know what Jewish life really meant and did not know how to cope with it, either personally, politically, or

---

85. Erich Reiss, who founded his publishing house in Berlin in 1908, produced beautiful and well-designed books. He also published theater periodicals. After 1933, he began to issue books of Jewish interest, but soon thereafter emigrated to the United States.
86. The German expression, "empfindlich wie eine Mimose," refers to a person who is oversensitive.

economically. I agreed to write such a book and to call it *We Jews*—and I decided to write it during our vacation in Bornholm.[87]

Hilde had to stay at home to take care of Michael and planned to come two weeks later. We were a group of fifteen people or so, among them my closest friends, Gerhart Jacobson, Benno Cohn[88] and Hans Levy,[89] all of them very talented people and intimate friends—all of them former members of the Blue-White movement. We had lived together for such a long time that we had a common language and terminology. It was almost like a sect. We had a great time together that summer. We drank a great deal of aquavit and ate marvelous food at the hotel. I took my typewriter into the cliffs above the ocean and every day I wrote ten or more pages. I would then take these pages to my friends in the evening and read to them what I had written. There would be critical analysis of these pages and I made corrections that were suggested. But the book was of such immediate concern to me and had to be written in a language that conveyed the urgency of the problem that there were few such corrections. It began with a poetic introduction about the wandering Jew, Jewish destiny, and Jewish fate.

Two weeks later Hilde came via Copenhagen. I was very glad to see her, but it was not very easy for her to adjust to our group. She was, after all, an outsider, and my friends, particularly Benno, were not very tactful. No one really understood that she was just a kid, nineteen years old, who came into a group that had been in existence for more than ten years. We had our own language, which she did not understand, our own jokes, and our very own relationships, men and women mixing together without any conventional considerations. The island was so beautiful, however, and my work so satisfying, that I hoped in the end she would also enjoy it although she was full of anxieties that I have not yet forgotten.

My publisher was very fearful that I might forget about the book and not deliver the manuscript in time. But I did, and he was very happy with it. German publishing houses did not have editors. No changes were made. The book went into print immediately and three months later it was on the market. It was an instant success and sold over 100,000 copies. It became the bible of the Jews who lived under the Hitler regime and it established me as a writer. Jewish publishing houses, which were among the most important in

---

87. *Wir Juden. Besinnung, Rückblick, Zukunft* (Berlin: Erich Reiss, 1934). It is dedicated to "the friends."

88. Benno Cohn (1894–1975), a Zionist politician, left Germany for Palestine in 1939. He represented the Liberal Party in the Israeli Parliament from 1961 to 1965.

89. Hans Jochanan Levy (1901–1945) left Germany as early as 1933 for Palestine, where he received a professorship at the Hebrew University in the field of classical antiquity.

Europe, went out of business since they were not permitted to publish German literature or even foreign literature in the German language. The great writers were left without a publisher. Many of them left Germany in order to live in freedom under most difficult conditions in other countries, whose languages they did not know. Some of them committed suicide; others continued to write their books in German and have them translated. An outstanding example of a great writer living in a foreign country, not knowing its language but continuing to write great books, was Thomas Mann, who was married to the daughter of Prof. Pringsheim, a converted Jew.[90] I met him here in this country.[91] He had not changed at all, remaining a member of the German literary nobility until his death in Switzerland.

During the four years of the Hitler regime that I lived in Berlin, I had almost daily experiences that translated a political situation into the very personal terms of a human life. The first of many such experiences, all of which I will not be able to describe, was the death of one of my most brilliant students. His body was found in the street, the story being that a storm trooper had pushed him from the windowsill of his home. A few days later the funeral service of this boy, who was nineteen years old, took place. I came to the service, to be conducted in the hall of our central cemetery, with great apprehension. Entering the park, I saw a man sitting on a bench crying bitterly and singing at the same time. He repeated again and again in Hebrew the sentence from the great prayer of the High Holy Days: "Our Father, our King, avenge the blood that was innocently shed."[92] It was the boy's father. He was immediately taken to an insane asylum and I hope he died soon thereafter. There was still enough misery at the service itself and so much crying that I decided not to deliver a eulogy. We buried him quietly; I have forgotten the location of his grave nor do I even remember his name.

Another case, which was rather bizarre, was that of a famous physician. He had been the army physician in charge of high-ranking officers, and I met him through Hilde's Uncle Ludwig, who had been with him in Belgium during the First World War. The doctor was married to a member of the famous Cassirer family, which owned a large gallery.[93] Each member of the family had a large collection of Impressionists, and when I visited the doc-

90. Alfred Pringsheim (1850–1941), a mathematician, had been a professor at the University of Munich until his retirement in 1922. He emigrated to Zurich in 1939.

91. Thomas Mann (1875–1955) lived in Pacific Palisades, California, from 1938 to 1953.

92. The exact text is: "Our Father, our King, avenge (before our eyes) the blood of Your servants that has been shed." It is generally omitted from Liberal prayer books.

93. Probably Erich Cassirer (1890–1963), who owned a Berlin gallery specializing in old Chinese art until it was expropriated by the Nazis.

tor's elegant home I found that he possessed some of the most precious examples of that school of painting. He had become the physician of the German aristocracy. For all practical purposes, he had no Jewish patients. As a matter of fact, although he was a Jew by blood and family, he was completely inactive Jewishly, did not participate in any activity, and was totally assimilated. Nevertheless, he owned a little Hebrew prayer book that he kept on his night table. He showed it to me and said, "This is my bridge to my people. I have no other." Once, during the first year of the Hitler regime, I received a message from this doctor. It was conveyed to me through Ludwig Bendix.[94] He invited me to come to his house because he had to discuss an important matter with me. He informed me that on the first of April, the day of the Hitler boycott, his shingle had been covered with antisemitic slogans. In accordance with Nazi law, he was thrown back into the Jewish community and had to consider himself a Jew, although in reality he was not a Jew at all. He had therefore decided to commit suicide. His reason for seeing me was to inform me that in two weeks he would be inviting 150 of his friends and their wives to a dinner party. But around midnight he would ask the people to listen to him and he would then without any further explanation tell the story of his life. "In reality," he said, "I am doing that for you. On the morning after the party I shall shoot myself. I am a very good shot, you know. When I will be buried, I do not want you to hear the story of my life from anyone else. But I will be dead and I don't want my wife or anybody else to tell you who I really was. My story will probably be long, but it will be very honest. A few days later, when you bury me, I want you to say the things that I consider to be important."

It was a ghoulish idea and I hesitated to go to his very elegant house and join the 150 gay people in a fantastic meal of French food, the most costly wines, and altogether have a marvelous time. But I did go, and from time to time I looked at the physician. He seemed to be enjoying himself tremendously, going from one couple to the other, telling jokes, and joining in the frolicking mood of the affair. At midnight he asked his guests to sit around and listen to him. This, too, was a rather strange idea, using the midnight gimmick of fairy tales in order to inform only one of the people there about his life. I don't think anyone suspected he would commit suicide. I know that his wife did not have the foggiest idea as to what he planned to do. I sat there in a corner listening carefully to what was in reality material for my eu-

94. Hilde's uncle, Ludwig Bendix, shortly thereafter emigrated to the United States, where he became a Wall Street banker.

logy. I still did not think he would do what he had intended. At that last moment I hoped he would not be able to commit suicide.

On the next day, at eight o'clock in the morning, I was called by his wife who informed me that her husband had committed suicide. She was completely unprepared. I conducted the service, which was attended by hundreds of people. Since he had been the physician of the general staff of the German army and had not yet been dismissed as a Jew, six German aircraft circled around the cemetery overhead while he was carried to his grave. I never told his wife about my meeting with her husband. She was not aware that the story of his life, which he told at the party, was premeditated, although she had certain suspicions. She was not very bright, but she was bright enough to understand that the time had come for her to leave Germany. A few months after her husband's funeral she moved to South Africa where she died, an old, rich woman, who left her precious collection to her children.

Another case I remember vividly is that of another physician. It was early in 1933. He, too, was a completely assimilated Jew, married to a non-Jewish woman with several children, all of them reared in the Protestant faith. He had served as a high-ranking officer in the German army and was a super-patriot. One day a patient came to him and he prescribed some castor oil for her to cure an intestinal illness. She told him she did not like castor oil, and in jest he replied, "Why don't you sing the Horst Wessel song, the National Socialist anthem, three times while you take it, and you won't feel a thing." She left his office and immediately went to the headquarters of the storm troopers, informing them of what she considered to be an insult to the sacred anthem of the Hitler regime. The doctor was arrested and taken to a certain well-known cellar the name of which I have forgotten, but known as a cellar of death where hundreds of people had been slain. The doctor was forced to undress and then several storm troopers used steel whips on him. He fainted and his entire body was bleeding. Then the commander of the storm troopers assembled some twenty men and ordered them to urinate on the man's open wounds as he was already dying. He died of poisoning. I saw his death certificate: it read that he had died of pneumonia.

I will never forget the funeral service. His Christian wife came to me. She was more Jewish than her husband ever was. She told me what had happened, piecing together bits of information she had received. I agreed to officiate at the funeral service. It was one of the first of many for victims of the Nazi regime at which I officiated. The congregation that assembled there to pay their respects to the man seemed to consist only of Christians. I was not aware that one Jewish man was among them. I began my eulogy with the following words: "I am about to bury a man, a human being, who was also a caring and skillful doctor. His patients are in this room. They came here to express their gratitude to him. But if you would open the coffin, you would understand that I am not merely burying a man. I herewith bury German civilization. You cannot see it, but in this coffin lie Bach and Beethoven, Goethe and Hölderlin." We buried him quietly and nothing happened.

However, a year later I was arrested by the Gestapo. The one Jewish man who had attended the service had been arrested and told the arresting officer that it was not right to take him to Gestapo headquarters while Dr. Prinz was still free in spite of the fact that he had insulted the German nation in his eulogy for the physician slain by the storm troopers. He quoted me verbatim. Fortunately, I was warned by my friend Kuchmann, the Gestapo agent, that I would be arrested because of the eulogy. I was therefore prepared when I appeared at the appointed time and was interrogated for many hours. I had my own method of acting during such interrogations, which I underwent hundreds of times during the four years. I knew the German mentality, and I used that knowledge profusely. I looked at the interrogating officer and said to him, "You will understand that I am a Ph.D. of a German university and therefore you know that I am not dumb. I want to ask you one question. Would a man of my intelligence be so dumb as to use the phrases that I was quoted as having spoken in the presence of several hundred Aryans who attended the funeral service?" I looked at him sternly and waited for the effect of my argument, which I had expressed with particular emphasis. After a few rather anxious moments, he said to me, "You are right and you are free." It was one of many such experiences that taught me what it meant to live under the Hitler regime. Still, I was doing the most outrageous things, violating every law of the land and dancing on a volcano, not noticing any dangers or being frightened by what might happen to me. I lived under divine protection. That in the end nothing happened to me, that I never saw a concentration camp, that I was not killed by the Nazis, is ample proof of it.

In those days the Nazis were discussing among themselves what to do with the Jews, as they had not yet decided on what was later called "The Final Solution." There were still intellectual groups among the higher-ranking SS officers who believed in a civilized solution to the Jewish problem. They relegated this question to the Department of Culture, headed by Dr. Goebbels.[95] It was there that they created a Jewish subdivision. The head of this

95. Goebbels was officially propaganda minister, but included culture under his aegis.

division was Dr. Hans Hinkel,[96] a rather strange man, and I believe a homosexual. (Homosexuality was altogether a very widespread phenomenon, particularly in the SS.)[97] Hinkel's idea was that the Jews should have their own cultural sphere. The Jewish actors had been eliminated from entertainment and theater, Jewish musicians could no longer be members of a symphony orchestra, most of the great conductors had left the country and the remaining ones were not able to get jobs. It was Hinkel's idea that the Jews, wherever they could, should form their own cultural groups. After all, in spite of the fact that there were no walls, we did live in a ghetto wherever we lived.

The structure decided upon by the Department of Culture was an organization called the Jewish Cultural Association (Jüdischer Kulturbund). A group of Jews who were in the entertainment and theatrical professions formed a board that was concerned with programs for the entire country. The leading spirit of this group was Dr. Singer, a rather talented man in many of the cultural fields.[98] The Kulturbund arranged for theatrical performances, symphonic music, and lectures. If I am not mistaken, it also purchased books from time to time. It was a going concern and extremely successful. Some of the well-known conductors became the leaders of newly formed Jewish orchestras, which offered a full program of classical music. The orchestras, of course, were not as good as the original symphony orchestras of Germany, but they were good enough and performed frequently. Thus jobs were created for Jewish musicians, conductors, and players of all instruments. The non-Jewish orchestras had great difficulty in getting non-Jewish musicians since, as is true of most symphony orchestras in the world, the majority of the players in Germany were Jewish.

I was the main lecturer of the group, spoke all over the country, and was very well paid for it. I could not fill all the engagements, but it gave me the opportunity to meet with the Jews even in smaller communities. It is impossible for me to describe now the extraordinary longing of the Jews for Jewish entertainment on every level and for Jewish lectures, particularly on problems of Jewish history and the present situation. The Nazi ghetto was, after all, a traumatic experience, which required some form of escape.

Along with the services in the synagogues, the activities of the Kultur-

96. Hans Hinkel, an early member of the Nazi party, served under Goebbels with special responsibility for overseeing Jewish cultural activities.
97. Prinz probably means the SA, among whose members homosexuality was common.
98. Kurt Singer (1885–1944) was a neurologist and also a music critic and choir director. From 1935 to 1938, he directed the National Association of Jewish Cultural Associations. He perished in Theresienstadt.

bund became the center of Jewish life. The Jews were culturally completely isolated. Wherever they lived, they were not permitted to attend theatrical performances, operas, and concerts.[99] In small towns they could not even go to movie theaters. In cities such as Berlin, which had a population of several million, we did not attend performances because it was very unpleasant to find yourself sitting next to an SS officer, and there was always the danger of violence against Jews in the audience. The entertainment offered through the Kulturbund—by actors, musicians, and lecturers—was therefore of enormous importance. I was invited to give a course on Jewish history. Seven thousand people registered for the course so that we had to rent a hall seating three thousand. I taught the same material twice a week to the largest audience I ever had for an adult course. The hunger for Jewish knowledge was beyond description. To most of the people who came, Jewish history was something completely new. But now, under the Hitler regime, they had become living witnesses to a Jewish history of which previously they knew nothing.

In those days, the Jewish Agency for Palestine quickly discovered that Germany was a country from which immigration could be expected. And indeed the year 1934 was the beginning of a large and important wave of German-Jewish immigrants. It no longer mattered who was a Zionist and who was not. The idea of getting out of the country was much more important than membership in an organization. Among the most successful new settlers in what was Palestine were anti-Zionists who turned into great patriots of what later became the Jewish state.

The Jewish Agency created an office in Berlin, which was called the Palestine Office. In addition to the German-Jewish staff, they sent two *shlichim*[100] to Berlin. Both of them were to become very important in later years. During their stay in Berlin for several years we became well acquainted and one of them began to play a very important role in my personal life. Their names were Levi Shkolnik and Enzo Sereni. Shkolnik was a very quiet man who worked systematically without any fanfare. Because of that we always thought of him as the less effective of the two. But that was not entirely fair. In his own quiet manner he reached a great many people and imparted the message of the State[101] with great sincerity. After the State was founded, he became secretary of the treasury, and then a few years later

99. A general prohibition was not issued until November 12, 1938, apparently because the cultural performances would not have been able to survive without attendance by Jews.
100. The Hebrew word for *emissaries*.
101. Prinz either means the *yishuv* (the Jewish settlement in Palestine) or the *idea* of a Jewish state.

prime minister of Israel, having changed his name to Eshkol.[102] He was a good and loyal friend, and later during the period when he was prime minister, he proved his friendship to me. I cherish a letter he sent to me after the Six-Day War, thanking me for what I had done as chairman of the Presidents Conference.[103]

Enzo Sereni was a completely different kind of person. He came from an ancient Roman family. His father, grandfather, and great-grandfather had been physicians to the king of Italy. They were a fully assimilated Italian family and Enzo was very Italian indeed. He spoke German with a strong Italian accent, but since he was linguistically very talented and a great speaker, his foreign accent did not disturb people but rather attracted them. When later he came to America to tell the story of Palestine and to enlist people in the Zionist movement, he was a complete failure. American Jews did not know that Italian Jews were almost more Italian than Jewish. His Italian accent in English reminded the Jews of the neighborhood barber, and he had to give up speaking in America. Knowing him was one of the most exciting experiences of my life. My house became the headquarters for the inner circle of the Zionist movement. We ate and drank together and, at times, when things became dangerous or when any of us returned from jail, we had drinking parties that almost resembled orgies. I remember that he preferred to drink Benedictine, which was very sweet, and often got drunk on it. He was a man of extraordinary charm, and women went wild over him; he, in turn, was wild about women. After his return to Palestine at the end of 1934, he founded the beautiful kibbutz of Givat Brenner. He married a girl from Rome and raised a family there. After the outbreak of the Second World War he suggested that a group of Palestinian Jews, who were trained as parachutists, should be dropped into various countries in order to counteract antisemitic activities and get people to Palestine. Since he had once been an officer in the Italian army and trained in parachuting, he volunteered to be one of the Palestine Jews who were selected for this dangerous job. As he was very valuable to the Jewish Agency, they tried to dissuade him, but they did not succeed; and so he parachuted with the others. He wanted to get to Italy where he would not be recognized as a Jew and be able to work with the Italian underground. The Roman Jews had not yet been deported; the Germans had not yet penetrated into Rome. By some accident that still

102. Levi Eshkol (1895–1969) served as Israeli secretary of the treasury from 1952 to 1963 and as prime minister from 1963 until 1969.
103. From 1965 to 1967, Prinz chaired the Conference of Presidents of Major Jewish Organizations, the principal representative body of American Jewry.

remains unexplained, Enzo landed behind the German lines where he was immediately arrested and sent from one concentration camp to the other. I understand that he was tortured in many of them. He was finally taken to Dachau where, according to some reports, he was shot.[104] To me and to those who worked with him and knew him he will remain unforgotten.

It was during the time that Shkolnik and Sereni worked with us that the Kulturbund was to have its first annual meeting, to be attended by Jews from all over the country. They had to get permission from Hinkel, the head of the Jewish Department of Goebbels's ministry, and they received it. It was suggested to me that I should be the keynote speaker. I thought that if I were to do that I should deliver a basic and major address on the life of the Jew under the Hitler regime. I therefore asked for an audience with Hinkel. I told him that I wanted to have an opportunity to speak freely and without any inhibitions, and that he should guarantee that I would not be arrested because of my speech. He said that he and his staff intended to attend the annual meeting and that he would be very happy indeed if I would deliver that kind of speech, which was needed, not merely for the Jews, but for the Nazis as well. As the spokesman for German Jewry, I should not feel in any way restricted and should say whatever I pleased, however critical it might be. He would discuss the matter with Goebbels and would guarantee my safety to prevent any kind of action against me.

The great day came. I deliberately dictated my speech, which was critical of the Nazi regime (it was later published).[105] Hinkel and his staff were present and seemed to be very much interested in what I had to say. I talked about the antiquity of German Jewry and the fact that the first synagogue built in Germany was in the year 324.[106] I spoke about Yiddish as a German dialect and that the caftan which Eastern European Jews wore as their garment had been worn by German peasants in the fourteenth century. I also spoke about Jewish values, the eternity of the Jewish people, and how the plan to exterminate the Jews of the world was an illusion since we would ex-

104. Enzo Sereni (1905–1944) served as an emissary of Palestinian Jewry to Germany and other European countries from 1931 to 1934. His visit to the United States must have taken place after Prinz was already living there. Sereni was indeed shot in Dachau on November 18, 1944. The kibbutz Netzer Sereni is named after him.

105. The speech at which Hinkel was present took place at a national convention of the cultural associations and was entitled "The Cultural Situation of the Jews in Germany and the Jewish Theater." It is mentioned in *Israelitisches Familienblatt*, September 10, 1936, and was printed there in the issue for October 7, 1936. Prinz had spoken for the Berlin association as early as 1934.

106. Prinz may be thinking of the Epistle of Emperor Constantine to the Cologne magistrates from the year 321, which contains the first mention of Jewish settlement in Germany.

ist forever, regardless of how many of us would die. The Jews who were sitting in front of me trembled because they were fearful that something would happen, not merely to me but to them, too. But nothing did. It was in the middle of my speech that the door suddenly opened and in marched a group of Gestapo agents headed by my friend Kuchmann. It was a demonstration of the tension that existed between the Gestapo and Goebbels's department. There were a great many such tensions between various Nazi establishments, and very often the left hand did not know what the right hand was doing. The Nazi regime was not always very efficient and the organization did not always function properly. I was very familiar with that conflict between the two Nazi establishments, so the presence of the Gestapo meant to me that it wanted to supervise Hinkel and not me. But the Jews in the audience, which consisted of something like five hundred people, did not know anything about it; the presence of a well-known agent was an additional threat to them. However, the meeting ended very peacefully. My speech was a great success because it was considered a challenge to the Nazi regime, and the Jews liked that.

In 1934 Hilde and I decided to go to Palestine. During the first year of the Hitler regime, and after that, hundreds of my pupils had gone to Palestine under the auspices of the program which was then already called Youth Aliyah. Miss Henrietta Szold, who was the president of Hadassah, became the great protector of the movement. I met her in Berlin; she was an extraordinary person. Her grandfather had been a rabbi in Baltimore when Lincoln was president.[107] She came from an old German-Jewish family that had settled in America at the beginning of the nineteenth century. She was very American and very Jewish, tremendously effective and incredibly humble.

Hilde and I went by train to Nice on the French Riviera because our boat was to leave from its harbor. It was a ship owned by the Cunard Line, one of the large passenger boats. It so happened that Hilde's Uncle Ludwig was vacationing in Nice, and we stayed with him at one of the famous luxury hotels. A few days later we sailed for Palestine.

On the boat was a large group of American Jewish passengers who were also going to Palestine for the first time in their lives. It was my first contact with American Jews—the women were all members of Hadassah. Many of them I would meet again later in America. We had a great time. After all, we were very young; Hilde was twenty-one and I was thirty-two. The company

107. Not her grandfather, but her father, Benjamin Szold (1829–1902), who came to the United States with his wife from his native Hungary in 1859 and served as rabbi of the conservative Oheb Shalom Congregation. Henrietta was born in Baltimore in 1860 and died in 1945.

was pleasant, the food was excellent (we, of course, traveled first class), and the anticipation of coming to Palestine, a country about which I had spoken for so many years, added a happy tension and expectation to the gaiety that prevailed on the boat. The fact that we were not in Germany and subject to all the restrictions of the Hitler regime was an additional bonus, which we enjoyed tremendously.

To be in Palestine for the first time in our lives was a great and indescribable experience. Our big boat landed in Jaffa since Haifa was not yet a harbor that could be used. Since our ship was too big to land in the port, we were taken to shore in little boats and then taken from the harbor to our small hotel in Tel Aviv. It was called *Dan* after the name of the owner, Kathe Dan. It was a little bit of a hotel, but except for the King David in Jerusalem, there were no big hotels in Palestine. Kathe Dan had been a member of my youth movement and was very happy to see us. The charge for a hotel room with breakfast was one pound, including the usual Palestinian breakfast. We began to see all of the country which, of course, was much smaller than Israel is today.[108] But Jerusalem was not divided and the Wailing Wall was not yet as commercialized as it is today. Jerusalem was the most important and most impressive experience. We went to all the little synagogues that existed in the Old City, some of them going back to the eighteenth century, as well as the marvelous places in Safed. But our main purpose was to see the young people who had been my students, for whom I had written the children's Bible and to whom I had told all the stories that, after all, happened in this country called Palestine.

I remember visiting a large group in En-Harod. The name of the place was taken from the well from which Gideon drank and the kibbutz was not far from the mountain on which Jonathan and Saul were killed.[109] So I told them the stories again, but now in a very real setting. What must have sounded like fairy tales when I told the stories in Berlin here became a living reality. We visited many other kibbutzim, and wherever we went we had friends, although the German-Jewish immigration was not yet in full swing. Several thousands of our people had come to Palestine, and I knew them all. After three weeks and many meetings we had to return to Jaffa to board our boat.

Both Hilde and I went downstairs to our cabin. We were too emotional

---

108. Prinz must be referring to the area of Jewish settlement, not to the boundaries of the British Mandate.
109. En-Harod is mentioned in Judg. 7:1. The modern En-Harod was founded in 1921. Two kibbutzim have existed by that name in the same vicinity.

to see the boat leave Palestine, and both of us literally cried when it finally happened. We were very eager and determined to return to Palestine and to settle there. I would have done it immediately had I not known that my job was with the German-Jewish community, which I thought needed me more urgently than did the Jews of Palestine. All the leaders of the Jewish Agency in pre-State Palestine were old friends and comrades of mine. I saw Ben-Gurion, Moshe Shertok, and Golda Meir and all the others who later were to become the top leaders of the new State of Israel—with which I will deal later on. We came back to Germany, to a situation that had become much more difficult.

There are some things that I have omitted until now but which were important to me. I remember that on Saturday, April 1st, the day of Hitler's boycott, my house looked like Grand Central Station. People walked in and out to get help because they wanted to leave Germany and they did not have enough money. In those days I gave of my own funds freely and went into debt in order to meet the people's needs. I was altogether quite irresponsible with money. Although it brought me a great deal of grief, I do not regret it at all now, because it was worthwhile. In the afternoon of the 1st of April there appeared at my house a tall, blonde, and blue-eyed lady, a Wagnerian figure, and definitely not a Jewess. I was very angry on that day. I said to her, "I am in no mood to see German Aryans in my house. I want you to state your case, but I will not offer you a chair to sit down." She seemed to be unimpressed by what I said and, standing up, said the following sentences: "My name is Claire Todtman. I am a German and a Christian. I am ashamed of both. I am married to a Jewish man who is not a member of the Jewish community. We are rich and ashamed of the fact that there is nothing we can do for the Jewish people. We have therefore decided that I should give you this." Thereupon she handed me two envelopes. One contained money equivalent to ten thousand dollars; the other contained a deed made out to me for a large piece of property containing several houses and a lake. It must have had about twenty acres of land. Then she said to me, "This is a little money that I want you to use and a deed to property that we have owned for a long time. I want you to work out a plan by which you can save Jewish children from the cruelty of the German streets so that they may have a place of refuge."

With that she left. I held these two envelopes in my hand. I was completely overwhelmed. This was exactly what I had in mind to do. My youth group had a membership of approximately one thousand. I could no longer handle them on the premises of the synagogue. They needed something new and something infinitely better. I went to my pulpit the next Friday night and I told my congregation the story that I have just related. I asked them to help me by sending me money so that I could protect the children. On Monday morning I had about ten thousand marks in my mail. I immediately inspected the property. It was indescribably beautiful and not very far from where we lived. I began to engage personnel: nurses, a psychiatrist, and group leaders. The "estate" became well known as an important place. Young people came every day. We needed a flag for what was commonly known as the Prinz Club. I had a meeting with the kids and we decided to have a black flag with a large yellow badge on it, and that each of us should wear a yellow badge in our lapel. I ordered some yellow metal badges made. Unfortunately, I did not keep any, although I am sure that some of the members of the club, who are now grown up, have kept them. We had daily programs, our most impressive one being on Saturday nights. I invented a new style of havdalah.[110] We gathered a thousand people around a bonfire, said all the blessings, and then sang for hours on end. Later this celebration marking the end of the Sabbath and the beginning of the week became an important event, for on the morning following it many kids were taken by their parents to the station from which they left for Palestine. The parents, as they bade farewell, knew very well they would never see them again unless they hurried and emigrated, which was a very difficult decision.

In my report about the Kulturbund I forgot to mention a rather interesting meeting with Mr. Hinkel. I met him in his office, which was situated in the building of Goebbels's ministerial department. There were several people with us and I do not now recall what we discussed. After the people attending the meeting left, I was alone with Hans Hinkel. He then said to me, "I have always wanted to tell you that I was born in Worms in the Rhineland. This, after all, was the city of Rashi.[111] To us, who were born in that city, the fact that such an important and brilliant Jewish scholar who came from France used to live there and preach and teach there was a source of great pride. It was that for me, too, and since we are alone I must tell you that it still is. The synagogue in our city is, as you know, a Romanesque building that will celebrate its nine hundredth anniversary in 1936.[112] I will not be there, but you will. Since you are dealing with me, I want you to know where I really stand." At that moment someone entered the room and our conversation ended. Hinkel could not add anything. A week later I saw in an antisemitic Nazi paper that he had written a very hostile report about

110. Havdalah is the ritual marking the conclusion of the Sabbath on Saturday evening.
111. Acronym for Rabbi Shelomo ben Yitzhak (1040–1107), the most significant Jewish biblical and talmudic commentator of the Middle Ages. He lived in Troyes, in France, but had studied in Worms.
112. The synagogue in Worms was completed in 1034.

me. I thought back to our conversation and could only pity the schizophrenia from which people like Hinkel suffered.

In 1936 the Zionist Congress was held in Lucerne, Switzerland.[113] We German delegates asked permission from the Gestapo to attend. After many weeks of waiting, we were told that we would be permitted to go to Lucerne under the condition that none of us would deliver a speech against the Hitler regime and that we would go under the supervision and constant surveillance of Mr. Schwartz. I have now forgotten his first name, but Mr. Schwartz was an interesting person. He was one of four Jewish members of the Gestapo. He was extremely intelligent and even brilliant, spoke many languages fluently, and was in charge of supervising Yiddish and Hebrew literature. He had been bought by the Gestapo. I remember very vividly how I once came to be interrogated by the Gestapo and Mr. Kuchmann said to me, "Schwartz is in the clink. We found him violating the law of racial purity. He had some sexual dealings with an Aryan." But he was discharged soon thereafter. I distrusted him more than an Aryan Gestapo agent. He was, of course, hated by the other members of the Gestapo. Somehow there was some decency left in these people; they despised a man who obviously betrayed his own people and they had no respect for him. I remember very well that at the beginning of the Hitler regime Max Naumann, about whom I spoke earlier, wrote a letter to the Gestapo telling them that I was attacking the Nazi government every Friday night. I was called to the Gestapo headquarters for interrogation, which was held in a magnificent Baroque palace where I had attended many balls given by the artistic community of Berlin. When I arrived, Kuchmann showed me Naumann's letter and said to me, "We had the duty to call you since the accusation is serious. But all I want to tell you is that all of us here will disregard the letter. He is a swine."

We arrived in Lucerne with many apprehensions. The city, of course, is beautiful and situated on a magnificent lake. Whenever we had time, we went swimming, sunbathing, and I had very interesting and pleasant meetings with many people there. I recall vividly my meeting with Moses Smoira who later became the first chief justice of the Supreme Court of Israel,[114] and Felix Rosenblüth, who later became Israel's first minister of justice.[115] But

113. The Nineteenth Zionist Congress was held in Lucerne in 1935, the Twentieth in Zurich in 1937. Prinz is referring to the 1935 Congress, as is clear from the stamps in his passport.

114. Moses (Moshe) Smoira (1888–1961) held the position of presiding judge of the Supreme Court of Israel from 1948 to 1954.

115. Felix Rosenblüth, later known as Pinchas Rosen (1906–1985), one of the founders of the Zionist youth organization Blau-Weiss, played a large role in European Zionism. He was Israeli minister of justice from 1948 to 1961.

the most important meeting during the Congress was our first encounter with Jews from foreign countries from whom we had been separated since the beginning of the Hitler regime, particularly American Jews. Among the American Jews was a man whom I greatly admired. His name was Stephen Wise.[116] He had written to me often from the beginning of the Hitler regime on. Since he did not have any experience with dictatorial governments, he could not possibly know that every letter I received was opened by the Gestapo censor. He wrote on stationery without his name, but since he was in the habit of correcting every letter and wrote in green ink, remembering the fact that he was born on the 17th of March, St. Patrick's Day, the Gestapo was well aware of who wrote the letters. The first letter was written at the beginning of 1933, a few weeks after Hitler had come to power, inviting me to come to America and telling me that I had unlimited possibilities in this country. Stephen Wise knew very well what I was doing and he admired me greatly. I met him together with the American delegation, among whom were many members of Hadassah. He turned to them and introduced me by saying, "This is Joachim Prinz, the Stephen Wise of Berlin." I was young and fresh enough to turn to him and say to the ladies, "I want you to meet Stephen Wise, the Joachim Prinz of New York."

It was at that time that Stephen Wise asked me to see him privately and to report to him alone on what was going on in Germany. I agreed, but I told him that in order to get to his hotel I would have to take several taxis so as to avoid being followed by Swiss Gestapo agents who were working there under Mr. Schwartz's supervision. The time was arranged, and I did in fact take three taxis to get there. Before I did so, something rather dangerous happened. In my presence and in the presence of other members of the German delegation, Mr. Schwartz was arrested by the secret police of Switzerland. At the moment when he was told to surrender to the police, he gave me his passports and other papers. Later, when I looked at them, I discovered that he had five passports under five different names and different nationalities, all of them fabricated by a bureau of the Gestapo that specialized in forgeries. The head of our delegation, Dr. Siegfried Moses,[117] intervened with the Swiss secret police and asked them to release Schwartz. If this were not done,

---

116. Rabbi Stephen S. Wise (1874–1949) was one of the leading personalities in American Zionism as well as the founder of the American Jewish Congress and the World Jewish Congress.

117. Siegfried Moses (1887–1974) was an early Zionist and a Jewish community leader in Germany before his emigration to Palestine in 1937. In Israel he served as state controller, president of the Council of Jews from Germany, and international president of the Leo Baeck Institute.

we all would die and the members of our families would be arrested and sent to concentration camps. Schwartz was then released.

When I went to see Stephen Wise I carried the five passports in my pocket. He had asked the hotel to arrange for a special room in which he and I could have sufficient privacy, eat our dinner, and talk for many hours. This was done. Stephen Wise and I were alone and I reported to him at great length about the situation and about my conviction that Hitler was firmly established, that only a war which might defeat him could save European Jewry, that he would try to conquer all of Europe, and that I believed he was seriously determined to destroy world Jewry. Stephen Wise did not believe me. He, like all the other Americans, had rather naïve notions about Hitler. Some of the Jewish newspapermen who came from America told me that Hitler was suffering from cancer and would soon die; others said he was insane. I told them that even if he were indeed insane, he was much more dangerous that way than if he were sane. I left the hotel late at night and decided that on the next morning I would go to Mr. Schwartz's hotel to give him his passports. I found Mr. Schwartz around eleven in the morning. As I handed him the passports he looked at me and said, "I am grateful to you and I want to express my appreciation to you by giving you these pieces of paper which you may destroy. I decided not to send them to our headquarters in Berlin." I looked at the papers and to my amazement I found an almost verbatim report of what I had told Stephen Wise. "You are amazed," Schwartz said to me, "but you did not know that the waiter who brought you food was an agent of the Gestapo and was assigned to the job of supervising your activities."

One of the amazing and disturbing experiences during the Hitler regime was the utterly negative, or at least lackadaisical, attitude of the churches and their ministers. Pastor Niemöller,[118] the leading Protestant minister in Berlin, a former U-boat commander and a member of the Nazi party, never bothered to call me in order to find out whether I was still alive or to express any kind of sympathy with us. The only real encounter I had with ministers took place in July 1933. Of course, I had met many ministers during the preceding years, although it is important to mention the fact that there was no organization that dealt with Christian–Jewish relations. There was no ministerial association that opened its doors to ministers, priests, and rabbis

118. The Protestant pastor Martin Niemöller (1892–1984), although a defender of the church against the Nazi state supremacy, supported the Nazi party and failed to speak out for the Jews. When he criticized the regime in 1937, he was briefly imprisoned.

alike. Everyone lived in his own cubicle and minded his own business. There was, of course, a great deal of antisemitism in the churches, but there were also some outstanding ministers and priests who were free of prejudice and from whom I expected at least an inquiry as to what and how we were doing. I was therefore pleasantly surprised when I received a telephone call from an old friend, a minister whose church was situated in the district where workers lived, a man who had spoken to some of my groups, who had political leanings to the left, and whom I remember fondly. It was Pastor Rackwitz[119] who called to invite me to attend a meeting of the ministers scheduled for a Saturday at midnight. The meeting was to be held on the upper floor of his church in a room used for storage purposes. I was very glad to accept the invitation.

I drove to the simple church shortly before midnight and found some men standing in the doorways of three houses neighboring the church. I also found to my great amazement that the square in front of the church was being used by storm troopers for midnight exercises. The people in the doorways were representatives of Pastor Rackwitz, violently opposed to the Nazis, and were posted there in order to protect us and show us the way to the church. The meeting was a big secret. It was a violation of the law for ministers to meet with Jews or to hold a meeting that was clearly conspiratorial.

I finally reached the church and found people sitting in the lobby to direct me to a room that was really an attic. It was furnished but sparsely. There was a table with chairs around it. In a short time the room was filled with some twenty ministers sitting around the table. I was the only Jew. The atmosphere was tense and no one dared to speak. Some whispering went on, but everyone was shy about expressing any view or inquiring directly from me as to the situation in the Jewish community. Sitting there silently we suddenly heard the voices of the brown-shirted storm troopers down on the square. They sang the usual Nazi songs, and since we were high up in the church, the sounds were muffled but loud enough for us to understand what they were singing. Suddenly, my friend Rackwitz said to me, "We would like to start with a prayer and we invite you to say a prayer for all of us."

I told him that it was not in the Jewish tradition to say spontaneous prayers but that I was willing to read something to them. There was a big,

119. The Protestant pastor Arthur Rackwitz (1895–1980), a lifelong socialist and a member of the resistance against Hitler, sheltered opponents of the regime in his parsonage. He spent a few months in the Dachau concentration camp toward the end of the war.

well-worn Bible in front of me and I decided to open it at random. I would have read anything to them, since it was but a mere formality and an attempt to relieve the tension of the moment. Everyone was aware that this was the first Christian–Jewish meeting and everyone there was ashamed of that fact.

Miraculously, the Bible fell open at the 23rd Psalm. I began to read: "The Lord is my shepherd, I shall not want." As I read, the storm troopers began to sing a new song. It was the famous antisemitic anthem praising the night of the long knives when all the Jews would be murdered.[120] The knife had become a symbol of death to the Jews and the song spoke glowingly about the glorious moment of the blade and knife plunging into the heart of a Jew and the blood flowing from the body as though in an act of spiritual redemption. I stopped for a moment and then I began to read until I came to the sentence: "Thou preparest a table before me in the presence of mine enemies." I stopped there. I looked around and into the faces of the ministers. They began to understand, as I did, that this was no mere piece of poetry written some two thousand years ago but a very relevant piece to be read to all of us at this very moment. I interrupted the reading and I said to them, "In the presence of mine enemies, it says here, but they are not mine—not the enemies of the Jews, but the enemies of everyone. And the table is prepared not only for me and my people; I can assure you that it is also prepared for you and yours. As we will go down during the many nights of the long knives, so will you, and as we will perish, so will Christianity, for the meaning of our meeting is to understand this: we are all in one boat. Unless you understand this you understand nothing and you don't deserve the title of a minister of Christ, who, after all, were he alive today, would be among the victims of my people." I finished the reading of the psalm. And this opened our discussion. I later discovered that several of the men who had dark hair and looked a bit Jewish had been arrested and thrown into the river; all of them were determined to reject the Nazi doctrine and not to succumb to the power of the regime.

This was my first meeting with Christians. It was also my last. After that night in July 1933 not a single minister dared call me or, for that matter, any other Jew. The Christian church had succumbed. The Protestant

120. "Night of the Long Knives" was the designation given to the purge of the SA in 1934. Perhaps Prinz is thinking of the popular Nazi verse, "Wenn's Judenblut vom Messer spritzt dann geht's nochmal so gut" (When the blood of Jews squirts from our knives, things go twice as well).

churches were clearly divided into separate groups, one of which made an
official pact with the Nazis, while the other, called the Church of Confession,[121] held fast to Christian tradition without becoming politically active.
But one must not forget that among the people who rebelled against Hitler on the 20th of July in 1944 were a number of important Christian ministers, and together with other rebels they were caught and hanged. In the
meantime the Roman Catholic church entered into a formal treaty with the
Nazis, although later Cardinal Faulhaber of Munich became a very active
opponent of the Nazi regime. After the war, when I visited the concentration
camp of Dachau, I was told that fourteen hundred Catholic and Protestant
clergy, as well as nuns and monks, had been put to death there. I visited one
of the few survivors of that group, who had become an archbishop in Munich and who was a very courageous man. He had been forced by the Nazis
to spend a whole year in a cage that was too small for him to lie down in; he
had to stand up continuously and sleep standing up. But he was a powerful
man, survived it, and was in good spirits and proud of the fact that he had
defied the Nazi regime.

By 1935 our isolation was complete. It is very difficult for those who live
under a democracy to understand the daily difficulties of living under a dictatorship. I am not talking about the Jews, who had their special problems,
or the socialists, Communists, and liberal intellectuals who, of course, were
taken to prison or concentration camps. I am talking about the average citizens, most of them decent people, who suddenly found their family life torn
asunder. They continued to be what they always were. Most of them were
slightly to the right, nationalistic, and probably sick and tired of democracy.
But few of them would have approved of the cruel treatment that people
received. I am convinced that the majority of them simply did not know.
Their problem was quite different. They could not continue to work in either factories or offices without joining the National Socialist Party. Many
did that quite automatically and mechanically, but as time went on and the
radio subjected them to ongoing Nazi propaganda, those who had become
members of the party as a necessary prerequisite became slightly convinced
that Hitler was right. There was no doubt that the problem of unemployment was being solved. Domestically, Hitler was very successful from the
very beginning, and the mood of the people turned to one of victory over the

121. In Nazi Germany, the Protestant church was split into the Deutsche Christen (German
Christians), who supported the regime, and the Bekennende Kirche (Confessing Church), which
sought to maintain its independence.

evil forces of democracy. In that way even the good people became believing Nazis, whether they were initially or not.

Another problem began to disturb people greatly. It was the split in families, which occurred suddenly and quickly. Most of the young people had become members of the Hitler youth. That made the generation gap between parents and children much more severe than ever before. It was no longer the father who was the head of the family. This old German tradition of the father figure had now been replaced by Hitler, the great hero who was both obeyed and worshipped. Many people simply did not know how to cope with the situation. It was easiest to yield to the spirit of the new times since everything pointed to victory and success. New roads were being built. A new Hitler car came into being. In general, I found that from the very beginning of the Hitler regime the majority of the German people were enthusiastic about the new regime. This did not mean in all cases a break with their Jewish neighbors or a newly kindled hatred for the Jews. But it did mean a sense of distance; it was no longer proper to talk to Jews, to go to their homes and to continue to be their friends. The loneliness of the Jews cannot be described. There were, after all, no Jewish neighborhoods; our neighbors were usually non-Jews and we had had a friendly relationship with them. But now that no longer existed. My father once put it very succinctly when he said to me: "My neighbors have disappeared. They no longer look at me; they look through me."

This new situation created some very tender and difficult problems within the Jewish community, especially for the children. They were no longer permitted to attend public schools.[122] We had to create Jewish schools in a hurry. Since there were no textbooks, they had to be written and printed very quickly. These schools were under very strict and hostile supervision of the state authorities. The children who now attended Jewish schools very often came from assimilated families. Like their parents, they suddenly found themselves thrown in with the Jewish people, with whom they had never had any contact or shared identity. I remember cases where Jewish children met in a home as a group and locked themselves into a room. When the room was finally broken open, the parents found the Jewish children wearing brown jackets, carrying the swastika flag and singing Hitler songs. For a psychologist of children, this was a natural phenomenon. Children want to identify with the majority. The majority of the children were Nazis. This is what the Jewish children wanted to be. They did not have either the

122. Although quotas were introduced, Jewish children were not totally excluded from attending public schools until 1938.

conviction, the stamina, or the strength to withstand what was indeed the tendency and tenor of the times.

But it was not merely a problem of the children; it was also the problem of all Jews, most of whose families had lived in Germany for hundreds of years. Although I had always been a Zionist, and therefore had kept my distance from Germany itself and from German affairs, there is no doubt that all of us who had gone through German schools had a relationship to the country. Although we Zionists knew that the attitude of the Germans toward us was, to say the least, ambiguous, and often enough hostile, there remained the fact that linguistically and culturally we were German. My mother's family had been in Bavaria in the early seventeenth century, and probably even longer than that. My father's family had been in Germany for three generations. Although I have never been able to be a patriot in the ordinary sense and wherever I lived I have maintained my universal outlook on life unrestricted by national and linguistic boundaries, there is no doubt that my roots were in the country where my family had lived for so many generations.

In addition, I was also a German writer, having written eight books in the language of that country.[123] Because of my membership in the Jewish youth movement, I was very close to the German countryside, the landscape, the trees, the rivers, and the mountains. That could not be denied. But we were suddenly expelled from all that, not merely from society. Our problem was not just a political and social one. It was a very serious and unprecedented psychological problem. The ghettos of the Middle Ages had actually been separate towns that were ruled and governed by the Jews. The Jews had not been citizens. Their language was not a pure German, but a mixture that was later called Judeo-German. They had no relationship to the painting and architecture of the country, nor to its literature. All that had changed. But now we were suddenly thrown into a ghetto with invisible walls as thick and impenetrable as those of the Middle Ages. Wherever we lived there were barriers and roadblocks. We could no longer look at the scenery with innocent eyes. We certainly could not enjoy it even if we had been permitted to go on hikes unmolested and unhindered. The molestation was there, however, and so were the obstacles to any kind of free movement in the city, and in the country as well.

It was at that time that I decided to write down and analyze all these things. As I mentioned earlier, I wrote a piece that was called "Ghetto 1935."

123. See listing, Appendix C.

Two years later, in my farewell speech in Berlin in 1937, I tried to restate and redefine this condition. It was a strange kind of schizophrenia to want to belong, but not be permitted to do so. Gradually we became estranged from the German language. Of course, we still spoke it; no other language was as familiar to us as German. But during the Hitler years I always thought that the translation of the prayers that we said during the Jewish service from Hebrew to German was not merely inadequate but also incongruous. I therefore wrote a new prayer book for my congregation, which was printed in ten thousand copies. It was called "Friday Night," and only a few copies have survived.[124] In this prayer book I rejected the notion of a German translation and instead printed the prayers in Hebrew. On opposite pages I wrote an interpretation and commentary on the prayers that were being said or sung. I thought this to be a more adequate expression of the situation as it really existed.

Jewish newspapers were prohibited from using Gothic type. They had to replace their equipment and print in Latin letters. Jews were not allowed to perform classical dramas, such as those of Schiller. Heinrich Heine, probably one of the greatest and certainly the most influential of the German poets and writers, was on the blacklist for non-Jewish readers. His famous song about the Rhine was now printed as an anonymous folk song rather than the creation of that Jew Heine whose books had disappeared from the libraries and the German curriculum. I will never forget that day in the month of May 1933 when on one of the most important squares in the city a huge bonfire was erected where thousands of books by Jewish authors were thrown into the flames and burned. It was a medieval scene like the burning of the Talmud in Italy in the sixteenth century and is still unforgettable. Book burning was the beginning of a new medieval period as far as we were concerned. The external ghetto that had been invisibly established was part of a medieval world in the midst of the twentieth century, a cruel and gruesome island established in the midst of contemporary civilization. That civilization was to a very large extent the creation of Jewish writers and artists. But the art that they and Christians had created was now designated as "decadent." It was banned from the museums, ridiculed, and rejected. A new German classicistic art was hailed as the true expression of the German national character and was not to be contaminated by Jewish degenera-

---

124. *Der Freitagabend, tefilat arvit leshabat. Gebet und Sinn,* interpreted by Joachim Prinz (Berlin: Brandussche Verlagsbuchhandlung, [1935]). It is dedicated to "those who want to learn to be Jews."

tion. This was equally true for Jewish scientists. The majority of the German scientists who had received the Nobel Prize had been Jewish. Einstein was not merely forced to leave the country; his theory of relativity was considered un-German and a new kind of German physics was devised to replace it. All this was, I am sure, done to the horror of decent German scientists. It extended from the area of the natural and mathematical sciences to many other scholarly endeavors. But most of the scholars at the universities proved to be cowards, mainly interested in preserving their own prerogatives and teaching positions. As mentioned above, in 1929 I had become the Jewish chaplain of the Berlin University, the first and only one they ever had. But in 1933 I was summarily dismissed. Since all Jewish students soon had to leave every university, there would have been no position for me anyhow.

Although the Jewish community had to adjust by creating conditions under which the Jews would be able to live in their new situation, I could not say that the community was united. Many of the important functions were performed by the Zionist organization, particularly in the field of adult education. As I noted earlier, I had founded the Chaim Nachman Bialik Institute of Jewish Adult Education, which became a thriving organization. I taught a course there in Jewish history in addition to the one I have already mentioned. This one was only attended by some five hundred people and lasted for many months. There were other lecturers, as well, and we made a great contribution to the enormous and appalling state of affairs in the field of Jewish knowledge. People were totally ignorant. But to know that one was a Jew and why was a psychological necessity. It was the most gnawing problem of the day: to suffer but not to know why. Of course, the best way out of the situation was emigration. But the people who were least knowledgeable still held fast to the notion that Hitler was but an episode, that some day he would either die or be overthrown. Such opinions flew in the face of the realities that surrounded these people. They must have understood that Germany was never stronger than at that time. The army was very visible and the Nazi groups, which formed the illegal militia, were no less formidable. They were certainly responsible for the deaths of thousands.

The Jewish establishment was virulently anti-Zionist, a phenomenon that has never been thoroughly investigated. It stemmed not merely from the traditional anti-Zionism of German Jews; it had its real roots in the fact that Zionism was identified with emigration and that the businessmen at the head of the community were simply opposed to losing their customers. The more Jews emigrated the less assured was the existence of the community. The community had a very large staff of many hundreds of people who had the status of civil servants. Even the president of the community received a large salary, although in the case of Herman Stahl,[125] who was the wealthy president of the community during that time, he probably did not accept it.

A battle between Zionism and anti-Zionism was fought out on my back. I was not merely the most articulate and visible representative of the Zionist movement, I was also the most disturbed.[126] They tried to test me by giving me the largest synagogue of the community, which had 3,500 seats.[127] They were very sure I could never fill it. Unfortunately for them and for me, this synagogue had to be closed half an hour before the beginning of the service because all the seats had been taken. It was a marvelous synagogue, which I began to love very much, although it was in the eastern part of Berlin. Like all synagogues in Berlin, it was named for the street on which it was located. This one was situated on the Oranienburger Strasse. It was a fantastic building. The pulpit, a beautiful little building unto itself, was raised rather high and it took quite a while to get up there. Of course, there was no microphone in those days. It would have been considered undignified for us to use it anyway, but the acoustics of the building were so fabulous that I did not need a mike. The building had three balconies and my voice could be heard in the last row of the third one. This had something to do with the fact that the building was built in 1860 by a student and disciple of the great Baroque architect Schlueter.[128] After the war I saw the building, the inside of which was charred and burned. My pulpit was no longer there. Nothing was there when, as in 1946, I stood at the center of this once magnificent building. It had not been rebuilt. The synagogue survived Kristallnacht in 1938[129] since it was next door to the archives of the government and the Nazis feared that if they burned down the synagogue, the archives would burn down too. But it was hit by a bomb during the air attacks on Berlin. Only the shell remained standing, completely burned out, a great monument to the tragic period of burning, looting, and killing.[130]

125. Heinrich Stahl. See note 34, above. As Stahl was his sworn opponent, Prinz's misrecollection of his first name may not be incidental.

126. Prinz doubtless intends: "disturbing."

127. See note 36, above.

128. The design for the building was first laid out by Eduard Knoblauch in 1857, and architectural work continued by Friedrich August Stüler. The synagogue was not completed until 1866. The architects may have been influenced by the seventeenth-century architect Andreas Schlüter.

129. The pogrom on the night of November 9, 1938, when synagogues all over Germany were set on fire.

130. Although members of the SA lit a fire in the synagogue during Kristallnacht, the synagogue was only superficially damaged. Since it still possessed the status of a historical landmark, the fire was extinguished. The interior of the building was burned out during an air raid in February 1943.

The fact that I was able to fill the synagogue aggravated the Jewish community leaders ever more. Often I received a letter from them, particularly after I had been arrested by the Gestapo, warning me against being so careless as to be arrested. Once I received a letter from them because I had delivered a sermon on Theodor Herzl and had asked the organist to play "Hatikvah"[131] as an introduction to my sermon. In this letter I was accused of Zionist propaganda in the synagogue, of which I was indeed guilty. I was refused the right to hold meetings of my youth groups in my room of the synagogue building, for these, too, were considered Zionist propaganda.

The fight between the establishment and myself was bound to lead to something very drastic since they were looking for an opportunity to abruptly end my contract. My sermons were very political, very direct, and quite different from the solemn declarations that came from other pulpits. I was altogether much more popular, not merely as a preacher but also as a pastor. At that time I also had a very large psychiatric practice.[132] It was so extensive that I had to hold my usual sessions in a large room of the community building. We had to give out numbers to the people who waited and a secretary had to act in the same manner in which the secretary of a physician works. The cases varied from people who needed money to others who needed psychiatric help. I worked with two psychiatrists, for I was not permitted to do any therapy, but I was sufficiently trained to do proper diagnosis.

All this did not sit well with the community. They waited for the moment to get rid of me and that moment came. Among the people who were members of my youth groups was a young and pretty girl, Renate Alsberg, the daughter of the most outstanding criminal lawyer of Europe.[133] She was very much in love with me, and I cannot deny I liked her very much. The family was very rich. They had many servants and chauffeurs, several Rolls-Royces, and Renate, who was sixteen and not permitted to have a full-fledged automobile, had a white car with three wheels that came from England. She very often picked me up. The family had a house in Switzerland. Her father had committed suicide there, and her mother was living in that house together with Renate and her brother. They invited us to come to St. Moritz. Hilde and I went there for a few weeks. While I was there, I suddenly began to suffer from a case of sciatica and could hardly move. I had received permission from the community to stay away for two weeks. This was common

131. The anthem of the Zionist movement and later the national anthem of the State of Israel.
132. More likely, a counseling service.
133. The reference is to Max Alsberg (1877–1933). Upon dismissal from his position as a professor of criminal law at the University of Berlin in 1933, he immigrated to Switzerland, where he committed suicide.

procedure, if you wanted to go away when it was not ordinary vacation time. But since I was young and quite irresponsible and careless, I forgot to inform the community that I could not return because of illness. It took four instead of two weeks before I returned to Berlin. When I arrived, I found a letter informing me that I would no longer be permitted to serve as rabbi of the community and that after a few months I would have to leave.[134]

It was a difficult but in my case welcome decision. I had to rearrange my life. I immediately got many offers to work at a salary higher than I had received hitherto. I accepted one of the offers, which came from Salman Schocken, who at that time was the owner of five department stores. He was also very active in Zionist circles and in Jewish life generally. His offer was for me to become the European representative of the Hebrew University.[135] I was to travel a great deal and to raise funds. It was a very exciting job. Among other places, it took me to Yugoslavia where I traveled as a guest of the government. It was a very fascinating trip, which I undertook with Hilde, seeing the beautiful country from one coast to the other and meeting not merely the leading Jews but also the governors of the various provinces of the country, both Croatian and Serbian. It was a new world. The Jewish community was divided into two parts, Sephardim and Ashkenazim.[136] With the Sephardic community I usually spoke in French, with the Ashkenazic in German. I was very well known in Yugoslavia; everyone had read the articles and books I had written.

I also went to Switzerland and worked there for several weeks quite successfully, made friends, and learned something about a community that was rich and smug and acted accordingly. My experience with the Hebrew University as propagandist and fundraiser was, in general, of great help to me, for I learned something about the secular Jews who could not care less about organized religion, but who had to be educated to identify themselves with the Jewish people and do something for Jewish causes. I also became deeply interested in the work of the Hebrew University. When I was in Yugoslavia I discovered similarities between many of the problems with which the Jews of Palestine had to grapple and those of Yugoslavia. This was particularly true of the problems of water, climate, and other matters. In Yugoslavia, I was received by the faculty of Belgrade University and seated among professors

134. Prinz's job as a Liberal rabbi in the Berlin Jewish community was permanently and completely terminated as of the end of September 1935.
135. From 1934 (when he moved from Berlin to Jerusalem) to 1945, Salman Schocken (1877–1959) chaired the executive council of the Hebrew University.
136. The Sephardim are those Jews who trace their ancestry from medieval Spain; Ashkenazim are those who stem from Central Europe.

who wanted me to discuss the university and its problems. Among the professors was the head of the department of theology. They wore the very colorful garb of high Orthodox clergymen. I reported to them in French, since that was the language they preferred. After I had finished, the head of the department of theology arose; he cut an imposing figure, an old man with a flowing white beard. He said to the chairman, "Mr. President, Dr. Prinz's speech was so moving that I began to think of the miracle of a new Jewish state which someday might come into being in fulfillment of the ancient Hebrew prophecies. It is in his honor and in deep respect for the Jewish people and its aspirations that I want to recite in Hebrew the first Psalm." He did so slowly and solemnly, and I must say that I have never forgotten that moment, which was one of deep emotions. I found it very difficult to express my gratitude to this noble man for the sentiments he had expressed.

My work for the Hebrew University lasted less than a year. I did not want to do much traveling and I had received a very flattering offer from a German-Jewish weekly, which had been a family paper for over a hundred years. There was hardly a Jewish family in Germany that had not subscribed to this paper.[137] I began to discover that the new times called for more attention to political problems. Since the editor had decided to emigrate, the paper was now without a head and I was invited to become the chief editor. The offer was very attractive, and altogether my interest in journalism was great enough to prompt me to accept it. Thus a new kind of life began for me. For the first time, I had to go to an office at a certain hour in the morning and leave at night. I began to revamp the paper and became, in effect, its political editor as well. My editorials were published on the front page. I was particularly interested in adding a new artistic face to the new political aspects of the paper. Every week I designed a whole page with photographs and reproductions of paintings, and I wrote the text for it. I worked with a young journalist who served his apprenticeship with me. There was also a literary section of the paper, over which Dr. Kayser[138] presided. After his emigration to America, he became the first director of the Jewish Museum in New York.

This completely new world attracted me greatly. The people in Germany looked forward to receiving the paper every week and to reading my articles. I expressed my political convictions, urged people to leave the country, and

137. The reference is to the *Israelitisches Familienblatt,* which in 1935 transferred its editorial offices from Hamburg to Berlin. It continued there, except for a three-month prohibition that same year, until its closure after the November Pogrom in 1938. In 1937, it had a circulation of about thirty thousand.

138. The reference is to Stephen S. Kayser (1900–1988).

analyzed the situation as I saw it. The paper was politically neutral. It was neither Zionist nor anti-Zionist. These terms, however, had become meaningless. I expressed my views on Palestine and the return of the Jewish people to its homeland without any hesitation, and no one prevented me from doing that. I was completely free and my work was very much appreciated. I was most happy to be able to work with printers again. I had, as you may recall, done that while I was a student when I had been the editor of a Zionist weekly.[139]

In spite of what I did to earn a living, I did not neglect my rabbinical duties. I was no longer a rabbi of the Jewish community, but since I was an ordained rabbi I remained a rabbi, officiating at weddings and funeral services. During the High Holy Days I preached. The first year I was invited to preach at the private synagogue located in the very elegant villa of the Schocken family.[140] The congregation consisted of about a hundred people. We had a cantor and I conducted the rabbinical part of the service and preached the sermons. But these sermons were now no longer what they had been in the large synagogues because I was speaking to very well-educated, learned Jews, all of whom knew Hebrew well and were conversant with Jewish literature. It was a great pleasure for me to be able to preach on such a high level.

There were many groups within Berlin Jewry that protested vigorously against the action of the Jewish community in relieving me of my duties. Mass meetings were held, attended by hundreds of people, to express their vehement opposition. But it was of no avail, because the Jewish establishment was very happy to have gotten rid of an irritant that could not easily be controlled—and I myself was very pleased indeed to have been afforded the opportunity to do something completely different. Nevertheless, I participated actively in rabbinical affairs. The most important of these relates to a rather interesting but almost completely forgotten fact. The Nazi regime had neglected to look into the matter of ritual slaughter.[141] Even after the Nuremberg Laws were issued, Jews continued the ritual slaughter of animals. Suddenly, someone in the Nazi regime discovered that this Jewish custom was still being observed. They therefore issued a declaration according to which the ritual slaughter of animals was a violation of the laws that prohibited cruelty to animals. From now on, they decided, the ritual slaughter of ani-

139. The *Jüdische Zeitung für Ostdeutschland.*
140. Salman Schocken owned a villa in the elegant Berlin suburb of Schlachtensee.
141. As early as the Weimar period, some German states, including Bavaria, had prohibited Jewish ritual slaughter. The central Nazi government issued a prohibition on April 21, 1933. However, until December 1935, shortly after the Nuremberg Laws were introduced, kosher meat could still be imported from Denmark.

mals was no longer to be permitted. I attended meetings of Liberal rabbis, where together we discovered the meaning of the Jewish law of ritual slaughter.[142] The question was whether an animal could be anesthetized before being ritually slaughtered. We found, studying the Jewish law, that it did not prohibit the anaesthetizing of animals before slaughtering them. We discussed the matter with the German government. It was their decision that if an animal would be anaesthetized, and therefore be unconscious while it was being slaughtered, it could no longer be maintained that Jewish slaughter amounted to the torture of animals. We looked into the matter very thoroughly and found that it was possible to anaesthetize the animals electrically. Experiments with it proved to be very successful. Jewish butchers now announced in their windows that they were selling kosher meat of anaesthetized animals. We were very glad that we had saved the Jewish institution of dietary laws. You must understand that all of us observed these laws.

However, we were suddenly confronted, not with the opposition of the German government, but with that of Orthodox Jews. Although they had no legitimate legal ground for objecting to our procedure, they did so after having inquired from Orthodox rabbis in Vilna who decreed that no Jew who observed the dietary laws was permitted to eat the meat of animals that had been electrically anaesthetized before slaughter. We had to discontinue our method, which we knew would have saved an ancient Jewish tradition and which, as a result, caused the vast majority of Jews to eat meat of animals that were not slaughtered in accordance with Jewish law. This was the end of traditional Jewish life. The Orthodox Jews ate only dairy food and stuck to it stubbornly. But they constituted a tiny minority of the Jewish population. All the others, including myself, began to buy meat from regular butchers and gave up observance of dietary laws. It was a dramatic illustration of the inability of Orthodox Jewry to deal with emergencies in Jewish life. Later, when millions of them were in concentration camps, they ate what they got to eat, and there were a few Orthodox rabbis in these camps who told them they were not violating any Jewish law. Had the Orthodox Jews agreed with us, we would have saved a Jewish tradition. In addition, we would have comforted those Jewish people who had adhered to Jewish customs for many generations and who now felt conscience-stricken in violating them.

Altogether, things now became rather difficult. On one occasion, while sitting in my office I saw two Gestapo agents and heard them ask for me.

---

142. Prinz wrote on the subject in an article entitled "Grenzen des Ritualgesetzes. Jüdische Theologen fordern Klärung der Schechita-Frage," *Israelitisches Familienblatt,* March 4, 1937.

I was certain they had come to arrest me and take me to a concentration camp. Since I was not very fond of this idea, I left the office by a back door and did not return home. I called Hilde and we decided to stay with a friend of ours for a week or so. We did that immediately because I was informed that I was right in assuming that the Gestapo was about to arrest me and this time to keep me. It was a rather hectic week. I did not dare take taxis to my office, but worked instead with my secretary in a truck. At the end of a week, I returned to the office, trusting my old luck, and for no reason at all I was proven right. I had a talk with my friend Kuchmann of the Gestapo. He confirmed that he had had orders to arrest me, which had been withdrawn. But he wanted to tell me that things were getting very difficult and that I should know about it.

I felt very ill at ease, and when a few weeks later it was again clear to me that I would be arrested and not returned, I decided to take Hilde and the children and leave Germany. This could not be done in the regular fashion. We had our passports, but we could not possibly dare to have all our things, including furniture and library, packed and go to America as tourists. I decided to leave everything where it was, to take along whatever we could carry, and flee to Prague. I did not dare take a train. I asked my good friend Chaim Schein to drive us to the border. He did so without any hesitation. From there we took the train, arriving in Prague a few hours later. Lucie was five years old and Michael three;[143] both really did not know what was happening. To them it was just another trip. To us it was the difficult beginning of a new life. We went to a medium-priced hotel since our funds were limited. It was a Saturday and the decision had been made suddenly. We did not tell anyone where we were going, not even Hilde's parents whom we simply informed that we would leave the country. It had to be a quick farewell.

In Prague I contacted the Jewish community leadership, which knew me well. I still remember the first man I met. He was a member of the Czechoslovakian parliament whose name, if I am not mistaken, was Goldstein.[144] Then we met our old friend Kurt Blumenfeld[145] who happened to be in Prague at that time. He immediately offered me a position with the Keren Hayesod, of which he was the director. The amount of money I would re-

143. This trip must therefore have taken place after April 30, 1936, the date of Michael's third birthday.

144. Angelo Goldstein (1889–1947) was an active Zionist who served in the Czechoslovakian parliament beginning in 1931. He left for Palestine in 1939.

145. Kurt Blumenfeld (1884–1963) was one of the principal leaders of German Zionism. He had immigrated to Palestine as early as 1933, where in 1936 he became the director of the Keren Hayesod, the Palestine Foundation Fund that purchased land for Jewish settlement.

ceive was rather limited, but for the time being we did not have to worry about paying for the hotel since it was paid for by the refugee committee of Prague. We received Czechoslovakian money, which took care of the food we needed. During this time I felt rather awkward about having left so suddenly and without any preparation and money, having left the things I loved at home and having to start from scratch like every other refugee.

While I was thinking about my future and that of my family I received a telephone call from Berlin. I do not now remember who called me, but it was one of the leaders of the Zionist organization. He told me that he and a few friends would come to Prague to talk to me. They were to arrive on the following day. Looking very serious and disturbed, they informed me that the Gestapo had told them that if I did not return within forty-eight hours, the Zionist organization would be dissolved and its leaders taken to jail. Also, all members of my family would suffer. There was no way out. We had to return, and return we did.

We came home to beds that were still unmade. I do not recall what we did with our housekeepers. We called Hilde's parents and they came over. They told us that the Gestapo had come to their home inquiring as to our whereabouts. It was a rather comical scene that my father-in-law reported: Mr. Kuchmann had come to him and asked whether he knew where we were. My father-in-law replied that he knew we had left the country, but that I had not told him where we were going. Then Kuchmann, according to my father-in-law's report, said that he was lying, whereupon my father-in-law, who was a very decent and honest man, said to Kuchmann, "Did you serve in the German army, and what was your rank?" Mr. Kuchmann answered that he did indeed serve in the army, and his rank was that of a corporal. My father-in-law went into another room, brought out his military papers and showed them to Kuchmann, proving that he had served in the army for four years as a petty officer and therefore outranked him. He yelled at the Gestapo agent, telling him in no uncertain terms that he—my father-in-law— had never lied in his life, and that Kuchmann should get out of his house. Kuchmann, still an army man and very much bound to the old regime and its values, understood that the man who spoke to him was his superior, and so the Gestapo agents left.

Upon our return to Berlin I was immediately called to the Gestapo and told that if this were to happen again I would be expelled[146] or taken to a concentration camp. Also, in order to make similar incidents impossible, I

146. It is not clear why Prinz would have been expelled for having left the country.

was to deliver my passport on the following day so that I could no longer cross the border into a foreign country. Handing over my passport was an act of self-emasculation for me. Without a passport I felt unsafe, no longer able to move around as I wanted to do. The situation had become rather dangerous.

In spite of all that, I continued my activities. I preached during the High Holy Days in a huge hall that seated more than two thousand people.[147] Meetings where I spoke continued to draw large audiences. One of the largest, arranged by the Kulturbund, was held in the Philharmonic Hall. Since I knew that I would not be staying in the country much longer, I tried to deliver a programmatic talk, asking the Jews of Berlin to leave the country, and I analyzed the situation as I saw it. I spoke for an hour and a half to three and a half thousand people. As a result of this talk, many people left Germany. However, since leaving meant sacrificing at least 50 percent of one's capital, many hesitated, and for this hesitation they paid with their lives. I remember this meeting vividly, not only because I delivered an important speech, but because of a rather funny incident that happened after the meeting. I was sitting in the artists' dressing room of this hall, where people came to see me. Among them was an elderly couple who said to me in heavily American-accented German, "We bring you regards from Dr. Stephen Wise." Since they spoke German with great difficulty, I suggested that they speak English, which I also spoke. Whereupon they replied: "We speak no language; we travel all the time."

Studying English became a much practiced habit. Ever since Stephen Wise had invited me to come to America at the beginning of 1933, I tried to improve my command of the language. I had begun to learn English when I was thirteen years old and I had been a subscriber to the London *Times* for many years. I had also studied English in high school for six years, six days a week, and had no difficulties in expressing myself in the language. Nevertheless, since language was my way of making a living, I thought it very important for me to brush up on English and study it seriously for as long as I remained in Berlin.

In the meantime, however, I made an attempt to settle in Palestine. I had worked out a plan to create a private school there on a very high level and to become its director. It was a difficult enterprise, which required large sums of money and could therefore only be done with the help of the Jewish Agency or some other Jewish organization. I wrote a letter to my friend Chaim Weiz-

147. In the year 1936.

mann,[148] whom I had known for a long time, thinking he might be helpful. He responded immediately, found the idea to be very valid, but informed me that no money was available. He also said that the people who lived in Palestine could not afford to pay the kind of tuition required to send their children to a private school. The plan was canceled. To learn English became much more urgent.

The most popular English teacher at that time was an Englishman by the name of Mr. Baker. He was an interesting, intelligent, and talented language teacher. He was English with a decided British accent. I engaged him and asked him to come to my home every Saturday afternoon for lunch and work with me for four hours during the afternoon. When he showed up, I found him an attractive man. In the course of the many hours I spent with him we became very friendly. He had great talent as a mimic, and he was able to imitate every German dialect. For a Britisher this was quite an accomplishment. I recommended him to many of my friends, who likewise became his pupils. He was very expensive, but it was, after all, an important investment. Since my house was the headquarters of the Jewish leadership, he listened very often to our conversations about Hitler and the regime, which were, of course, not very flattering. We trusted him completely because he was an Englishman and therefore an ally. Naturally, he did not participate in our discussions, but we were convinced that he was an anti-Nazi who did not return to England simply because he was able to make a better living in Berlin than in London. I am very indebted to Mr. Baker, for when I finally came to America I was linguistically prepared to earn a living from the very first day. What I did not know for many years was that Mr. Baker was not British at all. He was a German and a member of the Nazi party. I learned about that only when I returned to Berlin in 1946 after the war. He was waiting for me after a speech that I delivered and asked me to help him in the matter of denazification. Together we went to the wine cellar where we had spent countless hours. As we emptied several bottles of wine, he gave me his real name, which I have forgotten, but I remember that he was a member of the German nobility, and that we were skating on rather thin ice when we took him into our confidence. I helped him in the process of denazification, and he was denazified. A few years later, when I was the guest of the Ger-

148. Chaim Weizmann (1874–1952) served as president of the World Zionist Organization (1920–1930 and 1935–1946) and then as first president of the State of Israel. Prinz wrote to Weizmann on September 26, 1933, proposing the establishment of a school in Palestine and asking him to lend his name to the project, which Weizmann declined to do for political reasons. In his letter Prinz does not mention that he would become the school's director, only that he would be responsible for raising the necessary funds from German Jewry.

man government and was interviewed on TV, I discovered that Mr. Baker worked for the television station.

I do not now recall how many times I had to go to the Gestapo. It was always a close call, and I remember that I often took a small packed suitcase with me in case I would be detained in prison. I had learned to handle the Gestapo. Once I was there for five hours and taken from one office to another, having to cross the backyard of the building. It must be understood that the Gestapo building was not a dungeon. It was a Baroque palace built in the middle of the eighteenth century, with a marble staircase and very elegant rooms. The Gestapo agents whom I saw were housed in a wing of the department that was called the Department for Jews, Homosexuals and Freemasons. Most stories about Gestapo agents at their offices picture them and their surroundings quite inaccurately. The Gestapo agents I saw—very often once or twice a week—sat behind desks in large and beautiful rooms; they watered their elegant houseplants. I remember one of them having a bird, which he treated with particular care. Among the pictures on the walls was a map of Palestine. I remember vividly coming there one time and being greeted with the salutation of "Shalom" and then being asked to show them on the map of Palestine where Petach-Tikvah[149] was situated.

When I was taken across the backyard I suddenly began to understand the enormous power of the Gestapo. I have never seen a courtyard of any building so thoroughly guarded and militarized. There must have been at least fifty heavily armed storm troopers, machine guns, and even artillery pieces. I still remember the palpitation of my heart when I saw that and was aware that any one of them could shoot and kill me for any wrong move I might make. I walked across rather gingerly, to be taken to another office where I was again subject to all kinds of interrogations and soon, thank God, emerged unscathed.

It is time to discuss with you one of the least known chapters of Jewish existence under the Hitler regime. I am referring to the situation of our Christian housekeepers. According to the Nuremberg Laws, Jewish householders were no longer permitted to have Christian servants.[150] The theory was that any Christian living with a Jewish family could be sexually attacked by the male members of the family since Jews were suspected of being not merely congenital rapists, but particularly eager to humiliate the Aryan race by sexual relationships. Based on this theory, which was, of course, not

149. Petach-Tikvah is a city on Israel's coastal plain, not far from Tel Aviv.
150. The Nuremberg Laws included a provision that Jews were not to employ in their households women of German blood under the age of forty-five.

borne out by facts at all, a certain time limit was set for our maids to leave us. It became clear to me that the only German Christians who had intimate relationships with Jewish families were those who served us in our homes. In a very large number of families, and probably the majority of homes, Christian cooks and chambermaids had served these families for a very long time; sometimes it was the daughter of a mother who had been with the Jewish family, and sometimes even a granddaughter. In our own case, those who served us stayed with us for a very long time. We had a cook by the name of Frieda who had once invited her sister Anna to visit with her. Anna was a very young peasant girl who, during the few weeks she stayed with us, developed such extraordinary ability to play with children that we decided to ask her to stay with us and be our chambermaid, taking charge of Lucie and Michael. She proved to be as inventive as if she had been trained as a pedagogue, and she was so pleasant that the children developed a most intimate relationship with her. Her sister had to leave us for some personal reason and Anna was then our only maid. She had become a member of the family, close to the children, and very close to us. I remember seeing her in Berlin for a few hours after the war. She had married in the meantime and her husband was missing in action.

The time for the maids to leave us was set for a given date at twelve midnight. Anna stayed with us that day, leaving the house at one minute before midnight. Lucie was four years old when this happened. After Anna had left tearfully, and with genuine feelings about soon parting from her own family, Lucie said, "If they can take Anna away from me, there will come a time when they will also take my mother." I thought that was a very apt and accurate description of how deeply we felt about having to separate from someone who was so much a part of our lives. I decided to write an essay on the role of the Christian housekeeper in the Jewish household, but I never got around to doing it. It still remains a topic to be discussed, for the encounter between Jews and gentiles was never as close, as intimate, and as telling as that between us and the people who worked for us in our homes.

The process of isolating the Jews grew more rapid from day to day. I wrote a piece called "Life Without Neighbors,"[151] which described the situation as it really was. Of course, there were exceptions. I remember that in the home of friends we used to meet actors and actresses. I will never forget one evening when many of them came to the house after having been received by Adolf Hitler. All of them were well-meaning people who were very far re-

---

151. This is the article mentioned earlier, note 74, above.

moved from antisemitism and had nothing in common with the National Socialist government. But I will not forget their excitement about their visit with the Führer. To me it was a revelation that can hardly be described. They were so deeply impressed with Hitler's charm, with his eyes, with the easy manner in which he talked to them. Suddenly they discovered, or seemed to have discovered, that he was not a beast and a brute, but a most charming and bewitching human being. I began to understand the influence of Hitler on tens of thousands of people. If he appeared in such a manner to anti-Nazis, to actors and actresses who ought to know human nature, how much easier was it for him to impress the uneducated, gullible masses of the German people. In many descriptions of Hitler, in the biographies that were published recently, there are testimonies of people who were similarly impressed by him. There is no doubt that he was a very complex man, artistic and sometimes charming, and at the same time a mass murderer.

Hitler, however, was far removed from us. There was no opportunity for any one of us to ever have an interview with him, nor would it have helped us. His hatred of Jews was so deeply imbedded in either his character, his upbringing, or his personal experiences with Jews in Vienna that it was beyond description. None of us ever asked for an interview with him, nor did anyone ever get close to him or his staff. As a matter of fact, there was no contact between the National Socialist leadership and the Jewish leaders. The only contact was, as I said before, through Hans Hinkel, and this referred only to cultural activities. Everything else was regulated by law.

It took the Jews a long time to understand that whatever had happened before 1933 was no longer valid. There were literally hundreds of thousands of Jews who found it impossible to understand the new situation. After all, it was a throwback to the medieval status of the Jew. However, we were very much part of the twentieth century and had made our extraordinary contribution to the civilization of the century. Modern Judaism itself, as it existed in Germany, was an attempt to adjust the religion to the needs of the twentieth-century man. Non-Orthodox movements, Reform and Conservative Judaism, were conceived and formulated in Germany. This was not a mere accident. German Jewry was altogether Jewishly very creative. The first Jewish histories were written there. The first modern seminaries for the training of rabbis and teachers began in Germany. Although German Jewry was small in comparison with Russian Jewry, it is difficult to study any scholastic problem of Jewish concern without referring to books written in German and published in Germany. It is one of the most amazing phenomena of Jewish history that a community that small, consisting of less than 1 percent of the entire German population, should have produced so much. All this has to be said because, in addition to Jewish creativity, there was, of course, a process of assimilation unparalleled in the Jewish world.

In order to understand the Jewish attitude under the Hitler regime, it is important to understand the nature of German-Jewish assimilation. If I think of my parents and grandparents, I have to think of Prussianized Jews. My grandfather, who was really part of the landed gentry, fought in the war between Prussia and Austria in 1866. He always wore his medals, which he received for bravery and because he had been wounded during the war. There was not the slightest doubt that he, who wore the beard of Kaiser Wilhelm I under whom he fought, was a German. I do not believe that he ever saw the inside of a synagogue. His character was completely Prussian, aristocratic, and disciplinarian. He was unable or unwilling ever to smile or laugh. He ruled over his little empire in a small town in which he owned a great deal of land. His large household consisted of more than a hundred people who worked the land or were in charge of his moving business, his dairy farm, and many heads of cattle. He also ruled over his wife and children, who hated him for it.

I sometimes find that the term *assimilation* is a misnomer. We are talking about a complete cultural and political integration and adjustment to the country in which the Jews lived. They were as German as the Germans, and sometimes even more so. Although antisemitism existed, particularly at universities and in heavy industry, it was a benevolent kind of antisemitism, and during the Hitler regime we used to talk often about the "good old antisemitism." Until 1918, the year of the democratic revolution, no Jew could be a full professor at a university, and many who aspired to that position converted to Christianity, which was the prerequisite for a full professorship.

I myself always had a sense of distance between myself as a Jew and the German people. I never sang the national anthem of Germany. Long before Hitler, I realized we were living in a fool's paradise. Although I had no personal experiences with antisemitism (I was almost always the only Jewish student in a class), I felt how very deeply antisemitism was part of the German character. In 1911 Hans Buehler,[152] the founder of the Free German Youth Movement, issued a declaration in which he advocated an attitude of racial superiority. It was at that time that I joined the Zionist youth movement. It was clear to us that we were not part of the German people.

---

152. Prinz apparently means Hans Breuer (1883–1918), a leading personality in the founding of the Free German Youth Movement. In 1913, the movement adopted the *Meißnerformel*, to which Prinz is referring.

Our parents were, but we were not. When we went on our long hiking trips during the two months of summer and met groups from the German youth movements, we greeted them with "Shalom," and they greeted us with "Heil." They were really the genuine forerunners of the Nazi movement. But we were a very small part of German Jewry, almost a family. Zionists knew each other personally and were laughed at by all the others. We were considered to be eccentric, queer, unreasonable, intransigent, and, of course, completely wrong. We were the prophets of doom, while the majority of German Jews looked to their future as the fulfillment of the great promise of emancipation. Everything in their lives pointed to that. The Jews were the great chemists and physicists, the mathematicians and philosophers, the publishers of newspapers and the most important publishers of books. They owned all of the important department stores and most of the private banks, such as the banks of Mendelssohn and Bleichröder.[153] After all, when France paid indemnification after its defeat in 1871, its financial transactions were handled by the Jewish bank of Rothschild in Paris and the Jewish bank of Bleichröder in Berlin. When the Kaiser abdicated in 1918, one of the leading Jewish industrialists, who owned a fleet of merchant ships, committed suicide.[154]

The illusion of being rooted in Germany ran very deep. During the First World War, there was a great deal of antisemitism in the army and the usual explanation was that Jewish officers, sitting in army offices, had desk jobs rather than fighting at the front. It took the Jews more than a decade to compile and publish a book with the names of twelve thousand German Jews who had been killed in battle.[155] They were very proud of this volume and presented it to the then president of the German Reich, Field Marshal von Hindenburg. To the Jews who went to see Hindenburg it was a great historic moment, and they presented the leather-bound volume to the German president with a great deal of pride. Hindenburg accepted it so coldly—almost with contempt for the Jews—that these Jewish leaders returned from the presidential palace downhearted and a little bit skeptical about their own conviction that they belonged where they were living. Of course, they had

153. Joseph Mendelssohn (1770–1848), the oldest son of the Jewish philosopher Moses Mendelssohn, had founded a banking business; the banker Gerson von Bleichröder (1822–1893) served as Bismarck's personal financial consultant.

154. Prinz is referring to Albert Ballin (1857–1918), a Hamburg shipping magnate and adviser on naval matters to Wilhelm II.

155. It took until 1932. In that year, the Reichsbund jüdischer Frontsoldaten published *Die jüdischen Gefallenen des deutschen Heeres, der deutschen Marine und der deutschen Schutztruppen, 1914–1918.*

lived there for sixteen hundred consecutive years, and they knew that the first synagogue had been built in Cologne in the fourth century when the Roman army had occupied the Rhineland. With a great deal of pride and as a proof of the genuineness of their claim, they exhibited the document of privilege that was bestowed upon the Jews of Cologne by Emperor Constantine in the year 324.[156] All this was historically correct. What the Jews forgot was that, of the sixteen hundred years, they had lived within ghetto walls for more than a thousand, that the year of their emancipation was only 1812, and that between 1812 and 1933, the year of Hitler's advent to power, there had been many antisemitic movements, some of them preparing the German people for the racial ideology of Adolf Hitler.[157]

It was very difficult to convince the majority of German Jews that geographic existence in a country is not identical with social and political acceptance. It took many years until it became apparent to the most stubborn among them that their exclusion from public and private life had reached proportions that were beyond their control and that the time had come for them to draw the consequences. Some of them left the country, a large number to little Palestine, others to countries where they had families. But only half of German Jewry emigrated; the rest waited for the terrible event of German Jewry's deportation to death camps, which took place in November 1938, a year after I left Germany.[158] In the four years that I lived under the Hitler regime, every day brought new difficulties and a greater awareness by the people that there was no longer a battle to be fought, that everything was lost. The German-Jewish leadership was unable and unwilling to express its opinions—and with good reason. Many of us were taken to prisons at the slightest provocation. Meetings with Jews outside of Germany were difficult and dangerous, but they took place even though no country in the world was willing to intervene on behalf of the Jewish people. The American ambassador to Germany[159] sent reports to his government that made light of the anti-Jewish persecution. Our ambassador in London, Mr. Joseph Ken-

156. See note 106, above.

157. Ghetto walls existed only for city-dwelling Jews and only for part of the time since their original settlement. The emancipation of 1812 was not complete and applied only to a portion of the Jewish population in Prussia.

158. Following the November Pogrom in 1938, thirty thousand adult male Jews were sent to concentration camps (not death camps) in Germany, from which they were released if they could show that they had received an immigration visa to another country. Mass deportations of German Jews to death camps did not begin until the fall of 1941.

159. William E. Dodd, the U.S. ambassador to Germany from 1933 through 1937, felt deep revulsion for the Nazi regime but found no effective response to the Jews' deteriorating position—which he took quite seriously. He was succeeded by the more accommodating Hugh R. Wilson.

nedy, flirted with the Nazis and sent reports that disregarded the persecution of non-Aryans and political dissenters. The American consulates were very often uncooperative and demanded documents that were no longer available.

There was a small group of Jews who lived in Germany that had come from Eastern Europe, mostly from Lithuania and Poland, but some also from Russia. Although few in numbers, they maintained their own life separate from the German-Jewish community. Most German Jews looked down on them as inferior people, and even inferior Jews. Although there were no Jewish neighborhoods in German cities, the poor Eastern European Jews created their own. There most of them lived their lives, religiously and socially, with neither concern nor interest in German-Jewish affairs. But there were some—artists, businessmen, scientists and professors—who shared the life of German Jewry though they maintained themselves as a unique group. I had a very close and intimate relationship with Eastern European Jewry. While German Jews did not recognize the existence of a Jewish people and considered themselves "Germans of the Jewish persuasion," I as a Zionist and my friends accepted the existence of the Jewish people as a premise of our Zionist ideology.

I remember that when I was still in high school, sleeping in a tent on an overnight hike, I was rudely awakened by a great deal of noise. I crawled out of the tent and saw a German policeman in the process of arresting a number of young men. I listened to the sounds and heard a language with which I was not familiar, but which I guessed to be Yiddish. I had never heard that language before. I walked over and persuaded the policeman to release the group into my custody. This he did. It turned out that these young Jews had decided to leave Poland and go to Palestine. They were not merely my fellow Jews but also my fellow Zionists. I took them home; several of them slept in our apartment, and others I took to Jewish families where they stayed and were taken care of. It was my first experience with Eastern European Jews and I found out how much I had in common with them. Although I did not understand Yiddish very well, the similarity with the German language was enough to make communication between them and myself possible. We had seen Eastern European Jews who came to our town once or twice a year asking for money and we associated them with poverty and professional begging. As we had no poor Jews in our community, we were very happy to provide money and clothing for these people who had left their towns hurriedly to milk another Jewish community. But this group of young Jews was different. They were well educated and determined to make a new life in a country that they knew would some day become the Jewish state.

When I moved to Berlin I immediately found new Eastern European contacts. There was a cafe called the "Romanische Café" situated in the center of the western part of the city, not far from the leading Protestant church. This café had become the headquarters of writers, intellectuals, and artists. I used to spend almost every evening there, either before or after the theater or a concert. We had our own table, which was occupied by Yiddish-speaking intellectuals and writers. It was a typical European café where no one disturbed you even if you didn't consume anything. A café was a place where people talked and discussed literary and political issues. Sometimes we stayed there until the wee hours of the morning. Since I had written a number of books, I was accepted as a fellow writer. I was very young and not very rabbinical, and to many of these Eastern European Jews I was a completely new phenomenon. It was in those days that I tried to live down my rabbinical dignity and probably exaggerated quite a bit in doing so. I wanted to be normal and like the others. Soon I was accepted as the first and only German Jew into the club of Yiddish writers, which was called the Sholem Aleichem Club.[160] The writers spoke Yiddish among themselves and I soon became attuned to the language.

By the end of the First World War several thousand Eastern European Jews had settled in Germany, most of them in Berlin.[161] They came to us after the Russian Revolution, but some of them were communists. Among them were Jewish writers who formed a very distinctive as well as distinguished group. They included Sholem Asch, David Bergelson, Chaim Nachman Bialik, and the Hebrew Hellenist poet Tchernichovski.[162] His non-Jewish wife always sat next to him, wearing a black dress and a necklace with a large cross. I remember a writer who came from Poland, Israel Joshua Singer (Isaac Bashevis Singer's brother), the author of *The Brothers Ashkenazi* and *Yoshe Kalb*. We sat around the table in the café and he read a manuscript to us. He was a great teller of stories. Sometimes we stayed until two in the morning, laughing all the time.

I remember one incident very clearly. One of the writers asked Singer to visit his mother in Warsaw. "I have not written to my mother in fifteen years," he began, "and would appreciate it if you would go to her and give her my regards." He gave him his mother's address and we waited for Singer's

---

160. Named after the prominent Yiddish writer, Sholem Aleichem (1859–1916).

161. There were close to one hundred thousand East European Jews in Germany in 1925.

162. Sholem Asch (1880–1957) was a Yiddish novelist; David Bergelson (1884–1952), a Russian Yiddish writer; Chaim Nachman Bialik (1873–1934) was best known as an outstanding Hebrew poet; Saul Tchernichovski (1875–1943), likewise a Hebrew poet, was influenced by classical Greek literature. All of them lived for a time in Berlin.

return a month or two later to give us a report on his visit. When Singer returned, we sat around the table and the writer, whose name I have forgotten, said to Singer, "Have you seen my mother?" This was Singer's reply. "I went to see your mother," he said. "I found her living alone in a small apartment. She is a very old woman but very bright, and when I sat down, she offered me a glass of tea and some cake. Only after I had drunk and eaten did she ask me about my mission. I told her that I was a writer, that I visited with fellow writers in Berlin, and that it was there I had met her son. She said, 'My son? I have several.' I said to her, 'I met your son Yossele.' 'Yossele,' she said, 'I did not know he was alive. What is he doing?' I said to her, 'Your son Yossele is a famous writer.' She asked, 'What does he write?' I was very hesitant to answer the question since I knew that Yossele was a writer of atheistic books. So I simply said to her, 'Your son Yossele is writing books.' But this did not satisfy her. She had little blue eyes, and they looked at me inquisitively. She paused for a while and then she said, 'What kind of books does he write?' It was now my turn to pause, and then I decided that I would have to tell her the truth. So I said to her, 'Your son Yossele writes books against God.' There was a long pause. She sat there in her chair, small, old, but very alert. Then she looked at me with her bright little eyes and smiled, saying, 'My son Yossele is writing books against God!' Then with a little sigh she said, 'Writing books against God. May God help him.'"

When I listened to this story I thought back to the time when I was a student and, as I mentioned before, was editing a Jewish weekly. The paper was poor and I shared an office with a friend of mine who was in charge of a social agency. It was in the year 1923.[163] The chief of police had issued identification cards for foreigners who lived in Germany as legal residents. I remember coming to my office one morning before my friend arrived and finding someone in his room whom I did not know. I looked at him and saw an Eastern European Jew with a white beard, sitting there patiently waiting for my friend. He was a Rembrandtesque figure. His face was as beautiful as Rembrandt's self-portraits. He sat erect in the chair. There was no servility, nor any impudence. He seemed to be a man of great dignity.

My friend finally arrived. He was very young, just a few years older than I, arrogant, and very much aware of the high position he thought that he held. He looked at the man with some contempt and then he spoke to him in a voice that I have never forgotten. It was the voice of the bureaucrat dealing with a client who wanted something from him. He was clearly annoyed by this visit, although it was his duty to receive these people and attend to their

163. Should read: 1924.

needs. The man evidently did not quite understand, and my friend repeated, "What is it that you came here for?" The man replied in a quiet voice which was that of a basso profundo, "I have come to you, sir, to ask you to see to it that I get a passport." My friend was visibly irritated and asked the man, "Don't you have a passport?" The man reached into his pocket and took out several passports. One was Polish, the other Lithuanian, and there were two more issued by other countries. My friend looked at these passports and then yelled at the man, "You have four passports and you have the audacity to come to me and ask for another!" When the man heard this, he rose from his chair. I noticed that he was more than six feet tall, slim, and impressive looking. He eyed my friend with some sort of pity. Then he touched his shoulders and said to him, "Young man, let me tell you one thing that I hope you will never forget. For a Jew it is better to have five passports rather than four." I thought of this sentence ten years later, in 1933, after Hitler had come to power, when a passport had become such a precious thing and when even the blindest Jew had to understand that for a Jew it is better to have five passports rather than four.

This whole scene has remained unforgettable for me until this very day. It was the expression of Eastern European wisdom based on bitter experience. Altogether I had a rather romantic attitude toward Eastern European Jews, which was not at all realistic. But here I was, a German Jew, full of envy for the particular wisdom of the Eastern European Jew who had lived through so much misery, still preserving his human pride and dignity. I became very close with several Eastern European Jews, one of them the musician and composer Chemjo Vinaver.[164] He had come from a Hasidic family in Lithuania; his uncle was a Hasidic rebbe. They lived in a Jewish shtetl[165] where he had stayed with his uncle. There was a group of young people there that rebelled against the world of Hasidism. They decided to express their rebellion, and the most dramatic way to do that was to violate the laws of Yom Kippur, a Jewish day of fasting. They determined they would eat non-Kosher food publicly and thus declare their rebellion against the Jewish community of the little village. But of course, there was no non-Kosher food available in the little shtetl. So then they decided to have a gathering in town on the eve of Yom Kippur and to eat candles made from animal fat. It was the only non-Kosher food they could think of. In order to dramatize the rebellion even more my friend Chemjo, who was the leader of the group, seduced the rebbe's daughter and made known to the community that he had

164. See note 18, above.
165. A small East European town, most or all of whose inhabitants were Jews.

had sexual intercourse with her. They were all expelled from the Hasidic community and together they left the country, Chemjo landing in Berlin. He was enormously musical although he had had no music training, nor did he have any money. He continued to live with the rebbe's daughter for a while, but then she found another man whom she married. Chemjo, however, went to concerts and to the opera every night and trained himself to become a musician and composer. When I first met him, I was attracted to his beautiful hands. They were almost transparent, as though they had been made of fine, thin porcelain. Soon after I assumed my responsibility as a rabbi in Berlin, I engaged him to be my music director and conductor of my choir. We became very close friends.

Another of my Eastern European friends was the writer David Bergelson, who had written many novels. He had also written a play, which was so powerful that it had been accepted by a famous Berlin theatrical producer whose stage was considered one of the most advanced theatrical stages in the world. The producer's name was Piscator.[166] He was not a Jew but he left Germany for America when Hitler came to power. Piscator had accepted Bergelson's play, which was called "The Deaf One."[167] The play was, of course, written in Yiddish and Piscator needed a German translator. It appeared that there was no one among the 175,000 Jews in Berlin who knew both Yiddish and German. It was at that time that an American Jewish writer, Abraham Reisen,[168] had come to Berlin, and the Jewish writers decided to arrange for a party honoring the famous man. I was invited to attend the party. It was held in Bergelson's home, which was on a large estate owned by a Russian Jew who was known as a patron of Yiddish literature. The latter had invented a certain derrick that became very important to the oil industry, and he was a very rich man. He was well familiar with Bergelson's work and invited him to occupy the gardener's house on his beautiful estate, situated not very far from my home in one of the most luxurious parts of Berlin. The house was large so that Bergelson could live there with his wife and young son. His wife was a secretary at the Soviet Embassy in Berlin. Later, when they returned to Russia, the son became a hero of the Red Army.

166. Erwin Piscator (1893–1966) was a left-wing modernist theatrical director. After a stay in the Soviet Union, he lived in the United States from 1939 to 1951.

167. David Bergelson's short story, entitled "Der Toyber," was dramatized in 1930 and performed in Yiddish in the Soviet Union and the United States. Bergelson moved to Berlin in 1920, where he lived off and on until he settled in Moscow in 1934. Together with other Yiddish writers, Bergelson was shot, on his sixty-eighth birthday, in 1952.

168. Abraham Reisen (1876–1953), a prolific Russian Yiddish poet and short-story writer, had moved to New York in 1914.

Bergelson himself, unfortunately, was among those Jewish intellectuals who were killed under the Stalin regime.

At the party the great event was discussed. The Yiddish play had been accepted by a famous German director, but no one could translate it into German. Abraham Reisen looked at me and then said to the group, "Prinz should translate it." I tried to assure him that I did not know enough Yiddish to do so. But there was a majority decision, and the next day I became a student of Bergelson's. He was my teacher in a language that I found increasingly interesting and even fascinating. As Yiddish is based on medieval German, I had some knowledge of it. I had studied medieval German and Gothic at the Berlin University for a whole year and I discovered the German roots of Yiddish while Bergelson was teaching me. I bought a German–Yiddish grammar, studied Yiddish every day for many weeks, and at the end of these many lessons began to translate the play. Since Bergelson used multiple Russian words, I needed his help very often for I knew no Russian. Soon the play was finished and taken to Piscator. This was at the end of 1932. It was never performed.[169] In January 1933, Hitler came to power. Piscator went to America, and Bergelson and his family returned to the Soviet Union.

One of the most colorful Eastern European Jews I met was the famous actor Alexander Granach.[170] He had been a baker by trade and was born in a village near Kolomea, Galicia. Sometimes he bragged about the fact that much of his youth was spent in the brothel of the little town where he was born. But this was part of a natural braggadocio. He always liked to act and he performed in the only Yiddish theater in Berlin. Apparently someone had told the great director and theatrical genius Max Reinhardt that among the actors of that little amateurish Yiddish theater there was a man called Granach who seemed to have a natural talent for acting. Reinhardt went to one of his performances, and it was he who discovered Granach, who was to become one of the leading actors of the most famous theatrical group in Europe. It is difficult to describe him. He was coarse and tender at the same time. I never knew which part he was playing, for he was acting all the time. He was always in love with someone and he had a harem of women. On the stage he was incomparably great. It was his great desire to play Shylock in

169. Likewise, Prinz's German version was never published and was apparently lost. According to his daughter Lucie, although Prinz loved the Yiddish language, his mastery of it left much to be desired.

170. Alexander Granach (1890–1945) came to Berlin from Galicia at the age of fifteen, where he joined Max Reinhardt's school and in 1908 the Max Reinhardt Theater. After a period spent in Poland and Russia, he settled in the United States in 1938, a few months after Prinz's arrival.

Shakespeare's *The Merchant of Venice*, but I do not think he ever did.[171] I remember some of his most unforgettable performances. He was one of the few actors who came to our café. He never denied his Jewishness and was proud of his roots in Kolomea. After Hitler came to power, he went to Russia because he thought himself to be a communist. But in reality he was not.

In Russia he landed in prison, but for some strange reason he was released and came to America, where we were among the first people he visited.[172] I advised him strongly against joining the Yiddish theater in New York, from which he received many offers. He went to Hollywood instead. There he played one of the three Russians in the film *Ninotchka* in which Greta Garbo was the star. He was extraordinarily successful and played in other films, as well. Later he was called to New York to play the Italian fisherman in *A Bell for Adano*. It was the fulfillment of his great dream, having his name in large illuminated letters on a theater marquee. He played many performances and received enthusiastic critical acclaim. But because he always thought of himself as a he-man who could not possibly ever get sick, he neglected to take care of an appendicitis attack from which he died in a New York hospital.[173] Together with Fredric March,[174] who was one of his great admirers, I buried him in New York. When we came to the cemetery, the coffin was taken to a certain part of the crowded place which was reserved for people who came from Kolomea. As we arrived at the gates I was gently pushed aside by a group of men who said, as in a chorus: "Alex, welcome to Kolomea, welcome home." My rabbinical functions had ceased; Alex had come home.

Berlin, the capital of Germany and German Jewry, had also become the capital of Eastern European civilization. There were many publishing houses that published in Hebrew and Yiddish. One of them was owned by the poet Bialik, who was known as a particularly unpleasant exploiter of Hebrew writers. Nevertheless, his publishing house, called Devir, flourished in the north of Berlin. Far removed from the Jewish intellectuals who met in the café every night was a little old man, frail, inhibited, reticent, and almost inaccessible. His name was Simon Dubnow.[175] He was writing the first

171. In fact, Granach did play Shylock to great acclaim, but not in a Reinhardt production.
172. Granach was accused of leading a dissolute life. He was released after the German-Jewish writer, Lion Feuchtwanger, wrote a letter to Stalin on his behalf. Granach had been invited to Kiev to direct the Yiddish theater there.
173. Gad Granach, Alexander's son, wrote that when Prinz saw his father in the hospital, he said to him: "Hey, Granach, don't do anything stupid. You acted the role well. Now get up!"
174. Fredric March (1897–1975) was a highly regarded stage and screen actor.
175. Simon Dubnow (1860–1941) settled in Berlin in 1922. He later moved to Riga, where a

modern Jewish history in which he conceived of the history of his people in the context of world history. He wrote it in Russian and it was translated into German by my friend Aaron Steinberg,[176] the brother of Isaac Steinberg, who had been the first Minister of Justice under the Kerensky regime in Russia.[177] It immediately became a best-seller, and at least fifty thousand copies of the ten volumes were sold very soon. It remains one of the great Jewish histories.

It was only natural that Jewish work should attract Eastern European Jews. They were generally much more knowledgeable than German Jews. I had very many and very close friends among them. One was Jacob Lestchinsky,[178] who had come from Russia in 1921. He was a socialist and statistician; in addition to that, he was a lovely, gentle and knowledgeable man. One of his daughters became my student. Michael Traub[179] was another. He had come from Lithuania and became one of the major propagandists of Keren Hayesod. He had the obsession to collect more money than anyone before him, and he did. He was a perfectionist and an extraordinary organizer. In 1938 I traveled with him throughout Canada, where he served as the Yiddish speaker. He was as successful there as he had been in Berlin. I spent the last days of his life with him prior to his death in New York of leukemia.

When Hitler had been in power for several years, many Jews from other countries came to see us in order to learn what the real situation was and to try to help. Some of them stand out in my memory. One of the first and most courageous to come was Henrietta Szold,[180] that American Jewess who had become president of Hadassah, which she had founded. She was particularly interested in saving children, and it was she who coined the term *Youth Aliyah.* She was extraordinary in her quiet devotion. I have never seen a more dedicated person before or since. I remember once boarding a train with her. I traveled first class, but she traveled third class. I asked her why she

Gestapo officer shot him. His ten-volume *World History of the Jewish People* appeared in German translation between 1925 and 1929.

176. The philosopher and Orthodox Jew Aaron Steinberg (1891–1975) had come to Berlin from Eastern Europe in 1922. Later he played a leading role in the World Jewish Congress, as did Prinz.

177. More precisely, Isaac Steinberg (1888–1957), as a member of the Social Revolutionary Party, served as Minister of Justice in the first Soviet government, headed by Lenin, from December 1917 to March 1918.

178. Jacob Lestchinsky (1876–1966) was a pioneer Jewish demographer and prominent Zionist Socialist. In 1938, he moved to New York and later to Israel.

179. Michael Traub (1891–1946) died while on a mission for Keren Hayesod.

180. See notes 53 and 107, above.

was doing that to herself. She really shamed me by saying that since she was traveling at the expense of the Jewish people, she preferred the cheapest way possible. If, however, she would be traveling at her own expense, she would travel first class. In addition, many others came. Chaim Arlosoroff[181] came from the Ukraine to Berlin, where he lived until 1924 when he went to Palestine. There he played a large role in the political life of the Labor Party. He visited us at the beginning of 1933 and called for all of us to come to Palestine. Shortly afterward, he was assassinated there, and Palestine was thereby deprived of someone who undoubtedly could have become its first prime minister.

From England came Rebecca Sieff,[182] the wife of my old friend Israel Sieff who later became Lord Sieff of Brimpton. Rebecca was very active in the Zionist women's organization. She was an extraordinary person, a very wealthy woman who preferred public life to the conveniences of a rich English lady. Soon after she came, another one of my friends arrived in Berlin. She was the Lady Reading,[183] a marchioness and lady-in-waiting to the Queen of England. She came to one of our meetings at which I was the main speaker. When she was informed that there were two Gestapo agents in the audience, she fainted and had to be carried out. Chaim Weizmann came, of course. Someone else came, whom until then we had only known as one of the activists in the Labor movement in Palestine. He was David Ben-Gurion, a Polish Jew who stopped in Berlin for a few days.

The year about which I am writing is 1936. It was a very difficult year. The Nuremberg Laws had become a reality. The walls of the ghetto had grown taller and thicker. Life was much more restricted than ever before. My closest friends were leaving Germany with my blessing. I had to stay back, since it seemed impossible for me to leave my people and my position while they continued to suffer. It was probably a romantic notion on my part or an exaggerated opinion of my importance. But I felt instinctively that I had to stay with them and accept whatever might happen to me. I was busy writing books, delivering speeches, doing my work on the newspaper, and involving myself in political affairs to the extent that it was possible. I continued to

181. Chaim Arlosoroff (1899–1933), a Ukrainian Jew and a principal leader of Labor Zionism, had grown up in Germany. In 1924, he settled in Palestine, where he was murdered under mysterious circumstances.
182. Rebecca Sieff (1890–1966) was the first president of WIZO, the Women's International Zionist Organization, an office that she held for more than forty years.
183. Eva Violet, Marchioness of Reading (1895–1973), though brought up as a Christian, returned to Judaism in the 1930s, became a Zionist, and later chaired the British section of the World Jewish Congress.

preach, but even this was very difficult. Wherever I spoke or preached, my two Gestapo friends were there. Several times during that period I received a telephone call or a letter from the Gestapo, informing me that I was no longer permitted to preach. For the next week or so I was permitted to conduct services and read prayers, but I was not to preach. I had to accept that decree. The Gestapo agents were there to watch that I did. I had to try to think of something that would replace the sermon, but which was of equal strength and importance. The first time that the prohibition against preaching was in effect I went to the pulpit, and at the moment when I was to deliver a sermon I said: "According to a decree of the government and its agencies, I am not permitted to preach tonight. I shall therefore read an ancient prayer to you." I read it in Hebrew and in translation. This is what I read:

> O my God! guard my tongue from evil and my lips from speaking guile; and to such as curse me let my soul be dumb, yea, let my soul be unto all as the dust. Open my heart to Thy law, and let my soul pursue Thy commandments. If any design evil against me, speedily make their counsel of no effect, and frustrate their designs. Do it for the sake of Thy name, do it for the sake of Thy right hand, do it for the sake of Thy holiness, do it for the sake of Thy law. In order that Thy beloved ones may be delivered, O save with Thy right hand, and answer me. Let the words of my mouth and the meditation of my heart be acceptable before Thee, O Lord, my Rock and my Redeemer. He who maketh peace in His high places, may He make peace for us and for all Israel, and say ye, Amen.[184]

I read it with great emphasis, and certain sentences I read so slowly that every word became important and applicable to the situation in which we lived. I repeated the sentence: "If any design evil against me, speedily make their counsel of no effect, and frustrate their designs." Everyone in the congregation knew what I was referring to. After the service, one of the Gestapo agents came up to me and said, "The prayer you read was much more dangerous than any sermon you could have delivered." I replied, "According to the letter I received, I was permitted to read the prayers that we usually read. This prayer is said every day. We have always said it, and I was within my rights to do so tonight." To the Gestapo agents who, after all, were Germans, this was a convincing argument. This prayer expressed an attitude about which I had spoken several times publicly. The time was ripe to say something to the Jewish people that would make them strong, for strength was needed. There was no longer any sense in consoling them about

---

184. This prayer is the concluding meditation that follows the petitionary prayers in the daily and Sabbath services. Prinz refers to a line from this prayer earlier. See note 79, above.

what was happening to them. The reality was stark enough. Many people had already perished. Although no mass deportation had taken place, thousands of people were in concentration camps, and the names of concentration camps began to be known. Auschwitz was, of course, not yet among them, for it was situated in Poland, and the war had not yet begun. But there were enough concentration camps within Germany, and the people who were taken there were not only Jews but socialists, Communists, intellectuals, and other rebels. There was a sufficient number of Jews among them, however, and families were already receiving little boxes containing the ashes of people who had been killed in the camps. The Nazis considered even that act of sending the ashes to be buried to be an act of kindness. What the Jews needed now was a different kind of strength.

There is a German proverb that says: "It is better to be an anvil than to be a hammer."[185] I began to develop the theory that it was morally superior to be an anvil, that to be a hammer necessitated the immoral act of cruelty. Much against my conviction, I began to extol suffering. Suffering was now the expression of the righteous and the decent; persecution was the tool of murderers and highway robbers. I don't know to what extent my argument was convincing. But I repeated it so often and in so many variations that I thought some people might get a bit of consolation from the fact that they were among the decent ones, and therefore they had to suffer. I developed this theory into the notion of a Jewish nobility. In this theory, the Jews were the aristocrats and the others were the barbarians. How I ever dared to say all these things in public and in the presence of my Gestapo supervisors I do not know. I only know that when in the trenches you are more daring than the onlookers from far away. I simply disregarded danger, for I was not always aware of it. I was also very young and aggressive, and it may well be that I was vain enough to play the role of one of the very few Jews who were willing to speak up.

The Jews began to call me the "Jewish Goebbels," referring to the Minister of Propaganda, who was a great orator. But the Jews meant it as a compliment. What they really wanted to say was that there was at least one Jew who could speak with the same brutal directness that the Nazis used. They really wanted Hitler,[186] and I am sure that if Hitler had not been antisemitic, a large part, even a majority, of the German Jews would have become National Socialists. After all, they were as German as the others, and all the

185. Perhaps Prinz intends the proverb: "Ein guter Amboss fürchtet keinen Hammer" (a good anvil fears no hammer).
186. Presumably, Prinz intends: "*a* Hitler," in itself a most radical statement.

German instincts of obedience and discipline were also in their blood; but since they could not do it, they had to accept me as a substitute. I realized all that at the time, and I did not think it was particularly flattering to me. But this was the role I had to play and I played it not merely as a good actor but as someone who understood what the people needed. I therefore assured them they were not outcasts and not bearers of the yellow badge. They were the ones discriminated against and excluded from the mainstream of life, but they were much better than their persecutors. They were the "knights of the anvil," and that meant they were chosen to be the aristocracy of the world. I hope it comforted them. It was the last theory I developed in Germany under the Hitler regime.

It was toward the end of 1936 that my Gestapo friend Kuchmann began to talk to me about emigration. He said it would be better for me to leave and he hinted at the possibility that I might be taken to a concentration camp and perish there. We had this conversation in a certain café to which he summoned me. He spoke to me unofficially, privately, and kindly. He told me he would find a way of forcing me to leave the country since I apparently did not want to do it voluntarily. Shortly thereafter, he came to inform me officially in the name of Adolf Eichmann, who had become his boss, that I was herewith expelled from Germany, that I should leave the country as soon as possible during the course of the year 1937. I feel sure I was told this at the end of 1936, but it might have been at the very beginning of 1937. I told him I would have to go to America to speak to my friend Stephen Wise and that I would need a permit from the Gestapo to do so. Stephen Wise was, after all, considered to be enemy number one. Kuchmann thought that he could obtain such a permit for me and he did. In the spring of 1937 I came to America as a visitor. It had become known that I would do so, and the president of the Red Star Line,[187] which was the first shipping line to introduce a one-class system, invited me to go to America as its honored, prominent guest. I accepted the invitation, for my financial situation was not very good. Soon I found myself on a lovely little ship, which took me to America, landing in—of all places—Hoboken, New Jersey. My first impression of America was dreadful. The harbor was not impressive, the houses were decrepit, and the streets were dirty. The richest country of the world did not present itself to me as a place of glamour and prosperity.

Yet the few weeks that I spent in America were very important for me. I had read about the country, but I did not know that New York would over-

187. The Red Star Line was at that time owned by a Jew, Arnold Bernstein (1888–1971).

whelm me as it did. I walked down Fifth Avenue and looked at the skyscrapers, feeling very small and insignificant, full of fears about a country so huge and with such a large population, with buildings so tall they reached into the heavens. I felt I would never amount to anything here and would never be able to make my presence felt. I had many moments of depression because I knew it was easy to live in a little country like Germany with a bit more than half a million Jews. New York, with its Jewish population of two million, frightened me.

I had informed Dr. Stephen Wise[188] that I would come. I called him on the first day and met him in his study. Although we had met before, this was the first time I saw him in his natural habitat. He was a towering figure. Immediately he invited me to deliver speeches all over the country in which I would attack Hitler and call him all kinds of names. It took me a long time to convince him that that was not possible because I wanted to return to Germany where I had a family and colleagues with whom I worked. Moreover, I could not possibly attack the German government publicly before I had left the country permanently. He seemed to be very disappointed, but invited me to talk informally to students of the Jewish Institute of Religion.[189] Although I knew English quite well, it was my first public address in a foreign country using the language, and I must have sounded quite alien to the young people. Yet it was a great success, and I felt better after having finished this report on German Jewry and on Hitler. After all, this was not a public meeting and I could speak quite frankly. I found at that time, as I did later, that American Jewry and Americans in general, accustomed to ways of democracy, could not conceive of a dictatorship and had very little knowledge of what life under a Fascist regime really meant. They were very eager for bloody stories, but the stories that I could tell them were very ordinary, very depressing, very urgent, but not always stories of mass murder.

I stayed with my brother-in-law who was working for a brokerage firm on Wall Street and sharing his apartment with a friend. This was my place of residence for a few weeks and I learned a great deal from them. I visited my first American restaurant, saw the museums, and tried to discover New York. I remember being particularly interested in Harlem. It was at that time that I heard for the first time what is now commonplace, namely speeches about

---

188. See note 116, above.

189. The Jewish Institute of Religion was a nondenominational rabbinical seminary that Wise had founded in New York in 1922. It merged with the Hebrew Union College in Cincinnati in 1950.

black nationalism. Upon my return to Germany I wrote an article that was entitled "Zionism in Black."[190] I had heard a black man on one of the street corners in Harlem delivering a speech about the relationship between black Americans and Africa and appealing for a return in large numbers to their homeland. It was my first encounter with black people, but I had no opportunity to speak to any of their leaders.

I also began to discover a little bit of American Jewry, went to services, listened to sermons and, above all, met with Stephen Wise and his colleagues very often. We began to talk very concretely about my coming to America. I signed a contract with the United Palestine Appeal according to which I was to receive the amount of $300 per month in return for delivering speeches plus $50 for each speech. These amounts sound very small today, but in 1937 they represented at least a foundation on which I could build my life with my family. A house could be rented at that time for $50 or $60 a month and food was cheap. I also met a large number of German-Jewish refugees. I spoke to them, understood their problems and their difficulties. All of them were struggling to keep alive. Many were dependent on charity extended by an organization created for that very purpose. Most found the language a major barrier, and few of them, including the physicians and particularly the lawyers, had been able to make a living for themselves. It was a small group of desperate people, most of them longing for the country they had left and not yet in any way integrated into their new homeland. They had no knowledge of the political situation in Roosevelt's America.

It was during my stay in the United States that the crown prince of Holland visited America. When I heard President Roosevelt say on the radio that he was particularly happy to greet the crown prince of Holland since he himself was a Dutchman, I was so struck by this observation because it was quite different from the political mentality of Europe. I knew that the Roosevelt family had come to this country in the seventeenth century. However, I was puzzled by the notion that someone whose family had lived in America for three hundred years could still consider himself a Dutchman. I began to understand the particular nature of American nationalism, and dimly but not completely I began to comprehend the nature of American pluralism, something utterly alien to me. It was impossible for anyone living in Germany, France, or any other continental country to express any kind of allegiance, however tenuous, to a country other than that in which he lived. I

---

190. It has not been possible to locate this article. Prinz may be thinking of his article entitled "Amerika—hast Du es besser?" that appeared in *Der Morgen*, June 1937, 104–111. But that article does not compare black nationalism with Zionism.

met several Americans who told me that they were half French and half English. I cannot begin to describe my amazement at this kind of political ideology, which would permit a person to acknowledge his or her origin from a country other than America. The term *I am an American* had to be defined since everyone in this country was, after all, an immigrant, either of yesterday or of three hundred years ago. That fact remained a part of the American mentality which I knew I had to understand if I was to live here.

I made many friends and met many people in the American Jewish establishment who knew my name. Some of them had read a few of my books. I felt very much at home with them because they were kind and friendly and very eager for me to come to this country. I left America after four weeks by the same route and on the same ship on which I had come. It landed in Holland where I met Hilde. Together, slightly trembling, we went to Berlin.

In Berlin I was immediately called by the Gestapo. They asked me to bring my passport and come to Gestapo headquarters because of an accusation that had been made against me to which I had to respond. I could not possibly imagine what that accusation was. In the Gestapo office, I met with a very angry and hostile group who said I was being accused of having caused the destruction of the zeppelin Hindenburg, which had occurred on the day of my arrival in America.[191] There was no doubt in their minds that the burning of the great German dirigible was my work. This was a very serious accusation, and if they could prove it I would have been killed immediately. It was only due to a strange accident that I could demonstrate my innocence. We had arrived in Hoboken around five in the afternoon when I heard over the radio that the Hindenburg had burned and all the people in it had died. But because we arrived so late we could not land and had to stay aboard the ship until the next morning. The date of my arrival in America was stamped in my passport. I showed it to the Gestapo agents and was immediately released. I don't have to tell you how relieved I was, for I had escaped certain death by virtue of a little accident. Had it not been for the fact that I could prove I had not landed in America on the day of the Hindenburg's destruction, I would not be alive today.

This was now the beginning of the end. I was spending my last months in Germany. We had moved from our home in the fashionable district of Dahlem to the much less posh district of Charlottenburg. We lived on the

191. The airship Hindenburg, pride of Nazi Germany, exploded in mid-air above Lakehurst, New Jersey, on May 6, 1937, killing thirty-four passengers and crew. However, Prinz's passport indicates that he arrived in the United States on March 16, and was back in Southampton on April 26, 1937. Prinz's account is therefore not credible, though it is conceivable that the Gestapo believed Prinz had somehow laid plans for a sabotage of the zeppelin during his stay in the United States.

same street as my parents-in-law. Since we had two little children, it made life easier. I now had to begin my preparations for departure. I had been officially informed that I was to leave by the summertime. My passport had been taken away from me, but I was promised it would be returned as soon as I needed it for emigration. I received an affidavit[192] from Hilde's uncle who was a wealthy stock broker.[193] In addition, Stephen Wise had written to the American ambassador to France, Mr. Francis Biddle,[194] who had sent me a very helpful letter for immigration. In reality, I did not need either, for as a rabbi I could have immigrated on a nonquota basis. But this would have necessitated a contract with an American Jewish congregation, which I did not have. I believe I could have gotten one from Stephen Wise, but I did not want to have any kind of subterfuge. Therefore I decided to immigrate on the regular quota, which necessitated the acquisition of an affidavit of support. I sent all these documents to the American consulate, which informed me that I could not immigrate to America before the summer. Altogether, the American consulates were not terribly helpful. Whether this was due to the antisemitic attitude of the individual consuls I do not know. I only know that in many of the American consulates in the world Jews who did not have the proper documents were turned away, although this meant certain death for them. I received reports about the American consulate in Marseilles, France, which was notorious for its anti-Jewish attitude. I simply could not understand it, for I had a romantic approach toward America, "the land of the free and the home of the brave."

In spite of all the preparations we had to make, life went on as usual. I received a contract from a publisher to present a manuscript of the lectures I had delivered in Berlin on the psychobiography of five cities: Alexandria, Cordova, Amsterdam, Frankfurt, and Prague. The book was called *Life in the Ghetto: Jewish Fate in Five Cities*.[195] I had a deadline to meet and the book had to be written in a few weeks. I engaged a secretary for this purpose, and remember that we worked six hours a day. While dictating the book, I played Beethoven's Seventh Symphony repeatedly until I knew it by heart. I always

192. American law required that an American citizen sign an affidavit guaranteeing the material support of new immigrants to the United States.
193. His name was Ludwig Bendix.
194. The American ambassador to France in 1937 was William Christian Bullitt. Anthony Drexel Biddle, Jr., was deputy ambassador in 1940 and may have been on Bullitt's staff in 1937. Francis Biddle was at the time head of the National Labor Relations Board. There is no extant Wise letter that could be the one to which Prinz is referring.
195. *Das Leben im Ghetto. Jüdisches Schicksal in fünf Städten* was published in 1937 by Erwin Löwe and dedicated to "Lucie."

needed music when writing. The book was printed just a few days before we left Germany so that I read the galleys on the boat that finally took us to America. It was an interesting and greatly successful book, published after I had already left Germany.

I had seen many American apartments and I was amazed at the backwardness of American furniture. Both architecturally and in many other ways, America was still in the nineteenth century. I knew that if we took our very modern furniture, some of it from the Bauhaus, to America, people would laugh us out of the country. It had to be sold. But selling anything under duress amounted to giving away most of it. I do not now recall the details of the disposal of much of our furniture, some of which we were determined to take to America, where it still exists. I was permitted to take my library and as much furniture as I wanted, although it had to be packed in a certain manner. There were several firms that specialized in shipping the furniture of Jews. I had to pay my taxes in advance, after which I was permitted to leave.

I was very curious to know the reason for my expulsion from Germany. Not that I minded it; I had many reasons to be grateful. Had I stayed any longer, there is no doubt in my mind that I would have been sent to a concentration camp and perished there. What kept me alive was a riddle to me, and I am still puzzled by it. I asked for permission to see the head of the Jewish department at the state police and was amazed that I was granted such permission. The man in charge of Jewish affairs was a young, high-ranking SS officer by the name of Dr. Carl Flesch.[196] I arrived at his office, which was situated in a huge building which was not that of the Gestapo but of the state police. Entering his large room, the first thing I saw was a human skull on his desk. The skull was the insignia of the SS. He received me in a friendly manner and I told him I had come to inquire as to the reason for my expulsion. He replied that he was very eager to see me. It was only toward the end of the meeting that I realized what he wanted. We began to talk about my expulsion and then he asked his secretary to give him the file on me. I was amazed to see a rather heavy file. He removed a paper from it and said to me, "A few months ago you delivered a speech in Leipzig in which you are quoted as having said: 'Now that the German people has rejected the teachings of Christ, we are accepting Jesus of Nazareth as an important figure in Jewish history.'" I looked at him in amazement and said, "Since we are sitting here without witnesses, I will take the liberty of asking you a question.

196. Prinz may mean Gerhard Flesch (1909–1948), who possessed a degree in law and was appointed in 1936 to the Gestapo, where he was in charge of religious sects in Germany.

We were born in the same year. We were both students at the University of Berlin. Both you and I received our Ph.D. degrees in the field of philosophy (I had inquired about his background before I saw him). I know that your family had a democratic background and that you are the only member of the family who joined the National Socialist party. But since we have the same backgrounds, our families having lived in this country for many generations, can I not assume that you agree with me that Jesus of Nazareth was of Jewish origin?" He paused, looked at me for a moment, and then he said this unforgettable sentence, "I may or may not agree with you. One thing, however, is clear. The Führer has not as yet made a public statement about it, and therefore you are not permitted to claim the Jewish origin of Jesus." After this astonishing statement, he came to the real purpose of the meeting. He invited me to become a spy for the Gestapo after my arrival in America and to inform him of events that might be important in both military and political terms. This was the real reason for my expulsion. They thought I could be useful to them in America. I must have been disappointed,[197] but, of course, I told him that I would be very happy to write to him from time to time. I did in fact write to him a few months after our arrival in America, but that was the only letter, and it was not to his liking, I am sure.

These last months in Berlin were rather exciting because I did a great deal of looking back on the past eleven years, reevaluating what I had done in various fields and looking forward with some hope, but much more anxiety, to my new life in America. In the rabbinical field I had developed my own approach to the various problems that confronted the practicing rabbi who works in a congregation, has a pulpit of his own, and is known to the people as one of the spiritual leaders of the community.

There are several fields in which I developed my own approaches. One, to which I alluded earlier, was the very important field of preaching. My sermons dealt with people's real problems and I was very eager to deliver them in such a manner as to make the sermon into a lecture rather than a pious exercise. The proof of the pudding is in the eating, and the proof of the sermon is in its acceptance by the people. I attracted thousands of people to my sermons. I must admit I was helped during the Hitler years by the eagerness of the Jewish people to come to the synagogue and to listen to something that had a bearing on the new situation in the country. I never avoided difficult and sometimes controversial subjects because I was, and still am, in favor of controversy as a creative and important element in intellectual enterprises of

197. Prinz apparently means to say that he must have disappointed the Nazi official.

any kind. My being a Zionist in a community that rejected Zionism in itself created very vehement and passionate controversy.

The second field in which I was particularly interested was that of people's personal problems. I was very familiar with pastoral psychiatry, which was developed by one of Sigmund Freud's early students, who was also a pastor in Switzerland.[198] But in addition to that, I had received a great deal of instruction that enabled me to deal with the problems of families and individuals. Very soon I realized that I was attracting many schizophrenics who had come to me as a psychiatrist of the poor. My pastoral practice grew to such an extent that I had to transfer it from my home to a room in the community building.

It is probably akin to my interest in pastoral psychiatry that I developed a new theory and practice with regard to the very difficult task of comforting mourners. I began to think in terms of a different architectural design for the chapel of the cemetery. My concept was that the pulpit should be on the same level as the seats of the mourners so that the rabbi would really be one of the mourners. I then developed certain theories about the influence of color and type of music on the psychological problem of mourning. I found that a dark color corresponded to a baritone voice or a cello, and I found that a tenor or soprano voice, or a violin, were not acceptable at a funeral service. I also developed a new kind of eulogy, one that would treat the person as he or she really had been. I cannot claim that I cured the people of sorrow and grief, but I thought it was possible to apply some instant therapy at the moment of the funeral service, and I know that people came to appreciate this new approach to a problem that was inevitable and that occurred in the life of every family. When I left Berlin, I had buried several thousand people.

I had also developed a particular relationship to the field of writing. When I left Germany, I had published seven books and, as I indicated, an eighth was about to appear after my departure. I was therefore known as a writer. Until this very day I have my happiest moments when I am writing and miss it during those months of the year that I do not write. In writing, too, I developed my own style, which was particularly apparent in the Jewish history that I wrote. Mine was the first modern attempt at writing history not as a ghetto experience, but synoptically within the context of the history of the world.[199] Since I had studied art history, I was always eager to include

198. Prinz may be referring to the Swiss psychologist and pastor Oskar Pfister (1873–1956).
199. In fact, Simon Dubnow had done this earlier, as Prinz himself admits. See text and note 175, above.

the art of each period, as reflected in its architecture, painting, and sculpture. The art, as it reflected the Jewish life of the time, would indicate its special spirit and its unique contribution to civilization.

But probably the most important development in my life occurred a year or two before Hitler came to power, and it was in the field of politics. It was necessary to become politicized. After all, our people's situation was of a political nature and it was no longer possible to preach, write, or think without consideration of the political problems that beset us. Of course, the fact that I was a Zionist had sharpened my political understanding of the problems. Zionism was a political movement based on a political analysis of the Jewish situation. But as this Jewish situation was dependent on the general political atmosphere and climate, I had to extend my interest beyond purely Jewish affairs to the affairs of the country and of the world. Very early in my life I had become a political man who thought in political terms. I began to discover how very unpolitical the average Jew was. He was unable to recognize an enemy when he saw one. Optimism was a general Jewish curse, and it prevented the Jew from understanding Hitler. He did not understand that one of the most important political prerequisites was objectivity. It was not possible for me to look at a political phenomenon strictly from the Jewish point of view. I had to understand the political problem of a certain time and then relate the Jewish situation to it. The Jewish reaction often not only lacked objectivity but indulged in hysterics. For the majority of the Jews, the main problem was antisemitism. A very large part of contemporary Jewish literature dealt with that. To me, antisemitism was always a problem of the gentiles, and I have never been able to conceive of a Jewish solution, provided by Jews, to a problem that is one of Christian attitudes and that cannot be solved by the Jews. I tried to make this clear from the pulpit in my lectures and books. I don't think I ever succeeded.

Preparations were now made for my departure from Germany. Many of my friends had already left. They wrote letters, mostly from Palestine, where they were making a brave attempt to build a new life. This was not always easy and the letters we received were not always very encouraging. But the freedom of a new life compensated them for the many dissatisfactions. Articles were published in Jewish newspapers about the fact that I was leaving, and the Zionist organization prepared for a huge farewell lecture. It was held in the month of May 1937 in one of the largest halls in Berlin.[200] Long before the scheduled start of the meeting, the hall was filled with several thou-

---

200. Actually on June 26, in the Brüdervereinshaus. Benno Cohn was one of the introductory speakers, along with Franz Meyer, Michael Traub, and Robert Weltsch.

sand people. I reported earlier that I discovered among my audience the face of Adolf Eichmann.[201] The fact that he attended my last speech became very important. For legal reasons, it was necessary to identify Eichmann when he was tried in Israel. Until such identification was made, he was only purported to be Adolf Eichmann. My friend Benno Cohn,[202] who at that time was a judge and had had dealings with Eichmann in Berlin, was asked to identify him legally and in the presence of witnesses. According to a report that was published in several books, Benno Cohn said to Eichmann at the trial, "I am glad to see you here. The last time I saw you was at the farewell speech that Rabbi Fried delivered." This was an attempt to elicit from Eichmann a correction of the name. Eichmann fell for it, and said immediately, "This was not Rabbi Fried but Joachim Prinz who delivered the speech." These words legally identified him as Adolf Eichmann.[203]

This farewell speech had another important consequence. Eichmann, who at that time was a minor official in the Gestapo, reported about the speech in a long memorandum that he sent to Himmler, the head of the SS and the actual leader of the Gestapo. In this memorandum, Eichmann pointed out the fact that my going to America rather than to Palestine was clear proof of his contention that in America I would become the head of an international Jewish propaganda bureau. The memorandum was written in such a convincing manner that Eichmann was called to Himmler and received a promotion. It was because of that that he became the influential figure who caused the death of hundreds of people. It made him one of the leading and most brutal figures of the Nazi regime.[204]

Unfortunately, I do not now have any report about my speech, which

201. At the Eichmann trial in Jerusalem in 1961, Benno Cohn testified as follows: "We held a valedictory meeting to take leave of Rabbi Dr. Joachim Prinz who was leaving the country. He was one of the finest speakers, one of the best propagandists in those years. So we held that meeting in his honour. The hall was packed full. The public thronged to the meeting. Suddenly I, as chairman of the meeting, was called to the door, and my clerk from my office told me: 'Mr. Eichmann is here.' I saw a man, for the first time, in civilian clothing, and he shouted at me: 'You are responsible for order here? This is disorder of the first degree!' There was much pressure from people trying to get in. And he threatened to take measures himself if I did not put some order into it all. He complained that he had received a blow in the belly from a Jew who did not know that he was from the Gestapo. He then came in with a whole group, quite a number of people, some four of them. I watched him all the time from my place in the chair."

202. See note 88, above.

203. This story, with some variation, is related elsewhere. However, the identification took place during proceedings before the trial itself.

204. It has not been possible to confirm this claim. However, it was in 1937 that Eichmann received an officer's commission in the SS.

was published in full.[205] Although, of course, I had no manuscript, several stenographers were there and reported it. It was an attempt to redefine the position of the German Jew. I dealt with the very complicated problem of our relationship to Germany, which had now been defined for us by the new German government. I really did not care whether I was being supervised by Gestapo agents—if in fact I was—or whether I was completely at liberty to speak my mind. I decided that I should speak freely. I said that there was no doubt that a people who had lived in a country for sixteen hundred consecutive years, generations that could trace their origin back to the German Middle Ages, had developed a relationship to the country in which they lived. The German Jew had never spoken anything but German, although during the Middle Ages the German language of the Jews was called Judeo-German. It was German nevertheless. One of the troubadours of the early Middle Ages was a German Jew from the Rhineland.[206] There was a relationship to the language. The Jew had made a considerable contribution to the development of modern German. Heinrich Heine, a German Jewish poet torn between Judaism and Christianity, was the creator of modern German, particularly journalistic German. But in addition to him, there were many writers who made a sizable contribution to German literature. The language was not the only relationship that had to be dealt with. I also probably spelled out a hidden fear that I would not be able to express myself in a foreign tongue, or that at least I would feel inhibited to speak it or write it.[207]

The other equally profound relationship was with the land itself. Since I had been a member of the youth movement whose main activity was hiking in the country, I had developed a great love for the countryside, the rivers, the mountains, the German forests, and particular parts of Germany where we used to hike during the summer months. We never used public transportation outside of the railroad. We slept in barns and were not permitted by the rules of the youth movement to ever sleep in a hotel. This gave us a closeness to the land that other people probably did not have. But I remember very vividly that in my farewell address I spoke at great length about this relationship that could not be replaced by the relationship with any new country. I was wrong, of course, but I was right at the moment when I expressed these thoughts, and I am sure they meant a great deal to the people.

205. The *Jüdische Rundschau* of July 27, 1937, contains some of what Prinz said in his farewell speech, as does the *Israelitisches Familienblatt*, July 1, 1937.
206. The reference is to Süsskind of Trimberg, a well-known Jewish Minnesinger of the thirteenth century.
207. Prinz said that the "exodus from the German language" would be difficult for him.

I did not realize that I would come to another country and live there longer than I had lived in Germany, with the result that I did develop a relationship to that new country as profound as that which I had with the old one.

At the end of the speech there was a standing ovation. I was deeply moved that so many people had come to bid me farewell and that the relationship I had established between myself and thousands of individuals had borne fruit. I was also leaving the community, or what was left of it, as an outspoken advocate of total emigration, as someone who had dared to speak out against the government at a time when everyone else seemed to be so intimidated as to be silent.

But it was not so easy to bid farewell to all our friends. Even the technical arrangements were complicated. We had to vacate our apartment; all the things we wanted to take to America had to be packed; the library, the most important of my possessions, had to be carefully put into many cases. It took us weeks before we finally left our home and moved to the lively apartment of a friend. Since he was a bachelor he was able and very willing to accommodate us, including our two little children. My wife Hilde was pregnant in her seventh month, which did not make things easier. The continuation of my professional life likewise proved extremely difficult. One of the most painful experiences was our encounter with the consul general of the United States. Our papers were in order, the affidavit had been filed, and the letter from the American ambassador to France had been sent to the consul general (who knew who I was and of my work); nevertheless, we had to appear there at a set time. On the other hand, we were very lucky that we did not have to wait in line with the hundreds of people who were applying for American visas.

The reception we received at the consul general's office was far from cordial. Altogether it was utterly unnecessary for him to have treated me as an ordinary immigrant, as I was entitled to a non-quota visa. However, he subjected me to all kinds of questions about Hilde's uncle who had made out the affidavit, especially with regard to how much I thought he was worth. I was interested in the linguistic aspects of the term "How much is he worth?" I had always thought of worth as a moral term, and it took me some time to realize that he was speaking about our uncle's financial situation. I told him immediately that he was a millionaire, and that seemed to satisfy him. He did not realize that I did not have the foggiest idea of how much money he really had. When I told him, as he could see from the affidavit, that this uncle lived in Rye, New York, in Westchester County, and had an office on Wall Street, he was ready to accept my statement.

We then had to be examined by the physician of the consulate. This procedure ran into two difficulties. My wife was pregnant, and according to an ancient American law, the doctor of the consulate was not permitted to examine a woman gynecologically. I was struck by the insanity of this provision, but, nevertheless, this is what was done, or rather, what was not done. I remember his putting into her health certificate the following strange sentence: "Mrs. Prinz has a tumor of the abdomen. In all probability, it indicates pregnancy." Her examination therefore was very quick, but mine took a little longer. The doctor asked me to walk and thereupon insisted that I had a fracture of the leg. I had, in fact, never fractured my leg, and it took me half an hour to convince him that his diagnosis was inaccurate. This got me so excited that when he asked me for a urine specimen I was unable to comply with his request and I almost did not get an American visa because of this technicality. The consul finally agreed that he could ignore this technical difficulty and we got a marvelous piece of paper called a visa of immigration to America.[208] We left the consulate in great elation, looking with much pity at the hundreds of people who were standing outside waiting to be awarded the great privilege of leaving this dangerous country and arriving in God's own country. I still had to get an exit visa from the Germans. That took much less time. I will never forget the wording of the stamp that was put on our passports. It indicated that we were permitted to leave the country and that we had no right to return. It also said that when in Paris we would not be permitted to visit the World's Fair, since Jews were not allowed to enjoy such pleasures.[209] We could only smile at this naïve stipulation, since when we arrived in Paris there would be no German police to watch our movements. Nevertheless, we returned to the apartment of our friend, happy that our formalities had been taken care of and that we were on our way to America. We booked a train to leave on the following Monday at eleven o'clock. As that was going to be the beginning of the next week, we decided to visit friends and make the best of the last days in the country in which we and our ancestors had been born.

Among the provisions made for the new country was an agreement I entered into with an enterprising young man who had taken films of a Jewish children's home in the resort town of Caputh.[210] Since Hilde's parents spent their summers there (Albert Einstein also had a house there), we visited it every summer. The children's home was particularly successful, so that the

208. The quota immigration visa, signed by the American vice consul, is dated July 16, 1937.
209. The text reads: "Valid for an uninterrupted journey through France during the Paris World's Fair of 1937, however only en route to embarkation in Le Havre by July 23, 1937."
210. It is located on a lake to the southwest of Berlin.

young man, whose name I have forgotten, had taken films that he thought could be shown in America as an illustration of Jewish life under the Hitler regime.[211] It was an altogether naïve plan, but since I needed money very badly, I agreed to show the film in America and to speak about the problem. I do not remember now what sum of money I received for it. This agreement was among the many papers that I took along to America. Stephen Wise had informed me that I should not come to America traveling second class. We therefore booked a first-class trip to the United States on the French luxury liner De Grasse. We decided that our baby nurse should come with us so that the first years of the little baby to be born in America would be under proper supervision. But according to German law we could not travel with her since she was an Aryan. So we made arrangements for her to sit in a certain compartment on the train and to meet us after we crossed the border.

The day of our departure was fast approaching. It was already Friday and we went to services. Saturday was set aside for special meetings and parties with friends. I was therefore amazed when on Saturday afternoon there suddenly appeared in my friend's apartment two agents of the state police who examined my luggage and told me that I was to be arrested. That came at a rather awkward moment because the day before I had discovered that my passport lacked one extra page on which the entrance visa for America could be placed. Chaim Schein had given me his passport and with great difficulty pasted another page from it into mine.[212] We had to do it very carefully because if the German police had discovered our deed I could have been sent to prison. We had just succeeded in doing it when the two policemen arrived. I inquired as to what the charge was. They told me the charge was high treason. I knew that meant I could be shot. I decided to take all my documents along, including the passports with the American visa, and some reading material. Since the policemen had no car, they asked my friend Chaim to drive us to the prison. Chaim agreed. He owned a white convertible, a very luxurious car. It was a most amusing scene to see him at the wheel, with me sitting between the two policemen in the rear seat. I always found such things amusing, although there was no reason to laugh about it since the danger of this being my last trip was very great. I remember him, as he stopped in front of the prison, waving to me as I walked into the station with the two policemen.

The only consolation I had was that I was not arrested by the Gestapo but by the state police. There was a great difference between these two orga-

211. Presumably, the plan was for Prinz to raise money for the home in America.
212. The extra page containing the entrance stamp is no longer a part of Prinz's passport.

nizations. The Gestapo was the secret police of the National Socialist party. The state police was an official organ of the government. The treatment received from each of the two organizations was quite different. The state police was still rather polite and did things in accordance with the law. The Gestapo was quick to shoot people or send them to concentration camps. I always experienced a strange sense of elation whenever I was arrested; I was always so sure I would be released. It seemed to be some sort of psychopathological attitude I had adopted at that time, but it was very helpful to me. I don't have to tell you with what feelings I left my family and in what kind of mood they found themselves, but I had no time to think of that. The doors opened and I was in the station house.

There I found rather jovial German policemen. Most of them had served under the old regime and many recognized and greeted me, slightly embarrassed that I should be a prisoner. But since the charge was high treason, there was no way out, and they put me into a steel cage that had been erected in the middle of the station house. I sat there alone, although later some thieves and criminals came to join me. We were not permitted to speak to each other. Since it was Saturday afternoon, the atmosphere was rather strange. As I had nothing to do, I observed the scene with some sense of humor. It was really like the first act of a theatrical play. The policemen, who, after all, were petty bourgeois, were making plans for the weekend and talked about it quite happily. They ate their afternoon meal with gusto, which made me particularly hungry. I asked one of the men if he could get me something to eat. They gave me a piece of bread without butter. I started to nibble on it, but it was so hard I could hardly eat it. Finally, the young man who was involved in the filming of Caputh appeared. I then began to realize that the whole accusation was due to a misunderstanding. I remembered that a meeting of German officers had taken place in Caputh.[213] They had in the meantime been arrested, but apparently the police had assumed I had been instrumental in that meeting. My telephone had always been bugged so that I had to speak rather carefully about political matters, but I did not hesitate to talk about the Caputh plan which, after all, involved only a children's home.

By now most of the policemen had left the station and it was getting dark. I was then taken to the prison. Since the charge was high treason I had to be in solitary confinement. It was a dingy, little place with a bed, and I was very tired. Before I was allowed to enter the cell, my shoelaces were removed

---

213. Prinz is apparently referring to an anti-Nazi conspiracy. However, it has not been possible to find corroborating evidence.

and all my valuables, including my papers, my wallet and the passport with the American visa had to be given to the jailer. I was then permitted to enter the cell, which was closed and locked. Shortly afterwards as I sat down on the only chair available, I heard noises from my fellow prisoners to the left and the right welcoming me to the society of outcasts. The jailer who took me to the cell knew me quite well and said something like "I don't like the new regime. That they could do this to a man like you is further proof to me that they have no right to call themselves a government. I want you to know that I regret having to do this to you." I comforted him as best as I could, but then I was all alone and decided to go to bed and sleep. There was nothing better to do. I had no reading material, nor was there anyone to talk to. I must have fallen asleep shortly thereafter. It was four o'clock in the morning when I was suddenly called. The door to the cell opened with a loud noise and a man said to me, "It was all a mistake and you are free." I don't remember ever dressing so quickly. Upon leaving the prison, I was given my shoelaces and all my papers that had been neatly stacked away in a large envelope. Reaching the street and breathing in the beautiful spring air, I went to the first public telephone box to call my wife and tell her that I was free. I also kept the big piece of bread I had in my hand and took it to America. It was the symbol of my freedom; tomorrow we would leave. I can't describe the joy with which I was greeted not merely by my wife but by my friends who had stayed up all night and tried through various channels to find out about my fate. Now I was home, and I think we emptied a whole bottle of cognac. Then wearily we went to bed, to get up the next morning, the great day of departure.

Although for good reasons we had told no one when we would leave Berlin, a small group of very intimate friends showed up at the railroad station from which we were to depart for Paris. It was a luxury express train, and although the farewell was tearful to a certain extent, it was also full of joy and hope. In those days emotions were very often mixed and it was very difficult to decide between the one or the other. It was, after all, good to leave Germany, for things had become too dangerous, and had we waited for another month or so, we would never have been permitted to leave. All of us would have been killed. The final experience of sudden arrest under the flimsiest of circumstances was a good warning for us, which told us to get out as soon as possible. Although I was, as usual, calm and unexcited about being arrested and having been taken to jail, I began to understand that I was suffering from the euphoria of those who fought in the front lines. But my wife and family were not in the front lines, and I can imagine the constant anxieties they had to live through. Hilde was helped a little bit by the fact that she was very young, strong, and concerned about the children. But I was not always certain how the children reacted to the kind of life we had to live.

Now we were settled in the compartment. Our baby nurse Maria Breiden was sitting in a different compartment, very well aware of where we were, but according to law unable to join us. We had accepted those strange anomalies of life, but thinking back on it now, it was such a profound expression of the period of degradation in which we had lived. I was also thinking of the many people who were left behind, some of them in important and responsible positions of Jewish leadership. The situation could only deteriorate and become increasingly difficult and dangerous for the Jews. A great many of those who remained in Germany had come to Berlin where it was safer than living in the small towns. The latter had been conquered by Hitler long before his advent to power, and the few Jewish families who lived in them were the targets of a great deal of cruelty and molestation. It didn't matter that their families had lived in that same town or little village for hundreds of years. Their neighbors had turned into enemies, and the number of Christian families who protected Jews was very small. Nor could anyone blame them for their cowardice and hesitation. It is easy to talk about courage under pressure, but anyone who has ever lived under a regime of dictatorship knows that these are pious sermons. It took not merely courage but daring and complete neglect of family responsibilities to assert oneself. It must also be borne in mind that families themselves were split. Cases were not too rare where children betrayed their own parents, thinking nothing of exposing them to the danger of death. National Socialism was not just a political movement. It was, after all, a new fanatical religion with an explicitly spelled out credo that had little respect for the ancient values of family and normal decency.

We all leaned out of the windows of the train. We traveled first class so as to have a comfortable trip. The windows were wide and permitted all of us to lean out. Lucie was six and a half years old and Michael was four. I can still see Lucie playing with her doll and Michael sitting there with a teddy bear, completely unaware of what was happening. Lucie was much more excited and probably realized that a new chapter in our lives had begun. But she was, thank God, too young to comprehend the gravity of it all. Finally, the train began to move and soon Berlin was behind us. Our tickets were checked ever so often, as is the habit on European trains. But there was no political control. At long last the train stopped in Cologne in the Rhineland, which was the last stop before crossing the French border. This was a moment of great danger. Here we were not merely checked by the railroad personnel, but storm troopers in their brown uniforms came into our compartment and looked at our passports and visas. This was the point of greatest possible anxiety. At that moment I was sure I would be arrested. The train stopped for a long time and our passports were taken from us, evidently brought to a central office to be scrutinized. I was still afraid of the possible discovery that the last page in my passport had been glued in, that therefore my passport would be rejected as being invalid and I would be sent back to Berlin. But after a while, which probably was not too long but which seemed to be an hour later, our passports were returned. The man even smiled at us as we put our passports and immigration visas in our pockets. Shortly afterwards, the train rolled on toward the French border. Although we were not completely at ease until we had crossed into France, we were fairly hopeful that nothing else would happen. As soon as the train did indeed cross the border, the door opened and Maria our nurse came in and we embraced each other tearfully. Her being with us was a symbol of our new freedom.

At long last we arrived in Paris. Although I had been there many times, this time it felt like coming home. We had reserved rooms in a little hotel not far from the Opera and took a taxi there. We were to stay in Paris for several days before our boat would leave from Le Havre. It is most difficult for me to describe our feelings: finally to be free, to move about without fear, not to have to whisper as we did at home, not to be in fear of the telephone, which could pick up some political remark that we might make. No one could arrest me here. We opened our passports and saw that stamp forbidding us to go to the World's Fair in Paris, as "Jews are not permitted there." We laughed about the Germans' stupidity in believing they had control over us in a foreign country. It was in happy defiance of this ludicrous prohibition that we decided to visit the World's Fair. We did so with a kind of gusto that I have rarely experienced before or since. We had to be careful with our money. We had some with us, but we knew that we would need it when we came to America. So we did not splurge. But the food in the French restaurants tasted marvelous and the atmosphere in the summer days in Paris was great. Although we were a bit hampered because the children were so little, we saw many of the famous places in Paris. But we were eager to leave for Le Havre, from where we would finally set out for New York.

That day finally came. Here was the huge luxury liner, which no longer exists but which at that time was the most luxurious boat of the French Line.[214] We must have had three or four cabins since the first class was almost totally empty. The cabins were very comfortable. The children slept with the

214. The De Grasse.

nurse, and I think there was still one empty cabin. The food was incredibly good and the service was typically French. I do not now recall those first days, but it must have been paradise. The weather was perfect and we spent a great deal of time on deck chairs. We still have photographs of that voyage, which must have taken at least ten days.[215]

Soon we discovered that the people in first class were so stiff and formal that it was very difficult to begin any kind of temporary friendship with our fellow passengers. I still remember there were a number of high-ranking Protestant English clergymen there. We made the best of the situation since, after all, we were a family of three grown-ups[216] and two children and were sufficiently busy with each other, enjoying the peace and rest, the food and drinks, and each other's company. I had received the galleys of my new book before we left, which gave me enough to do during the day. I also prepared a statement for our arrival since I knew that I would be met by the press. We talked about our new life. Since I had been to America before, I tried to explain to Hilde what we were bound to find there. I was full of optimism as to our future, but I was also full of fear. It was, after all, not merely a new, but a strange country, with a new set of values, and the kind of civilization that bore little resemblance to the Central Europe in which we had grown up.

Soon after our departure, we discovered that the second class was much livelier than the first, and although we took our meals in the first class and, of course, slept there, we began to spend a great deal of time in the merry, frolicking, and gay atmosphere of the second class. We had to have special permission to visit there, but it was not difficult to obtain. The great attraction in the second class was the Folies Bergère.[217] They were making their first trip to America and performed all the time. There was a great deal of dancing, drinking and laughing. I danced a great deal, but Hilde was already so pregnant that she did not feel like dancing. I remember making the acquaintance of a particular French girl, with whom I became very friendly. But I have forgotten her name or any other circumstance of our being together.

We also made the acquaintance of the manager of the Folies Bergère. He was a Romanian Jew, very happy to meet a German rabbi. In the first class, we had the most luxurious swimming pools and other athletic facilities of which we took advantage. There were special rooms for children to play in. The weather was perfect; there were no storms; and no one was seasick.

Finally we approached New York. As we passed by the Statue of Lib-

---

215. It took from July 23 to August 1.
216. Including the nursemaid, Maria Breiden.
217. The Parisian spectacle, featuring exotic, often nude dancers.

erty we dutifully went to the railing to ponder the symbolic meaning of that statue, which was the promise of a new life, a new freedom, and a new dignity. It made a powerful impression on us. Artistically, I did not like the statue; it was so very much an example of nineteenth-century pomposity. But who cared about aesthetics at that moment? We entered the gates of a new country. It was like the gates leading to heaven.

Temple B'nai Abraham in Newark, New Jersey, where Prinz served beginning in 1939. Courtesy of American Jewish Archives.

Abner ("Longy") Zwillman, Prinz's gangster acquaintance, in 1938. Courtesy of John Steinbach.

Prinz with David and Paula Ben-Gurion (undated). Courtesy of American Jewish Archives.

Prinz in front of the ruins of the Fasanenstrasse synagogue in Berlin, 1949. Courtesy of American Jewish Archives.

With Nahum Goldmann, president of the World Jewish Congress, in Geneva. Courtesy of American Jewish Archives.

With Rabbi Stephen S. Wise (third from left) and other Jewish leaders. Courtesy of American Jewish Archives.

Prinz and other leaders of the March on Washington, including Martin Luther King, Jr., meet with President Kennedy, August 28, 1963. Courtesy of American Jewish Archives.

Prinz speaking at the March on Washington. Courtesy of American Jewish Archives.

Joachim Prinz in old age, Brookside, New Jersey. Courtesy of the Prinz family.

3

Newark, New Jersey

WE LANDED IN NEW YORK and saw the skyscrapers from afar, Hilde for the first time. As an experienced traveler, I showed her this or that famous building (the skyline of New York in 1937 was a little less impressive than it is now). Both Hilde and Maria stood there in awe and fear. But we had little time to indulge our emotions because a group of photographers and press agents came for interviews. They wanted to take my picture and I pointed to Hilde who, after all, was my wife. But when they saw that she was very pregnant, they decided to take my picture alone. I gave a longish interview to the *New York Times* and other papers. I had not come to America to occupy a pulpit, but as a representative of the United Palestine Appeal.[1] I avoided answering political questions put to me. It was too dangerous to be critical of the Hitler regime at a time when so many of my people, including my parents, were still there. My brother Hanan[2] had already left for Palestine and was serving his apprenticeship as an agricultural worker with the parents of Moshe Dayan.[3] But since my parents were still in Germany, as, of course, were many of my colleagues and fellow workers, I had to be careful. On the next morning, August 1, 1937, the *New York Times* and other papers published my picture on the front page next to that of the ballerina of the Folies Bergère.[4] It was a funny combination. Members of the Jewish organizations had come aboard the ship to greet me, and I was made to feel very much at home. Hilde's uncle had sent someone to take us to a hotel on Riverside

1. The United Palestine Appeal was the American branch of the Keren Hayesod, which raised money for Jewish settlement in Palestine.
2. This is the brother who is earlier referred to as Hans.
3. Moshe Dayan (1915–1981) was born at Kibbutz Degania Aleph and grew up on the agricultural settlement of Nahalal.
4. A photograph and a very brief article appeared on page 4 of the *New York Times* for August 2, 1937, the day after his arrival. Perhaps another paper published his photo on the front page together with one of the ballerinas.

Drive. We thought that we had been invited as his guests since he was very rich. However, at the end of two weeks, we were presented with a bill. Apparently, generosity was not his main trait.

We had several rooms on one of the upper floors in the hotel, so that we looked down on the streets of New York. I remember seeing a police car pass by and hearing its siren or that of a fire engine. Lucie, upon hearing this strange noise, said quietly, "It sounds as though a thousand children are crying at the same time." I thought it a very accurate description of a sound to which we had to get used. For only in Paris could one hear a similar sound of a police car. The children had never heard it before. Since they were in good hands with Maria, I could take Hilde to see a bit of New York. That was a frightening experience. Everything seemed strange—the new foods, so many cars, and the buildings reaching into heaven. Her English was very limited. We went to stores to buy things and found everything rather cheap. But, above all, everything was so plentiful that it almost blinded us. I remember when the first thing I bought was some corned beef in a delicatessen store, Hilde was amazed at the large quantities I got and the fabulous quality of the meat. We took it up to our room and ate it with the bread we had bought. At first we didn't understand the man who had asked us what kind of bread we wanted. We did not know there was such a variety of bread. That, too, added to our impression of a fabulously rich country.

We now started to look for a permanent residence. Since we had friends who lived in Great Neck, most of them rather affluent or at least economically very secure, we visited them and found Great Neck to be a small village with a familiar kind of atmosphere. We were able to rent a little house, at a rent that I believe was in the neighborhood of $60 per month. When we were advised that our furniture was about to be delivered, we informed the firm of the new address, 6 Preston Road. We decided to move in on the same day that the furniture was delivered. Hilde, being in her eighth month of pregnancy, had to be kept out of this whole maneuver. Nonetheless, we stood in front of the sweet little house as the van arrived. The most difficult thing to accommodate was the library, but otherwise we were able in a single day to furnish the house sufficiently for us to live in. It was an exciting moment to move into a new house in a new country and to discover our neighbors, all of whom were very friendly and helpful.

The most annoying experience was the American summer. We had arrived on the first of August and found from that first day that American summers had little in common with the kind we were used to. It was not just hot, it was also very humid. European summers are not that hot and humidity does not exist. For a pregnant woman like Hilde it was more than annoying. As we moved into the house during the middle of August, the weather had not improved but worsened. Very often we sat in the shade of a tree in our new backyard, which was large enough for our children to play in and for us to enjoy nature. Air conditioning was hardly known at that time and we found the nights utterly unbearable. Soon we were talking about the birth of the new baby, which was expected in the middle of September, only four weeks after our arrival in Great Neck. Hilde, having attended a school that taught Latin and Greek but not English, refused to go to a hospital because of her linguistic limitations. She was generally rather apprehensive about our new life. So we decided to engage an obstetrician who had moved to America from Germany, a doctor recommended by Hilde's family. In consultation with him we decided to have the birth at home. We obtained a hospital bed and engaged a midwife. The doctor assured us the birth would be normal since the mother was young and strong and that there was no risk involved in her giving birth at home rather than in the hospital. Fortunately, he was right.

On the morning of September 20th I was asked to go to New York to attend to some matters. I did not realize that Hilde was already in labor and that she had sent me away so that I would not be present at the birth of the child. When upon my return from New York in the afternoon I saw several cars in front of our house, I realized that Hilde must have given birth. Entering the house, I heard the cries of a little baby. I went upstairs, and there was Hilde, smiling and happy on the sofa. Still unwashed was the little baby, who looked sweet and not at all like a newborn child. We decided to call him Jonathan. I immediately cabled to various people that Jonathan had been born. Since we did not know of any Jewish circumciser, we decided to have the baby circumcised by the physician and to have the ceremony afterwards in our living room. This is what we did, although the circumcision took a long time and our nurse, who attended it, fainted. But the party was very nice. Food in those days was rather cheap and we had discovered a large grocery store owned by a Dutchman who treated us with great respect as well as kindness and compassion. I remember buying a duck for one dollar and wine for very little money. All our friends came to welcome Jonathan as a member of our family.

When I had arrived at our hotel on the first of August, I had found a check in the amount of $300, the sum agreed upon with Stephen Wise. In return, as I mentioned, I was to deliver speeches for the United Palestine Appeal and be paid an additional $50 for each speech. Although I had not as yet delivered a single speech, on the first of October a check in the amount of $500 arrived with a little note written by Dr. Wise's secretary which read:

"Now that Jonathan has been born, you will need more money. Dr. Wise wanted you to have this amount from now on." It was one of the very many kindnesses for which Dr. Wise was famous, and it was done in such a manner that it was difficult to thank him. When I did so, he refused to accept any expression of gratitude, saying that it was only natural that I should have more money at my disposal. He visited us shortly afterward and we realized at that time that he was much more than my mentor and famous friend. He took a very personal and warm interest in the future of my family—and he began to talk to me about entering the American rabbinate.

Having seen and met a number of rabbis, I had come to the conclusion that it would be utterly impossible for me ever to be a rabbi in the United States. I found most of the American rabbis mediocre, not at all rabbis as I understood the term. They employed all kinds of gimmicks to attract people and were not even successful at that. Guest speakers were invited several times a month and various activities, most of them social and unrelated to Jewish life, were the order of the day. I was much more interested in being a freelance lecturer and later entering academic life than lowering myself to the status of an American rabbi. I must say that at that time there were still giants among the rabbis, and Stephen Wise was one of them. But the majority of congregations were unattractive and I found that I had little in common with those rabbis that I met.

My career as a lecturer began with a nationwide address that I delivered over the national hookup of a well-known radio station in New York.[5] Stephen Wise was to introduce me. I wrote a speech that was edited by the woman who later became my agent and who at that time was married to Henry Montor,[6] the leading spirit of the United Palestine Appeal, a man to whom I am deeply indebted for what he did for me during the first years of my life in the United States.

Of course, I had to read the speech. It was entitled "A Sermon to My Fellow Jews in Nazi Germany." I no longer have the manuscript, but it was evidently a very effective speech, for during the weeks that followed I received something like five hundred invitations to deliver lectures, not only to Jewish audiences but to universities and churches as well. I now had to have an agent to decide where and when I was to go. A very busy life began that took me through the entire country and afforded me an opportunity to under-

5. According to *Jüdische Rundschau,* October 1, 1937, the speech was broadcast on September 14, 1937, a day before Yom Kippur, and dealt with Palestine.
6. Henry Montor (1905–1982) was a prominent fund-raiser for Zionist causes, who was working for the United Palestine Appeal at the time Prinz came to the United States.

stand the special mentality of American audiences as well as the differences between Jewish and Christian ones. It also gave me practice in a language that I knew theoretically but not how to use in a speech. Moreover, I had learned British English and now began to discover that American English was a different language. Many of the terms I used were unknown to the American people. Even though many were attracted by my British accent, I knew I could not live in America without adjusting myself linguistically and culturally to the country that had now become my home.

Indeed, feeling at home in a strange country is easier said than done. I know of so many people who came to America as infants and had no difficulty becoming part of God's own country, as they called it; they grew into it almost organically and considered themselves native Americans, as the memory of their foreign birth was faint and uncertain. In our case, the situation was quite different. I came to America at age thirty-five and Hilde was twenty-four. However, our age was not the main factor that made our adjustment to the new country difficult. The principal difficulty lay in the fact that we had been brought up in a civilization that seemed ever more different the longer we lived in America. We came here with a linguistic and cultural package containing so many notions and convictions that we had grown up with as part of our very existence. It had formed our life and thought. I had attended universities that gave me a certain intellectual approach to problems and had taught me to think in a very specific way. I came from a Europe that had lived through a war and had, during the period between 1918, the end of the First World War, and 1933, the beginning of the Hitler regime, developed a very specific and extraordinarily prolific and productive civilization. I grew up with new concepts of literature, the new novel, the new literature of protest, and the rejection of old values. I came from a civilization that was based on a revolution in almost every realm: politics, economy, intellectual and artistic life. The birth of late Impressionism, which found its most eloquent expression in the paintings of Vincent van Gogh, had been followed by the period of Expressionism, an approach which was translated into painting, sculpture, architecture, and poetry. All this must be seen in the context of the political revolution that had begun in 1918, pitting a struggling democracy against the strong and organically rooted values of militarism and dictatorship. But the fact that this democracy was struggling and that I and my contemporaries had always been convinced that there was no other form of government than democracy only heightened its importance for us. It was a social democracy based on moral values, and neither bribery nor kickbacks nor any kind of immoral action or thought entered our minds. Democracy was to be pure. Socialism was a profound conviction based on the notion of justice and equality, and a socialist politician did not sell his rights at any price; he was an idealistic servant of the people.

It must be understood that the immigration of which we were a part, however small, had its own face, and therefore its own importance. It brought many Albert Einsteins to this country and was able to enrich various American universities with a very large number of creative thinkers. Although many brilliant scholars had to struggle with the language, their works had been translated and some of them had become part of modern American civilization long before their authors came to the shores of this country. In many respects we did not look at America as "God's own country." We were very grateful that it saved our lives and we knew enough about American literature and, to a certain extent, politics that we felt somehow at home from the very first day. But the longer we stayed here, the more foreign we felt. For years the people called us "refugees." We knew of many cases of very important and valuable refugees who had landed in the hands of the refugee bureaucracy and were treated without any compassion and knowledge of their particular value. Bureaucracy and compassion are altogether strange bedfellows and very rarely happy ones. Although people greeted us with friendliness, we were in a way citizens of inferior quality. Our wages were lower, although the experience of the sweatshops of the earlier century was, of course, not repeated. In a way we were deeply resented by the people who felt inferior to us, although they were so much better off economically. Since most of those with whom we came into contact had little intellectual background, it was particularly painful for us to realize that they were our fellow citizens. We could not possibly be expected to admire with gaping mouths the great technological advances of America. We had learned to distrust technology. It is true that the skyscrapers were a new experience, but they were only taller than our houses, and certainly not more beautiful. What I particularly missed in the new country was history and historical expression in terms of architecture and art. The homes were furnished in the most old-fashioned manner, and I found there was little appreciation, and certainly hardly any knowledge of art in architecture, sculpture, and painting. All this was to come much later. When we came, America was a very large, very rich, and very empty land.

People resented the fact that we did not admire America more openly and profoundly than we did. I am afraid that I, for one, did not hesitate to express disappointment. This was not always done tactfully. My greatest disappointment was the arena of American politics in its widest sense. I am not talking about American political parties, although there was enough in that field to be criticized and even despised; the Democratic party was still the party of Tammany Hall,[7] the rule of the old bosses, who bought votes during elections. It was something much more profound that disgusted me. I will never forget certain incidents that suddenly made me aware of the great difference between my political education and the political reality of the 1930s in America. It was the time when Franklin Delano Roosevelt was president. I had never been in the White House and was still far away from the mainstream of American political life. He was a great figure for us, but far away nonetheless, and we could hardly imagine that he was also a New York politician who was well aware of all the wheeling and dealing that was part of political life, and in which he himself played a very active role.

I was invited to address the meeting of a trade union. They were probably curious to hear a refugee speak about America. (Many years later I learned that they were among the most corrupt political institutions in the country.) I spoke as a socialist about socialist ideals, those with which I had been brought up and which now that I had been expelled from a country of dictatorship had become even more glamorous and more important to me as the nation's moral political goal. I spoke about equality and morality in politics. I began to talk about the role of the black man in America and the fact that socialist politics had to be based on moral convictions rather than political arrangements. The response to my speech was not merely negative but hostile. I found myself in the presence of crude, coarse, and uneducated men. They did not understand me at all. But not understanding a speech is not the greatest of crimes. What I considered to be criminal and what disheartened me to the point of despair was the open and unashamed rejection of the sacred credo of the political religion that called itself socialism. It was to them clearly a bread-and-butter issue, a matter of hours and wages. To me it was a matter of building a better society. I had spoken to the walls and to deaf ears, and I had received my first and most important lesson about American political life.

Among the hundreds of invitations that I received in America, there was a group of about twelve invitations to address meetings on consecutive nights in Atlanta, Georgia, a city that in 1937 was not what it is today. It was still a developing southern town and not yet one of the southern capitals of culture. No museum had been built as yet and no integrated society had been formed. Its main industry at that time was Coca-Cola. Many of the people I met were involved either in selling, bottling, or some other aspect of the important industry of a beverage of which I knew nothing. I went

7. Tammany Hall, the Democratic political machine in New York City, was considerably weaker in the 1930s than it had been in earlier years.

to Atlanta especially because it was the home of a man I had admired for a long time. His name was Prof. King.[8] I knew that he was a black man. But one must understand that my experiences with black people had been limited to the circus; there were no black men in Germany. Only in France did I see some on the streets of Paris who, after all, were citizens of France since they came from North Africa. For some strange reason I also was not aware of the problem of black America. Naïvely I took it for granted that blacks were equal and that in a democracy there was no problem of any kind of deprivation and discrimination. I walked into the black American problem like a child, naïve and uninformed, idealistic and even romantic. I knew that many of the black people were poor, but I was not aware of the causes of their poverty.

Prof. King was an Old Testament scholar. He had specialized in the poetry of the Old Testament and particularly that of the Hebrew prophets. Just a few months prior to my coming to America he had been in Jerusalem where he delivered a memorable scholarly address on the subject. His paper was so impressive that I decided to visit him. It took me some time to find out where Prof. King was. I then learned that he was teaching at the black theological seminary of Atlanta, Georgia.[9] I called him to announce my visit and found him not merely a most congenial and polite, reticent man, but also a man who interested me greatly; I spent more than an hour with him. Since after that he had to teach and I wanted to spend more time with him, I invited him to have dinner with me at my hotel. He hesitated, saying that it would be more advisable if we would take dinner in my room rather than in the hotel dining room. I did not quite understand the meaning of his words, but I agreed.

After I left the seminary it was time for me to go to a certain place to deliver an address at a luncheon given in my honor by three Zionist groups. I was greeted by the people in charge of the affair and shortly thereafter one of them said to me, "I understand that you visited that nigger in the black seminary and somebody told me that you invited him to have dinner with you tonight." I was completely speechless. I responded that it was true that I had invited that great scholar and that I had earlier had a very interesting time with him. But I could not help adding that I was amazed to hear such words from a Jewish group welcoming a Hitler refugee whose people had been per-

8. Prinz's reference is to Willis Jefferson King, a black Methodist bishop who had studied in Palestine under the auspices of the American School for Oriental Research. He was a Professor of Old Testament and Christian Sociology at Gammon Theological Seminary. When Prinz spoke with him in 1937, he was serving as Gammon's president.
9. Gammon Theological Seminary.

secuted in the country of their birth because of their race. I added that I simply did not understand nor had I known that Jews, the classical victims of racial persecution, could themselves be racists. I said that what was evidently happening to the black people of America was the very same thing that was happening to the Jewish people in Europe. No one replied. There was a pause of embarrassment and amazement on the part of my fellow Jews, and then in order to break the painful silence someone said to me: "Would you care for a drink?" There was nothing I would have liked better—a large and stiff alcoholic drink, not merely intoxicating, but anaesthetizing for a pain that I can hardly describe. I immediately said that I would like nothing better. Soon after, someone brought me a glass of Coca-Cola. I thought it was a glass of some intoxicating liquor and took the first sip. It was not what I wanted. That was the first time—and also the last time in my life— that I drank Coca-Cola. In all these forty years that have elapsed since 1937, Coca-Cola was for me a symbol of hatred and prejudice with which I did not want to be identified.

Altogether, the American Jews were a great disappointment to me. In 1937, little original Jewish creative literature had been published. Our textbooks for Jewish schools were old-fashioned and outmoded. The number of Jewish scholars was small and their station in Jewish life was not at all what I was used to. They were not the great nobility of our people; they were employees of institutions, poorly paid and hardly known. Organized Jewish religion was particularly obnoxious to me. The intellectual level of the average rabbi was rather low. Their backgrounds were extremely ghettoized and limited. Very few of them were really civilized people; they considered themselves and were treated by others as spiritual employees of Jewish institutions, usually headed by the richest and least educated man of the community. There was no creative Jewish music and the sermons I had to listen to were on the lowest possible level. With few exceptions, rabbis had neither a large income nor any kind of security and were dependent on the will and whim of ignorant people. Services were poorly attended and there was really very little to attract people. Those who were intellectually important stayed away from the synagogue and were still part of those secular Jewish groups that had come from Eastern Europe, the founders of the Yiddish theater and the Yiddish dailies. Yiddish was altogether still a very living and important language. Eastern European Jews lived in their own groups, very often continuing the traditions of the little towns from which they came. They were looked down upon by the German Jews who had come to America a few decades before them and had achieved social and economic status in the new country. To them the Eastern European Jew was an inferior being with whom they had no social contact and who was not part of their own crowd.

There was really nothing in Jewish life to attract me. This included the movement from which I had come and which to me was of such great importance. I am referring to the Zionist movement. In my experience, Zionism was the profound conviction of a small group of people who considered themselves guests in a foreign country in which they might have lived for centuries but which had rejected them. Zionism meant acceptance of the social rejection of the Jews. It was also rejection of the hope for the Messiah.[10] It was a very real thing, and it changed people's lives. Many of us young people had gone to Palestine well trained and extremely well prepared for the new life in the old–new land.[11] Since I was a well-known Zionist I was not merely invited to Zionist meetings but, if I recall correctly, became chairman of the National Administrative Committee less than a year after my arrival in America. However, what I found here was not merely different from what I had considered to be Zionism, but something that offered so little in terms of an idealistic goal that I became estranged from it. Although my friend Stephen Wise was one of the leaders, he, too, had only a limited concept of the great revolutionary, social, and intellectual ideal that was the very foundation of the Zionist movement. I began to realize that I was not dealing with the Zionist movement but with a Zionist organization that simply provided the opportunity for Jews to become somewhat active as Jews. It was an organization with which I had little in common.

My experiences with the Jewish community, and particularly with the Zionist movement, were so shocking that I found it difficult to adjust to this completely new situation. The Zionist movement to me meant something completely foreign to the average American Zionist. There was, for instance, no Zionist youth movement with concrete plans for transferring itself to what was then called Palestine.[12] The whole concept of aliyah[13] was not merely considered foreign to the American Zionist movement, but sometimes was even regarded as dangerous to the existence of the Jews in the United States. I remember heated discussions, particularly in Hadassah,[14]

10. In other words, Zionism was committed to dealing actively with Jewish issues rather than waiting passively for a divinely initiated redemption.

11. A reference to Herzl's Zionist novel, *Old-New Land*.

12. By the time Prinz came to America, there were Zionist youth organizations in the United States, such as He-Halutz and Ha-Shomer Ha-Tza'ir, which viewed pioneering settlement in Palestine as their ultimate goal.

13. Settlement in the Land of Israel.

14. The women's Zionist organization.

which even at that time was a very important part of the American Zionist movement. It was strictly forbidden to discuss aliyah, for the very term was considered a betrayal of American patriotism. The whole concept of Zionism, as they understood it, was in reality an attempt to solve the Jewish problem, which existed in some parts of the world, by transporting those Jews to a country in the Near East that they hoped someday might become a Jewish homeland. It was all as vague as that. Since ideology altogether was usually identified with some form of neurosis or even lunacy, nobody, or almost nobody, undertook to create an ideological underpinning or definition of the movement. There were a few attempts, but they were by small groups, certainly not by the leaders of the Zionist Organization of America.

In order for you to understand the difference between the world from which I had come and the world that I found, I would like to quote here a few pages from my book *We Jews,* which I published in 1934. The following paragraphs will explain the difference between my Zionist concepts and those that were enunciated by the various Zionist organizations. In order to be fair to them, though, I must say that these associations were politically much more active than we were in Germany. Their whole concept was not merely politically motivated, but geared to the kind of political action that was typical of American approaches to problems. One must not forget that the Balfour Declaration of 1917 was largely due to the many political activities and initiatives of American Zionists. Figures such as Wise and Justice Brandeis[15] are but two of a large number of people who took advantage of their relationship to the White House, the Congress, and the political parties in order to achieve American participation in the formation of the British policy toward Zionism during the First World War. This is certainly not to be belittled. Later, in the years before the creation of the Jewish state, their efforts bore fruit, and the same method was then applied to the problem of the creation of the Jewish state. I am therefore not degrading American Zionist efforts, but I want to emphasize the difference between them and the Zionist concepts with which I had grown up and which simply found no echo in American Zionist circles.

Here are the quotations from my book:[16]

15. Louis Dembitz Brandeis (1856–1941) combined a distinguished legal career, culminating in appointment to the Supreme Court, with key roles in American Zionism.
16. The following paragraphs are Prinz's rough translation of pages 162–167 of his 1934 book *Wir Juden.* In some spots, he purposely or subconsciously alters the text to make it more applicable to his present readers, to express a change of emphasis in his own views, or to avoid a passage that bears too critically on his own decision not to settle in Palestine.

The creation of a territory for the Jews of the world is the only concrete task for the Jew of today, although not so long ago it was considered to be sheer Utopia. Once upon a time it was a dream of a Jew who had left the world of journalism in order to become a Jewish activist.[17] Today, however, this Utopian dream is part of the longing of millions of people, and the dream itself has become a reality.

We should be afraid of starting with charitable institutions and welfare measures. We must not deceive ourselves, and in doing so, betray ourselves. All these are attempts to drown out and negate our own responsibility. "The problem of our people cannot be solved philanthropically. It is a political problem, and its solution must be political."[18]

Since these words were written, the old Jewish homeland has become a reality. The soil of Palestine has created new people. In reality, we can already speak of a new, radically new, Jew. Today there are Jewish farmers, artisans and workers. This new Jew has a new pride and a calm and sure attitude toward life. This is the Jew of the new Palestine. The whole world will understand and respect him because work is respected all over the world. The Jew who is a farmer will speak with his counterparts in the world, and so will the artisan and the worker of Palestine. Everybody will know: this is a Jew. He lives in his own land. He tends to his fields there as I do here. He builds his home there, as I build it in my land. This is, in reality, the only possible concrete foundation of mutual understanding. This kind of understanding is not artificial, but is derived from the organic and natural sources that create an international brotherhood of farmers, artisans and workers. What we need is a healthy Jew. We can't have him anywhere but in his own land. Only there can we have a Judaism which is not demonstrative but natural and organic.

Our sages used to say: the air of Palestine will make us wise. Today we know that it also makes us normal.

To really comprehend all this requires an inner revolution of Jewish thought that will have to be accepted by world Jewry.[19] This means that at this moment it is important that all of us look back and think of the great Jewish figures of antiquity, the strong Jews who worked and thought straight, and were therefore capable of being creative. If we do this, we will begin to understand the degree of our degradation. We will awaken within ourselves a new sense of honor and honesty; and we can then ask ourselves whether the end of Jewish history has really come and the Jewish people are to sink so low as to become the people without rights and decency. There is no other response to this question than to say to ourselves that we will have to begin anew and create a new concept of Jewish decency.[20] But it should be clear to all of us that such a beginning can only take place in our own country.

This beginning in our own land is already being made. The sacred heri-

17. Theodor Herzl.
18. Prinz does not supply a source for this citation, but it is in the spirit of Herzl.
19. The original text has "Western European Jewry."
20. The original does not mention honesty; in place of *decency* it has *prosperity*.

tage of Theodor Herzl is beginning to bear fruit. Anyone who would like to see it can go there and see whether it is true that there exists a new type of Jew who lives his own life. He will also, if he is intellectually and morally honest, see all the great difficulties. There are many political and economic obstacles that will render the new beginning more difficult than many believe. I am speaking of the problem of the Arabs and our co-existence with them,[21] the economic difficulties, the great task of forging a community of Jews who come from many countries of the world. I am talking about the question of labor and its integration into the new country. All these are questions that are difficult, and some of them exist in other countries as well. But in Palestine they will prove to be particularly difficult. The cowards who will go there and realize all this will leave the country and come home again. They will understand that life in Palestine is hard and not terribly convenient.[22] Two thousand years of exile have made an enormous impact upon the Jewish people. We should not prevent the cowards from leaving the new country.

Palestine is not a country for those who want luxury and conveniences. It is altogether not a country for cowards. It is a land for those of our people who understand the real reason for the creation of a Jewish homeland. The main concern is not our own personal happiness. We are not concerned with our own life. The real concern is that our children may be permitted to live in decency and honor. The goal is to create peace for a people that has been denied serenity for many thousands of years. We are not talking about a Jewish problem; we are talking about a world problem. The world has an obligation to give to this ancient Jewish people a land that will create for it an opportunity to develop its own strength and then join the family of nations. Our interest is to create a new, honorable and decent name for the Jewish people. We have had enough intellectuals[23] and peddlers. What we need is the soil, the smell of the fields, our own space, in which we can breathe anew and in a new freedom. We need all that for the sake of our own life, but also for the sake of the life of the nations of the world.

The time has come for you to understand that it is now that we must work toward the solution of an international problem. Intellectual solutions are no longer possible. We simply have no time for that anymore. The Jewish problem is becoming gigantic. The question is pressing and burning.

The solution to the Jewish problem is often conceived as some sort of an enterprise of transporting Jews from one place to another. Many people believe that you can simply transport Jews from an antisemitic country to a land that is not yet dangerous for them. But the term "not yet" means that it is only a matter of time until this new land, too, will become unbearable. Therefore any concept of mere transportation from one country to another is an irresponsible attempt to postpone the solution. We simply leave it to the coming generation. This is not the kind of solution I have in mind.

---

21. The words "and our co-existence with them" are added.
22. Prinz omits the following sentence: "They will not feel that the Orient is their home."
23. Literally: hair-splitters.

The attempts to create for Jews who have lost their economic existence in one country new jobs in another, either in Europe or in the colonies, may be an honest attempt to solve the problem. Although there is the danger of transporting not merely Jews to a new country, but with them antisemitism, there is no doubt that it could help solve individual Jewish cases. However, one must understand that all this is a solution for individuals and of economic problems; it is not the solution to the Jewish problem.

Solving the Jewish problem presupposes that we have the willpower to end the process of assimilation and Jewish dissolution. It is not only simply a matter of settling Jews in their own country, but also the creation of a new Judaism. Every attempt at a solution to the Jewish question must therefore include the goal of creating a new Jewish renaissance. If this is not done, the settlement itself is meaningless. No one has a right to deny that settlement itself has its value; no one has a right to belittle it. But no one who is really concerned about a people and its fate has a right to overestimate the value of settlement. There is no help for the Jewish people unless it includes the creation of conditions for a Jewish renaissance and a new Jewish creativity.[24] All projects that are now under discussion have their economic importance. However, they cannot be considered contributions to the solution of the Jewish problem unless they include our determination to create a strong Jewish civilization together with a clearly defined new Jewish national consciousness. To forget this means to overlook the importance of the problem.

The solution to the Jewish problem must be based on the exciting and passionate will of the Jew not to save himself by creating a new Jewish island, but by building a land of his own for the purpose of beginning a new Jewish history. This consciousness of a new beginning of the entire people and its history, this understanding of the fundamental world-historical importance of the settlement in Palestine, is in reality the profound meaning of this new and revolutionary undertaking.[25]

I quote these few pages from my book in order to make it understood why I have never been able to feel at home within the American Zionist movement. It is so completely different from my own ideas. I found that American Zionists simply did not deal with the important problems of a Jewish state in the making. Whenever at their meetings I began to discuss the necessity of taking the anti-Jewish problem seriously, my ideas were always rejected as being irrelevant and unimportant. In a way, they felt my strangeness and that I was talking and thinking in the context of a foreign world. They were quite right, and I must admit that much of the misunderstanding was due to my own inability to understand the uniqueness of American Jewish life and the specific mentality of American Jews, including the Zionists.

24. Here it is clearly apparent that Prinz's Zionism was influenced not only by the political Zionism of Theodor Herzl but also by the cultural–spiritual Zionism of Ahad Ha-Am.
25. The original text reads more simply: ". . . is the meaning of the rebuilding of Palestine."

It was, after all, a young country and an even younger Jewish community, while I had been part of a Jewish community that was in existence for sixteen hundred years. I had now come to live among Jews whose history really started around 1900. The differences—social, economic, and political—among the various groups that constituted American Jewry were still very real. I remember that in one of the first weeks after we came to America I delivered several speeches in Baltimore, Maryland. While there, I asked one of the leaders of the community to show me the city and tell me about the Jewish community. At that time I was particularly interested in the problem of intermarriage, which had been one of the larger problems of European Jewry in the early twentieth century. He told me very seriously that he, too, was interested and worried about intermarriage because in Baltimore it had happened recently that a young man from a good German Jewish family had married a young woman who was the daughter of an Eastern European Jew. I told him that I did not consider that to be intermarriage, but he was adamant in his view.

All this is why I never became part of the Zionist organization and never assumed any leadership in the movement even though I maintained my membership, as I will report later, and was one of the delegates to the first Zionist Congress to be held after the Second World War.[26]

It was very important for me to discover America for myself. No literature could help me. I had to become part of the country and the Jewish community, but I could not do so except through personal experience. I was very unhappy about the prospect of becoming an American rabbi. I had been used to a particular system of Jewish community governance. There had been no "congregations" in Europe; the rabbi there was both an official of the entire Jewish community serving all its people and also a civil servant whose position was guaranteed by the government. In many cases, the government of the state in which the rabbi lived paid his salary. From the first day on, a German rabbi had a life contract that entitled him to receive his full salary as his pension when he left community service at the age of sixty-five. The salaries paid to us in Berlin were very large. We received the same remuneration from the government as the secretary of foreign affairs, and whenever he received an increment, so did we. This made the rabbi completely independent, and in very many cases he did not even know the president of the community personally. When I came to America, I noticed that American religious life was completely fragmentized. Congregations of every possible type were dominated by lay leaders who to a very large extent

26. The 22nd Zionist Congress, held in Basel, December 9–24, 1946.

were Jewishly illiterate and had been selected only because of their economic status in the community.

But my discovery of Jewish life in America had to come from personal experiences, so I was particularly grateful that I started my life in the United States as a lecturer. I spoke in more than forty states, and although my stay in the cities of these states was rather limited, my contact with various groups, Jewish and non-Jewish, proved very helpful. What impressed me most negatively was the fact that the Jews lived among themselves. Although they were citizens of the United States and very proud of it, their life after six p.m. was restricted to their Jewish friends. I discovered to my amazement that there was a thing called the Jewish neighborhood. Since I came from a city where Jews lived all over and where no Jewish ghettos existed, I had never heard of anything like that. But here in America I began to understand that it was not merely a result of antisemitic social rejection; it also came from a very deeply felt desire on the part of the Jews to be among themselves. During those days, Jewish country clubs came into being. They were a reaction to the fact that Jews were not admitted to general country clubs. But one must not forget that the Jews were very happy to be among their old friends and really had no desire to mix with others.

The Jews' wish to be among themselves was repeated hundreds of times by other groups who had their own psychological and social need to be "among themselves." Nevertheless, it caused the Jewish group to become isolated, provincial, and ill at ease about their natural rights of citizenship. Many of them were still politically very timid. Although two Jews, Brandeis and Cardozo,[27] served on the Supreme Court and were later joined by others, these positions were still considered to be "Jewish positions." All this puzzled me greatly, but the more I learned about American Jews the more I realized that they were a completely new phenomenon. Not only was the Jewish community young, but it also had shed many of its European characteristics and embarked on a new adventure in Jewish history. I also found American Jews poorly informed about Jewish affairs. Very often when I spoke about the Hitler regime, I found that the audience had little knowledge of the horrible realities we had experienced between 1933 and 1937. They were very disappointed when I did not tell them stories of bloody persecutions, of murder in the streets, but rather tried to analyze the political problems that lay behind all those extraordinary events.

My contacts with the general American climate of opinion usually came

---

27. Benjamin Cardozo (1870–1938) was appointed to the Supreme Court by President Herbert Hoover in 1932.

via churches and universities and various other American organizations that invited me to speak to them. They were hardly aware of the Jewish problem under the Hitler regime and were psychologically and politically far removed from Europe and the people who participated actively in the solution of the problems. Most of them were genuine isolationists. Although I am speaking here of a time only four years removed from the official declaration of war, I found the majority of the Christian people unaware of the dangers of Hitler and uninformed about what had happened to the Jews, to Christian dissenters, to the trade unions, and to Germany itself. It frightened me to talk to university groups and be confronted with students, as well as faculty, who were only superficially involved and interested in the affairs of nations three thousand miles away from this country.

Yet my experiences as a lecturer were of extraordinary importance to me. I had to learn the specifically American way of delivering a speech. It was not unusual for a European audience to listen to a lecturer for an hour or two. I remember vividly one of my first speeches, in Chicago, when I spoke for over an hour. I was amazed that during the latter part of my speech many people left the hall. It was a shattering experience for me to realize that I had to develop a new method of addressing an audience. Everyone waited for a humorous remark at the beginning of a speech, and the speech had to be at the level of the audience, not that of the lecturer. I remember how very difficult it was for me to get used to that. But there was no doubt that I had to do it if I was to become a successful lecturer, if indeed I was to live in America and make my living by delivering speeches and sermons. It was hard for me to learn this, but it did not take me too long to finally "catch on" and become an American lecturer.

Although lecturing was an important experience that permitted me to see much of America, traveling from coast to coast, meeting all kinds of people, Jews and non-Jews, it was, nevertheless, an extraordinarily difficult burden to bear. My schedule was irregular and dependent on the booking of lectures by my agent, who received a certain percentage of my income. Although the income was very important, I had to leave my family so often that I was hardly at home. Jonathan, who was born in September of 1937, was growing up practically without a father. Hilde was left alone with the three children, which was very difficult for her, although we had a few good friends who made her life a little easier. In the meantime, my parents had left Germany and settled in the Land of Israel.[28] Since they left without any funds and I was the only one of their children who was earning some money,

28. Joseph Prinz and his second wife, Gertrude, left for Palestine in 1938.

I was their sole monthly support. This was an additional financial burden and not an easy one. During these difficult years, my brother Kurt and his family arrived and stayed with us for many months.[29] He, too, had left Hitler's Germany without any money and had become my responsibility. But the main reason for my decision to change my life was the fact that traveling from coast to coast on such an irregular and unpredictable schedule, repeating most of the speeches, which dealt mainly with the Hitler regime, had become quite unbearable. I decided to talk to Wise about the possibility of accepting a position that would keep me in New York. As I did not want to go into the rabbinate, I was ready to work with any Jewish organization that could offer me a decent job.

As always, Stephen Wise was very helpful and understood immediately why traveling about was not the easiest way of making a living. He looked around and offered me the position of educational director of the American Jewish Congress[30] at a very decent salary. I was to develop a cultural and educational program for the organization of which he was the president. I had many interviews and was very eager to begin that kind of work, which would have given me an opportunity to develop my experience and knowledge in this field. I signed the contract and informed my lecture agent that all the lectures booked for 1938 had to be canceled immediately. (As lectures had to be booked almost a year in advance, this meant that with the acceptance of the invitation from the American Jewish Congress the source of my regular income for the whole coming year was canceled.) I was not merely rash in my decision, but also quite naïve. I was unfamiliar with organizational politics, personal rivalries, and ambitions. It was much too late when I found out that one of the leaders of the American Jewish Congress, a man whom I had admired greatly and with whom I had a very personal and friendly rapport, vetoed my election to the post because he was very eager to give it to his mistress.[31] There was nothing that Stephen Wise could do about it or that he wanted to do. I was his friend, but only a new friend and a foreigner; that American Jewish leader who claimed the job for his mistress

29. The family then settled in St. Louis.
30. The American Jewish Congress was established by Stephen S. Wise in 1928 as a permanent Jewish organization concerned mainly with Jewish political affairs both nationally and internationally.
31. Wise had a different explanation. On July 29, 1938, he wrote to Prinz's relative, Ludwig Bendix: "We had, and continue to have, under contemplation his [Prinz's] serving as head of the Department of Education of the Congress. The difficulty, however, is that we have no funds to meet a salary for him, which would have to be about five thousand per year." (Wise Papers, American Jewish Archives, microfilm 2356.)

was an old friend and an important figure in American Jewish life. I was a nobody. I was then informed that my contract was canceled and everyone regretted the fact that I no longer had any real income. Everyone was aware of the fact that the amount I received from the United Palestine Appeal was not sufficient to maintain my family, both here and abroad. No one realized how much of a catastrophe this was.

The year 1938 proved to be one of the most catastrophic years of my life. I tried to get a position anywhere in the Jewish world, but was unsuccessful. The fact that I was a Hitler refugee prompted many organizations to offer me the most menial jobs. I remember the Zionist Organization offering me a job at $25 a week. I was unable to pay my rent regularly. Moreover, payments to my parents had to be made since they had no other income. My family had to eat and to exist; the children had to be brought up, and there simply wasn't money to do all that.

It was during this year that my old friend Alexander Granach,[32] the great actor, came to us from Russia. He would come to our house often, spend the weekend with us, and cook for us. We had very little money and he had none, so the food we ate was peasant food like that I remembered having eaten in my childhood home, and which was very tasty and nourishing. We drank as much liquor as we could afford and had a marvelous time in all the poverty and with all the problems.

The great event of 1938 for me was a sudden invitation by the Jewish community of Canada to head the Canadian campaign for Palestine. I was to be the English speaker who traveled together with Michael Traub, a man with whom I had worked in Berlin, a Lithuanian Jew who was a great organizer and a fantastic fund-raiser.[33] I received a rather large sum for two months' work, and since all my expenses were paid for, my trip throughout Canada, which took me from the Maritime provinces to Vancouver Island, enabled my family to take advantage of an additional and most welcome income. My experiences in Canada were a valuable addition to my American ones. Here I met with a completely different Jewry, one that was closely knit and deeply ghettoized. Most if not all of them were Russian Jews, some of them pioneers of early Canadian life, builders of railroads, and early settlers.

I was also profoundly impressed with the Jews of the Canadian prairie. The small Jewish community of Moose Jaw[34] and similar communities con-

32. See Chapter 2, note 170.
33. See Chapter 2, note 179.
34. A town in Saskatchewan, just to the west of Regina.

sisted of twenty or thirty Jewish families. They were, of course, all natural Zionists, and most if not all of them spoke Yiddish. Their hospitality, I must say, was an experience unto itself. I remember our appearance in Winnipeg, one of the largest and most interesting Jewish communities in the Western world. I found the Jewish inhabitants completely committed to the Jewish people and to Judaism. Their children spoke Hebrew and attended the excellent Jewish schools of the community, which in itself was interesting, since the city was populated by ethnic groups that maintained their own exclusive ethnic identities. Winnipeg's resident groups all lived in the city and worked for it, but socially they were completely separated from each other and each lived in its own world.

It was here that I made my first contact with the Bronfman family. The Bronfmans, who were already very much involved in the liquor industry, were to become the founders of the Seagram liquor empire and the richest Jews in Canada—probably in all of North America. They had all been born in Winnipeg.[35] Some members still lived there. They showered me with gifts and spoiled me with their hospitality. There was also a group of people in Winnipeg whose main occupation was to maintain the memory of Sholem Aleichem, which they did by meeting regularly to read the stories of the great Jewish humorist who was considered the Mark Twain of the Jewish people. I was fascinated by the community. Our meetings there were extremely well attended and we were very well received.

At the end of the campaign, we had succeeded in raising the largest amount of money ever raised in Canada. It sounds ridiculous in terms of today's fund-raising, but in 1938 Michael Traub and I were looked upon as the great heroes of Canadian Jewry. We had raised $100,000 from the entire country. They had never done that before. While I was traveling through Canada looking at the prairie cities shortly after they had been hit by a sandstorm, I met the Canadian branch of the Amish, called Mennonites, who invited me to spend a day with them.[36] I soon fell in love with Canada and decided that we should leave America and settle somewhere in Canada. I liked Canada because it was still a pioneering country and the Jewish community was so much smaller than that of the United States. I felt that I would have a better chance to get ahead there and become one of their leaders.

I returned home to the family in Great Neck, still living in that big[37]

---

35. The Bronfman family did have its North American beginnings in Manitoba, but not in Winnipeg. Samuel Bronfman (1891–1971) was born in Brandon, to the west of Winnipeg.
36. The Amish are a highly conservative division of the Mennonite Church.
37. The first house in Great Neck was small, the second one much larger.

house, still beset with terrible financial problems from which there was evidently no escape. In my desperation I decided to enter the American rabbinate. I was told there was a synagogue in New York, a rather unimportant congregation, that had a vacancy. At that time I became very friendly with Rabbi Jonah B. Wise, who had married into the Sulzberger family of the *New York Times*.[38] He was a very congenial, happy-go-lucky man who was very eager to meet with me, for he loved to drink a glass of beer and was one of the admirers of German Jewry. He talked me into accepting an invitation from that congregation to deliver a sermon, which in reality was a trial sermon, based on which the congregation would either accept or reject me. It had been announced that I would deliver the sermon on a particular Friday night. The synagogue was rather small, seating about six hundred people, but since it was known that I would preach, it was crowded with many Hitler refugees and there was not a single empty seat. Jonah B. Wise was in the congregation. I delivered my sermon, which was considered successful, and everyone was excited about it. All the people came up to me to shake my hand, many of them having known me from Berlin. I was certain that I would be accepted as the rabbi of the congregation. I was therefore shattered and downhearted to be informed of the congregation's decision not to engage me because I would attract mainly Hitler refugees who had no money to pay dues. In their letter, the officers paid me a high compliment for my oratorical ability, but that was little comfort at a moment when I needed more than consolation. I needed the money.

The year 1938 brought many other events that were not particularly encouraging or even interesting. I was sure that I would never make it in America and that my experiment, which had begun so gloriously, had failed. Even Stephen Wise got annoyed with me for having become a burden to him. I delivered some lectures, but nothing was enough to maintain my family. I went into debt. I owed rent for many months and took loans from banks to which I owed what constituted a large amount of money in those days. I planned to write books, one of them on Hitler, but I received a letter from Germany to the effect that it had become known I was offering a manuscript to Viking Press, whose president I knew. The letter made it clear that if I were to write a book on Hitler it would, of course, be cultural, or my friends would be sent to concentration camps. So this plan, so readily ac-

---

38. Beginning in 1925, Jonah B. Wise (1881–1959), a son of Isaac Mayer Wise, was the rabbi of Central Synagogue in Manhattan. He was active in the Joint Distribution Committee's efforts on behalf of German Jewry. His sister, Effie Miriam Wise, married the newspaper publisher Adolph S. Ochs. Their daughter Iphigene later married Arthur Hays Sulzberger.

cepted by Viking Press, also failed. I then planned to write a book for children that would be called "This Is Your World, My Child." It was not supposed to be a Jewish book but an attempt to familiarize the American child with the workings and the aims of American democracy. But in writing the book, I began to realize that I myself knew too little about the subject and therefore would never be able to write a convincing book. So that plan, too, failed. I was left in a state of complete desperation. Hoping to earn a little money, I formed a German-Jewish congregation, holding High Holy Day services in the mosque on 55th Street in New York. It was attended by more than two thousand people. However, we had to charge very little for the tickets, and although the excitement was great, after we paid the cantor and choir and the rent for the hall, little was left for me. On the second day of Rosh Hashanah, Stephen Wise appeared and preached a sermon. It was a great and marvelous gesture on his part, even if I do not know whether the people of my congregation understood an English sermon. Still, I appreciated his friendship. He was very much aware of how desperate I was, but he was unable to offer any solution to my problem. At that time I thought I should continue to work toward the creation of a German-Jewish congregation in New York. We rented a little office down on Pearl Street downtown, and I engaged a man whose name I have now forgotten to help me organize the congregation. It was all very pitiful though. I was not used to begging for membership and after months of incredible struggle I simply gave up.

The year 1939 was approaching. The situation in Europe had become dangerous. It was quite clear to me that we were about to enter a second world war, but no one believed me. America was still optimistic, and optimism was considered the American creed. I remember very vividly an experience I had at the beginning of my life in America. I was invited by Rabbi Abba Hillel Silver to deliver a speech in Cleveland.[39] It was an extremely well-attended meeting, and I was asked to deliver my analysis of European events. In my speech I predicted the downfall of European Jewry. I argued that Hitler would begin a campaign of conquest, that few understood him, and that he would find it easy to conquer most of the world. I also predicted that in the course of such events European Jewry would be murdered and simply disappear with the world standing idly by and offering no help. The audience was stunned. At the end of the speech, Silver came up to me to thank me for the address, but it was an expression of gratitude bordering on complete rejection. I noticed immediately that he was not merely unhappy

39. Abba Hillel Silver (1893–1963) was the rabbi of a Reform congregation in Cleveland and the rival of Stephen S. Wise for the leadership of American Zionism.

with my speech but very critical of what I had said and regretful of having invited me to speak. If Silver, a leading Zionist, did not understand, who would? I left Cleveland heartbroken.

A few days later, after returning home, I received a telephone call from Stephen Wise asking me to meet with him at his office on West 68th Street. He looked at me and said, "I received this letter and I want you to read it." It was a letter from Abba Hillel Silver in which he said that since Stephen Wise was my mentor and had invited me to come to America, he should be informed of the fact that "Prinz was a pessimist who had the audacity to predict European Jewry's destruction. The time has come for us to teach him that America's creed is one of optimism and that he should begin to talk optimistically about the Jewish future or leave the country." I was flabbergasted and told Wise that I had expressed my profound conviction that Hitler would mean the end of all Jewish history in Europe and the death of millions of Jews. Wise said, "I believe this is your conviction. I feel very close to it although I cannot as yet express it as clearly as you do, but I want you to see a copy of the letter which I sent to Silver." With that, he gave me a letter that I will never forget. It read: "I have invited Joachim Prinz to America because he could no longer live in a country that was not free. He has come to the 'land of the free.' I believe in that freedom, which includes his freedom to express himself in accordance with his convictions. This is what he has done. He may be right that the time has come for us to forget about the American creed of optimism and understand in pessimistic terms the fate of our people. Those who do not agree with him are at liberty to say so. But I have no doubt that he is at liberty to say what he believes in and I do not regret having invited him to live among us in a country that guarantees freedom of speech to everyone who lives here." It was more than a letter. I do not know whether I still have it somewhere in my files.[40] I cherished it greatly because it really was a characteristic expression of the great man that Stephen Wise was. It encouraged me to express myself as freely and sincerely as I wanted instead of repeating the shallow and false slogans that tried to lull the Jewish people into false confidence in a future that simply did not exist.

Just as I was interested in the specific character of an American Jewry that had not yet developed a tradition of its own, so too was I greatly puzzled by America itself. It took me many years to understand the mentality of America as a country and the American people as a nation. I had been brought up to accept the definition of an entity called a nation as composed of individuals who had been living in a given country for hundreds and

---

40. Neither the Silver letter nor the Wise reply could be located.

sometimes thousands of years and which had absorbed those who had immigrated into that country to such an extent that they were no longer distinguishable. It was therefore difficult for me to understand a country in which nationalities had endured for many generations. It was a strange process of integration that maintained even linguistic identification with the country from which the grandparents had come to America. I found it puzzling that one could be an American patriot but carry the Irish flag on St. Patrick's Day and the Italian flag on Columbus Day. A few years after our arrival in America, I was invited to deliver a speech at the hundredth anniversary of the creation of the Italian state under Cavour.[41] I spoke about the Italian Renaissance and the great contribution Italy had made to the world and its civilization. I am sure my Italian listeners were very pleased with it, but then suddenly the governor of the state, who was the second speaker, spoke about the creation of Italy and invited the people to sing the Italian national anthem. They did it with gusto, and after that they sang the national anthem of America. In any European country such a demonstration of loyalty to the "old country" would have been considered high treason. Here it was taken for granted, and the singing of "Hatikvah" together with the national anthem was an equally interesting and puzzling experience of a dual loyalty that Americans accept as something very natural, while I continued to be amazed by it. It took me many years before I began to understand that America was a marvelous experiment unequaled in the world, and that the American people had succeeded in creating a great and not merely powerful nation with national instincts that were the result of a combination of many backgrounds and civilizations. It was a nation unlike France or Germany, and the Jews were part of that nation as much as they were part of the Jewish people.

The year 1939 proved to be of very great importance. My lecture career had been all but ruined and our existence during 1938 had been, as I mentioned, extremely precarious. I was now determined to accept a position as a rabbi or as anything else provided I would get a salary on the first of the month so that I could take care of my family without incurring debts. It was in this mood that I received a telephone call from Stephen Wise, who invited me to come to his office because he had an important message for me. Arriving there, I found three gentlemen who had come from the city of Newark, New Jersey. They were looking for a rabbi to replace the man who had served them for many decades but with whose services they were dissatisfied. I remembered that I had delivered a lecture at that congregation, whose name

41. Camillo Cavour (1810–1861) was the chief architect of Italian unification.

was Temple B'nai Abraham. But since I had delivered so many lectures during those years, I had no real recollection of it. Stephen Wise had asked the librarian of the Jewish Institute of Religion to bring up all the books I had written and they were piled up on his desk. Eight of my books were there, evidently to impress the delegation from the congregation.

After I met the three gentlemen, who later were to become close friends of mine, I heard Stephen Wise say to them: "There are only two people who can save your congregation. I could do it and Dr. Prinz could do it. There is nobody else who could undertake such a difficult job. Unfortunately, I am not able to come since I have a congregation, but Dr. Prinz is free and I hope he will accept your invitation." I was flabbergasted at the way he formulated this rather unrealistic alternative. But the men were rather impressed with both what he said and the fact that I was the author of so many books. They then asked to meet me in another room. Dr. Wise remarked that he would have to leave anyway, and so we stayed in his lovely study and began to talk. I informed the delegation from B'nai Abraham that I would emphasize education as the heart of congregational life and that I could not accept the invitation without being assured by them that I would be able to work in complete freedom, be completely independent, and that I would not be involved in a popularity contest but rather be the leader of the congregation in every respect. I also assured them I had no knowledge of administration and that they would have to manage the congregation in its financial and organizational affairs without my help. I was amazed at myself, for I really was in no position to stipulate any conditions. I should have been very happy to get a position that would pay me a certain salary and stabilize my situation, which had become so tenuous and so dangerous. But apparently because I was firm and insisted upon my concept of the congregation as a prerequisite of my engagement, they invited me immediately to come to them and be their rabbi. They were, as they told me, in very bad financial shape. My contract would call for a salary of $6,000 and the contract would be for one year. Also, I would have to buy or rent my own house. I accepted immediately. In 1939, $6,000 was not a large salary, but it was adequate and probably compared favorably with the average rabbi's salary at that time. I told them I would come to Newark to discuss matters with the staff and the lay people and that I would begin my work on July 1st of that year.

I remember that I did not have enough money to go to Newark and that I borrowed a few dollars from a friend of mine so that I could buy the railroad ticket to get there and back home. It was a humiliating experience, but it had symbolic value. I really had accepted the invitation of B'nai Abraham in desperation and as a solution to evidently insoluble problems. I had not been a success and had come to the end of my American tether. Hopeful at the beginning, I was desperate now.

I will never forget my first impression of the temple. It was a huge building with a seating capacity of two thousand. Apparently, it had been built by an ingenious architect who eliminated the pillars and columns that usually obstruct people's views by inventing a method of building a hanging roof. The space above the ceiling was about as large as the synagogue itself. I was a little disturbed by the theatricality of its pseudo-Baroque style, but I had to admit that it was impressive architecture. I went to the pulpit and realized that I would be able to see every person seated in the pews and upstairs in the balcony. I also learned that the congregation had dwindled in numbers to something like three hundred families who were members and that their situations were as precarious as mine. In addition to the synagogue, I saw a social hall, a gymnasium, and a swimming pool. The synagogue had been built in 1924, at a time of great prosperity. A few years after the dedication, the Depression came and most of the members of the congregation, who had pledged large contributions, lost their money and were no longer able to remain with B'nai Abraham. The lay leadership was an extraordinary group of people. It included Louis V. Aronson, the founder of Ronson Corporation;[42] Michael Hollander, the head of the famous empire of fur dyers;[43] and Michael A. Stavitsky, a former social worker, who had become a realtor and was one of the leaders of the community.[44] The group that formed the board of trustees was equally impressive. All the people were completely dedicated to the synagogue. It was their dream to have one of the largest and most impressive synagogues in the country, but they were saddled with a debt of $100,000 and the recognition they were unable to pay off the huge mortgage of almost $700,000. The building had cost $1,250,000. Still, they were very hopeful that with my help a new chapter in the history of B'nai Abraham would begin and that the congregation could be revived. Its rabbi was a former cantor. He had not been ordained by any recognized rabbinical school, but had nevertheless been quite successful in the community. He was abroad at the time that I inspected the building. I was never told that he was sent a cable informing him that he should consider himself rabbi emeritus.

---

42. In 1886. Louis V. Aronson (1869–1941) founded a metalworks company, The Ronson Corporation, which became known for its cigarette lighters.

43. The firm of A. Hollander and Sons, established in Newark in 1889, engaged in dyeing and dressing furs. Michael Hollander was one of the founder's sons.

44. Michael "Mike" Stavitsky was the chairman of the board of trustees of Congregation B'nai Abraham when Prinz was appointed in 1939.

They had pensioned him off against his will, or at least without his consent. I am very glad I was never told about this, for had I known I would never have accepted the invitation to serve as their rabbi.

It was agreed that I would begin officially on July 1st, but we also decided that I should start to work during the next few months in order to prepare myself for the difficult job. I agreed to spend one day every week at B'nai Abraham; this gave me an opportunity to look into the congregation, which was not merely financially bankrupt but also had no program that would attract members. My predecessor was mainly interested in the rabbinate as a means of making money, and although he had published prayer books for the congregation, he had no scholarly interest at all and no concept of what a congregation in the twentieth century should be like.[45] I had given a great deal of thought to the situation of organized religion in our time. After all, I had eleven years of experience behind me, almost four of them extremely difficult years under the pressure of the Hitler regime. I had been successful there, but I knew my success had something to do with the fact that I had strong convictions and that I had made my convictions the basis of the program of the congregation. I distinguished very clearly between a Jewish organization and a Jewish congregation. Joining a Jewish organization was a rather mechanical act. Membership in a Jewish congregation, however, was a declaration of Jewish and human commitment. This concept included every possible area of human interest and concern. It was the very opposite of a restricted ghettoized Judaism that was only involved with parochial Jewish problems and concerns. I never had any respect for what was called the sanctity of the pulpit. I excluded no topic—political, economic, literary, or anything else—from those to be discussed. The pulpit was a forum; the synagogue was not a church but a house of assembly for the Jewish people. I believed that the majority of the people were sick and tired of the cursed solemnity of both the sermons and the services. I rejected these notions and placed squarely before my people my own concept of an all-embracing, universal Judaism that acknowledged the existence of the Jewish people as well as the relevance of the Jewish faith.

Although most people seemed to have overcome the period of the Depression and had reestablished themselves in their old or new businesses, Prohibition was very much alive. The law had been revoked and restrictions had been lifted, but I discovered very soon after my arrival in Newark that the experience of the Prohibition period was an integral part of the col-

45. Prinz's predecessor was Julius Silberfeld, who served as rabbi from 1902 to 1939.

lective memory of the community with which I had to deal.[46] Newark altogether was both a very ugly and a very interesting town. It lived greatly in the shadow of New York. In the days when transportation to New York was not available, when the highways had not yet been built and no trains took people to the great metropolis, Newark had played a significant role as a city in its own right. Important theatrical performances were tried out there before opening up in the big city; industries developed there that made Newark the headquarters for costume jewelry and the hat-making business. In addition, several important beer breweries existed in those days. All this had made Newark a prosperous community. However, this situation had changed. As highways were built and trains and buses took people to New York in no time, Newark shrank in its cultural and to some degree in its economic importance. Yet it must not be forgotten that Newark remained the place where important industries, many of them chemical and pharmaceutical, had established large plants; where tanneries, a business which was started in the seventeenth century, remained intact; and where there were still important establishments in the fields of jewelry and insurance. Still, there is no doubt that the city had a very difficult time maintaining a cultural life of its own. The theaters, museums and concerts were in New York so that people traveled there whenever they wanted that kind of entertainment. Newark, or for that matter New Jersey, did not have an orchestra of its own. The Newark Museum was small and remained so. Although the entire system of library administration, and particularly the system of library cataloguing, was invented in Newark, New York was the large supplier of scholarly information.

We found a little house in the Clinton Hill section, not far from the synagogue. We paid $65 per month in rent and soon established ourselves. All our neighbors seemed to be Jewish and all of them were members of Temple B'nai Abraham. Many were very kind to us from the very beginning and tried to make life easier for us. All this was very pleasant, but certainly not fascinating. What fascinated me most there was the memory and aftermath of the Prohibition period.

I soon discovered that a certain elegant apartment house situated at 299 Clinton Avenue, in the very heart of the city, was the headquarters of the people who had played an important role during Prohibition as well as a source that could supply me with sufficient information. Almost everybody who was anybody lived in elegant apartments in this building. I remember

46. Prohibition had been instituted by the Eighteenth Amendment to the Constitution in 1919 and repealed through the Twenty-first Amendment in 1933.

that in the evening the doors of every apartment were open. You just walked in for a drink, found good company, a great deal of hilarity and, above all, the warmth and friendship that we needed so much being strangers to the city and foreigners in a new country. We found all that in large measure. We got used to meeting with a small group of people who had formed a friendship club for good drinks, good food, and the kind of comradeship and mutual concern that evidently all of us needed. It was in this small but distinguished circle of people that I began to understand the role that Newark and New Jersey had played during Prohibition. The main figure in all of this was a man who also lived at 299 Clinton Avenue, whose name was Abner Zwillman. Since he was more than six feet tall, he was generally known as "Longy."[47] I was not aware of the fact that he was the king of the underworld, controlled many businesses in New Jersey and other states of the union, and exerted extraordinary influence not merely over businesses but over very important organizations such as some of the most influential labor unions. My first contact with him was rather typical of later encounters. I was told that he was very rich and very eager to help. I knew of a family of German Jews who had arrived under the most difficult circumstances via Russia and China and were penniless. They turned to me immediately for help, and since institutional help was not sufficient, I called Mr. Zwillman to ask him whether he would be willing to contribute $2,000. As I began to tell him the plight of the family he grew rather angry, telling me that whenever I needed his help I should be sure not to tell him the stories of those whom I wanted him to help. He would take my word for it and send any amount of money I needed. Within two hours, a messenger arrived bringing me $2,000 in cash so that I was able to help the family immediately.

This was typical of the man, with whom I was to have many dealings. He was one of the most interesting men I ever met. Soft-spoken, well read, very hospitable, and charitable, he governed city and state and many other affairs with some degree of dignity, and certainly no signs of violence. I was later told that he had been accused of killing someone and that he maintained a triggerman to do his dirty jobs for him. None of that was in any way discernible to me. I met him over a period of several years without knowing who he really was, and he considered me to be his spiritual adviser. Whenever anything happened in his family, he called me, inviting me to officiate at various occasions, happy or sad. But I heard so many whisperings that I

---

47. Abner "Longy" Zwillman (1904–1959), Newark's most notorious gangster, was a very wealthy bootlegger during Prohibition and a founding member of the Murder Inc. crime syndicate. His violent death was either a suicide or a mob murder.

began to inquire about him, and although the responses I got were always very evasive, I soon put all the pieces together and arrived at the conclusion that Mr. Zwillman was one of the most powerful men in the country. During the Kefauver investigation into the network of the American underworld, he appeared on television, again well-spoken, and of course claiming to be completely innocent of any of the charges raised against him.[48]

I remember very vividly an incident that brought me rather close to Zwillman. I was sitting in my study when I received a telephone call from Mr. Sam Teiger, who was the most famous restaurateur in the state. He operated and owned The Tavern Restaurant, probably one of the best eating places in the vicinity and far superior to most restaurants in New York.[49] It was much later that I learned it was Mr. Zwillman who had helped him to establish the business. Also I learned that during Prohibition, Sam Teiger used to have a stand at which he sold French toast, which was one of his inventions and which remained a famous dish on his menu. The restaurant had been established for the purpose of having a speakeasy on the upper floor where a great many important and secret meetings took place. It was clear that there had to be a relationship between Mr. Zwillman and the liquor industry, of which many important representatives were members of my congregation.

Mr. Teiger himself was one of the most colorful figures of the community. One day he telephoned me to come immediately to his taxi, which was waiting in front of the synagogue, and to bring my robe and rabbinical book. I asked him the purpose of all this, but he responded that he would explain it to me on our way in the taxi. I met him downstairs and, when I entered the taxi, he told me he had come on behalf of Mr. Zwillman.

I was very curious about the cause. He then told me that Mr. Zwillman's triggerman was supposed to get married at this hour, that the synagogue was filled with hundreds of people waiting for the ceremony to be performed, but that the rabbi refused to officiate. This synagogue had been built by Mr. Zwillman in memory of his parents. It was situated on Bergen Street and still a rather new building. The son of the rabbi who had been Mr. Zwillman's parents' spiritual leader had been flown in from Canada to officiate at the ceremony, and it was he, a young, Orthodox rabbi, who refused to officiate. As we approached the synagogue, the car stopped sud-

48. Senator Estes Kefauver's committee conducted televised hearings to expose organized crime in 1950–1951. Zwillman appeared before the committee on March 26, 1951. The next day, newspapers reported that he had been a "telegenic hit."

49. Sam Teiger's very successful The Tavern Restaurant, which opened in 1923, catered especially to the Newark Jewish community in which Teiger himself was very active.

denly and Mr. Zwillman entered. He thanked me profusely for my willingness to perform the ceremony. We stopped in front of the synagogue, he held the door open for me, I entered the synagogue and went to the upper floor where the couple and the rabbi were waiting for me. From that balcony I looked down and saw at least five hundred people, of whom I knew some, waiting for the ceremony to begin. I understood they had been waiting for more than two hours, but no one dared to leave because all of these people were dependent upon "Longy" Zwillman. I met the young rabbi, who was very anxious about this whole matter, and asked him why he was not willing to perform the ceremony. He told me that he could not possibly do so because the bridegroom, whose name was Mr. Stacher (and who, because of his illiteracy was called "Doc" Stacher) was a "Kohen," a member of the priestly tribe, that the bride was a divorcee, and that according to biblical law, which he observed, a priest could not marry a divorcee.

I looked at the bride, a woman past her prime, and Mr. Stacher, a rather undistinguished-looking man. The bride was very eager to show me the Hebrew document of her divorce, which had not impressed the young rabbi and which I did not have to see. I turned to the rabbi and asked him to define for me what a "Kohen" was. He expressed his amazement at my ignorance. I told him it was not my ignorance that prompted me to ask the question but my interest in having his definition so that I could make the proper judgment. He then proceeded to tell me that a "Kohen" was a member of the Jewish elite and that he represented the best of Jewish tradition. He grew rather enthusiastic about it and began to describe to me the limitations of this tradition. I then pointed to Mr. Stacher and said to the rabbi, "Do you know Mr. Stacher?" He conceded that he did. I then asked, "Are you aware of what Mr. Stacher has done throughout his life, what his function is, and that he is indeed considered to be Mr. Zwillman's triggerman?" He conceded that too. I followed with, "Does Mr. Stacher's life appear to be a fulfillment of the glorious description that you gave me of the 'Kohen,' a member of the Jewish elite?" After a long pause the rabbi replied that Mr. Stacher did not represent a "Kohen" of the classical nobility. I then said to him, "I herewith declare in my capacity as an ordained rabbi that Mr. Stacher, because of the kind of life he has led, is not a 'Kohen.' As he is not a 'Kohen' he may marry a divorcee." Turning to Mr. Zwillman, I said, "I will perform the ceremony with the provision that the rabbi who came here from Canada will be fully reimbursed as though he himself had performed the ceremony and that I will not take any honorarium. I will perform the ceremony only under these circumstances." Mr. Zwillman nodded and we decided to begin the ceremony.

The whole scene reminded me of *The Threepenny Opera.*[50] Mr. Zwillman, more than six feet tall, was to be the ring bearer. A formal procession started, the groom and the blushing bride walking down the center aisle of the synagogue. Everyone rose, and I could feel an air of fear and anxiety when Mr. Zwillman, carrying the ring in his big hands, passed by a row of people who I was given to understand were the leading croupiers of gambling establishments from Maine to California. Reaching the altar where the canopy had been properly set up, the couple and Mr. Zwillman followed me. There we were, about to begin the ceremony, when the little rabbi from Canada came in. I whispered to him, "I thought you did not want to participate in the ceremony." He replied to me in Yiddish, "I decided to sing a little bit, because if I don't, he may not pay me." This only added to the hilarity of the whole scene. I performed the ceremony, tongue in cheek. It was a brief ceremony and everyone breathed a sigh of relief when the happy groom broke the glass and kissed the bride with whom he had shared a bed and room for many years before the wedding.

This was only an interlude, and a happy one in a way. Some time later, Mr. Zwillman sent me his tailor, asking me to permit him to make three suits for me as compensation. I informed the tailor I had no need for these suits and that he should tell Mr. Zwillman I had entered into an agreement with him, which he was violating. Later I was also invited to a wedding party that took place in the old Essex House, which was owned by another member of the Zwillman clan. I found out later that this was the most elegant and unusual party ever held in the city, but I was glad that I was not part of the gay gathering.[51] It took me quite some time to discover how many of my friends had been or still were very close associates of Mr. Zwillman, who in the meantime had established many legitimate businesses.

During the war, which started after my arrival, I became aware of the fact that Mr. Zwillman controlled the telephone union. When I had need of an additional telephone during the war, and when no one could obtain one, I reported my plight to Sam Teiger, who told me that the "tall man" would have a phone delivered to me within twenty-four hours. This was done. I began to talk to my close friends. There was not a single one who had not played some role in the Zwillman empire. One of them, who later became a rich man, had been in charge of labeling illegal whisky bottles in a garage on Kinney Street. Many decades later, when he bought up a large number of parking lots in New York, he called it, sentimentally, the Kinney System,

---

50. Berthold Brecht and Kurt Weill's sardonic musical masterpiece.
51. We are not told why Prinz was happy not to be there.

which still exists today. There were others I never suspected of having anything to do with illegal activities of that tragic period in American life, but to my amazement I began to discover that most of them played some role. None of them had ever forgotten it, nor did Mr. Zwillman permit them to do so. A Jewish mayor ruled Newark at that time.[52] He was a very bright man, good-looking, witty, articulate, and very capable, but everyone knew that it was not he who governed the city, but that Mr. Zwillman was the real mayor and that the man who was known to be the mayor of Newark was financially and otherwise completely dependent upon Mr. Zwillman and his henchmen. Innocently, I often accepted invitations to do invocations at meetings of this or that labor union only to discover Mr. Zwillman sitting at the head table and that it was he who determined the policy of the union.

It was decades later that I buried Mr. Zwillman. He had been in trouble with the law, and it finally caught up with him. He owed the Internal Revenue Service one million dollars. He was accused of having bribed a juror in one of his trials and was sentenced to serve a term in prison. Once he told me he had never been a prisoner in jail and that he would never be one. I was in my office in New York when I was called and told that Mr. Zwillman had died. According to the report given to me, he had hanged himself in the basement of his lovely home. He had never touched any liquor, but before he committed suicide he had emptied a bottle of bourbon whisky and then hanged himself. I was puzzled that a man so tall could manage to commit suicide in this manner in a basement the ceiling of which almost touched his head. Later I was told that he had been murdered, but his influence was still great enough to force the doctor to note on the death certificate that he had died as a suicide.

I will never forget the moment that I entered his house that evening. There were several well-known personalities who had been Longy Zwillman's close friends, such as Toots Shor[53] and others. They surrounded his widow, a member of a distinguished New York family. Among the guests in the house was a high-ranking Catholic priest who said that in my eulogy I should not forget to mention how charitable Mr. Zwillman was. I informed him that there would be no eulogy. Mr. Zwillman was entitled to be buried in accordance with Jewish law, and the prayers for the dead would be read, but I could not preach a eulogy without mentioning facts of his life

52. Meyer "Doc" Ellenstein, Newark's mayor from 1933 to 1941, was a childhood friend of Zwillman. He was twice tried on charges of corruption, but was not convicted.
53. Bernard "Toots" Shor owned a well-known restaurant in New York that drew famous athletes, politicians, and Broadway stars.

that were not flattering. The funeral service itself was unforgettable. Television crews were outside the funeral home. It had been arranged for me to arrive in a car that was not my own so that the TV men could not photograph me. At the cemetery they tried to take pictures, but I told them they were violating the law, which prohibits the disruption of a religious ceremony. Strangely enough, they obeyed, but Longy Zwillman's death was reported at great length in all the papers of the country. The *New York Times* published an obituary covering almost an entire page.

Not everyone lived in the shadow of Longy Zwillman. I watched with amazement and great admiration the manner in which the lay leaders of the Jewish community organized a community that had been utterly chaotic. Among these leaders were some unforgettable men. The most creative was probably Michael A. Stavitsky, who had been a social worker but upon the advice of another important member of the Jewish community of Newark decided to become a realtor and was very successful in his new field. When I became the rabbi of Temple B'nai Abraham, he was elected its president and remained in this office for ten years. I spent almost every day with him and found him to be a man of great understanding for the kind of program I had in mind. The fact that he had become a rich man had not entirely wiped out his training as a social worker and he understood that a congregation, and indeed organized religion, would have to declare its bankruptcy if it were not able to develop creative programs. He helped me set up the first large Jewish adult school in the country, which from the very beginning was extremely successful and which exists until this very day. Mike Stavitsky was married to Eve, who was a great lady and was helpful to him because she was critical and loving. Mike had a very bad temper, was obstinate and often contemptuous of people, but the Jewish community is indebted to him for his organizational talent. He was the founder of the Jewish Education Association of Essex County, of which he was the first and I the third president. Hilde and I became particularly close to Mike and Eve Stavitsky when an automobile accident killed their young son Ethan, who was nineteen years old and their greatest hope. I will never forget the morning he called to inform me of his son's death. He had arranged his whole life around this boy, who was a very shy, reticent, and beautiful human being. I brought the body from their lovely home in Murray Hill, near Summit, and I shall always remember how Eve knelt down at the cemetery and kissed the coffin in which their beautiful son was laid to rest.

Mike died in a nursing home after having spent four years completely oblivious of anything around him. He was a man who had been bright and creative and was suddenly bereft of every ounce of his intelligence. There he sat in the nursing home of New York Hospital, surrounded by three friends: Leppy Rich, a childhood friend; Dr. Meyer C. Ellenstein, the former mayor of Newark; and Mr. McDonald,[54] the first American ambassador to Israel. I saw these four men sitting together. No one spoke to the other. It was a tragic commentary on the frailty of human life. When I buried Mike, I did so almost joyfully. For his wife and me to see him in a state of complete senility was more painful than the knowledge that he was now at peace with himself and the world.

The second among the leaders was a man of extraordinary importance and one who fascinated me greatly. He was born in London into a poor family and had to earn a living for the family when he was twelve years old. He was practically illiterate, or at least, as I know from his own lips, did not know how to write properly. He was the founder of a great fur-dyeing empire and his name was Michael Hollander.[55] He was one of those who lived at 299 Clinton Avenue. Once in a while I heard him speak publicly. It was a unique experience, for he spoke with much feeling and without any sentimentality. I remember coming to his office to ask him to finance a plan of mine that called for a luncheon meeting with the Christian ministers of the town. I asked him for a contribution of $1,000, which in those days was a great deal of money. He looked at me with amazement, even anger, and scolded me for having come down to his office for such a puny amount instead of phoning him to say that I needed the money. I felt a bit ashamed of myself, but very proud of the man who was one of the most generous people I ever knew, and who died much too young.

The third one was Mr. Louis V. Aronson, the founder of Ronson Corporation, a company which at that time specialized in the manufacture of their famous cigarette lighters. He was a very interesting character. I must say it was good that I buried him in 1941, only two years after I came to the congregation. I would not have been able to live with him; he was one of the vainest men I ever met. With his vanity went a sense of power and dictatorship that made the members of his family tremble. Nevertheless, he was a great man who had started his large and extremely successful business by manufacturing metal buttons for the Belgian army during the First World War. He then invented a rather crude lighter, which was used in the trenches

54. James Grover McDonald (1886–1964) had been a supporter of Zionism and a proponent of the admission of Jewish refugees from Germany to the United States. He served as U.S. Ambassador to Israel from 1949 to 1950.
55. Prinz is thinking of Michael Hollander's father, Adolph, who was the founder of the enterprise.

by many soldiers during that war. This is how he laid the foundation for an enormous fortune that long after his death dwindled because the patent for his lighters had run out and the Japanese had begun to manufacture and sell them at a price far below that charged by Ronson.

These three characters must suffice for our purpose here. Many others could be added, but these three were the most outstanding, or at least the most interesting. There were others in the community who were not members of Temple B'nai Abraham, but it can be said with all honesty that those who were the leaders of B'nai Abraham were also the leaders of the community. It helped me greatly that I had come to a congregation whose leadership understood that congregations, Jewish or Christian, could not afford to live on an island of their own parochial solemnity, but had to be active in building the community at large as well as the Jewish community. All of them were highly respected citizens of the city of Newark.

Once in a while, I had lunch with the founder of Bamberger's, one of the great department stores of America, which later merged with Macy's. Louis Bamberger[56] was a man who had come from Baltimore in 1902, and had built his large department store on a site where in the nineteenth century a modest building of Temple B'nai Abraham had once stood. When we sat together in the store's dining room, he never permitted a waitress to wait on him before serving the customers. He came from a wealthy German Jewish family, never married, and when he died left his entire fortune for public purposes: the Institute for Advanced Studies at Princeton University, the Newark Museum, and Protestant and Jewish charities. I will never forget his last will. It started with the sentence: "I came to Newark in 1902 and prospered. Now that I am no longer among the living, I am paying back from that which I earned that which I owe to the people of my community."

But all the personal matters and even building the congregation, which took a long time and a great deal of effort and which caused many disappointments even as it reached achievements—all of this suddenly moved into the background. From the first months of my work with the congregation I was mindful of the fact that while we were doing all the local things and being involved in all these parochial matters, the world was aflame and the war was going on. Since I was familiar with the German army and the mentality of the German people and had never underestimated Hitler, I knew that it would be a long and bloody war with rapid conquests and with very doubtful results. The democracies of the world were ill prepared for

---

56. Louis Bamberger, the founder of L. Bamberger and Company, sold his large and very successful department store to R. H. Macy in 1929. He was a generous donor to both Jewish and general community causes.

this kind of adventure, and one country after the other fell. I watched the tragic events in Europe with growing anxiety, while the people with whom I was dealing belittled Hitler's successes and were certain that he would be defeated soon. I was always amazed at the naïveté or ignorance of the vast majority of the American people. They simply had no ability to judge the realities that faced the world. After all, Europe was far away, not merely geographically, but in every other respect as well.

I remember that I was attending a meeting of B'nai Abraham on Sunday afternoon, December 7, 1941, when I was told that America had been attacked by Japan, that the tragedy of Pearl Harbor had taken place, and that we were now participants in the war. I recall very vividly taking home a judge, who was a highly respected member of the community. On the way there he told me boastfully that the war with Japan would last three weeks, that the American might would come down on those "Japs" and smash them. I tried to convince him that he was wrong and that I was afraid the war would take a long time. I said that tens of thousands of our men would be killed and that it would take years before Hitler would be defeated. He told me that I was, after all, a foreigner and knew very little about the power of the United States. He assured me that this would be a war of weeks and not years. Many years later he had to admit to me that he was wrong and that I, alas, had been right.

We were now at war and things changed rapidly. Young men were called to the colors of their country and were training hurriedly. It did not take many more months until the bad news arrived that this or that young man had fallen in battle. I remember many of these cases and the sadness that suddenly descended upon the country. Most Americans seemed to be dealing with something beyond their understanding. The reality was so stark, however, that they soon began to comprehend that there was a man in Europe, altogether insane, who would not stop before devastating most of Europe and conquering the majority of its lands.

There came a time when the civilian population at home started to become involved in the war. My wife became a nurse's aide at the Newark Beth Israel Hospital, and so did many other women. Rationing began, but the black market flourished. Soon many people were making huge sums of money, waxing rich on the misery of the world. D-Day was not merely a day of great elation and triumph; it was also a day of mourning for the thousands of young men killed in this first great step toward final victory. But Hitler was still the master of Europe for a subjugated Holland and Belgium, France and Italy, Poland and Romania, and large parts of North Africa. The German army proved far superior to the democratic forces, which had indulged themselves in one illusion after the other. I was particularly worried about the fate of the Jewish people. It was at that time that I received frequent reports about what was happening to the people who since 1938 had been taken to concentration camps, which in most cases were death camps.[57] It was quite clear to me that all of the three and a half million Jews in Poland would perish.

It was during these years that I became active in the American Jewish Congress. I worked closely with Stephen Wise and was soon elected chairman of the administrative committee. I was still ill prepared for the parliamentary procedures used at meetings and the whole structure of the organization. But I overcame my limitations and welcomed the opportunity to be of service to our people. I was never satisfied with just being the rabbi of a congregation. Rabbinical work was very often frustrating. There was not enough satisfaction in being close to individuals and families, serving and helping them whenever possible. I was always driven into public life and all my life I have been a public man. This was not really a desire for publicity; my main interest was the political development of our people. Very soon I became deeply involved and interested in international affairs. At that time, the American Jewish Congress was very closely connected with the World Jewish Congress,[58] which had, as it still does, an office in Geneva. I was with Wise when he received a cable from Dr. Gerhart Riegner, the secretary of the World Jewish Congress in Geneva, informing him of the situation in the concentration camps. There was an additional sentence stating that the large industrial firms of Germany had built plants in close proximity to concentration camps and that they were using the fat from Jewish corpses for the manufacture of soap.[59] Holding the cable in his hands, Wise began to cry. He showed the cable to me and said, "I have to go to Washington to

57. See Chapter 2, note 158.

58. The continuous history of the World Jewish Congress, established as an association of Jewish communities and organizations, began in 1936 with the purpose of furthering Jewish interests throughout the world.

59. The cable that reached Wise was sent by the representative of the World Jewish Congress in England, Samuel Silverman. Dated 8/29/42, it read (punctuation added): "Have received through Foreign Office following message from Riegner Geneva. 'I received alarming report that in Führer's headquarters plan discussed and under consideration: All Jews in countries occupied or controlled [by] Germany, number 3-1/2 to 4 million, should after deportation and concentration in East at one blow [be] exterminated to resolve once for all Jewish question in Europe. Action reported planned for autumn. Methods under discussion includ[e] prussic acid. We transmit information with all necessary reservation as exactitude cannot be confirmed. Informant stated to have close connexions with highest German authorities and his reports generally reliable. Inform and consult Newyork. Foreign office [h]as no information bearing on or confirming story.'" There is nothing in the telegram about industrial plants or plans to use fat from Jewish corpses for manufacture of soap. Although it was long believed that soap was produced from Jewish corpses, no evidence of such use has been discovered.

see to it that our government intervenes." I left the room, as I thought that Wise wanted to be alone. Later he told me of his visit with the Under Secretary of State, the late Mr. Sumner Welles, who said to him, "We have not received any confirmation of this matter and I don't want to publicize it." Wise told me that he yielded but was very unhappy about it. It was much later that I learned that the State Department deliberately withheld information about concentration camps for more than a year. Welles, whom I met only twice, gave Wise permission to talk about it publicly only half a year after his visit. I said to Wise, "All this makes me very unhappy because it smells of an American conspiracy to withhold information and to postpone action." At that time I did not know how right I was. Wise was a great American and a great Jew. His close relationship to Roosevelt stemmed from Roosevelt's being beholden to Wise because of his activity during Roosevelt's campaigns for the governorship in New York and later the presidency. But Wise was also a great Jew, most deeply involved in Jewish affairs and very much in love with the Jewish people. Often there were conflicts between the two allegiances, and one was not always sure which would prevail.

It was only natural that I should be more deeply concerned with the affairs of our people in Europe since they were, after all, my people. In the month of November 1938, all of German Jewry had been arrested and taken to concentration camps.[60] Thirteen members of my family were among them. Many of my former students were gassed in various camps and I felt guilty about the fact that I was a survivor. I was unable to understand why I had been singled out for life and survival while others were sent to their death. I tried to convey that to Wise and other people. I found in the World Jewish Congress a number of extraordinary people, some of them of European descent, who understood me fully and shared my anxieties and sorrow. Still, it was difficult to penetrate the American Jewish community. My pulpit became more and more a political forum, although some people may not have liked it that way. I believed that organized religion would go under unless it became a potent force in society, and that meant in political life. Unless religion became the guardian of decency and morality in the community and in the country, it had no right to exist. I am sure that many people in the congregation found it difficult to accept that kind of a sermon, but I persisted. It became part and parcel of my life and a very important element of my thought and action.

Dispatches from the war were very discouraging. The list of people killed in action grew longer. Food rationing began. Americans who were ac-

---

60. Thirty thousand Jewish men had been arrested, not all of German Jewry. The mass deportation to death camps in the east began only in the fall of 1941.

customed to being spoiled and getting everything they paid for complained bitterly about restrictions on purchasing sugar, butter, and similar items. To me, the attitude of the people seemed ridiculous. The food restrictions in America could not compare with the rationing in Europe long before the war began.

With the defeat of Adolf Hitler and the end of the war, the year 1945 would mark the beginning of a new chapter in human history. For me, too, that year was of special significance. I was unanimously elected to serve as chairman of the United Jewish Appeal of Essex County. I was the first, and so far the only, rabbi who ever held that position. Of all the opportunities I have had to serve the community and become acquainted with it and with all kinds of people from every walk of life, this was the greatest. Although I retained my office in the temple and continued to work for it, it was no longer the center of my life. The year 1945 was dedicated to the UJA. The chairman before me had raised $200,000 from the entire community, but I had promised that I would raise a million dollars, the first million ever to be raised in the community. It was considered an unattainable goal. I formed a cabinet with whom I met every day, and moved my activities to downtown Newark where I discovered a world completely unknown to me, in many ways alien, but in every respect fascinating and interesting. The campaign was divided into departments, which brought various operational and professional groups together, and I worked with every one of them. In those days I must have delivered three or four speeches a day. I met people I had never seen before and established friendships that have lasted to this day or to the death of that person. The vast majority were not members of my congregation, but I established relationships that were to endure and gave me an insight into the private lives and professional habits of literally thousands of people. Looking to the end of the war, I was able to arouse their enthusiasm, promising them a Jewish state soon thereafter and stressing that the displaced persons following the end of the war would be the major problem that required great Jewish concern.

At the end of the campaign I had raised just a bit under a million dollars and was considered the great hero of the community. I did not need that title; the community had given me something for which I could not thank them enough. I was now not merely the rabbi of a congregation but a spiritual leader of the entire community. Although people could not pronounce my first name or had other reasons not to call me by it, there were cases where I was able to establish a relationship of human intimacy such as I never thought possible. It was a good introduction to the specific character of the American Jewish community. I am sure that my role in American Jewry would have been quite different without the experience of 1945.

The war was reaching its conclusion. After incredible sacrifices in terms of human life and energy, the Allied troops had been able to achieve victory in North Africa over one of the greatest military geniuses of history, the German General Rommel; then came the invasion of Sicily, the campaign in Italy, and finally the conquests of France and Germany. All of us followed these events every hour and there was no more popular radio program than the hourly news. At that time there were newscasters of great prominence. Newscasting was not merely a factual report of what had happened, but an interpretation of the events that could only be performed by men of great ability, such as Edward Murrow[61] and many others. We stayed glued to the radio since television did not exist in those days. Finally Berlin fell, and the war was over.

The progress of the war stimulated my own thoughts and impressions. I was flabbergasted to see that General Eisenhower yielded Berlin to the Russians. This act had something to do with the fact that Americans were not familiar with the geography of Germany and that Eisenhower never understood the symbolic importance of Berlin. This very fact must be interpreted in terms of the political naïveté or ignorance that led to the division of Germany, one of the tragic circumstances of postwar history. But it could not be helped. It was done. Roosevelt was dead; Harry Truman had taken over. I was reminded of the day when Stephen Wise spoke at Madison Square Garden in Roosevelt's campaign[62] and on behalf of his old friend FDR. After speaking, Wise came down to our seats and asked me to leave with him. At that moment Harry Truman, the candidate for the vice presidency, began to speak. Wise insisted upon leaving, but I finally convinced him to stay because I thought it improper to leave while a vice presidential candidate was speaking. He consented and we remained standing in the aisle; then turning to me he said, "This man is mediocre but decent and a man of integrity." I reminded him of this sentence some time later when Harry Truman proved to be one of the great presidents of the country, a man of decision and great courage. But I will also not forget the day Roosevelt died. We had a romantic notion about Roosevelt. There was something messianic about him and many of us forgot that he was, after all, a New York politician, a man of many human frailties. But when his voice had been stilled and the voice of Harry Truman was heard for the first time, we could not believe that he would ever amount to much or be able to lead the people as Roosevelt had done.

In later years I would become very close to Mrs. Roosevelt. I had little knowledge of their tragic marital problems and only much later did I begin

61. Edward R. Murrow (1908–1965) worked for CBS news broadcasting during the war.
62. In 1944.

to realize that she came into her own only after her husband's death. I had the great pleasure of performing the wedding ceremony of her physician, David Gurevitch, in her Manhattan home and being invited to a small dinner for Indira Gandhi. I established a rather close relationship with Mrs. Roosevelt and consider her one of the greatest women who has ever lived. I will not forget that when I came to perform the ceremony of her personal physician, which was to take place early in the morning, I found her with two pillows in her hands. I asked her what she intended to do with them and she replied, "I thought that since you were not a Reform Jew, you would kneel during the wedding ceremony." I was amazed. She who was so involved in Jewish causes and had so many Jewish values told me she had attended only one Jewish wedding ceremony. It had taken place in Hyde Park in the home of her friend Henry Morgenthau, Jr., the secretary of the treasury.

The war, which had destroyed a considerable part of Europe and decimated the Jewish people by six million, was now ended. It had become apparent to every thinking person how very tragic the victory was. The enemy was defeated, but so was mankind, and the consequences of the Second World War are still with us. The entire world had changed. One could see that Hitler was successful in that regard, though not in the way he had envisaged. It was not Germany that now ruled the world. Communist regimes had been extended from the Soviet Union to half of Europe; the entire political framework had changed. Although Germany was defeated, she was to establish herself as one of the most powerful and prosperous nations of the world. All this was done with the help of American capital and a political concept that called for the establishment of a strong Germany as a bulwark against the forces of Communism. The Jewish situation created by the Second World War was so overwhelming that it was difficult to think of a solution to the problem. We had lost half of our people. But statistics, which deal with numbers, do not reveal the reality that the death of so many people had created. Among the six million Jews who perished (the number is not exact and has been established as an approximation of the losses that were sustained) were the most devout and learned of Jews, particularly of Eastern Europe. Their loss was irreparable; the wound will never heal. No Jewish community in the world can reconstitute the piety and knowledge of the Jews of Eastern Europe; two million children were among the victims. The Holocaust still remains beyond explanation. No interpretation can enable thoughtful people of any faith to reconcile it with their concepts of decency and piety.

There were, of course, hundreds of thousands of survivors. We still lack an analysis of their mentality, the reasons for their survival, and their attitudes toward mankind and Judaism. Some of them remained in Germany where their moral record is not particularly encouraging testimony to their qualities as human beings.[63] Many survived because of their shrewdness and put that quality to good and sometimes cruel use.[64] But the majority survived as people who will forever bear scars of body and soul. They will remain embittered about a humanity that is forgetting the tortures of the 1930s.[65] Because of the need to deal with displaced persons and the hope for the establishment of a Jewish state, the new Jewish situation became much more complicated than ever before. American Jews began to emerge as the major hope for those who needed help. Although it took a long time before they realized the magnitude of the problem, they became the major contributors, in large measure successfully addressing overwhelming needs through their generosity.

A year after the defeat of Hitler, the World Zionist Organization called the first Zionist Congress to be held after the war.[66] It met very much in the shadow of the Holocaust and in the hope of establishing a Jewish state. I was elected a member of the American delegation to the Congress, which was to be held in Basel, the town in Switzerland where the first Congress had been held.[67] Although Switzerland had not been involved in the war, it had suffered to the point that although the Congress was held during the winter, we slept in unheated rooms. Since hotel facilities were not available in sufficient numbers, I and many others had to be satisfied with rooms in private homes that, of course, lacked heat and provided very little food. But this was not the main problem of the Congress. I went to Switzerland with my friend Stephen Wise who, like myself, did not identify with the views of the American delegation. The American Zionists were led by Abba Hillel Silver, who was not merely a right-wing Republican but also a right-wing Zionist. It was at that time that the Jews living in Palestine began to fight the British occupation forces. Jewish terrorists had sprung up, among them the Stern Gang, as well as the Irgun.[68] Quietly but systematically the Haganah, which

63. Prinz is apparently thinking of the black market activities engaged in by some Jews in displaced persons camps in Germany.

64. A reference to those who, in saving themselves, caused the deaths of others.

65. He omits the 1940s!

66. See note 26, above.

67. Prinz's name does not appear on the list of delegates nor do the congress bulletins mention him as a speaker. He may have been an alternate delegate.

68. "Stern Gang" was an epithet given to the "Fighters for the Freedom of Israel" (Lehi), headed by Avraham Stern, which considered any means of struggle against the British in Palestine to be legitimate. The Irgun, the "National Military Organization" (Etzel), was a similarly inclined, if somewhat less extreme, Jewish military underground in Palestine.

was later to become the Israeli army, prepared for a great battle with the British. Abba Hillel Silver sided with the terrorists[69] and many American Jews supplied them with arms. Stephen Wise and I, and possibly a few others of the American delegation, allied ourselves with Hadassah, which fought for the Haganah and against any terrorist activity in Palestine. From the very beginning, both Wise and I were excluded from meetings of the inner circle. I never saw Wise so angered and so embittered as in those days.

We stuck together as we were of the same political opinion; very often we attended meetings of other groups since we were not admitted to the caucuses of the American delegation. Because of his anger, Wise delivered some of his worst speeches during the Congress. His words were no longer taken seriously. I don't think he ever spoke to Silver or Emanuel Neumann[70] during the entire Congress.

During the Congress, I recall our learning of a meeting to be held by former concentration camp inmates. We stumbled into a smoke-filled room where every seat was occupied. As we entered, we heard a young, red-haired man speaking in Yiddish with a kind of oratorical passion I have never heard before or since. Since Stephen Wise's knowledge of Yiddish was very limited, I had to translate for him. We listened with great attention because these were our people who had survived the camps. The room conveyed a peculiar kind of reality. It was as though those present had not yet recovered from the kind of life that forced them to face death every day and provided them with barely the necessary food to maintain themselves. It was a world unparalleled anywhere in the universe. Yet they had survived and now were full of anger, bitterness, resentment, and thoughts of revenge. Each of them had a number tattooed on his or her arm. Their eyes showed the only outward sign of the anger that burned in their souls. We began to listen to the young man who had apparently been speaking for quite a while. And then we heard the following sentences: "You must understand that we had to develop our own underground language in the concentration camps so that the Nazi guards would not be able to understand us. A great deal of trade and illegal activities were conducted in Auschwitz where I spent the last years. Somehow we received dollars and spoke a great deal about America from where the help had come. But so that the Nazis should not understand us, we called dollars *Stephanim* and we called America *Stephania* since, for us, America was

69. Although he did not support terrorism, Silver did side with the right-wing Zionist Revisionists. At the Congress he called for an "undivided and undiminished" Palestine.
70. Emanuel Neumann (1893–1980) was for many years a leading figure in American Zionism and a close associate of Abba Hillel Silver. Although on the right wing of the Zionist political spectrum, he was not an active supporter of Jewish terrorist groups.

identified with Stephen Wise." I did not have to translate this to Wise. He was sitting next to me and he began to tremble. His face pale and with tears running down his cheeks, he said to me, "This is the greatest compliment that was ever paid me. I know I do not deserve it. If people in concentration camps even thought of me, I must consider that a greater honor than the Legion of Honor I received from the French Republic, greater than anything ever done for me."

We decided to take a boat back to America together. Mrs. Wise[71] was with us. I have not written about her, and this might be a good opportunity to do so. She was very petite and fragile, a member of the Waterman family, wealthy German Jews who were known as manufacturers of very expensive canned vegetables. Wise had met her when he was a young rabbi in Portland, Oregon. I read the many love letters that were published after she died.[72] Wise's letters were full of flowery compliments in the style of nineteenth-century poets. He was deeply in love with her and so was she with him. I am not sure the Waterman family was very happy about their daughter marrying a rabbi, but even in Portland, Wise was a pioneer, particularly in his attack on child labor. He was tall and good looking and his voice was to become famous throughout the land. From the very beginning, he was an extraordinary preacher. Although he was never ordained by a theological seminary, nor was he ever a Jewish scholar of any kind, he was, nevertheless, a passionate Jew, who had attended the Second Zionist Congress.[73] Born in Hungary, he was the son of a Hungarian rabbi. In introducing me shortly after I came to America, he said, referring to my birth in a foreign country, "I have been an American for only sixty-nine years, but I have been a Jew for three thousand years." Louise Waterman married that kind of a man. He was an homme à femme who, I understand, had many affairs with women even after his marriage. But that did not bother Louise at all. She, the daughter of one of the richest Jews in America, was a radical liberal. Although she was never a member of the Communist Party, she certainly was a radical socialist. She had very little knowledge of Jewish customs, and for her to be married to a rabbi was a rather strange accident in her life. I don't know how many services she actually attended, but she adored Stephen. They had two children: James, who started to study theology but never finished and

71. Louise Waterman Wise, who died in 1947, two years before her husband, came out of Felix Adler's Ethical Culture movement, which had moved her to a life of social activism.
72. In Justine Wise Polier and James Waterman Wise, eds., *The Personal Letters of Stephen S. Wise* (Boston, 1956).
73. The Second Zionist Congress was held in Basel in 1898.

remained a Bohemian almost all his life, certainly until the death of his father; and Justine, who became a famous jurist and a judge of Family Court in New York.

Louise Wise was, of course, well educated, having gone to the most prestigious colleges. She knew French and German very well. Once she translated my book *We Jews* into English, a translation I did not want to be published since the book had been written for the Jews living under the Hitler regime. She and Stephen had discovered the book in a bookstore in London at a time when we did not know each other. She also translated Aimé Pallière's book into English, a book that was published.[74] Very often she showed me letters, in French, to people in France that she wanted me to correct, but very few corrections were necessary. When the first German-Jewish refugees came to America, she became very active on their behalf. She bought two houses next to the Institute of Jewish Religion, which were called Congress houses and which offered shelter and food to hundreds of refugee families for the first weeks or months of their stay in the new country. All or most of these refugees were from the upper middle class and appreciated the facilities, which were better than welfare care.

She was also a rather competent painter and I am very proud that I own one of her original paintings. Although she was mainly a copyist, going to the various museums and copying with great skill some of the works of the classical painters, she did a number of her own paintings, whose subject matter was mainly social problems. She was a woman with a very large heart, capable of passionate love for humanity. There are hundreds of anecdotes about her and her complete lack of understanding of Jewish traditions. The Wises, of course, did not observe the dietary laws in their home, and I remember Wise once telling me of calling his wife to tell her he would bring three Orthodox rabbis home for dinner. He asked his wife to have the cook prepare a fish dinner. When they arrived home, which at that time was in a hotel on Fifty-Seventh Street, and the dinner was about to be served, the maid brought in a beautifully arranged platter of shrimp. I remember that when she died, old and very ill and ready to fall asleep, we took her body to the cemetery of the Free Synagogue,[75] which is situated in Westchester County. There she had designed a mausoleum for the family, which had not yet been used; she was the first to be buried there. The burial services were

74. Aimé Pallière (1875–1949) was a French Catholic writer and theologian who was a Zionist and came close to converting to Judaism. His book, *The Unknown Sanctuary: A Pilgrimage from Rome to Israel,* appeared in an English translation by Louise Waterman Wise in 1929.
75. The Free Synagogue was the name of Stephen Wise's congregation in Manhattan.

private. Only the family and a few others were permitted to attend the services at the cemetery. I stood next to Wise, and when the coffin was lowered into the grave, heard him say in German, "Auf Wiedersehen, Louise."

This was typical of Wise's naïve piety. Theologically, he could not possibly have believed in resurrection after death, but often he expressed the religious feelings of a child. Louise Wise once told me the following story. When Stephen Wise received the Legion of Honor in Paris, she was watching the ceremony, which involved the president of the Republic of France, from a balcony of her hotel. After the ceremony she said to her husband, "I wish your parents could have seen this great and solemn scene, with the president of France embracing and kissing you on both cheeks." He turned to her and said simply, "They did, my dear, they did."

Shortly after I returned from the Zionist Congress, I received an invitation from the Jewish community in Great Britain to be the American speaker during a fund-raising campaign for Palestine.[76] Of course I accepted immediately, although it would necessitate my being in England for two months. It was not easy to arrange for a substitute to take my place in the congregation. I do not now recall what I actually did about it, but I suppose I had an assistant at that time who simply took over and performed all the functions that were usually mine. In those days it took between sixteen and eighteen hours to get to London since there were no jet flights. We stopped overnight in Newfoundland where we slept in army barracks. Constant repairs and refueling were required. I had bought the *New York Post* in the evening, which I wanted to show my listeners in London. Upon arrival, I was met at the airport and taken to one of the most elegant and luxurious hotels in London, the Dorchester, where Chaim Weizmann used to have an apartment. London was still a living witness to the brutal air attacks by the Germans. There was rubble in almost every street, and food was rationed. The tiny slivers of meat we received and the complete lack of fruit and eggs were a sad commentary on a nation that was supposed to have been victorious. She was still suffering the aftermath of a terrible and costly war. There was hardly a family that had not been affected, and hundreds of private dwellings lay in ruins. The people's clothing was shabby; altogether, it was a rather sad experience.

I arrived in London in the afternoon, and my first speaking engagement was to be in the evening at one of the synagogues in the West End. At that time Ernest Bevin was serving as the Prime Minister of Britain, a man who

---

76. Prinz has the sequence wrong. He raised funds for the United Palestine Appeal in England during the summer of 1946, five months *before* the Zionist Congress.

was one of the most stubborn, unbending advocates of limiting Jewish immigration to Palestine.[77] He still held fast to Great Britain's role as the mandatory power in Palestine and was determined to prevent a Jewish state from coming into being. America was at odds with England over this issue and the Jews of England stood up courageously against their own government. The newspaper I brought from America carried on its front page a very critical and violent rejection of Bevin's stubbornness and a solemn identification of the American government with the Jewish dream of a national homeland.[78] The tragedy of all this was that 1946 was just one year after the defeat of Hitler. Hundreds of thousands of people were lingering in displaced persons camps, longing to get out after having spent so many years in concentration camps. As there seemed to be no understanding of this situation on the part of the British government, everything had to be done to attack it and subject it to international criticism. In addition to raising funds, this was indeed my task in England. I showed the newspaper to my audience in St. John's Wood Synagogue.[79] The meeting began with a rather humorous experience. The rabbi of the congregation, whose name I do not recall,[80] introduced me by saying that I had come to England in order to criticize the government and join British Jewry in doing so. And then he added, "Dr. Prinz is coming to us in the spirit of an ancient Jewish tradition. We have never yielded to any government when it came to moral issues. Does it not say in the Psalm: 'Do not put your trust in princes?' " He did not notice that the audience was beginning to snicker and giggle. But when he said the last sentence immediately after the biblical quotation, "I now take great pleasure in introducing to you Dr. Prinz," there was loud and hilarious laughter. I myself was quite amused at the lack of a sense of humor on the part of the rabbi, who simply did not understand why both the audience and I were rather amused by his introduction.

The two months in England, which took me all over the country, were quite interesting because I came into contact with the British Jewish com-

77. Ernest Bevin (1881–1951) served as foreign secretary (not prime minister) of Great Britain from 1945 to 1950. From 1945 to the establishment of Israel in 1948, he kept legal immigration to Palestine to a minimum and dealt severely with Jewish refugees who sought to enter the country by illegal means.

78. As reported by the London *Jewish Chronicle* (June 21, 1946), the newspaper Prinz brought with him contained an advertisement signed by 150 prominent Americans expressing objection to Bevin's policies and support for the Jewish homeland in Palestine.

79. Although the reference could be to the Orthodox synagogue by that name, it is most likely to the principal congregation of Liberal Judaism in England located on St. John's Wood Road.

80. The rabbi was probably Philip Cohen, the third minister of the synagogue following Israel Mattuck and Maurice Perlzweig.

munity. In particular, I had a close relationship to the German-Jewish refugees who had come to England in large numbers. There is hardly a Jewish community in the world that has behaved as beautifully and generously to these unfortunates as have the Jews of England. The refugees were welcomed and even pampered at a time when the English people themselves had very little to spare. To give them work, the British Jews had established a complex of small industrial firms in Wales, near the city of Cardiff. I visited them and found a number of old friends who were very happy to see me after so many years. Many had been liberated from concentration camps. Some had had to spend the war years in a camp set up by the British government for "enemy aliens," situated on the Isle of Man. It was probably one of the most ridiculous projects engaged in during the war.[81]

One of the most important experiences for me, which came through my work, was meeting the young and very attractive widow of General Orde Wingate.[82] It was just two years after Orde, who became known as "Wingate of Burma" because of his daring assaults upon the enemy there, had been killed in an airplane crash. When they found his body, he was holding a Hebrew Bible. He had come to Palestine in 1937 and fallen in love with the Jewish people, identifying himself completely with the concept of a Jewish state. Earlier he had studied Arabic and other Semitic languages. Born in India and a very unconventional man, he was particularly active in helping poor Jews. Although he was part of the British occupational army, he was in constant touch with the Jewish settlers and assisted the Jewish leadership. He began to speak Hebrew and the people of Palestine got used to calling him *Ha-Yedid* (the friend). For a time he trained the special night squads of the illegal Haganah. He was brutal in attempting to teach his military students the laws of discipline and caution. Modeling his military method on the biblical story of Gideon, who sent most of his troops home and kept only the bravest, Wingate trained a small group thoroughly and thereby achieved amazing victories. This was Wingate's thesis: "A small people can overwhelm large numbers of opponents if they are well trained; although inferior in quantity, they could be superior in quality." Orde Wingate is still remembered in Israel as a friend; a kibbutz bears his name.[83] He died at the age of

81. Worried that "enemy aliens" (including German Jews) might act as spies for Germany, the British government, in September 1939, set up an internment camp for them on the Isle of Man.

82. Orde Charles Wingate (1903–1944) was a British army officer who served in Palestine from 1936 to 1939, where he fought against Arab terrorists and espoused the Zionist cause. His wife, Lorna, was for a time a leader of Youth Aliyah in England.

83. Yemin Orde, a youth aliyah village in the north of Israel.

forty-one, but his widow was determined to carry on what she considered to be her husband's mission.

While I was in England, her son, who was born a few months after his father's death, was christened in Westminster Abby.[84] A report about the christening in the London *Times* mentioned as present at the ceremony, together with a number of Lords, three members of a kibbutz in Palestine. Lorna Wingate had become a passionate Jewess. Coming from Scotland, she and her mother, Mrs. Paterson, had embarked upon a systematic campaign to hurt the English because of their bad behavior in Palestine and to do as much as they could for the Jewish people. Many a time Lorna shared a platform with me at God knows how many meetings. Very often she appeared in my hotel with eggs she had bought on the black market. She said things about Jews that I could not accept, such as the frequently repeated story that it made her very happy to see a Jewish pawnbroker cheat a "goy." She was very angry at the "goyim," who had killed so many Jews, and at the English who were now preventing the survivors from having their own homeland. I rebelled against this kind of philosemitic utterance but drew no conclusions about her from it. I saw her almost every day and we established a rather close relationship. Much later I learned that she had remarried and turned against the Jewish people. I have no way of ascertaining whether or not this was true. But it seems psychologically sound for someone who showed all the characteristics of a convert to a cause to suddenly turn around and do the opposite of what her "conversion" had taught her. The Patersons had a castle in Scotland, and for a year or so a Hebrew teacher from Palestine would come to that place every morning to teach Mrs. Paterson the secrets of the Hebrew language.

The year 1946 was in many respects a tragic one. The terrorists of Palestine fought the occupational army without mercy. It was during the time that I was in London that the newspapers published pictures on their first page of forty-six young British soldiers who had been killed by Jewish terrorist groups when they blew up part of the King David Hotel.[85] It was not easy to sit in the compartment of an English train and observe people who were in deep mourning for what had happened to these innocent young people. I could well understand the anger of the British people, which should have been directed against their own government, but which instead was, of course, directed against the Jews and the terrorist bands in Palestine. I re-

84. The son, born May 11, 1944, was christened Orde Jonathan.
85. The King David Hotel explosion, which occurred on July 22, 1946, resulted in the deaths of 92 Britons, Arabs, and Jews. The British Mandatory Government Secretariat was located in its southern wing.

member that I saw David Ben-Gurion, an old friend, during those days,[86] and I will never forget his saying to me after I read him the newspaper article and he had gotten additional information from Palestine, "I feel deeply ashamed of being a Palestinian Jew."

Ben-Gurion had asked me to come to the office of the Federation of British Zionists, which was at 77 Great Russell Street. Although this address may not mean anything to people today, it meant a great deal to me. It was a very old and not very luxurious office with a number of little rooms. This is where British Zionism was born. It was Chaim Weizmann's office, where the whole idea of the Balfour Declaration had been conceived. It was, as you know, written by Arthur Balfour who was at that time the Prime Minister of England.[87] The text, however, was prepared by Chaim Weizmann. The letter was addressed to Lord Rothschild. When the Declaration arrived at the Zionist office at 77 Great Russell Street, Dr. Weizmann asked one of the office boys to deliver it to Lord Rothschild. This was in 1917. Many decades later, at a dinner at the Waldorf Astoria, I was to meet a famous magician who was entertaining there, a person whom I admired greatly. Apparently, someone had told this magician that I was in the audience and he came over to our table, saying he had always wanted to meet me because he wanted me to know that he was the errand boy who had taken the Balfour Declaration to Lord Rothschild. We spent a lovely and interesting evening together following his performance.

I had never been to 77 Great Russell Street, where Ben-Gurion was now situated in a small room, his desk covered with countless books and papers. He was not as yet the Prime Minister of Israel because the state had not yet been created. He was one of the leading men in the Jewish Agency and one of the leaders of the *yishuv*, the Jewish settlement in Palestine. I had seen him in Germany during the Hitler regime when he visited us as he passed through Berlin from Warsaw on his way to Palestine. At that time, he had felt that as a Zionist leader he should visit the beleaguered Jewry of Germany and we had shared the platform one night. As some of you might recall, he had a very tinny, high voice and was not the greatest of speakers. But everyone listened to him with great respect, and what he had to say was meaningful and relevant. It was an invitation to German Jewry to settle in Palestine. I had also seen him when he was in America, and this is how he

86. On June 19, 1946, Ben-Gurion had met in London with the Colonial Secretary, to whom he expressed his grief at the kidnapping of some British officers by Jewish extremists in Palestine.
87. Arthur James Balfour (1848–1930) signed the Balfour Declaration on November 2, 1917, in his capacity as foreign secretary (not prime minister) of Great Britain.

knew that I would be in England. The topic of our conversation was to be of a very intimate nature.

Ben-Gurion informed me that his son Amos had served in the British army in the special contingent that had been created for Palestinian Jews and that he had been wounded in battle. Having to spend several months in a British hospital, Amos met and apparently fell in love with a British nurse who took care of him. After his discharge from the hospital, he continued to see her and an affair developed between the two of them. They planned to marry; however, the nurse was not Jewish. She had been born to a very devout Christian family on the Isle of Man. Amos insisted on marrying her regardless of whether she converted or not. Ben-Gurion himself had no opinion about that and did not care about it. What was important to him was his son's happiness. But this was not the opinion of his wife Paula, who was a very determined and aggressive woman. Ben-Gurion began his conversation with me by showing me ten cables that had arrived from Paula every day in which she said quite plainly that Amos should not dare come to Palestine with a non-Jewish wife unless she had converted to Judaism. Ben-Gurion said he was in a predicament and hated to impose on me. The English rabbis, who were organized in the United Synagogue, a rather conservative body, insisted upon a preparation for conversion that took a whole year. This, of course, was out of the question. The only Reform rabbi in England at that time was Rabbi Israel Isidore Mattuck, the minister of the Liberal Jewish synagogue and the organizer of the World Union for Progressive Judaism.[88] He was known as one of the most rabid anti-Zionists, who preached against the movement and the establishment of a Jewish national home. Ben-Gurion told me that "it is beneath my dignity to go to this man although he could be helpful; I will not lower my standards and honor this man who deserves no honor. I want you to help me by converting my future daughter-in-law. Her name is Mary and I will see to it that she visits with you."

I agreed and the following day Mary visited me in my hotel. She was a very English-looking young woman, not overly attractive, but very pleasant and, above all, very determined. I had decided to convert her without much ado and without any ceremony. My thought was that I could establish a new halakhic principle based on the famous sentence found in the Bible: "I shall live among my people."[89] I said to her, "I understand that you and Amos

---

88. Israel Isidore Mattuck (1883–1954), a co-founder of the World Union for Progressive Judaism, was the leading Liberal rabbi in England at the time. British Liberal Judaism was more radical and anti-Zionist than the contemporary British Reform Judaism.

89. Second Kings 4:13. The words are spoken by the Shunammite to the prophet Elisha, but in the present tense: "I live among my people."

want to get married and that you are willing to convert to Judaism. There is no time to convert you in the proper way, to teach you the foundations of Judaism. I have therefore decided to convert you if you assure me now that you want to be a Jewess." It took some time before she answered with "I am going to Palestine to live there with Amos. I will live among the Jewish people. I do not know whether I will stay. But if I decide to stay with Amos and his people, I would very much like to become part of that people, to understand their beliefs, and to share their fate." It seemed to me a very solemn and sufficient declaration. I then began to question her so as to make it easier for me to issue a document of conversion. I asked, "Have you been to a church service lately?" She replied, "No, I have not been to church for several years." I was relieved, but she quickly added, "But this is only due to the fact that I am a nurse and I simply have had no time to go to church services." I began to probe a little further. She told me she did not believe in the Immaculate Conception, the Holy Trinity, or the divinity of Christ. This was helpful to me. I then said to her, "When you lived on the Isle of Man with your family, I suppose you attended church services very rarely since you do not accept the creed of the Christian church." Hearing this she became very adamant and aggressive, and replied, "No, sir. When I was yet living on the Isle of Man, my family and I were in the habit of attending church services every Sunday morning, noon, and night. My family and I were very regular churchgoers." This left me speechless, but after a while I said to her, "Since you reject the Christian creed, it will be easy for you to accept Judaism and its beliefs. I want you to know that when you go to Palestine you will change your name from Mary to Miriam, for this is the Hebrew equivalent of Mary." Thereupon she rose rather primly and answered, "Doctor, my name is Mary. I was baptized Mary, and as long as there is breath in my body I shall remain Mary. Good day, Doctor."

I was left flabbergasted, but I had given my promise to David Ben-Gurion. I firmly believed that Mary would not stay in Palestine so that the conversion would be a mere formality and serve mainly to appease Paula. I made out a certificate of conversion in which I gave all the information about my rabbinical training, my ordination, and the name of the Jewish scholar who had ordained me. I wanted the document to be clear proof of my authority to convert her and of the fact that she was indeed a converted Jewess. I omitted the matter of the name and until today Mary remains Mary Ben-Gurion. But a great miracle occurred. Although Paula Ben-Gurion never accepted Mary as a Jewess and repeatedly told me so, Mary became, according to David Ben-Gurion and others, "the only real Jewess in the Ben-Gurion family." Until this very day she lights candles on the eve of the Sabbath, attends services, and observes every Jewish holiday. During the War of Independence in 1948, just two years after her conversion, she fought with her fellow Jews, a rifle in her hand, without any fear and completely identifying with the Jewish people. The conversion, which was performed in violation of every possible ruling, proved to be one of the most successful conversions I have ever performed.[90]

The year 1947 was coming to an end, but the end was to be most dramatic. A commission had been set up to inquire into the future of Palestine, for it was evident that the Balfour Declaration would not solve the problem. The tension between the Jewish people of Palestine and the English army of occupation, as well as the government of Great Britain, was as bad as the relationship between the Jews and the Arabs. In April 1947, the United Nations General Assembly had established the special committee on Palestine, which consisted of representatives of eleven states.[91] After several months, the committee unanimously recommended that the mandate over Palestine be terminated, that Palestine be granted independence as soon as possible, and that the country should be partitioned into a Jewish state, an Arab state, and a separate city of Jerusalem. This report, rejected by some and accepted by others, stirred an enormous amount of new activity among Jews. The decisive meeting of the United Nations General Assembly was to take place on November 29th of that year. At the time, Dr. Weizmann was no longer the president of the World Zionist Organization. The movement was in turmoil. The Zionist Organization of America was in disarray. Weizmann stayed at the Plaza Hotel, slowly growing blind and altogether in rather bad physical shape. But he knew that the Zionist movement and the Jews in general would have to prepare for that meeting.

November 29th was a Saturday. I had received an invitation from Prof. Fabregat of Uruguay[92] to attend the meeting. No one knew what would happen. We were sure of a number of votes, including those of the United States and the Soviet Union, but many other votes were in doubt. The membership of the United Nations at that time was rather small. Hilde and I and some friends, who were fortunate to have gotten tickets for the afternoon plenary

90. On June 28, 1946, David Ben-Gurion wrote to his wife Paula: "This week the conversion ceremony took place and Mary already has a proper certificate attesting that she is a Jew. There were some difficulties because our rabbis in England have some strange customs in this regard. But I finally overcame the difficulties and Mary will reach the land of Israel as a Jew." (Ben-Gurion archives webpage http://bgarchives.bgu.ac.il/bgarchive/img/0043-69.gif.)
91. In April 1947, the United Nations Special Committee on Palestine (UNSCOP) was appointed. It recommended termination of the British mandate and the partition of Palestine.
92. Enrique Rodriguez Fabregat represented Uruguay in UNSCOP. He was a firm supporter of the partition resolution.

session, went there in great anxiety. We sat behind a whole row of Arabs, who wore their traditional Arab garb. The only business of the meeting was the vote on Resolution 181, which suggested the partition of Palestine and guaranteed the creation of a Jewish state. The vote was one of the most dramatic occasions of my life. We anxiously awaited each "yes," "no," or "abstention." The final vote was thirty-three in favor, thirteen against, with ten abstentions. The Arabs, both in the audience and those who served as delegates, stormed out of the hall. The Jews and their friends broke into thunderous applause. As the new building of the United Nations had not yet been erected, the meeting took place in Flushing Meadows. We left, embracing each other, and drove to New York City. It was decided that someone should go to the Plaza Hotel to visit Weizmann, who was confined to his bed. He had a little radio on his night table and had listened attentively and excitedly to the proceedings. My old friend Josef Cohn,[93] who had served as Weizmann's private secretary for many years, was sent to see Weizmann. He came back with the report that Weizmann was lying in bed crying.

To celebrate that great day we planned to meet late in the evening at Nahum Goldmann's apartment.[94] No official Zionist would be present as we were not part of their group, nor were they part of ours. The only familiar Zionists who were there were the leaders of Hadassah, who had sided with us since that famous postwar Zionist Congress in Basel. Moshe Sharett[95] (whose name at that time was still Shertok) and his wife Zippora were there. We had taken Lucie, our daughter, along and she got Moshe's autograph. Then Prof. Fabregat and another South American delegate arrived. The mood was gay but also solemn, for no one really knew what the future would bring. Meyer Weisgal[96] and his wife joined us and, finally, Chaim Weizmann and his wife Vera came. This was the highpoint of the evening. We wanted to do something unusual together, so we danced the hora,[97] with the two Christian South Americans joining us. I can still see Chaim and Vera Weizmann standing outside the circle of their dancing friends. Weizmann was

---

93. Josef Cohn had been Weizmann's translator in Berlin in 1929. He served as Weizmann's personal secretary from 1933 to 1948.

94. Nahum Goldmann (1895–1982) was among the foremost Jewish political leaders of the twentieth century. Together with Stephen S. Wise, he was an organizer of the World Jewish Congress, in which he played a leading role. Though a lifelong Zionist, he did not settle in Israel, whose government he frequently criticized.

95. Moshe Sharett (1894–1965), a moderate Zionist, served first as foreign minister and then as prime minister of the State of Israel.

96. Meyer Weisgal (1894–1977) served as Weizmann's personal representative in the United States and later headed the Weizmann Institute in Rehovot, Israel.

97. The folk dance of the Jewish settlers in Palestine.

visibly moved. It was difficult for him to stand for such a long time, but he did, for the moment was of more than symbolic importance.

History had been made; the two thousand years of exile were over. Soon a Jewish state would be established. The great powers would guarantee implementation of the overwhelming vote of the United Nations, and this was most encouraging. We analyzed the vote and came to the conclusion that it was the expression of a bad conscience by the Christian nations who had looked on while Hitler was killing our people. Now they had found an opportunity to do something for a persecuted people, to finally give them some space in which to live. This was not the time to talk about the great dangers of this adventure. We knew Weizmann was very much opposed to proclaiming the Jewish state soon. We also knew that very important members of the State Department were opposed to this Jewish state. Later I heard from Adlai Stevenson,[98] an important member of the American delegation to the United Nations, that he himself, together with others, would have liked to have voted against the resolution, but that the White House, represented by Harry Truman, directed that the United States vote for it.

It was quite clear to us that we needed some further outlet and relaxation. Upon the advice of Meyer Weisgal, who was always the gayest of us all, we decided to go to the Lower East Side. There was a famous café called the Café Royal,[99] which was the hangout of Jewish writers and intellectuals. I took Moshe Shertok and his wife in my car, and together with Hilde and Lucie, we went downtown. Approaching the café in the Jewish section of the Lower East Side, where we were to spend an hour surrounded by so many Jews who recognized and congratulated us on the establishment of the Jewish state, we saw large groups of Jews dancing in the streets of New York. As we left the car, Moshe Shertok said to me, "Look at them. They are dancing now. They do not realize, thank God, that from tomorrow on there will be bloodshed in Palestine."

It was during 1947[100] that I accepted an invitation from a prosecutor at the Nuremberg Trials to interrogate one of the Nazi prisoners. Unfortunately, the name of the man escapes me now,[101] but he was in charge of Nazi propaganda in foreign countries. He was a German by birth and training, but had lived in Cairo for many years. It was from there that he had directed

98. The unsuccessful Democratic presidential candidate in 1952 and 1956.
99. The Café Royal on Second Avenue and 12th Street was the intellectual center of Yiddish-speaking New York. It closed in 1953.
100. On the basis of the following paragraph, the correct date must be 1946.
101. It may be that this was a man named von Hohmeyer, an editor, formerly in Cairo, who was put in charge of transoceanic press propaganda.

the propaganda apparatus, which was extremely well financed by the German government. His case was not dealt with at any of the Nuremberg Trials. He had been arrested, as had hundreds of other Nazis, but in the end I believe he was released. He had committed no crime other than serving the party of which he had been a member for many years.

My long talk with him was interesting because, having been informed that I would interrogate him, he had prepared a long memorandum for me, in which he offered his services to the Jewish people to become the head of an organization that would fight antisemitism. He was as cocky as the others, and when I told him that I considered his offer an insult to the Jewish people, he pretended not to understand. I left him with a sense of disgust and went into the main hall where I saw the leaders of the Nazi party sitting in the dock.[102] I saw Goering in the first row together with all the others, including Mr. Streicher,[103] that very incarnation of brutal and vulgar antisemitism. Most of the people I saw there were executed. It gave me a very strange sensation to look at these men for the first time in my life. These were the lords who had been in charge of the most effective mass murder organization in the world. There they sat, meekly as well as arrogantly, accused of crimes against mankind and probably quite aware of the fact that the end of their lives had come, that their careers had proven to be short-lived. It is difficult for me now to describe what I felt as I sat through the session. I experienced no feeling of satisfaction, for whatever happened at the Nuremberg Trials was trivial as compared with the world historical events that had taken place under the leadership of these prisoners.

I made plans to visit several displaced persons camps as well as the Jewish community of Berlin and asked the military government of the American occupation army to place facilities at my disposal. I was given the rank of colonel for the time of my stay in Germany. As I traveled by train to Berlin, I looked out of the windows continually and saw the destroyed cities. The train stopped in Cologne, where I decided to spend a few days. Cologne was founded by the Roman army, and it was there that the oldest Jewish community in Germany was located. The ruins of its ancient synagogue had been exposed by the thorough bombardment of the city. The city itself hardly existed any longer, though the huge Gothic cathedral, by some accident or miracle, was only slightly damaged and remained standing. The

102. This could only have occurred during the duration of the trial, from November 1945 to October 1946.
103. Julius Streicher (1885–1946) was the editor of the notoriously antisemitic weekly *Der Stürmer*. He was hanged following his trial.

city resembled the theatrical setting of a modern play. The people, many of them walking on crutches, moved like ghosts through streets that were no longer recognizable. The main hotel had been bombed and had no roof, but there were still a number of rooms available for members of the American army, and I was able to find a room there. Given the shortage of food, I had to resort to the American PX where one could buy things that, of course, were not available in Germany. American cigarettes were accepted as currency. Among the destroyed buildings were some of my favorite Romanesque churches, which had been built in the eleventh century. I sought out the church of St. Gereon, which used to be one of the gems of Romanesque architecture; it was now completely flattened. In the center of the rubble was a crucifix with the image of Christ who, as is often the case in Romanesque buildings, looked like a Jew. I walked around the ruins of the church and was constantly attracted to this Jew, Jesus of Nazareth. He had become the symbol of a destruction. He was also a symbol of Jewish survival, for amidst all the ruins there was that Jewish brother of mine who seemed to have survived the destruction of his sanctuary.

Later I visited some of the displaced persons camps. I was particularly interested in Bergen-Belsen; it was from this camp that our daughter Jo,[104] whom we adopted after the war, had been liberated. I was also acquainted with the leader of the displaced persons camp, Mr. Josef Rosensaft,[105] whose life later ended tragically, but was no doubt a man of extraordinary leadership qualities.

The old concentration camp of Bergen-Belsen had been destroyed and all that was left was the cemetery where more than one hundred thousand people were buried. The mass graves carried small markers that indicated the number of people buried in each grave. The smallest number was twenty thousand. Standing in front of these markers, I began to understand how impossible it was to interpret the catastrophe of the Holocaust to normal people in the world. To contemplate that where I stood twenty thousand skeletons of human beings were buried was beyond my comprehension. In later years I was involved in the attempt of the French government to exhume French bodies from these mass graves. Having been there, I knew how utterly ridiculous it was to assume that one would be able to differentiate between men and women, let alone determine nationality. The whole

104. Jo Seelman, a relative who lived for a while in the Prinz house, beginning in June 1947, was adopted by the Prinz family.
105. Josef Rosensaft (1911–1975) chaired the camp committee of Bergen-Belsen survivors as well as the Committee for Displaced Persons in the British Zone of Germany. He died relatively early of a stroke at the age of sixty-four.

bankruptcy of our Western civilization became quite apparent to me while I visited the cemetery. The people buried there were nameless and only God knew how many geniuses of science, literature, and art there were among them.

The displaced persons camp for survivors of Bergen-Belsen was a former German army camp with rather sturdy and comfortable houses. A few thousand displaced persons were living there under the supervision of the British army. I was welcomed by an old friend of mine who represented the Jewish Agency in the camp. He asked me to stay at his house so that he could inform me of the real situation. It must be borne in mind that I had served as chairman of the United Jewish Appeal in 1945 and had delivered many speeches about the misery of the displaced persons. Here for the first time, though, I was to meet them in the flesh.

And for the first time I met a new breed of human beings. They were the survivors. There was no sense in asking why they had survived. It was certain, however, that their experiences in the concentration camp had made them the most selfish and most determined people I ever met. These were not the people about whom I had spoken in the propaganda speeches for the United Jewish Appeal; they had nothing in common with the miserable creatures who had been suffering in camps. They had elected a group of leaders with well-defined goals, who ruled the camp with the kind of discipline that can only be seen in army camps. Most of the people I met were Zionists, and many of them wanted to go to Palestine as soon as possible. I need to emphasize that the leadership and the inmates were not merely human beings and Jews, but also members of one or another Jewish political party. This led to what to me were the most ridiculous consequences, but parties were taken very seriously by the residents of Bergen-Belsen. I remember that while I was visiting with some people in their little comfortable home, a small naked baby walked into the room. When I inquired about him and his family, the man I was visiting said to me, and very seriously, "Don't talk to him. He is a member of Mapam."[106]

I had arrived on Thursday. On Friday morning my friend told me to go with him in order to experience something completely unexpected. He took me to the open marketplace of Bergen-Belsen, where German farmers offered their wares: vegetables, meat, duck, and geese. I saw the women of Bergen-Belsen walk from stand to stand, carefully buying what they needed for the Sabbath meal. I also saw them drive German cars to the place where they were to receive their weekly packages containing coffee and cigarettes

106. Mapam was the Marxist Zionist party on the extreme left wing of the movement.

sent them by American Jewry. I soon realized that this displaced persons camp was actually a trading post. My friend took me to the warehouse, which contained radios and other appliances in large quantities, together with other commodities that were scarcely available in Germany. Every one of the inmates had large sums of dollars. As I discovered, with the help of certain American Jews, they had used the money to buy up large quantities of cigarettes and coffee, which they sold on the black market. This was not a camp of miserable displaced persons. It was a very comfortable and profitable place where Jews could wait until they found a place to settle either in Palestine or in another country. I later discerned the involvement of American Jewish officials in the criminal activities that caused some of the leaders to leave the camp as millionaires.[107]

I had eaten food in German restaurants that hardly deserved the name of food. I knew millions of people were starving, but in Bergen-Belsen the main dish was filet mignon. The menu served to guests, of whom I was one, could very well have been presented in a fashionable and luxurious French restaurant. I learned that one of the displaced persons camps, in the vicinity of Frankfurt, was engaged in the diamond trade and that it established the price of diamonds in the world. This was a new breed of Jew, determined, as they told me, to destroy the German economy and take revenge for what the Germans had done to them. My feeling for the Germans was one of disgust and contempt, but I must admit that what I saw in the displaced persons camps, of which I visited several, did not arouse in me a sense of sympathy, compassion, or admiration.

The year 1948 promised to be a year of decision. There was no doubt that the British Mandate in Palestine had to come to an end. The British had been harassed by the Jewish terrorist groups in Palestine and had lost a great many of their soldiers. The people in Britain were impatient: the governments of the world had expressed the conviction that the Mandate was no longer valid and could not be maintained much longer. The British government agreed to withdraw its troops in the month of May. As I mentioned, Chaim Weizmann was opposed to an immediate proclamation of the Jewish state because it was quite clear to him, as it was to all of us, that as soon as the British soldiers left the country the bloodshed, which had started at the end of November 1947, would escalate and the Arab nations would use their arms against the creation of a Jewish state. I know that the State Department, particularly its Near Eastern desk, which at that time and for

107. Although black market dealings were not uncommon in the displaced persons camps, few, if any, of the survivors emerged as millionaires.

many years to come was occupied by the sons of Christian missionaries who had served in Arab countries, was utterly opposed to the creation of a Jewish state. They considered it a calamity for the United States and the world. But David Ben-Gurion and his group, who were in charge of the Jewish Agency, thought otherwise. On the 14th of May, he proclaimed the Jewish state and called it Israel. Originally, it was supposed to be called New Judea. It was a stroke of genius by David Yellin,[108] who determined the use of new words in the Hebrew language, that it be called Israel, a name that conjured up memories of ancient Israel. The Jewish people were flabbergasted, excited, and at a loss about how to express their feelings. It was, after all, only three years after the defeat of Hitler and the period of degradation and death for the Jewish people. Suddenly they had a flag and a place to go, a country they could call their own. It was all a bit too much for them to digest. Indeed, they have not really digested it until this very day. But the flag of Israel, which was once the flag of the Zionist movement, was now flying from the mast of the Waldorf-Astoria Hotel where Chaim Weizmann was staying. We were all intoxicated by the news, and those of us who had been Zionists since our youth could hardly comprehend that the age-old dream of a Jewish national homeland had become a reality. What the reality was we scarcely understood, and what the consequences of the existence of the Jewish state would be in terms of the Jewish people in many countries of the world was still unclear.

I remember having three wedding ceremonies on that day,[109] and I decided not to have a glass broken as has been the Jewish custom for a long time. After all, the interpretation of the breaking of the glass was "in commemoration of the destruction of the ancient Temple in Jerusalem." For me, the Temple of Jerusalem had been reestablished. The Jewish state was a reality and the Jewish people, in my imagination if not in reality, were dancing in the streets of a thousand cities and towns all over the world. At one of these weddings I met an old friend, Mr. Charles Ehrenkrantz, who had been the principal of my Hebrew School for many years and was a veteran Zionist. I remember that when we saw each other we embraced. We had never done that before, but it was a natural instinct to embrace someone who had shared your own hopes and dreams.

Now that the state existed, the Jews were at a loss to understand what they should do. Very soon after its creation, the United States, as well as

108. As the linguistic scholar David Yellin had died in 1941, it seems unlikely that he was directly responsible for the adoption of the name *Israel,* though he may have proposed the possibility.
109. More likely on the following Sunday.

the Soviet Union, recognized the state, and diplomatic relationships were established. Israeli embassies began to exist in many countries. The anti-Zionist organizations in America and across the world began to understand that anti-Zionism was no longer a valid option and distanced themselves from their ideological platforms. Stephen Wise, David Petegorsky,[110] and I planned for a long session in order to think through what the consequences of the new event meant and how we, as the American Jewish Congress, and other movements should react to it. It took many months and many sessions, reaching into 1949, until we came to the conclusion that a completely new era unparalleled in Jewish history had begun and that nothing existing before this era was valid any longer. David and I decided to take a year off to barnstorm around the country and inform the people of our interpretation of the event and that the Jewish people, now coexisting with the new Jewish state, required radical decisions and actions. Zionism as we knew it, and particularly the Zionism that had been formulated by Theodor Herzl, no longer had any validity. We knew that something entirely different had to be created. We began to formulate our ideas, and accordingly, I published an article in *Congress Weekly* that was titled "This Jewish Revolution."[111] A few years after it was written, I again formulated my position at a national meeting of the American Jewish Congress held in Philadelphia, and to the consternation of many people here and in other parts of the world, I said, "Zionism is dead. Long live Israel and the Jewish people." I was attacked by almost everyone, and my friend Nahum Goldmann, who at that time was the president of the World Zionist Organization, did not speak to me for a whole year. Others who had vested interests in the preservation of the Zionist Organization attacked me in their newspapers and magazines. I still believe I was right; I still think I am more right than ever.[112]

The Jewish state was proclaimed on May 14, 1948, and the World Jewish Congress planned to hold its first international convention[113] in the month of July of that same year. Jewish leaders had not seen each other since the war, with the exception of those who attended the Zionist Congress about which I spoke earlier. We looked forward to this occasion with great anticipation. It was the first time that the Jewish state would be rep-

---

110. At that time, David Petegorsky (1915–1956) was serving as the executive director of the American Jewish Congress.

111. It was published in the issue for April 4, 1949.

112. At this point in the autobiography, Prinz introduces the full article, adding: "It is now forgotten, but I want you to remember it." However, the text has been excised here since it is readily available and because it severely interrupts the flow of the narrative.

113. It was, in fact, the Second Plenary Assembly, the first having taken place in 1936.

resented as part of the Jewish people, and we would also have an opportunity to meet Jews from Eastern European countries who in the meantime had sided with the Communist world. I was to lead the American delegation in my capacity as chairman of the executive of the American Jewish Congress,[114] which was the founder of the World Jewish Congress. Although Stephen Wise appeared there as the president of the World Jewish Congress, I was the leader of the American delegation. Wise was already in Europe at that time, and I was to take his son-in-law Shad Polier[115] to Europe. It was an adventurous and exciting experience. Shad was one of the brightest and most honest men I have ever met. He was also one of the most unbearable. He indulged in constant disturbances at the meetings, and although his observations were always pertinent and proper, he used such an arrogant tone that he antagonized more people than anyone else. In addition to that, he was a provincial American. He was born in the South and remained a southerner all his life. Europe to him was just an unimportant annex to the great power that was America, an annex that had to be fed through the Marshall Plan and would never amount to anything. His relationship to the Jewish people was tenuous. Although he was the son of an immigrant family, he had completely assimilated and everything was measured by the yardstick of the American experience. He knew no Yiddish or Hebrew. I had to introduce him to Europe. After an eighteen-hour flight via Sabena Airlines, we reached Brussels, from which we had to go to Montreux, Switzerland by train. Having a few hours at our disposal in Brussels, I took him to see this marvelous city. I showed him not merely the royal palace, but also the Grand-Place,[116] which is a marvel of Renaissance architecture. All this was very strange to him. He had never seen buildings that had been built in the sixteenth century and marveled at the fact that they were still standing. I treated him to the famous Brussels grapes, which he enjoyed like a child. But this enjoyment was guarded, for he suddenly found himself in a strange and alien atmosphere that he really did not trust even if he endured it with some pleasure.

Finally we reached Montreux. We had rented the large and elegant Grand Hotel for the occasion, and there was Stephen Wise, standing in the center of a huge room. He embraced us and in his inimitable fashion cautioned us, "When you boys use the bathroom for serious purposes, I want

114. More precisely: Chairman of the Administrative Council of the American Jewish Congress.
115. Shad Polier (1906–1987) himself played leading roles in the American Jewish Congress and World Jewish Congress.
116. A group of remarkable public and private buildings dating mostly from the late seventeenth century.

you to be careful with the toilet paper here. If you are not, you'll cut your balls." He was not far from wrong, for the postwar quality of paper and food was not too good. Very helpful at these meetings was David Petegorsky,[117] Canadian by birth and of Orthodox, immigrant parents, well-to-do, and perhaps the brightest young man I have ever met. Unfortunately, he was to die at the age of forty-one. I had a very intimate and close relationship with him, and Stephen Wise considered him his right-hand man. During those years very few things Wise wrote were not prepared by David; they had developed a relationship of mutual respect and admiration. Shortly before David died, I asked him about the great influences in his life. He said, "There were three men who influenced me: Rabbi Meir Berlin,[118] Prof. Harold Laski[119] of London, and Stephen Wise." He was a graduate of the London School of Economics. David was to be of great help to me during these difficult sessions. Together we prepared my speech, which I was to deliver in German since we had no interpreters and could not assume that people coming from all over the world would understand English.

The meeting started with my address.[120] I looked around. There were some two or three hundred delegates. In front of each delegate was a small sign indicating the country from which he came. For the first time in my life I saw the Jewish people as an entity. Until then, it had been merely a concept and an ideology, but here and now it was a reality. Our people had come from the United States and Canada, South Africa and Australia, all the Eastern countries with the exception of the Soviet Union, and above all, from the State of Israel. It was the first time in its history that Israel sent a delegation to an international Jewish meeting, and there was the little sign saying simply "Israel." We all looked at it in amazement and with little prayers of thanksgiving for having lived long enough to witness this great day. Israel was represented by its Minister of Transportation, Moshe David Remez,[121] and Moshe Sneh.[122] Both men were quite different from each

117. See note 110, above.

118. Meir Berlin (later Bar-Ilan; 1880–1949) was a leader of Mizrachi, the religious Zionist movement.

119. Harold Laski (1893–1950), a British socialist and political theorist who taught for many years at the London School of Economics, became an active Zionist in the years immediately preceding the establishment of the State of Israel.

120. In fact, the meeting began on June 27, 1948, with addresses by Stephen Wise and Nahum Goldmann. Prinz spoke, in German, on June 29 as part of the General Debate.

121. Moshe David Remez (1886–1951) had settled in the Land of Israel as early as 1913, where he played a major role in the Jewish labor union, the Histadrut.

122. Moshe Sneh (1909–1972) settled in the Land of Israel in 1940 after an active Zionist career in Poland. In 1947 he joined Mapam, the Zionist Marxist party.

other in temperament, in convictions, and in the delivery of their speeches. Remez was a solid citizen, a very close friend of Golda Meir. Sneh, who had come to Israel from Poland, was a left-wing socialist who later joined the Communist movement and was one of the most fascinating speakers I have ever heard in my life.

We were equally fascinated with a new breed of Jew: the Yiddish-speaking Communist. The most important delegation was from Poland, which was led by a large number of people, who had gone through the dialectical school of Karl Marx. They were all hostile to the State of Israel and the Zionist movement, and they knew very well how to express their political views. I remember that whenever we adopted a resolution praising the State of Israel or expressed Zionist ideas, the whole delegation would walk out. Nevertheless, we learned to respect them; and although they gave us many difficult moments because they were great and able fighters, sometimes fighting over a word or even a comma in a resolution, we came to know each other and even gained mutual respect. This new breed of Jew had little in common with whatever we had known before. Sometimes we called them antisemites in the Yiddish language, since some of their thoughts, which were expressed in passionate speeches, were not very flattering to the Jewish people. Nevertheless, they were supporting a Jewish theater and a Jewish press, and they were convinced that under the Communist regime in Poland they could establish a Jewish community that would function and even create. That this creativity would be hostile to the Jewish religion and alien to the Jewish state did not seem to worry them. This was a new era, and therefore a new type of Jew had to be created. They were pioneers and they knew it. They carried this new distinctive burden with a great deal of dignity and pride as well as incredible arrogance.

Within the Polish delegation was a rabbi who had been a classmate of mine in Breslau. We embraced most heartily. He was wearing the uniform of a colonel of the Polish army, and since he was a clerical dignitary, the Polish government had placed an automobile and a chauffeur at his disposal. Although he was quiet during most of the sessions, he did deliver some sort of an official speech, which was of no consequence.[123] Romania had a small delegation that was led by another rabbi. The Romanian rabbi was quite different. He was young, wore a red yarmulke, and turned out to be a captivating speaker. No one trusted him. We thought him a spy and repre-

---

123. The reference is most likely to Dawid Kahana, who studied at the Jewish Theological Seminary in Breslau from 1925 to 1930. During the war, he was the Jewish chief chaplain in the Polish army and, beginning in 1949, a chaplain in the Israeli army.

sentative of the Communist government, which he repeatedly praised. His name was Moses Rosen,[124] who today is the very distinguished and very successful chief rabbi of Romania. I very often reminded him of those days in Montreux when we all thought he was a Jewish traitor, but in reality he turned out to be the savior of Romanian Jewry.

Stephen Wise was to speak at the last session. We were terribly worried about him since he had, as we knew, a malignancy of the spleen. He suddenly took ill and we were sure he would die. He was in great pain. Fortunately, there was a physician by the name of Dr. Tenenbaum[125] in the American delegation. He treated Wise and we thanked God that he saved his life. Wise was very weak during the entire meeting and used to lean on me. Nahum Goldmann was there, of course, but he spoke very little and left it to Wise to represent the organization as its president. The moment came for Wise to speak. It was almost the last speech he ever delivered, since less than a year later he died. The speech was delivered in English, for this was the only language he knew well. He knew very little Yiddish, and we were afraid that nobody would understand him. This speech, incidentally, was recorded and can still be heard today. It was a most fantastic, oratorical exhibition. Wise spoke about the fact that he had not ever hoped to see the establishment of the Jewish state. He reminded the people that he had been a delegate to the second Zionist Congress, which was held in the last century when he was a very young man and probably the only Zionist rabbi in the United States. He said that he would, for as long as he lived, watch the development of the state. He then added a little sentence that I will not forget. He said, "I will watch it for as long as I live, but that cannot be long." I was amazed to notice that all the people in the audience who claimed not to know any English were carried away by the pathos of a man who, in reality, was a nineteenth-century Shakespearean actor. But through all this acting there shone the sincerity, the warmth, and the greatness of a man who was not merely an outstanding Jew, but a very outstanding human being.

Returning from the convention of the World Jewish Congress, we began to realize for the first time that the Jewish world of the postwar era had now radically changed, as had the world in general. The situation of the Jewish people seemed more complicated than ever before. We had extended an invitation to Soviet Jews to attend the meeting, but we had not even received a reply. I suggested to Stephen Wise to leave two rows of seats vacant in order

124. Moses Rosen (1912–1994) had become the chief rabbi of Romania as early as 1948. Beginning in 1957, he also served in the Romanian parliament.
125. Joseph L. Tenenbaum (1887–1961) was a urologist and Zionist leader.

to indicate symbolically that we were without Soviet Jewry and that these empty seats were waiting for them to come. Although Wise was usually very eager to accept such dramatic proposals, it was not carried out.

The Jewish world now had three separate and different parts: the Jews of the free world, the Jews of the State of Israel, and the Jews of the Communist world. None of the three really knew what to do. Israel was hoping for a very large immigration, and in the end the six hundred thousand Jews who were living in Israel at the end of the War of Independence grew to three million.[126] But with this, the problems grew. Israel had to establish itself as a sovereign nation and, as such, all the trappings of statehood had to be put in place. This meant an enormously large and extraordinarily costly diplomatic apparatus. I still remember the very solemn ceremony at which Abba Eban,[127] who was Israel's representative at the United Nations, fastened the flag of the new state to one of the empty flagpoles in front of the old building of the United Nations. This was a great, exciting, and emotional period. I will never forget the moment when the first Israeli plane of the El-Al Line landed at what was then Idlewild Airport.[128] Soon the first Israeli stamps appeared. We began to understand that what Israel was striving for was the establishment of a normal society as well as a state that imitated whatever other states did. Of course, it had to learn from scratch since hardly anyone, with the exception of Weizmann, was familiar with the habits and customs of sovereign states. Israel, we realized, was to be the major problem of world Jewry during our entire lifetime. None of us had solutions.

The second entity of the Jewish world consisted of communities that lived under Communist regimes. These included the rather small Jewish community of East Germany, which contained a goodly part of Berlin, a city now split into two political and economic entities. Many years later I witnessed the building of the wall between the two cities, a symbol of separation, but also of hostility. Czechoslovakia was not yet fully Communist and Austria remained part of the free world. But all these Jewries had been reduced to small numbers. Their leadership had been killed by Hitler. Many of their buildings had been destroyed, their libraries burned down, their rabbis had perished. No one knew what would happen to them in terms of their participation in the future of a meaningful Jewish life. The most glaring example was that of Polish Jewry. At the convention they were the most

---

126. By the first years of the twenty-first century, that figure had risen to well above five million.
127. Abba Eban (1915–2002) was later Israel's ambassador in Washington (1950–1959) and served in various political capacities including foreign minister (1966–1974).
128. Today, John F. Kennedy Airport.

articulate and the brightest. We trusted none of them but had to arrive at some kind of modus vivendi. Here was a Jewry whose leadership was totally dedicated to the Marxist ideal of a doctrinaire Communist regime. The average people themselves probably had very little to do with Communist ideology, but they also had no say in the matter. Jewish life was completely supervised by the government and the leadership was totally subservient to it. The secret police did its proper job, and more often than not, Jews were members of the secret police, supervising Jewish activities. The population had dwindled from 3,500,000 to 23,000. There were whole towns without functioning synagogues and Jewish cemeteries were neglected, although before the war Jews had constituted the majority in these places. An understanding between the free world and the Communist regimes was practically out of the question: whenever we made an attempt, we discovered we were not speaking the same language nor thinking the same thoughts. Here was a new Jewish task: to help the people build their communities without identifying with their ideology and their spiritual goals. Jewish religion became the belief of old people, the synagogues stood empty, and we knew that it would not be long before the older generation would die out. Nothing would be left. But the Jews were true to the flag and the meaning of the Communist regimes.

The third and largest entity was, of course, the Jewry of the free world. Until this very day we are wrestling with the problem of defining the relationship between Israel and the Diaspora. People began to talk about the "centrality of Israel." It was an alluring slogan but, nevertheless, it remained a slogan; for although Israel began to absorb the secularized forces in world Jewry, it could not possibly claim the ability to solve our problems, many of which were central: Jewish assimilation, Jewish education, the problem of intermarriage, the growing ignorance of the Jews, and many others. In terms of priority, the first thing to be done was the creation of a Jewish Marshall Plan, which would finance the Jewish communities in the world that had been destroyed by Hitler and help them rebuild the lives of their people.

It was at this time[129] that a rather important episode in modern Jewish history took place. The negotiations with the German government for reparations to be paid to the Jewish people began with a fantastic discovery in London that the defeated Germany possessed more gold in the Bank of England than did England, the victor. This discovery led to the logical conclusion that the Germans, who had robbed the Jews of whatever they possessed,

129. Although Chaim Weizmann had demanded reparations from Germany as early as September 1945, no progress was made until 1951.

would have to indemnify the Jewish people collectively and the Jewish Nazi victims individually. The real founder of what was to become a very complicated and very helpful system was a Russian Jew whose name is now forgotten but who should be remembered forever. It was Noah Barou,[130] an economist and adviser to the Bank of England. It was he who made the first contact with representatives of the West German Federal government and established the principle of Germany's moral responsibility toward the Jews as a people and toward those Jewish individuals who had suffered. Under the leadership of Dr. Nahum Goldmann and the World Jewish Congress a system was worked out according to which the State of Israel was to receive an amount of $12,000,000 for twelve years[131] and every Jew or non-Jew who had been victimized by the Nazi regime was to receive an ample amount of money for the duration of his or her lifetime. This arrangement has cost the German government five billion dollars so far and will continue for as long as Nazi victims are alive. The Conference on Jewish Material Claims against Germany was created; it was later replaced by the Memorial Foundation for Jewish Culture.[132] It can be said without exaggeration that without this system neither Israel nor Jewish life in the world could have existed. At first there was an outcry by the former inmates of concentration camps who refused to accept money from Germany. I myself was attending a meeting in the early days of the Claims Conference when a large number of people stormed into the meeting hall, disrupted the meeting, and cursed us. We knew how justified all this was, how very understandable it was in theory that one ought not to accept money for something that could not be made good by any amount. But the opposition quieted down as soon as they realized how much they would benefit by this plan. Indeed, the lives of tens of thousands of people have been changed and made secure by virtue of the fact that they receive large sums of money from the German government.

At the beginning of 1949, Stephen Wise took ill and it was very clear to him that he would not live for very long. He had written an elaborate piece about his funeral service, giving exact instructions as to where he would lie in state, what kind of music should be played, and that David Petegorsky should deliver his eulogy. He had done all that a few years earlier when Louise Wise died. At the beginning of spring, a few weeks before Passover, he was taken to the Lenox Hill Hospital. Everyone of us knew that his last

---

130. Noah Barou (1889–1955), an East European left-wing Zionist living in England, was one of the founders of the World Jewish Congress.
131. The actual figures rose much higher.
132. Prinz is in error. These are two separate institutions.

days had come. We were sitting at the seder table, together with Dr. Nahum Goldmann and his family, who usually attended our seder when they were in town, when a telephone call interrupted the reading from the Haggadah. It was Stephen Wise's son-in-law, Shad Polier, who told us that Wise had taken a turn for the worse and that it was only a matter of time before he would die. I remember how difficult it was to continue reading the Haggadah, and I do not now recall whether we actually did. Although Stephen Wise was old, had been sick for a long time, and all of us realized he would soon die, he was so much a part of our lives that it was difficult to imagine living without him. I went to the hospital the next day, but I could no longer see him. A few days later he died.

As soon as word spread that Stephen Wise had passed away, it was as though the heart of New York suddenly stood still. The news of his death was not published on the usual obituary page of the *New York Times* but on the front page, and the obituary itself covered a whole page. There was much to report. That the voice of this eloquent, articulate, and forever controversial man should now be stilled was something not easily to be comprehended. I went to the hospital[133] immediately. The first telegram of condolence came from the Red Caps of Pennsylvania Station, who always carried his luggage whenever he made a trip and who adored him as one of the great New Yorkers whom they loved. As we sat with Justine, Wise's daughter, two representatives of the State of Israel came: my friend Arthur Lourie,[134] who served as Israel's ambassador to the United States, and one of his colleagues whose name I have forgotten. Stephen Wise did not want to be buried on the day following his death. It took several days, perhaps three at least, before the body was taken to Carnegie Hall. It was a dreary spring day. The sky was cloudy and the rain came down as though the heavens were crying. The three thousand seats in Carnegie Hall were all taken; many of the people waiting for the service to begin cried softly. We took him to lie next to his wife Louise. Only a few people were permitted to go to the cemetery. Hilde and I were among them.

133. Perhaps Prinz means Wise's home.
134. Beginning in January 1947, Arthur Lourie (1903–1978) served as director of the New York office of the Jewish Agency. In that capacity, he presented the Zionist cause before the United Nations. After the establishment of the State of Israel, he served as the Israeli Consul General in New York.

APPENDIX A
CHRONOLOGY

1814	birth of maternal great-grandfather, Joachim
1853	Temple B'nai Abraham founded
1870	birth of father, Joseph
1877, Sept. 2	birth of mother, Nani Berg
1901	marriage of parents, officiated at by Leo Baeck
1902, May 10	Joachim born in Burkhardsdorf (Bierdzan), Upper Silesia
1902, July	birth of Lucie Horovitz (first wife)
1903	birth of brother Kurt; emigrated to United States in 1938
1905	birth of brother Hans (Hanan); emigrated to Palestine in 1937
1910	family moves to Oppeln
1913, July 24	birth of Hilde Goldschmidt (second wife)
1915, Feb. 15	birth of sister, Dorothea (Thea); emigrated to Switzerland in 1937
1915, Feb. 15	death of mother in childbirth
1915, May	Bar Mitzvah
1916	father, Joseph, remarries
1917	joins Zionist youth movement (Blue-White)
1918	graduates from first part of high school
1918	apprentice at department store in Breslau
1921	graduates from high school in Oppeln
1921	at Jewish Theological Seminary, Breslau; studies at University of Breslau
1922	studies at University of Berlin for one year
1924, Jan. 21	Ph.D. dissertation in philosophy accepted by University of Giessen
1924, Feb. 22	begins editing *Jüdische Zeitung für Ostdeutschland*
1925, Dec. 25	marries Lucie Horovitz
1926	begins work as rabbi at Friedenstempel, Berlin
1926	takes exam for rabbinate
1927, Jan. 7	installation sermon in Berlin
1927	dissertation published
1929, Jan. 27	date of ordination certificate
1929	Friedenstempel merged into community
1929–1933	Jewish chaplain at Berlin University
1931, Jan. 1	first child is born (named Renate, later Lucie)
1931, Jan. 14	death of Lucie, the mother
1931	speaks in Ulm, warning about Hitler; trip to Italy

1932, May 24	marries Hilde Goldschmidt
1933, Jan. 30	Hitler becomes German chancellor
1933, April 1	Nazi boycott of Jewish stores
1933, April 30	birth of son Michael
1933, July	meeting with Christian ministers
1933, August	vacation in Bornholm; writes *Wir Juden* there
1933	lectures for Jewish Cultural Association
1934, Feb.–March	trip to Palestine with Hilde
1935, March	suspended as community rabbi; starts work for Hebrew University
1935, May 17	the controversial sermon
1935, June	in Switzerland raising money for Hebrew University
1935, summer	lectures in Essen, Bremen and elsewhere
1935, Aug. 20–Sept. 4	Zionist Congress in Lucerne; gets to know Stephen Wise
1935, Sept. 30	end of Prinz's employment by Berlin Jewish Community
1935, Nov.	political editor of *Israelitisches Familienblatt*
1935–1936	speaks in Yugoslavia, Hungary, Czechoslovakia, Romania
1936	conducts High Holy Day services in Beethoven Hall for Zionist Organization
1936, end of	begins talking about emigration
1937, March 6	leaves for four-week visit to the United States
1937, March 16	arrives in the United States
1937, April 17	begins return voyage to Germany
1937, April 26	arrives back in Southhampton
1937, June 26	farewell event (Adolf Eichmann in attendance)
1937, July 23	embarks on emigration voyage from Le Havre
1937, Aug. 1	arrival in New York on steamship De Grasse
1937, Sept. 20	birth of son Jonathan
1937	gives speech in Atlanta—meets Willis King; speaks in Canada
1938	forms German-Jewish congregation for High Holy Days
1938, Nov.	Joseph and second wife, Gertrude, emigrate from Oppeln to Palestine
1939, July 1	rabbi at Temple B'nai Abraham, Newark, replacing Julius Silberfeld
1939, Sept. 9	installed at B'nai Abraham
1945	elected chairman of United Jewish Appeal of Essex County
1946	elected to Executive Board of American Jewish Congress
1946, summer	fund-raising campaign in Great Britain; meets with Ben-Gurion
1946	visits displaced persons camps in Germany
1946, Dec. 9–24	attends World Zionist Congress in Basel
1947, June	Jo Seelman, a Holocaust survivor, comes to live with Prinz family
1947, Nov. 29	attends meeting of UN special committee on Palestine
1948, June–July	attends World Jewish Congress Plenary Assembly in Montreux
1948	leaves Zionist Organization of America
1949, April 19	death of Stephen S. Wise
1952	daughter Deborah born

1954	death of father in Israel
1958–1966	president of American Jewish Congress
1959	honorary degree from Hebrew Union College-Jewish Institute of Religion
1963, Aug. 28	March on Washington
1965–1967	chair of Conference of Presidents of Major Jewish Organizations
1967, July	Newark race riots
1967–1969	chair of World Jewish Congress Governing Council
1973	congregation moves from Newark to Livingston
1977	retirement from rabbinate
1988, Sept. 30	death at age 86
1994, May 16	death of wife Hilde

APPENDIX B
PRINZ'S SPEECH AT THE LINCOLN
MEMORIAL, AUGUST 28, 1963

I speak to you as an American Jew.

As Americans we share the profound concern of millions of people about the shame and disgrace of inequality and injustice which make a mockery of the great American idea.

As Jews we bring to this great demonstration, in which thousands of us proudly participate, a twofold experience—one of the spirit and one of our history.

In the realm of the spirit, our fathers taught us thousands of years ago that when God created man, he created him as everybody's neighbor. Neighbor is not a geographic term. It is a moral concept. It means our collective responsibility for the preservation of man's dignity and integrity.

From our Jewish historic experience of three and a half thousand years we say:

Our ancient history began with slavery and the yearning for freedom. During the Middle Ages my people lived for a thousand years in the ghettos of Europe. Our modern history begins with a proclamation of emancipation.

It is for these reasons that it is not merely sympathy and compassion for the black people of America that motivates us. It is above all and beyond all such sympathies and emotions a sense of complete identification and solidarity born of our own painful historical experience.

When I was the rabbi of the Jewish community in Berlin under the Hitler regime, I learned many things. The most important thing that I learned under those tragic circumstances was that bigotry and hatred are not the most urgent problem. The most urgent, the most disgraceful, the most shameful and the most tragic problem is silence.

A great people which had created a great civilization had become a nation of silent onlookers. They remained silent in the face of hate, in the face of brutality and in the face of mass murder.

America must not become a nation of onlookers. America must not remain silent. Not merely black America, but all of America. It must speak up and act, from the President down to the humblest of us, and not for the sake of the Negro, not for the sake of the black community but for the sake of the image, the idea and the aspiration of America itself.

Our children, yours and mine in every school across the land, each morning pledge allegiance to the flag of the United States and to the republic for which it stands. They, the children, speak fervently and innocently of this land as the land of "liberty and justice for all."

The time, I believe, has come to work together—for it is not enough to hope together, and it is not enough to pray together—to work together that this children's oath, pronounced every morning from Maine to California, from North to South, may become a glorious, unshakeable reality in a morally renewed and united America.

APPENDIX C
BOOKS BY JOACHIM PRINZ

Helden und Abenteurer der Bibel (Berlin-Charlottenburg: Paul Baumann Verlag, 1930).
Jüdische Geschichte (Berlin: Verlag für Kulturpolitik, 1931).
Illustrierte Jüdische Geschichte (Berlin: Brandussche Verlagsbuchhandlung, 1933).
Wir Juden. Besinnung, Rückblick, Zukunft (Berlin: Erich Reiss, 1933).
Die Geschichten der Bibel (Berlin: Erich Reiss Verlag, 1934).
Die Reiche Israel und Juda: Geschichten der Bibel (Berlin: Erich Reiss Verlag, 1935).
Der Freitagabend: Gebet und Sinn (Berlin: Brandussche Verlagsbuchhandlung, [1935]).
Das Leben im Ghetto: Jüdisches Schicksal in fünf Städten (Berlin: Erwin Löwe, 1937).
The Dilemma of the Modern Jew (Boston/Toronto: Little, Brown, 1962).
Popes from the Ghetto: A View of Medieval Christendom (New York: Horizon Press, 1966).
     Reprinted as a Schocken paperback in 1968.
The Secret Jews (London: Vallentine, Mitchell, 1973).

INDEX

Michael A. Meyer is Adolph S. Ochs Professor of Jewish History at the Hebrew Union College–Jewish Institute of Religion in Cincinnati, Ohio, and international president of the Leo Baeck Institute, devoted to the history and culture of German-speaking Jewry. He is author of *Response to Modernity: A History of the Reform Movement in Judaism* and editor, together with Michael Brenner, of the four-volume *German-Jewish History in Modern Times*.